HIGH COURT CASE SUMMARIES

TORT LAW

Keyed to Dobbs and Hayden's Casebook on Tort Law, 5th Edition

THOMSON

WEST

Mat #40424072

© 2005 Thomson/West
      610 Opperman Drive
      P.O. Box 64526
      St. Paul, MN 55164–0526
      1–800–328–9352

Printed in the United States of America

ISBN 0–314–16623–8

 TEXT IS PRINTED ON 10% POST CONSUMER RECYCLED PAPER

Table of Contents

	Page
CHAPTER ONE. Tort Law: Aims, Approaches, and Processes	**1**
Prosser v. Keeton	3
Holden v. Wal-Mart Stores, Inc.	5
Estevez v. United States	7
CHAPTER THREE. Establishing a Claim for Intentional Tort to Person or Property	**11**
Van Camp v. McAfoos	13
Snyder v. Turk	15
Cohen v. Smith	17
Leichtman v. WLW Jacor Communications, Inc.	19
Garratt v. Dailey	21
Hall v. McBryde	23
Polmatier v. Russ	25
White v. Muniz	27
Cullison v. Medley	29
Koffman v. Garnett	31
McCann v. Wal-Mart Stores, Inc.	33
Brown v. Muhlenberg Township	35
CHAPTER FOUR. Defenses to Intentional Torts—Privileges	**37**
Great Atlantic & Pacific Tea Co. v. Paul	39
Katko v. Briney	41
Brown v. Martinez	43
Surocco v. Geary	45
Wegner v. Milwaukee Mutual Ins. Co.	47
Vincent v. Lake Erie Transportation Co.	49
CHAPTER FIVE. The Prima Facie Case for Negligence	**51**
Stewart v. Motts	53
Wilson v. Sibert	55
Robinson v. Lindsay	57
Creasy v. Rusk	59
Roman v. Estate of Gobbo	61
Chaffin v. Brame	63
Rains v. Bend of the River	65
Wright v. Brown	67
Impson v. Structural Metals, Inc.	69
CHAPTER SIX. Negligence: The Breach or Negligence Element of the Negligence Case	**71**
Indiana Consolidated Insurance Co. v. Mathew	73
Stinnett v. Buchele	75
Bernier v. Boston Edison Co.	77
United States v. Carroll Towing Co.	79
Santiago v. First Student, Inc.	81
Upchurch v. Rotenberry	83
Thoma v. Cracker Barrel Old Country Store, Inc.	85
Wal-Mart Stores, Inc. v. Wright	87
The T. J. Hooper	89
Byrne v. Boadle	91
Giles v. City of New Haven	93
Warren v. Jeffries	95
Widmyer v. Southeast Skyways, Inc.	97
CHAPTER SEVEN. Harm and Causation in Fact	**99**
Preston v. Cestaro	101
Salinetro v. Nystrom	103

	Page
Landers v. East Texas Salt Water Disposal Co.	105
Anderson v. Minneapolis, St. Paul & Sault Ste. Marie Railway	107
Dillon v. Twin State Gas & Electric Co.	109
Summers v. Tice	111
Lord v. Lovett	113

CHAPTER EIGHT. Negligence: The Scope of Risk or "Proximate Cause" Requirement **115**
Medcalf v. Washington Heights Condominium Ass'n, Inc.	117
Palsgraf v. Long Island Railroad Co.	119
Hughes v. Lord Advocate	121
Derdiarian v. Felix Contracting Corp.	123
Sheehan v. City of New York	125
Ventricelli v. Kinney System Rent A Car, Inc.	127
Marshall v. Nugent	129

CHAPTER NINE. Contributory/Comparative Fault **131**
Butterfield v. Forrester	133
Sollin v. Wangler	135
Wassell v. Adams	137
Mercer v. Vanderbilt University	141
Bexiga v. Havir Manufacturing Corp.	143
LeRoy Fibre Co. v. Chicago, M. & St. P. Ry.	145

CHAPTER TEN. Assumption of the Risk **147**
Moore v. Hartley Motors	149
Crews v. Hollenbach	151
Turcotte v. Fell	153

CHAPTER ELEVEN. Defenses Not on the Merits **155**
Crumpton v. Humana, Inc.	157
Schiele v. Hobart Corp.	159
Doe v. Maskell	161
Hoery v. United States	163

CHAPTER TWELVE. Carriers, Host–Drivers and Landowners **165**
Gladon v. Greater Cleveland Regional Transit Authority	167
Bennett v. Stanley	169
O'Sullivan v. Shaw	171
Minnich v. Med–Waste, Inc.	173
Rowland v. Christian	175
Pagelsdorf v. Safeco Insurance Co. of America	177

CHAPTER THIRTEEN. Duties of Medical and Other Professionals **179**
Walski v. Tiesenga	181
Vergara v. Doan	183
Velazquez v. Jiminez	185
Smith v. Knowles	187
States v. Lourdes Hospital	189
Ybarra v. Spangard	191
Harnish v. Children's Hospital Medical Center	193
Arrington v. Wong	195
Horizon/CMS Healthcare Corp. v. Auld	197

CHAPTER FIFTEEN. Governmental Entities and Officers **199**
Loge v. United States	201
Maas v. United States	203
Riss v. City of New York	205
Harry Stoller and Co., Inc. v. City of Lowell	207
Thompson v. County of Alameda	209
Vaughn v. Ruoff	211
Navarro v. Block	213

CHAPTER SIXTEEN. Nonfeasance **217**
Yania v. Bigan	219
Wakulich v. Mraz	221

Page

Farwell v. Keaton 223
DeShaney v. Winnebago County Dept. of Social Services 225

CHAPTER SEVENTEEN.   Contract and Duty **229**
Thorne v. Deas 231
Mobil Oil Corp. v. Thorn 233
H.R. Moch Co. v. Rensselaer Water Co. 235
Paz v. State of California 237
Florence v. Goldberg 241

CHAPTER EIGHTEEN.   The Duty to Protect From Third Persons **243**
Posecai v. Wal-Mart Stores, Inc. 245
Marquay v. Eno 247
Tarasoff v. Regents of University of California 251
Brigance v. Velvet Dove Restaurant, Inc. 255

CHAPTER NINETEEN.   Emotional Harm **257**
GTE Southwest, Inc. v. Bruce 259
Homer v. Long 261
Grube v. Union Pacific R.R. 263
Boucher v. Dixie Medical Center 265
Sacco v. High Country Independent Press, Inc. 267
Potter v. Firestone Tire and Rubber Co. 269

CHAPTER TWENTY.   Prenatal Harms **273**
Remy v. MacDonald 275
Chaffee v. Seslar 277

CHAPTER TWENTY–ONE.   Death **279**
Smith v. Whitaker 281

CHAPTER TWENTY–TWO.   Vicarious Liability **285**
Hinman v. Westinghouse Electric Co. 287
Edgewater Motels, Inc. v. Gatzke 289
Lisa M. v. Henry Mayo Newhall Memorial Hospital 293
Kastner v. Toombs 295
District of Columbia v. Hampton 297
O'Banner v. McDonald's Corp. 299
Pusey v. Bator 301
Otero v. Jordon Restaurant Enterprises 303

CHAPTER TWENTY–THREE.   The Development of Common Law Strict Liability **305**
Weaver v. Ward 307
Brown v. Kendall 309
Bamford v. Turnley 311
Rylands v. Fletcher 313

CHAPTER TWENTY–FOUR.   Tort Liability for Defective Products **315**
Moorman Manufacturing Co. v. National Tank Co. 319
Lee v. Crookston Coca-Cola Bottling Co. 321
Knitz v. Minster Machine Co. 323
Honda of America Mfg., Inc. v. Norman 325
McCarthy v. Olin Corporation 327
Liriano v. Hobart Corporation 329
Lewis v. Lead Industries Ass'n 333
Turpin v. Merrell Dow Pharmaceuticals, Inc. 335
Bowling v. Heil Co. 337
Hughes v. Magic Chef, Inc. 339
Reid v. Spadone Machine Co. 341
Boyle v. United Technologies Corporation 343
Newmark v. Gimbel's Inc. 347
United Blood Services, Division of Blood Systems, Inc. v. Quintana 349

CHAPTER TWENTY–FIVE.   Settlement and Apportionment **353**
Gleason v. Guzman 355
Ascheman v. Village of Hancock 359
Safeway Stores, Inc. v. Nest-Kart 361

Page

Hymowitz v. Eli Lilly and Company 363
Cartel Capital Corp. v. Fireco of New Jersey 367
D'Amario v. Ford Motor Co. 369
Board of County Comn'rs of Teton County v. Bassett 371
Turner v. Jordan 373

CHAPTER TWENTY–SIX.   Damages **375**
Martin v. United States 377
McDougald v. Garber 379
Mercado v. Ahmed 383
Keans v. Bottiarelli 385
State Farm Mut. Auto. Ins. Co. v. Campbell 387

CHAPTER TWENTY–EIGHT.   Worker's Compensation **391**
Jaeger Baking Co. v. Kretschmann 393
State Industrial Commissioner v. Leff 395
Carvalho v. Decorative Fabrics Co. 397
Harris v. Board of Educ. of Howard County 399
Martin v. Lancaster Battery Co., Inc. 401
Kerans v. Porter Paint Co. 403

CHAPTER TWENTY–NINE.   Public Compensation Systems, Including Social Security **405**
Heckler v. Campbell 407

CHAPTER THIRTY.   Private Insurance Solutions **411**
Licari v. Elliot 413

CHAPTER THIRTY–TWO.   Communication of Personally Harmful Impression to Others **417**
New York Times Co. v. Sullivan 419
Gertz v. Robert Welch, Inc. 421
Friedman v. Dozorc 423
Solano v. Playgirl, Inc. 425

CHAPTER THIRTY–THREE.   Communication of Commercially Harmful Impressions to Others **427**
Jeffrey v. Cathers 429
Brunson Communications, Inc. v. Arbitron, Inc. 431
Alyeska Pipeline Service v. Aurora Air Service 433
Caruso v. Local Union Number 690, International Brotherhood of Teamsters 435
Qualitex Co. v. Jacobson Products Co. 437
Sears, Roebuck & Co. v. Stiffel Co. 439

CHAPTER THIRTY–FOUR.   Misrepresentation and Other Misdealings **441**
Ultramares Corp. v. Touche, Niven & Co. 443
Gauerke v. Rozga 445
Pinnacle Peak Developers v. TRW Investment Corp. 447
Ollerman v. O'Rourke Co., Inc. 449

Alphabetical Table of Cases

Alyeska Pipeline Service Co. v. Aurora Air Service, Inc., 604 P.2d 1090 (Alaska 1979), 433

Anderson v. Minneapolis, St. P. & S. S. M. Ry. Co., 146 Minn. 430, 179 N.W. 45 (Minn.1920), 107

Arrington v. Wong, 237 F.3d 1066 (9th Cir.2001), 195

Ascheman v. Village of Hancock, 254 N.W.2d 382 (Minn. 1977), 359

Bamford v. Turnley, 122 Eng.Rep. 27 (Exch.Ch.1862), 311

Bennett v. Stanley, 92 Ohio St.3d 35, 748 N.E.2d 41 (Ohio 2001), 169

Bernier v. Boston Edison Co., 380 Mass. 372, 403 N.E.2d 391 (Mass.1980), 77

Bexiga v. Havir Mfg. Corp., 60 N.J. 402, 290 A.2d 281 (N.J.1972), 143

Board of County Comn'rs of Teton County v. Bassett, 8 P.3d 1079 (Wyo.2000), 371

Boucher v. Dixie Medical Center, 850 P.2d 1179 (Utah 1992), 265

Bowling v. Heil Co., 31 Ohio St.3d 277, 511 N.E.2d 373 (Ohio 1987), 337

Boyle v. United Technologies Corp., 487 U.S. 500, 108 S.Ct. 2510, 101 L.Ed.2d 442 (1988), 343

Brigance v. Velvet Dove Restaurant, Inc., 725 P.2d 300 (Okla. 1986), 255

Brown v. Kendall, 60 Mass. 292 (Mass.1850), 309

Brown v. Martinez, 68 N.M. 271, 361 P.2d 152 (N.M.1961), 43

Brown v. Muhlenberg Tp., 269 F.3d 205 (3rd Cir.2001), 35

Brunson Communications, Inc. v. Arbitron, Inc., 266 F.Supp.2d 377 (E.D.Pa.2003), 431

Butterfield v. Forrester, 11 East. 59, 103 Eng. Rep. 926 (1809), 133

Byrne v. Boadle, 2 H. & C. 722 (1863), 91

Carroll Towing Co., United States v., 159 F.2d 169 (2nd Cir.1947), 79

Cartel Capital Corp. v. Fireco of New Jersey, 81 N.J. 548, 410 A.2d 674 (N.J.1980), 367

Caruso v. Local Union No. 690 of Intern. Broth. of Teamsters, 100 Wash.2d 343, 670 P.2d 240 (Wash.1983), 435

Carvalho v. Decorative Fabrics Co., 117 R.I. 231, 366 A.2d 157 (R.I.1976), 397

Chaffee v. Seslar, 751 N.E.2d 773 (Ind.App.2001), 277

Chaffin v. Brame, 233 N.C. 377, 64 S.E.2d 276 (N.C.1951), 63

Cohen v. Smith, 269 Ill.App.3d 1087, 207 Ill.Dec. 873, 648 N.E.2d 329 (Ill.App. 5 Dist.1995), 17

Creasy v. Rusk, 730 N.E.2d 659 (Ind.2000), 59

Crews v. Hollenbach, 358 Md. 627, 751 A.2d 481 (Md.2000), 151

Crumpton v. Humana, Inc., 99 N.M. 562, 661 P.2d 54 (N.M. 1983), 157

Cullison v. Medley, 570 N.E.2d 27 (Ind.1991), 29

D'Amario v. Ford Motor Co., 806 So.2d 424 (Fla.2001), 369

Derdiarian v. Felix Contracting Corp., 434 N.Y.S.2d 166, 414 N.E.2d 666 (N.Y.1980), 123

DeShaney v. Winnebago County Dept. of Social Services, 489 U.S. 189, 109 S.Ct. 998, 103 L.Ed.2d 249 (1989), 225

Dillon v. Twin State Gas & Electric Co., 85 N.H. 449, 163 A. 111 (N.H.1932), 109

District of Columbia v. Hampton, 666 A.2d 30 (D.C.1995), 297

Doe v. Maskell, 342 Md. 684, 679 A.2d 1087 (Md.1996), 161

Edgewater Motels, Inc. v. Gatzke, 277 N.W.2d 11 (Minn. 1979), 289

Estevez v. United States, 72 F.Supp.2d 205 (S.D.N.Y.1999), 7

Farwell v. Keaton, 396 Mich. 281, 240 N.W.2d 217 (Mich. 1976), 223

Florence v. Goldberg, 404 N.Y.S.2d 583, 375 N.E.2d 763 (N.Y.1978), 241

Friedman v. Dozorc, 412 Mich. 1, 312 N.W.2d 585 (Mich. 1981), 423

Garratt v. Dailey, 46 Wash.2d 197, 279 P.2d 1091 (Wash. 1955), 21

Gauerke v. Rozga, 112 Wis.2d 271, 332 N.W.2d 804 (Wis. 1983), 445

Gertz v. Robert Welch, Inc., 418 U.S. 323, 94 S.Ct. 2997, 41 L.Ed.2d 789 (1974), 421

Giles v. City of New Haven, 228 Conn. 441, 636 A.2d 1335 (Conn.1994), 93

Gladon v. Greater Cleveland Regional Transit Auth., 75 Ohio St.3d 312, 662 N.E.2d 287 (Ohio 1996), 167

Gleason v. Guzman, 623 P.2d 378 (Colo.1981), 355

Great Atlantic & Pacific Tea Co. v. Paul, 256 Md. 643, 261 A.2d 731 (Md.1970), 39

Grube v. Union Pacific R. Co., 256 Kan. 519, 886 P.2d 845 (Kan.1994), 263

GTE Southwest, Inc. v. Bruce, 998 S.W.2d 605 (Tex.1999), 259

Hall v. McBryde, 919 P.2d 910 (Colo.App.1996), 23

Harnish v. Children's Hosp. Medical Center, 387 Mass. 152, 439 N.E.2d 240 (Mass.1982), 193

Harris v. Board of Educ. of Howard County, 375 Md. 21, 825 A.2d 365 (Md.2003), 399

Harry Stoller and Co., Inc. v. City of Lowell, 412 Mass. 139, 587 N.E.2d 780 (Mass.1992), 207

Heckler v. Campbell, 461 U.S. 458, 103 S.Ct. 1952, 76 L.Ed.2d 66 (1983), 407

Hinman v. Westinghouse Elec. Co., 88 Cal.Rptr. 188, 471 P.2d 988 (Cal.1970), 287

Hoery v. United States, 64 P.3d 214 (Colo.2003), 163

Holden v. Wal–Mart Stores, Inc., 259 Neb. 78, 608 N.W.2d 187 (Neb.2000), 5

Homer v. Long, 90 Md.App. 1, 599 A.2d 1193 (Md.App.1992), 261

Honda of America Mfg., Inc. v. Norman, 104 S.W.3d 600 (Tex.App.-Hous. (1 Dist.) 2003), 325

Horizon/CMS Healthcare Corp. v. Auld, 985 S.W.2d 216 (Tex. App.-Fort Worth 1999), 197

H.R. Moch Co. v. Rensselaer Water Co., 247 N.Y. 160, 159 N.E. 896 (N.Y.1928), 235

Hughes v. Lord Advocate, A.C. 837 (H.L.1963), 121

Hughes v. Magic Chef, Inc., 288 N.W.2d 542 (Iowa 1980), 339

Hymowitz v. Eli Lilly and Co., 541 N.Y.S.2d 941, 539 N.E.2d 1069 (N.Y.1989), 363

Impson v. Structural Metals, Inc., 487 S.W.2d 694 (Tex.1972), 69

Indiana Consol. Ins. Co. v. Mathew, 402 N.E.2d 1000 (Ind. App. 3 Dist.1980), 73

Jaeger Baking Co. v. Kretschmann, 96 Wis.2d 590, 292 N.W.2d 622 (Wis.1980), 393

Jeffrey v. Cathers, 104 S.W.3d 424 (Mo.App. E.D.2003), 429

Kastner v. Toombs, 611 P.2d 62 (Alaska 1980), 295

Katko v. Briney, 183 N.W.2d 657 (Iowa 1971), 41

Keans v. Bottiarelli, 35 Conn.App. 239, 645 A.2d 1029 (Conn. App.1994), 385

Kerans v. Porter Paint Co., 61 Ohio St.3d 486, 575 N.E.2d 428 (Ohio 1991), 403

Knitz v. Minster Mach. Co., 69 Ohio St.2d 460, 432 N.E.2d 814, 23 O.O.3d 403 (Ohio 1982), 323

Koffman v. Garnett, 265 Va. 12, 574 S.E.2d 258 (Va.2003), 31

Landers v. East Texas Salt Water Disposal Co., 151 Tex. 251, 248 S.W.2d 731 (Tex.1952), 105

Lee v. Crookston Coca–Cola Bottling Co., 290 Minn. 321, 188 N.W.2d 426 (Minn.1971), 321

Leichtman v. WLW Jacor Communications, Inc., 92 Ohio App.3d 232, 634 N.E.2d 697 (Ohio App. 1 Dist.1994), 19

LeRoy Fibre Co. v. Chicago, M. & St. P. R. Co., 232 U.S. 340, 34 S.Ct. 415, 58 L.Ed. 631 (1914), 145

Lewis v. Lead Industries Ass'n, Inc., 342 Ill.App.3d 95, 276 Ill.Dec. 110, 793 N.E.2d 869 (Ill.App. 1 Dist.2003), 333

Licari v. Elliott, 455 N.Y.S.2d 570, 441 N.E.2d 1088 (N.Y. 1982), 413

Liriano v. Hobart Corp., 170 F.3d 264 (2nd Cir.1999), 329

Lisa M. v. Henry Mayo Newhall Memorial Hospital, 48 Cal. Rptr.2d 510, 907 P.2d 358 (Cal.1995), 293

Loge v. United States, 662 F.2d 1268 (8th Cir.1981), 201

Lord v. Lovett, 146 N.H. 232, 770 A.2d 1103 (N.H.2001), 113

Maas v. United States, 94 F.3d 291 (7th Cir.1996), 203

Marquay v. Eno, 139 N.H. 708, 662 A.2d 272 (N.H.1995), 247

Marshall v. Nugent, 222 F.2d 604 (1st Cir.1955), 129

Martin v. Lancaster Battery Co., Inc., 530 Pa. 11, 606 A.2d 444 (Pa.1992), 401

Martin v. United States, 471 F.Supp. 6 (D.Ariz.1979), 377

McCann v. Wal–Mart Stores, Inc., 210 F.3d 51 (1st Cir.2000), 33

McCarthy v. Olin Corp., 119 F.3d 148 (2nd Cir.1997), 327

McDougald v. Garber, 538 N.Y.S.2d 937, 536 N.E.2d 372 (N.Y.1989), 379

Medcalf v. Washington Heights Condominium Ass'n, Inc., 57 Conn.App. 12, 747 A.2d 532 (Conn.App.2000), 117

Mercado v. Ahmed, 974 F.2d 863 (7th Cir.1992), 383

Mercer v. Vanderbilt University, Inc., 134 S.W.3d 121 (Tenn. 2004), 141

Minnich v. Med–Waste, Inc., 349 S.C. 567, 564 S.E.2d 98 (S.C.2002), 173

Mobil Oil Corp. v. Thorn, 401 Mich. 306, 258 N.W.2d 30 (Mich.1977), 233

Moore v. Hartley Motors, Inc., 36 P.3d 628 (Alaska 2001), 149

Moorman Mfg. Co. v. National Tank Co., 91 Ill.2d 69, 61 Ill.Dec. 746, 435 N.E.2d 443 (Ill.1982), 319

Navarro v. Block, 72 F.3d 712 (9th Cir.1995), 213

Newmark v. Gimbel's Inc., 54 N.J. 585, 258 A.2d 697 (N.J. 1969), 347

New York Times Co. v. Sullivan, 376 U.S. 254, 84 S.Ct. 710, 11 L.Ed.2d 686 (1964), 419

O'Banner v. McDonald's Corp., 173 Ill.2d 208, 218 Ill.Dec. 910, 670 N.E.2d 632 (Ill.1996), 299

Ollerman v. O'Rourke Co., Inc., 94 Wis.2d 17, 288 N.W.2d 95 (Wis.1980), 449

O'Sullivan v. Shaw, 431 Mass. 201, 726 N.E.2d 951 (Mass. 2000), 171

Otero v. Jordon Restaurant Enterprises, 119 N.M. 721, 895 P.2d 243 (N.M.App.1995), 303

Pagelsdorf v. Safeco Ins. Co. of America, 91 Wis.2d 734, 284 N.W.2d 55 (Wis.1979), 177

Palsgraf v. Long Island R. Co., 248 N.Y. 339, 162 N.E. 99 (N.Y.1928), 119

Paz v. State of California, 93 Cal.Rptr.2d 703, 994 P.2d 975 (Cal.2000), 237

Pinnacle Peak Developers v. TRW Inv. Corp., 129 Ariz. 385, 631 P.2d 540 (Ariz.App. Div. 1 1980), 447

Polmatier v. Russ, 206 Conn. 229, 537 A.2d 468 (Conn.1988), 25

Posecai v. Wal–Mart Stores, Inc., 752 So.2d 762 (La.1999), 245

Potter v. Firestone Tire & Rubber Co., 25 Cal.Rptr.2d 550, 863 P.2d 795 (Cal.1993), 269

Preston v. Cestaro, 2001 WL 254343 (Conn.Super.2001), 101

Prosser v. Keeton, 143 Unrep. Case 1113, 3

Pusey v. Bator, 94 Ohio St.3d 275, 762 N.E.2d 968 (Ohio 2002), 301

Qualitex Co. v. Jacobson Products Co., Inc., 514 U.S. 159, 115 S.Ct. 1300, 131 L.Ed.2d 248 (1995), 437

Rains v. Bend of the River, 124 S.W.3d 580 (Tenn.Ct.App. 2003), 65

Reid v. Spadone Mach. Co., 119 N.H. 457, 404 A.2d 1094 (N.H.1979), 341

Remy v. MacDonald, 440 Mass. 675, 801 N.E.2d 260 (Mass. 2004), 275

Riss v. City of New York, 293 N.Y.S.2d 897, 240 N.E.2d 860 (N.Y.1968), 205

Robinson v. Lindsay, 92 Wash.2d 410, 598 P.2d 392 (Wash. 1979), 57

Roman v. Estate of Gobbo, 99 Ohio St.3d 260, 791 N.E.2d 422 (Ohio 2003), 61

Rowland v. Christian, 69 Cal.2d 108, 70 Cal.Rptr. 97, 443 P.2d 561 (Cal.1968), 175

Rylands v. Fletcher, L.R. 3 H.L. 330 (1868), 313

Sacco v. High Country Independent Press, Inc., 271 Mont. 209, 896 P.2d 411 (Mont.1995), 267

Safeway Stores, Inc. v. Nest–Kart, 146 Cal.Rptr. 550, 579 P.2d 441 (Cal.1978), 361

Salinetro v. Nystrom, 341 So.2d 1059 (Fla.App. 3 Dist.1977), 103

Santiago v. First Student, Inc., 839 A.2d 550 (R.I.2004), 81

Schiele v. Hobart Corp., 284 Or. 483, 587 P.2d 1010 (Or. 1978), 159

Sears, Roebuck & Co. v. Stiffel Co., 376 U.S. 225, 84 S.Ct. 784, 11 L.Ed.2d 661 (1964), 439

Sheehan v. City of New York, 387 N.Y.S.2d 92, 354 N.E.2d 832 (N.Y.1976), 125

Smith v. Knowles, 281 N.W.2d 653 (Minn.1979), 187

Smith v. Whitaker, 160 N.J. 221, 734 A.2d 243 (N.J.1999), 281

Snyder v. Turk, 90 Ohio App.3d 18, 627 N.E.2d 1053 (Ohio App. 2 Dist.1993), 15

Solano v. Playgirl, Inc., 292 F.3d 1078 (9th Cir.2002), 425

Sollin v. Wangler, 627 N.W.2d 159 (N.D.2001), 135

State Farm Mut. Auto. Ins. Co. v. Campbell, 538 U.S. 408, 123 S.Ct. 1513, 155 L.Ed.2d 585 (2003), 387

State Industrial Commissioner v. Leff, 265 N.Y. 533, 193 N.E. 307 (N.Y.1934), 395

States v. Lourdes Hosp., 762 N.Y.S.2d 1, 792 N.E.2d 151 (N.Y.2003), 189

Stewart v. Motts, 539 Pa. 596, 654 A.2d 535 (Pa.1995), 53

Stinnett v. Buchele, 598 S.W.2d 469 (Ky.App.1980), 75

Summers v. Tice, 33 Cal.2d 80, 199 P.2d 1 (Cal.1948), 111

Surocco v. Geary, 3 Cal. 69 (Cal.1853), 45

Tarasoff v. Regents of University of California, 131 Cal.Rptr. 14, 551 P.2d 334 (Cal.1976), 251

The T.J. Hooper, 60 F.2d 737 (2nd Cir.1932), 89

Thoma v. Cracker Barrel Old Country Store, Inc., 649 So.2d 277 (Fla.App. 1 Dist.1995), 85

Thompson v. County of Alameda, 167 Cal.Rptr. 70, 614 P.2d 728 (Cal.1980), 209

Thorne v. Deas, 4 Johns. 84 (N.Y.Sup.1809), 231

Turcotte v. Fell, 510 N.Y.S.2d 49, 502 N.E.2d 964 (N.Y.1986), 153

Turner v. Jordan, 957 S.W.2d 815 (Tenn.1997), 373

Turpin v. Merrell Dow Pharmaceuticals, Inc., 959 F.2d 1349 (6th Cir.1992), 335

Ultramares Corporation v. Touche, Niven & Co., 255 N.Y. 170, 174 N.E. 441 (N.Y.1931), 443

United Blood Services, a Div. of Blood Systems, Inc. v. Quintana, 827 P.2d 509 (Colo.1992), 349

United States v. _____ (see opposing party)

Upchurch v. Rotenberry, 761 So.2d 199 (Miss.2000), 83

Van Camp v. McAfoos, 261 Iowa 1124, 156 N.W.2d 878 (Iowa 1968), 13

Vaughn v. Ruoff, 253 F.3d 1124 (8th Cir.2001), 211

Velazquez v. Jiminez, 172 N.J. 240, 798 A.2d 51 (N.J.2002), 185

Ventricelli v. Kinney System Rent A Car, Inc., 411 N.Y.S.2d 555, 383 N.E.2d 1149 (N.Y.1978), 127

Vergara v. Doan, 593 N.E.2d 185 (Ind.1992), 183

Vincent v. Lake Erie Transp. Co., 109 Minn. 456, 124 N.W. 221 (Minn.1910), 49

Wakulich v. Mraz, 322 Ill.App.3d 768, 255 Ill.Dec. 907, 751 N.E.2d 1 (Ill.App. 1 Dist.2001), 221

Wal–Mart Stores, Inc. v. Wright, 774 N.E.2d 891 (Ind.2002), 87

Walski v. Tiesenga, 72 Ill.2d 249, 21 Ill.Dec. 201, 381 N.E.2d 279 (Ill.1978), 181

Warren v. Jeffries, 263 N.C. 531, 139 S.E.2d 718 (N.C.1965), 95

Wassell v. Adams, 865 F.2d 849 (7th Cir.1989), 137

Weaver v. Ward, Hob. 134, 80 Eng. Rep. 284 (K.B.1616), 307

Wegner v. Milwaukee Mut. Ins. Co., 479 N.W.2d 38 (Minn. 1991), 47

White v. Muniz, 999 P.2d 814 (Colo.2000), 27

Widmyer v. Southeast Skyways, Inc., 584 P.2d 1 (Alaska 1978), 97

Wilson v. Sibert, 535 P.2d 1034 (Alaska 1975), 55

Wright v. Brown, 167 Conn. 464, 356 A.2d 176 (Conn.1975), 67

Yania v. Bigan, 397 Pa. 316, 155 A.2d 343 (Pa.1959), 219

Ybarra v. Spangard, 25 Cal.2d 486, 154 P.2d 687 (Cal.1944), 191

*

CHAPTER ONE

Tort Law: Aims, Approaches, and Processes

Prosser v. Keeton

Instant Facts: The original owner of a stolen watch brought suit against the man who purchased the watch from the thief, seeking its return.

Black Letter Rule: The law may give the good faith purchaser title to property if there is a legitimate policy reason to do so, even if a thief could not give title.

Holden v. Wal-Mart Stores, Inc.

Instant Facts: A customer sued Wal–Mart (D) when she fell and injured her knee in a store parking lot.

Black Letter Rule: An award of damages may be set aside on appeal as excessive or inadequate, but only when it is so excessive or inadequate as to be the result of passion, prejudice, mistake, or some other means not apparent in the record.

Estevez v. United States

Instant Facts: A two-year old who was severely injured in an automobile crash caused by a United States Postal Worker sued for compensation for his injuries.

Black Letter Rule: When a party is injured, awards can be made for past medical bills, future medical expenses, future pain and suffering, and future lost earnings.

Prosser v. Keeton

(Watch Owner) v. *(Buyer of Stolen Watch)*

143 Unrep. Case 1113

SOCIAL POLICY TRANSCENDS THE QUESTION OF JUSTICE

■ **INSTANT FACTS** The original owner of a stolen watch brought suit against the man who purchased the watch from the thief, seeking its return.

■ **BLACK LETTER RULE** The law may give the good faith purchaser title to property if there is a legitimate policy reason to do so, even if a thief could not give title.

■ **PROCEDURAL BASIS**

[Hypothetical] Appeal of a lower court decision finding the purchaser of a stolen watch liable for conversion.

■ **FACTS**

Prosser's (P) watch, valued at about $500.00, was stolen by a thief named Thurlow. Claiming that he needed to sell the watch to pay for his mother's medical care, Thurlow sold the watch to Keeton (D) for $500.00. Approximately one month later, Prosser (P) saw Keeton (D) wearing the watch and identified it as his by means of a secret mark on the back. Prosser (P) demanded a return of the watch and Keeton (D), arguing that he had paid for it, refused to return it. Prosser (P) brought suit seeking its return.

■ **ISSUE**

Can a purchaser of stolen property gain valid title to the property by operation of law even though a thief could not pass it to him?

■ **DECISION AND RATIONALE**

(Allen, J.) No. The thief did not have title to the watch, and as such he cannot transfer title to the watch. And if the thief cannot transfer title to the watch, then Keeton (D) did not get title to the watch from the thief, even though he paid for the watch. Since Keeton (D) has no title, he has no right to the watch and is liable to Prosser (P) as a converter.

■ **DISSENT**

(Bateman, J.) A rule of law should work justice between the parties. In this case, neither Prosser (P) nor Keeton (D) were guilty of wrongdoing, but as the thief has disappeared, someone must bear the loss. Watch owners are in a better position to guard against theft than purchasers are to discover it. Therefore, justice requires that we find in favor of Keeton (D) and grant him good title by operation of law.

■ **DISSENT**

(Compton, J.) The law may give the good faith purchaser title if there is a legitimate policy reason to do so, even if the thief could not give title. There is no reason in justice to make Prosser (P) bear the loss here—no evidence has been presented to establish that he, or any other watch owner, can protect himself from thieves any better than a purchaser can. Justice, therefore, does not help us. However, social policy, which transcends the question of justice, demands that exchange of goods be fostered. If every buyer had to investigate the provenance of the goods he or she has purchased, the process of buying and selling would be made much more costly, if not stopped altogether. Social policy, therefore, requires us to hold that Keeton (D) should be given title to the watch. [The case does not correctly state any rule of law—so don't rely upon it in that regard.]

Analysis:

This hypothetical case demonstrates the interplay and interaction of justice and policy in the law of torts. Both are important, but sometimes one may take precedence over the other, as in this case where social policy was deemed to be more important and more significant than justice (to "transcend" it). Many tort cases deal with issues of justice and social policy, and in some cases those issues contradict one another.

■ CASE VOCABULARY

CONVERTER: One guilty of conversion (the wrongful possession of another's property).

GOOD FAITH PURCHASER: One who purchases an item with absolutely no knowledge of wrongdoing on the part of the seller; one who purchases an item with a reasonable belief that he or she is purchasing it from the true owner.

OPERATION OF LAW: The way in which a right or liability, regardless of a party's intent, is created for a party.

PROVENANCE: An item's history of ownership.

TITLE: The legal right to ownership in a particular piece of property.

Holden v. Wal-Mart Stores, Inc.

(Injured Customer) v. *(Department Store)*

259 Neb. 78, 608 N.W.2d 187 (2000)

COMPENSATORY DAMAGES ARE THE PROPER AWARD IN MANY TORT CASES

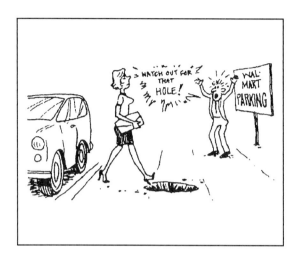

■ **INSTANT FACTS** A customer sued Wal-Mart (D) when she fell and injured her knee in a store parking lot.

■ **BLACK LETTER RULE** An award of damages may be set aside on appeal as excessive or inadequate, but only when it is so excessive or inadequate as to be the result of passion, prejudice, mistake, or some other means not apparent in the record.

■ **PROCEDURAL BASIS**

Certification to the Nebraska Supreme Court of a jury decision awarding a personal injury plaintiff only $3,600 after a fall in a store parking lot.

■ **FACTS**

In July of 1992, Holden (P) was injured when she fell in the parking lot of a Wal-Mart in Scottsbluff, Nebraska. Holden (P) had, at the time of injury, an extensive history of knee problems, one for which she received a handicapped parking permit from the state. After getting out of her car, Holden (P) accidentally stepped into a hole in the parking lot, which caused her to twist her foot and injure her knee. She was taken to the emergency room and subsequently underwent knee replacement surgery. At trial, Dr. Diane Gilles, an orthopedic surgeon, testified that Holden's (P) knee replacement surgery, which she would have eventually needed anyway, was sped up by 5 to 10 years as a result of the fall. Dr. Mark Alan McFerran, the orthopedic surgeon who performed Holden's (P) knee replacement, similarly testified of a hastening of the need for the surgery. Gilles charged Holden (P) $646.75, and McFerran charged her $24,707.91. McFerran also testified that, in approximately 15 to 20 years, Holden (P) would need another replacement surgery (as the parts in her knee would wear out) which would cost her between $40,000 and $50,000, barring complications. The jury found that Holden (P) was 40% negligent and Wal-Mart (D) 60% negligent for Holden's (P) fall. The jury found total damages of $6,000, and thus Holden was awarded $3,600. An appeal followed.

■ **ISSUE**

Can an appeals court overturn a jury's award of damages to a particular plaintiff?

■ **DECISION AND RATIONALE**

(Connolly, J.) Yes. Holden (P) argues that the jury made a mistake in its computation of damages. It is true that an award of damages may be set aside on appeal as excessive or inadequate, but only when it is so excessive or inadequate as to be the result of passion, prejudice, mistake, or some other means not apparent in the record. Such is not the case here. Evidence was presented regarding Holden's (P) previous knee problems, and the conflicting evidence regarding the effect of the fall on this preexisting condition. Holden (P) testified of the additional pain that resulted from the injury, and her doctors indicated that the fall sped up the need for her to have replacement surgery. However, there was also evidence that Holden (P) had been having similar knee pain causing difficulty in her life prior

---

to the fall—pain that she had not reported to her doctors. Also, the evidence was strong that she would, at some point, have undergone knee replacement surgery regardless of the fall. When she might have done so was unclear. The jury could have reached any number of conclusions. A jury is entitled to determine what portion of a claimed injury was proximately caused by the incident and what portion of the medical bills was reasonably required. In this case, the jury certainly could have, and did, determine that the fall was the proximate cause of only a small part of Holden's (P) damages. The evidence supports that conclusion, and we will not disturb it on appeal. Affirmed.

Analysis:

There are a number of remedies available to plaintiffs in the many actions that can be brought under tort law. In some cases the proper remedy is an injunction. In other cases it is punitive damages. In many others, compensatory damages is the remedy awarded to a victorious plaintiff (and in some cases, all three might be granted). *Holden* demonstrates the simple principle of compensatory damages, as Holden (P) was awarded money to compensate her for the injury that she received at the hands of Wal-Mart (D). There are a number of different types of compensatory damages. Some might include recovery of lost wages and medical expenses, as well as compensation for pain and suffering resulting from the tort. There can be recovery for future damages and emotional injury as well, in certain cases. The party bringing suit—the injured party—always bears the burden of proving the extent of damages caused by the other side's tort, as demonstrated by the fact that, in this case, it was Holden (P) who was presenting the jury with evidence of injury. There are other important points that can be gleaned from this case. First, it is the job of the trier of fact to determine the amount of compensatory damages that should be given to a particular party. And second, in certain cases it is permissible for a court of appeals to overturn a damages award because of mistake, passion, or prejudice.

■ CASE VOCABULARY

COMPENSATORY DAMAGES: Damages in the nature of compensation awarded for injury.

INJUNCTION: A court order that commands or prevents a particular action.

LIABILITY: A state of obligation or responsibility.

NEGLIGENCE: A failure to use that measure of care that a reasonable person would have used in the same circumstances.

PROXIMATE CAUSE: The cause of an event.

PUNITIVE DAMAGES: Damages awarded in addition to compensatory damages with the intent of punishing the opposing side for certain wrongdoing.

Estevez v. United States

(Injury Victim) v. *(United States Government)*

72 F.Supp.2d 205 (S.D.N.Y.1999)

IT IS PERMISSIBLE FOR A TORT CLAIMANT TO RECEIVE COMPENSATION FOR FUTURE LOSSES, COSTS, AND PAIN AND SUFFERING, AS WELL AS FOR PAST LOSSES, COSTS, AND SUFFERING

■ **INSTANT FACTS** A two-year old who was severely injured in an automobile crash caused by a United States Postal Worker sued for compensation for his injuries.

■ **BLACK LETTER RULE** When a party is injured, awards can be made for past medical bills, future medical expenses, future pain and suffering, and future lost earnings.

■ **PROCEDURAL BASIS**

A family brought suit in federal district court for injuries stemming from a car accident caused by an employee and agent of the United States.

■ **FACTS**

Joseph Estevez (P), a two-year old, was severely injured when his parents' car was involved in a collision with a postal truck. After the crash, Joseph (P) was taken to the hospital where he remained for approximately five weeks. During that time he underwent the following surgical procedures: (1) exploratory laparotomy, bowel resection, and repair of perforations in the bowel wall; and (2) aortic endartectomy, thrombectomy, and patch angioplasty. The first surgery was due to a perforation in a section of the small intestine, an abdominal wall hernia, and a tear or fracture of the lower pole of the right kidney. The second was a result of an intimal tear to the inner lining of the aorta. Joseph (P) also underwent a spinal fusion. Joseph (P) sustained the following injuries or underwent the following additional treatment: (1) he wore a special spinal fracture brace for seven weeks for a compression fracture; (2) he was placed on high blood pressure medication as a result of renal injuries; (3) he was intubated with an endotracheal breathing tube; (4) he was forced to utilize a nasogastric feeding tube; and (5) he has a foot drop. As a result of the last injury he underwent extensive physical therapy. The trial court found the United States (D) negligent and then considered damages.

■ **ISSUE**

Can a tort claimant receive payment for future costs, losses, and injuries?

■ **DECISION AND RATIONALE**

(Scheindlin, J.) Yes. The parties agree that Joseph (P) has incurred $138,000 in past hospital and medical costs. With respect to future injuries, this court heard testimony that Joseph (P) is at high risk for the development of intestinal adhesions, which can lead to intestinal obstructions. He is also at a risk of suffering an infection of the Gortex patch or of developing pseudoaneurysms of the aorta. Finally, he will be at risk of developing endocarditis, though this last risk may be preventable through prophylactic treatment and early diagnosis. The government agrees that Joseph (P) will require an annual echocardiogram, 13 of which will occur as a child and 55 of which will occur as an adult (based on Joseph's (P) life expectancy of 67.5 years). The total cost of these procedures will be $85,415. Joseph (P) will also need a scannergram and x-ray of his leg every 18 months during the next five

---

years, which will cost a total of $1,800. There is some disagreement on the future cost of treatment for the foot drop, but at a minimum Joseph (P) would require an orthotic shoe insert, which over his lifetime will cost over $40,000. There is also the possibility of physical therapy, which will cost Joseph (P) approximately $11,700 per year. Surgery is also a possibility, though there was no testimony as to the cost on the record. Joseph (P) is entitled to an award for future medical expenses. Based on the evidence in the record, Joseph (P) is awarded a total of $220,815 in future medical expenses. Joseph (P) is entitled to an award for future pain and suffering. Though the setting of such an award is speculative, based on my review of the evidence I conclude that an appropriate award is $750,000. I reach this conclusion based on the totality of Joseph's (P) medical problems and his long life expectancy. Joseph (P) also requests an award for future lost earnings. He claims that as a person with a disability, his earning capacity is diminished as compared to people who have no disability. He relies on the testimony of Andrew Gluck, who performed a vocational economic assessment. Mr. Gluck made several assumptions. First, he assumed that Joseph (P) has a permanent, non-severe disability. Second, given the education of Joseph's (P) parents, he assumed that Joseph (P) is likely to obtain a college degree. He next assumed, based on statistical tables, that disabled males with a college degree are likely to earn $10,000 less per year than non-disabled males ($54,526 as opposed to $64,610). Finally, he concluded that occupationally disabled people have a shorter work life expectancy than non-disabled people. He testified that on average occupationally disabled people work 6.67 years less than those who have no disability. I agree with the government (D) that there is no principled way to conclude that Joseph's (P) earning power will be any less than that of a healthy person. Nonetheless, I disagree with the government (D) with respect to work life expectancy. Based on the evidence, I conclude that Joseph (P) has a less than average work life expectancy. Given the $64,610 average annual salary of a 45-year old college educated male, I conclude that Joseph (P) is entitled to a future lost earnings award of $432,887 ($64,610 x 6.7 years). Joseph (P) is therefore entitled to a total award of $1,993,902.

Analysis:

The significance of *Estevez* lies not in any legal principles that it teaches, but in the way in which it demonstrates computation of damages in a tort case. This case demonstrates the way in which the judge addresses the computation of past medical damages, as well as the manner in which future medical, pain and suffering, and lost wage damages are calculated by the court. This case also demonstrates that an award for future damages will only be given to the degree that an amount is ascertainable, though there will be awarded some damages for speculative future needs or costs, such as future pain and suffering and future lost wages, even when the amount truly necessary cannot be concretely determined.

■ CASE VOCABULARY

AORTA: A part of the heart that carries blood from the heart to the arteries.

AORTIC ENDARTECTOMY: The surgical removal of a blood clot from inside the aorta.

BOWEL RESECTION: The surgical removal of part of the intestine.

ECHOCARDIOGRAM: An examination of the structure and functioning of the heart.

ENDOCARDITIS: An inflammation of the lining of the heart and heart valves

ENDOTRACHEAL BREATHING TUBE: A breathing tube that is placed within the trachea (the part of the respiratory system in which air passes to and from the lungs).

EXPLORATORY LAPAROTOMY: An exploratory cutting of the abdominal wall.

FOOT DROP: An inability to flex the foot.

INTESTINAL ADHESIONS: An abnormal uniting of tissue within the intestines.

INTESTINAL OBSTRUCTIONS: An obstruction of the intestines resulting from the growth of intestinal adhesions.

INTIMAL TEAR: A tear in the innermost layer or coat of an organ.

INTUBATED: Having a tube placed inside a hollow organ.

NASOGASTRIC FEEDING TUBE: A feeding tube reaching the stomach by means of the nasal passages.

ORTHOTIC SHOE INSERT: A shoe insert made for the purpose of aiding and taking strain off of weak joints and muscles.

PATCH ANGIOPLASTY: The surgical patching or repair of a blood vessel.

PERFORATION: A hole or holes, in this case in the intestinal wall.

PROPHYLACTIC TREATMENT: Preventative treatment.

PSEUDOANEURYSMS: An abnormal dilation of blood vessels, particularly in an artery, resulting from disease of the artery.

RENAL INJURIES: Injury to the kidneys.

SPINAL FUSION: A surgical fusion of portions of the spinal cord required by injury thereto.

THROBECTOMY: The removal of a blood clot from a vein.

CHAPTER THREE

Establishing a Claim for Intentional Tort to Person or Property

Van Camp v. McAfoos

Instant Facts: A woman injured by a young child on a tricycle sued the child to recover compensation for her injuries.

Black Letter Rule: It is not enough, to survive a motion to dismiss, to simply plead that one person touched another and injury resulted there must also be a claim of fault, negligence, or wrongdoing on the part of the party doing the touching.

Snyder v. Turk

Instant Facts: A nurse sued a doctor for battery when he grabbed her during an operation and yelled about her incompetence.

Black Letter Rule: A person is subject to liability for battery when he acts intending to cause a harmful or offensive contact, and when a harmful or offensive contact results.

Cohen v. Smith

Instant Facts: A woman sued her nurse and the hospital when, against her wishes, the nurse saw her unclothed and touched her naked body.

Black Letter Rule: An actor commits a battery if he acts with an intent to cause harmful or offensive contact to another and such a contact results.

Leichtman v. WLW Jacor Communications, Inc.

Instant Facts: An anti-smoking advocate brought suit for battery against a radio talk-show host when the host intentionally blew cigar smoke into his face.

Black Letter Rule: A battery is committed when one person intentionally blows cigar smoke into another's face.

Garratt v. Dailey

Instant Facts: A woman brought suit against a young boy when she was injured in a fall that resulted from his pulling a chair out from underneath her.

Black Letter Rule: When a person has knowledge to a substantial certainty that harmful or offensive contact will result from a certain action, a battery occurs if that action is taken, even if there is no intent to cause harm to another.

Hall v. McBryde

Instant Facts: Hall (P) was struck by a stray bullet in crossfire between McBryde (D) and other gang members.

Black Letter Rule: A battery occurs if someone acts with the intention of causing a harmful or offensive contact with the person of another, or an imminent apprehension of such contact, and a harmful or offensive contact with a third person directly or indirectly results.

Polmatier v. Russ

Instant Facts: The wife of a murder victim brought suit against her insane son-in-law, the killer, for her husband's wrongful death.

Black Letter Rule: The reasons and motives that form a defendant's intentions to act in a certain way need not be rational in order for the defendant to have the intent to invade the interests of another; irrational motives and reasons can provide the intent to commit a battery.

White v. Muniz

Instant Facts: A supervisor at a care facility for the elderly sued a resident when she was slapped for trying to change the resident's diaper.

Black Letter Rule: In order to find a mentally deficient person liable for an intentional tort, a jury must find that the actor subjectively intended offensive or harmful consequences.

Cullison v. Medley

Instant Facts: Cullison (P) sued the Medleys (D) for assault after they intimidated him while Mr. Medley was armed.

Black Letter Rule: Assault occurs when one acts intending to cause a harmful or offensive contact with the person of the other or an imminent apprehension of such contact.

Koffman v. Garnett

Instant Facts: Garnett (D), an adult football coach, lifted Koffman (P) and threw him to the ground to demonstrate proper tackling technique.

Black Letter Rule: Assault consists of an act intended to cause either harmful or offensive contact with another person or apprehension of such contact, and that creates in that other person's mind a reasonable apprehension of an imminent battery.

McCann v. Wal–Mart Stores, Inc.

Instant Facts: Three store patrons sued Wal–Mart for false imprisonment when two store employees backed them into a corner and held them there for over an hour while waiting for a store security guard to arrive.

Black Letter Rule: The tort of false imprisonment occurs when conduct by one party serves to confine another within certain boundaries fixed by the actor and the victim is conscious of the confinement or harmed by it.

Brown v. Muhlenberg Township

Instant Facts: A Muhlenberg Township (D) police officer shot and killed Brown's (P) dog when it escaped from its fenced yard.

Black Letter Rule: Under the Fourth Amendment, all people have the right to be secure in their persons, houses, papers, and effects against unreasonable searches and seizures.

Van Camp v. McAfoos

(Injury Victim) v. *(Toddler on a Tricycle)*
261 Iowa 1124, 156 N.W.2d 878 (1968)

WHERE AN ESSENTIAL ELEMENT OF THE CAUSE OF ACTION IS MISSING, THE QUESTION IS NOT WHAT MAY BE SHOWN UNDER THE PLEADING BUT WHETHER A CAUSE OF ACTION HAS BEEN PLED

■ **INSTANT FACTS** A woman injured by a young child on a tricycle sued the child to recover compensation for her injuries.

■ **BLACK LETTER RULE** It is not enough, to survive a motion to dismiss, to simply plead that one person touched another and injury resulted—there must also be a claim of fault, negligence, or wrongdoing on the part of the party doing the touching.

■ **PROCEDURAL BASIS**

Certification to the Supreme Court of Iowa of a trial court decision granting a motion to dismiss in a civil battery action.

■ **FACTS**

Mark McAfoos (D), a three year-old, injured Van Camp (P) when he ran into her with his tricycle while on the public sidewalk. The collision caused injury to Van Camp's (P) right Achilles' tendon, which injury required surgery. Van Camp (P) sued, the trial court granted McAfoos' (D) motion to dismiss, and Van Camp (P) appealed.

■ **ISSUE**

In order to state a cause of action, is it sufficient to simply plead that the plaintiff was touched by the defendant and injured, with no claim of fault, negligence, or wrongdoing against the defendant?

■ **DECISION AND RATIONALE**

(Becker, J.) No. The trial court stated the following: "It is not alleged that the defendant was negligent. It is not alleged that the action of the defendant was willful or wrongful in any manner. Under these circumstances it is difficult to see how the Division as now set out states any basis upon which the plaintiff could recover." We agree. Van Camp (P) argues that invasion of her person is in itself a wrong and she need plead no more. She argues that a person has a right not to be injuriously touched while using the sidewalk, and since she was struck by McAfoos (D), no more need be pleaded. She would impose liability without fault. We are not prepared to extend this concept to acts by children. Van Camp (P) insists on a right to recovery by proof of an accident caused by another, independent of fault or wrongdoing. Where an essential element of the cause of action is missing, the question is not what may be shown under the pleading but whether a cause of action has been pled. Intentionally wrongful or negligently wrongful use of the tricycle is neither pled nor can it be made out from the bare allegation that McAfoos (D) "operated a tricycle on said public sidewalk and drove the tricycle into the rear of the plaintiff without warning." Finally, Van Camp (P) cites many cases from other jurisdictions holding that a young child may be liable in tort. All of her cases, however, involve the fault concept; each case has fault as one of the essential elements of liability. We need not disagree with those authorities. Affirmed.

Analysis:

Van Camp stands for a very simple proposition: in order to hold a defendant liable in tort for battery (and most other torts), a plaintiff must show fault on the part of the defendant. In this case, Van Camp (P), as the court points out, was struck by a tricycle and injured. In her legal pleadings (which the court had to adhere to strictly as it was reviewing a motion to dismiss), she simply relied on the fact that she was hit by a tricycle. She did not allege negligence, fault, or wrongdoing on the part of the child, but simply wanted to collect based on the fact that she was struck—she wanted strict liability. The court held, however, that in order to hold a defendant liable in tort, a plaintiff must show fault on the part of the defendant—in order for McAfoos (D) to be held liable for the injury, Van Camp (P) would have to allege fault on his part. This she did not do, and as a result she lost on appeal.

■ CASE VOCABULARY

SINE QUA NON: Latin phrase meaning "without which not," or a condition on which something else necessarily relies.

STRICT LIABILITY: Liability for injury that does not require negligence or intent, but is based purely on the breach of some duty.

Snyder v. Turk

(Scrub Nurse) v. *(Surgeon)*

90 Ohio App.3d 18, 627 N.E.2d 1053 (1993)

A BATTERY IS AN INTENTIONAL, UNCONSENTED-TO CONTACT WITH ANOTHER

■ **INSTANT FACTS** A nurse sued a doctor for battery when he grabbed her during an operation and yelled about her incompetence.

■ **BLACK LETTER RULE** A person is subject to liability for battery when he acts intending to cause a harmful or offensive contact, and when a harmful or offensive contact results.

■ **PROCEDURAL BASIS**

Certification to the Court of Appeals of Ohio of an appeal of a directed verdict entered in favor of the defendant in a civil battery action.

■ **FACTS**

Dr. Turk (D) was performing a gall-bladder operation with the assistance of Snyder (P), a nurse. The operation was not going smoothly and Dr. Turk (D) was frustrated. Feeling that Snyder's (P) mistakes were a major reason that the operation was not going as he would like, Dr. Turk (D) grabbed her at one point, forced her head down toward the surgical opening, and said "Can't you see where I'm working? I'm working in a hole. I need long instruments." Snyder (P) sued for battery.

■ **ISSUE**

Can grabbing someone in a way offensive to personal dignity constitute a battery under tort law?

■ **DECISION AND RATIONALE**

(Wilson, J.) Yes. Dr. Turk (D) contends that there is no liability on his part for the commission of a battery against Snyder (P) absent proof of an intent to inflict personal injury upon her. He further argues that the directed verdict entered in his favor was proper because there was no evidence of his intent to inflict personal injury on Snyder (P). A person is subject to liability for battery when he acts intending to cause a harmful or offensive contact, and when a harmful or offensive contact results. Offensive contact is any contact which is offensive to a reasonable sense of personal dignity. In this case, the issue is the propriety of the directed verdict. A motion for a directed verdict assumes the truth of the evidence supporting the facts essential to the claim after giving the non-moving party the benefit of all reasonable inferences from the evidence, and refers the application of a reasonable-minds test to such evidence. Here, we believe that reasonable minds could conclude that Dr. Turk (D) intended to commit an offensive contact. Reversed.

Analysis:

Snyder is important in that it demonstrates the two different ways in which a battery can take place. Certainly, as Dr. Turk (D) argued, a battery occurs when one person intentionally inflicts personal injury upon another, such as when one person punches another. A second way in which battery can occur, as this court points out, is by the offensive touching of another person, or the intentional touching of another person in a way that a reasonable person would find offensive to personal dignity. In this case, the appellate court found that reasonable people could find grabbing someone and pushing them toward an operating table in order to demonstrate their incompetence to be an offensive act, and therefore battery was found. It is important to note that the views of the one committing the battery and the victim are not dispositive, but it is the view of the reasonable person that controls. Thus, if Snyder (P) were simply a hypersensitive person, and no reasonable person would find pushing her face toward the table to be offensive, there would be no battery—the fact that she was personally offended would not matter. Nor did it matter that Dr. Turk (D) did not find his own actions to be offensive to anyone.

■ CASE VOCABULARY

BATTERY: An intentional, unconsented, and offensive touching of another person.

Cohen v. Smith

(Pregnant Woman) v. *(Male Nurse)*
269 Ill.App.3d 1087, 207 Ill.Dec. 873, 648 N.E.2d 329 (1995)

PROTECTING PERSONAL INTEGRITY HAS LONG BEEN VIEWED AS AN IMPORTANT BASIS FOR THE LAW OF BATTERY

■ **INSTANT FACTS** A woman sued her nurse and the hospital when, against her wishes, the nurse saw her unclothed and touched her naked body.

■ **BLACK LETTER RULE** An actor commits a battery if he acts with an intent to cause harmful or offensive contact to another and such a contact results.

■ **PROCEDURAL BASIS**

Certification to the Appellate Court of Illinois of a trial court decision to grant a motion to dismiss in favor of the defendant in a civil battery case.

■ **FACTS**

Patricia Cohen (P) was admitted to St. Joseph Memorial Hospital to deliver her baby. After she was told that she would need a cesarean section, Cohen (P) allegedly informed her doctor, who informed the hospital staff, that her religious beliefs prohibited her from being seen unclothed by a male. The doctor assured her that the beliefs would be respected. During the procedure, Roger Smith (D), a male nurse, allegedly observed and touched Cohen's (P) naked body. Cohen (P) sued Smith (D) and the hospital. The trial court granted Smith's (D) motion to dismiss, and Cohen (P) appealed.

■ **ISSUE**

Can contact that does not cause injury but does cause offense provide grounds for a tort action in battery?

■ **DECISION AND RATIONALE**

(Chapman, J.) Yes. A trial court may dismiss a cause of action for failing to state a claim only if it is apparent that no set of alleged facts can be proven which will entitle a plaintiff to recovery. The Restatement (Second) of Torts provides that an actor commits a battery if: "(a) he acts intending to cause a harmful or offensive contact with the person of the other or a third person, or an imminent apprehension of such a contact, and (b) a harmful [or offensive] contact with the person of the other directly or indirectly results." Restatement (Second) of Torts, § 18 (1965). Liability for battery emphasizes the plaintiff's lack of consent to the touching. Offensive contact is said to occur when contact offends a reasonable sense of personal dignity. As such, a defendant is not only liable for contacts which do actual physical harm, but also for any contacts which, however trivial, are offensive or insulting. This application of battery to remedy offensive and insulting conduct is deeply ingrained in our legal history. Although most people in modern society have come to accept the necessity of being seen unclothed and being touched by members of the opposite sex during medical treatment, the Cohens (P) had not accepted these procedures and, according to their complaint, informed Smith (D) and the hospital of their convictions. Although others may not share these convictions, the courts have consistently recognized individuals' rights to refuse medical treatment or, in this case, determine the scope of medical treatment. Accepting as true the Cohens' (P) allegations that they informed Smith (D) and the hospital of their beliefs and that Cohen (P) was still treated as a patient without those beliefs, we conclude that the trial court erred in dismissing the battery claim. Reversed.

Analysis:

Cohen presents the Restatement (Second) view of battery, which is a view much the same as that found in *Snyder* and other cases. Indeed, the Restatement (Second) supports the idea that an offensive touching, though not physically harmful, can result in a battery. One slight difference between the two cases, however, can be found in the way in which it is determined whether there has been offensive conduct. *Snyder* clearly states that conduct is only offensive when a reasonable person would find it to be offensive. *Cohen* is slightly different, however, in that it finds offensive conduct even where a reasonable person might not, so long as it is reasonable that a person would take offense. The difference is that under the first, the court looks to whether a reasonable person would be offended, while under the second it looks to see whether it was reasonable for the offended person to get offended. It is possible that, as in this case, a reasonable person would not be offended while it is still reasonable for another, because of circumstances (or in this case religious beliefs), to be offended at particular conduct. In *Cohen,* the court clearly states that most people have accepted the fact that one must be seen unclothed and be touched during medical procedures. Thus, a majority of people would not likely find the touching that took place in *Cohen* offensive Indeed, it is only a small minority who do find it offensive. Even though this is true, the court still accepted the actions as offensive because the Cohens found them offensive. Thus, the test for offensiveness used here is not that of the reasonable person, but of the subjective view of the one touched.

■ **CASE VOCABULARY**

OFFENSIVE CONTACT: Contact that offends a reasonable sense of personal dignity, or contact that a reasonable person would find offensive to personal dignity.

Leichtman v. WLW Jacor Communications, Inc.

(*Anti-Smoking Advocate*) v. (*Radio Station*)

92 Ohio App.3d 232, 634 N.E.2d 697 (1994)

ONE WHO IS PRESENT AND ENCOURAGES OR INCITES THE COMMISSION OF A BATTERY CAN BE HELD LIABLE FOR THE BATTERY JUST AS THE ONE COMMITTING THE ACTUAL BATTERY WILL BE

■ **INSTANT FACTS** An anti-smoking advocate brought suit for battery against a radio talk-show host when the host intentionally blew cigar smoke into his face.

■ **BLACK LETTER RULE** A battery is committed when one person intentionally blows cigar smoke into another's face.

■ PROCEDURAL BASIS

Certification to the Court of Appeals of Ohio of a trial court dismissal of a battery count, stemming from the intentional blowing of smoke into an anti-smoker's face.

■ FACTS

Leichtman (P), a self-proclaimed "nationally known" anti-smoking advocate, was invited to appear on the WLW Bill Cunningham radio show on the date of the Great American Smokeout. He was invited for the purpose of discussing the harmful effects of smoking and breathing second-hand smoke. While Leichtman (P) was in the studio, Furman, another WLW (D) talk-show host, lit a cigar and repeatedly blew smoke in Leichtman's (P) face "for the purpose of causing physical discomfort, humiliation and distress."

■ ISSUE

Does intentionally blowing smoke into another's face for the purpose of harassing the other constitute a battery?

■ DECISION AND RATIONALE

(Authoring Judge Not Stated) Yes. Leichtman (P) contends that Furman's (D) intentional act constituted a battery. In determining whether a person is liable for battery, the Ohio Supreme Court has adopted the rule that "[c]ontact which is offensive to a reasonable sense of personal dignity is offensive contact." The word "offensive" has been defined as "disagreeable or nauseating or painful because of outrage to taste and sensibilities or affronting insultingness." Furthermore, tobacco smoke, as a particulate matter, has the physical properties capable of making contact. When Furman (D) intentionally blew cigar smoke in Leichtman's (P) face he committed a battery. No matter how trivial the incident, a battery is actionable, even if damages are only one dollar. With respect to Cunningham (D), at common law, one who is present and encourages or incites the commission of a battery by words can be equally liable as a principal. With regard to WLW (D), an employer is not legally responsible for the intentional torts of its employees that do not facilitate or promote its business. While we do not approve of trivial lawsuits, absent circumstances that warrant sanctions for frivolous appeals, we refuse to limit one's right to sue. Reversed.

Analysis:

Leichtman addresses the "contact" aspect of battery. Under the general definition of battery, there must be some contact or the "touching" of the victim by the one committing the battery. In this case, the court found contact even though Furman never actually touched Leichtman's body with his own because "tobacco smoke, as a particulate matter, has the physical properties capable of making contact." This is in the vein of cases holding that a bullet from a gun or a rock thrown from the hand are extensions of the person pulling the trigger or holding the rock. In this case, the smoke particles were considered an extension of Furman, and were therefore capable of being used to commit a battery. *Leichtman* also briefly addresses the issue of liability for one who incites another to commit a battery, holding that Cunningham, who apparently encouraged the smoke blowing, could be held liable for the battery along with Furman.

■ CASE VOCABULARY

OFFENSIVE: Offensive contact is that contact which is "disagreeable or nauseating or painful because of outrage to taste and sensibilities or affronting insultingness."

Garratt v. Dailey

(Young Boy) v. *(Older Woman)*
46 Wn.2d 197, 279 P.2d 1091 (1955)

WHEN A MINOR COMMITS A TORT WITH FORCE HE IS LIABLE AS ANY OTHER PERSON WOULD BE

■ **INSTANT FACTS** A woman brought suit against a young boy when she was injured in a fall that resulted from his pulling a chair out from underneath her.

■ **BLACK LETTER RULE** When a person has knowledge to a substantial certainty that harmful or offensive contact will result from a certain action, a battery occurs if that action is taken, even if there is no intent to cause harm to another.

■ **PROCEDURAL BASIS**

Certification to the Supreme Court of Washington of a trial court finding that there was no battery in a suit brought by an adult woman against a young boy.

■ **FACTS**

Ruth Garratt (P) suffered a fractured hip and other serious and painful injuries when, on July 16, 1951, she fell to the ground while trying to sit down in a lawn chair. How she came to fall was the subject of dispute. Garratt's (P) sister, who was present during the fall, testified that Brian Dailey (D), a five year-old boy, deliberately pulled the chair out from under Garratt (P) as she was about to sit in it. Dailey (D) testified that he had moved the chair and was about to sit in it when he saw Garratt (P) sitting down (with nothing underneath her). At that time, he jumped up and tried to move the chair to a position underneath her so as to prevent injury. Garratt (P) brought suit against Dailey (D) for the injuries. The trial court found in favor of Dailey (D), stressing that he did not have any intent to injure Garratt (P) when he moved the chair, and therefore did not commit a battery. Garratt (P) appealed.

■ **ISSUE**

Can a battery occur if there is no intent to injure another but there is a knowledge that a certain action will result in harmful contact and that action is taken?

■ **DECISION AND RATIONALE**

(Hill, J.) Yes. Brian (D), whether 5 or 55, must have committed a wrongful act before he can be held liable for Garratt's (P) injuries. Garratt (P) argues that the act of moving the chair constituted a battery, which is defined as the intentional infliction of a harmful bodily contact upon another. The rule used in determining liability for battery is found in 29 Restatement (First) of Torts § 13, which states: "An act which, directly or indirectly, is the legal cause of a harmful contact with another's person makes the actor liable to the other, if (a) the act is done with the intention of bringing about a harmful or offensive contact." The comments to this section further state that in order for an act to be done "with the intention of bringing about a harmful or offensive contact .... [it] must be done for the purpose of causing the contact ... or with knowledge on the part of the actor that such contact ... is substantially certain to be produced." Had Garratt (P) proved to the satisfaction of the trial court that Brian (D) moved the chair while she was in the act of sitting down, his action would have been with the intent of causing her injury, and she would be entitled to a judgment against him. The trial court did not so find, but accepted Brian's (D) version of the facts. It then considered whether a battery was established under the facts as it found them. In this connection, we quote another section of the comments to the Restatement: "It is not enough that the act itself is intentionally done and this, even though the actor realizes or should realize that it contains a ... risk of bringing about the contact or apprehension. Such realization may make the actor's conduct negligent or even reckless but unless he realizes that to a substantial certainty, the contact or apprehension will result, the actor has not that intention which is necessary to make him liable under the rule stated in this section." Thus, a battery would be established if, in addition to Garratt's (P) fall, it was proved that, when Brian (D) moved the chair, he knew with substantial certainty that she would attempt to sit down where the chair had been. The mere absence of any intent to injure Garratt (P) or to play a prank on her or to embarrass her, or to commit an assault and battery on her would not absolve him from liability if in fact he had such knowledge. Without such a knowledge, however, there would be no wrongful act and thus no liability. We believe that before Garratt's (P) case can be dismissed, there should be no question but that the trial court addresses this issue; hence, the case should be remanded for clarifications of the findings to specifically cover the question of Brian's (D) knowledge, because intent could be inferred therefrom. If the court finds that he had such knowledge the necessary intent will be established and Garratt (P) will be entitled to recover, even though there was no purpose to injure or embarrass her. The only circumstance where Brian's (D) age is of any consequence is in determining what he knew, and there his experience, capacity, and understanding are material. Remanded.

Analysis:

Garratt stands for the proposition that, in some jurisdictions, a battery can occur even when there is no intentional and offensive touching, which is the normal definition of battery. Under *Garratt,* a battery will occur despite a lack of an offensive intentional touching when a person has knowledge to a substantial certainty that harmful or offensive contact will result from a certain action. Thus, in this case, it was found that Brian (D) might have committed a battery even though he never touched Garratt (P); the fact that he knew pulling the chair away might cause her harm was enough for the court. Some jurisdictions accept the Washington view of battery laid out in *Garratt,* but many others still require an actual touching of the battery victim. With respect to the remand ordered by the Supreme Court of Washington, the trial court later found that Garratt (P) was actually in the act of seating herself when the chair was moved, and that Brian (D) knew what she was doing. On that ground, the trial court ruled in favor of Garratt (P).

Hall v. McBryde

(*Neighbor*) v. (*Gang Member*)
919 P.2d 910 (Colo. Ct. App. 1996)

INTENT TO COMMIT BATTERY UPON ONE PERSON CAN TRANSFER TO ANOTHER

You hurt me, you hurt them.

■ **INSTANT FACTS** Hall (P) was struck by a stray bullet in crossfire between McBryde (D) and other gang members.

■ **BLACK LETTER RULE** A battery occurs if someone acts with the intention of causing a harmful or offensive contact with the person of another, or an imminent apprehension of such contact, and a harmful or offensive contact with a third person directly or indirectly results.

■ **PROCEDURAL BASIS**

On appeal to review a judgment entered for the defendant.

■ **FACTS**

McBryde (D) was a high school student who lived with relatives in hope of avoiding involvement in gang activity near his parents' house. While at his parents' house to collect some clothing, he noticed a car with several youths approaching. He went under his parents' bed, retrieved a handgun belonging to his father, and went back outside. When the youths in the car began shooting at him, he returned four shots at the car, striking Hall (P), who lived next door. Hall (P) sued McBryde (D) for battery. The trial court entered judgment for McBryde (D) without determining whether the bullet that struck Hall (P) was fired by McBryde (D). Hall (P) appealed.

■ **ISSUE**

Did the court err in concluding that McBryde (D) did not intend to make harmful contact with Hall (P) when he shot at the car in which Hall was riding?

■ **DECISION AND RATIONALE**

(Hume, J.) Yes. "An actor is subject to liability to another for battery if he or she acts intending to cause a harmful or offensive contact with the person of the other or a third person, or an imminent apprehension of such a contact, and a harmful or offensive contact with the person of the other directly or indirectly results." The trial court decided that there was no evidence that McBryde (D) intended to shoot at another person as opposed to the passing vehicle, requiring judgment for the defendant. However, the intent requirement for battery does not require an intent to contact another, but merely the intent to put another in apprehension of such contact. Similarly, the doctrine of transferred intent establishes that Hall (P) need not be the object of McBryde's (D) intent so long as McBryde (D) intended to contact or place another person in apprehension of contact. While the trial court incorrectly failed to consider whether McBryde (D) intended to place the youths in the passing car in apprehension of harmful bodily contact, it is clear that he did so as a matter of law. By firing the gun at the automobile to protect his house, McBryde (D) intended to place the youths in apprehension of harmful or offensive contact, establishing the intent requirement for battery against Hall (D). Because the trial court failed to determine whether the bullet striking Hall (P) was in fact fired by McBryde (D), the case is remanded.

Analysis:

The tort of battery is an intentional tort, requiring a plaintiff to establish the defendant's intent to commit the act to recover for her injuries. Some commentators question whether the doctrine of transferred intent is required in today's legal culture, given the liberal application of negligence law. The reasonable person standard, it is argued, enables a plaintiff's recovery under a negligence theory, making transferred intent a legal fiction. In this case, for example, regardless of whether McBryde (D) intended to strike somebody with a bullet, Hall (P) may recover from McBryde (D) for negligence if his act of firing the gun deviated from the conduct expected of a reasonable person under the circumstances.

■ CASE VOCABULARY

BATTERY: The intentional and offensive touching of another without lawful justification.

TRANSFERRED INTENT: Intent that has been shifted from the originally intended wrongful act to the wrongful act actually committed. For example, if a person intends to kill one person but kills another, the intent may be transferred to the actual act.

Polmatier v. Russ

(Wife of Murder Victim) v. *(Killer)*
206 Conn. 229, 537 A.2d 468 (1988)

INSANE PERSONS CAN BE HELD LIABLE FOR THEIR INTENTIONAL TORTS

■ **INSTANT FACTS** The wife of a murder victim brought suit against her insane son-in-law, the killer, for her husband's wrongful death.

■ **BLACK LETTER RULE** The reasons and motives that form a defendant's intentions to act in a certain way need not be rational in order for the defendant to have the intent to invade the interests of another; irrational motives and reasons can provide the intent to commit a battery.

■ **PROCEDURAL BASIS**

Certification to the Supreme Court of Connecticut of a trial court decision in a wrongful death action involving the actions of an insane man.

■ **FACTS**

On November 20, 1976, Norm Russ (D) and his two-month-old daughter went to the home of Arthur Polmatier, Russ' (D) father-in-law, and his wife Dorothy (P) and their son. While there, Russ (D) attacked his father-in-law, beat him on the head with a beer bottle, and shot him twice in the chest. Polmatier died as a result of the gunshots. Russ (D) was taken to a local hospital and later transferred to the forensics ward of a mental institution. He was charged with murder, but found not guilty by reason of insanity. When questioned about the homicide, Russ (D) told police that his father-in-law was a heavy drinker and that he wanted him to suffer for his bad habits. He also told police that he was a supreme being who had the power to rule the world, as well as the power to make his bed fly out of the window. Russ (D) provided additional bizarre reasons for his actions when questioned by psychiatrists. Dr. Walter Borden, a psychiatrist, testified in Russ' (D) behalf in his criminal trial and in a civil trial for wrongful death, brought by Dorothy Polmatier (P). Dr. Borden testified that Russ (D) was legally insane and could not form a rational choice, but that he could make schizophrenic or crazy choices, and that he was not in a fugue state.

■ **ISSUE**

Can an insane person who intended to injure another, but did so because of psychotic delusions, be held liable for battery?

■ **DECISION AND RATIONALE**

(Glass, J.) Yes. A majority of the jurisdictions that have considered the issue have held that insane persons can be held liable for their intentional torts. This rule has been applied to cases involving intentional homicide. In this case, Russ (D) argues that for an act to be done with the requisite intent, the act must be an external manifestation of the actor's will. Russ (D) further argues that because his "activities were the external manifestations of irrational and uncontrollable thought disorders these activities cannot be acts for the purposes of establishing liability for assault and battery." We disagree. The reasons and motives that form a defendant's intentions to act in a certain way need not be rational in order for the defendant to have the intent to invade the interests of another; irrational motives and reasons can provide the intent to commit a battery. In this case, the trial court found that Russ (D) could not form a rational choice, but that he could make a schizophrenic or crazy choice. Considering his statements to the police and to Borden that he intended to punish Polmatier and to kill him, we are persuaded that Russ (D) intended to beat and shoot him. Because he was found not guilty by reason of insanity, it is uncontested in this civil action that he was incapable of forming the intent necessary for criminal responsibility for Polmatier's death. Under Connecticut's wrongful death statute, however, intent is not an essential element of the cause of action. Affirmed.

Analysis:

Polmatier stands for the proposition that the insane are generally liable for their torts, and that the fact that their intentions to commit a battery are based on irrational beliefs does not absolve them of liability for the tort. In the opinion, the court, citing the case of *Seals v. Snow,* 254 P. 348 (1927), a Kansas Supreme Court case provides the reasons that underlie the majority rule that the insane are liable for their torts. The Kansas Court wrote, "This liability has been based on a number of grounds, one that where one of two innocent persons must suffer a loss, it should be borne by the one who occasioned it. Another, that public policy requires the enforcement of such liability in order that relatives of the insane person shall be led to restrain him and that tort-feasors shall not simulate or pretend insanity to defend their wrongful acts causing damage to others, and that if he was not liable there would be no redress for injuries, and we might have the anomaly of an insane person having abundant wealth depriving another of his rights without compensation."

■ CASE VOCABULARY

FUGUE: A disturbed state of consciousness in which a person, seemingly fully aware of what he or she is doing, engages in certain acts, but upon recovery cannot remember doing them.

TORTFEASOR: A person who commits a tort.

White v. Muniz

(Representative of Insane Person) v. (*Care Facility Supervisor*)

999 P.2d 814 (Colo.2000)

INSANITY IS NOT A DEFENSE TO AN INTENTIONAL TORT, BUT IT IS A CHARACTERISTIC THAT MAY MAKE IT MORE DIFFICULT TO PROVE THE INTENT ELEMENT OF BATTERY

■ **INSTANT FACTS** A supervisor at a care facility for the elderly sued a resident when she was slapped for trying to change the resident's diaper.

■ **BLACK LETTER RULE** In order to find a mentally deficient person liable for an intentional tort, a jury must find that the actor subjectively intended offensive or harmful consequences.

■ **PROCEDURAL BASIS**

Certification to the Colorado Supreme Court of a state appellate court reversal of a jury verdict based on its belief that the jury was provided with an erroneous instruction.

■ **FACTS**

In October of 1993, Barbara White (D) placed her grandmother, Helen Everly, in an assisted living facility. While there, Everly exhibited erratic behavior, becoming easily agitated and aggressive towards others. A doctor diagnosed her with having progressive dementia, loss of memory, impulse control, and judgment; and a degenerative dementia of the Alzheimer type. On November 21, 1993, the caregiver in charge of Everly's wing asked Sherry Lynn Muniz (P), a shift supervisor, to change Everly's diaper, an effort in which Everly was not cooperating. Everly refused to allow Muniz (P) to change the diaper, and when Muniz (P) reached for the diaper, Everly struck her on the jaw and ordered her out of the room. Muniz (P) sued Everly and White (D), Everly's representative, for assault and battery. Following the presentation of evidence at trial, the judge instructed the jury that a person may suffer from dementia and still act intentionally, a person can be held to have intended an act even though her reasons and motives were entirely irrational, and that, in order to be liable for battery, a person "must have appreciated the offensiveness of her conduct." Muniz (P) objected to the last part of the instruction, the jury found for Everly, and Muniz (P) appealed. The appellate court overturned the jury verdict because it felt that the instruction was erroneous. White (D) appealed to the state supreme court.

■ **ISSUE**

Must a person appreciate the offensiveness of his or her conduct in order to be held liable for battery?

■ **DECISION AND RATIONALE**

(Kourlis, J.) Yes. It is generally agreed that an intentional tort requires some proof that the tortfeasor intended harm or offense. According to the Restatement (Second) of Torts § 13, "An actor is subject to liability to another for battery if (a) he acts intending to cause a harmful or offensive contact with the person of the other ... and (b) offensive [or harmful] contact ... directly or indirectly results." Traditionally, the actor had to understand that his contact would be harmful or offensive. The actor need not have intended, however, the harm that actually resulted from his action. Thus, if a slight punch to the victim resulted in traumatic injuries, the actor would be liable for all damages even if he

---

only intended to knock the wind out of the victim. More recently, some courts around the nation have abandoned this dual intent requirement in an intentional tort setting, that being an intent to contact and an intent that the contact be harmful or offensive, and have required only that the tortfeasor intend a contact with another that results in a harmful or offensive touching. Under this view, a victim need only prove that a voluntary movement by the tortfeasor resulted in a contact which a reasonable person would find offensive or to which the victim did not consent. Colorado requires a dual intent, so we reject Muniz's (P) argument and find that the trial court delivered an adequate instruction to the jury. Operating in accordance with the instructions, the jury had to find that Everly appreciated the offensiveness of her conduct in order to be liable for the intentional tort of battery. We presume that the jury looked into the mind of Everly, and reasoned that she did not possess the necessary intent to commit an assault or a battery. A jury can, of course, find a mentally deficient person liable for an intentional tort, but in order to do so, the jury must find that the actor intended offensive or harmful consequences. As a result, insanity is not a defense to an intentional tort according to the ordinary use of that term, but is a characteristic, like infancy, that may make it more difficult to prove the intent element of battery. Reversed.

Analysis:

White makes clear that while mentally deficient persons can be held liable for torts, they must be able to comprehend the offensiveness of their actions before that liability can attach. Because Helen Everly could not comprehend that her actions were offensive—the jury found that she was simply too far gone to understand that slapping Muniz (P) would be offensive—there was no liability, and Muniz (P) had no claim for damages. Under the rule in *White,* the same result would likely occur even if Muniz (P) was seriously injured and incurred large medical bills as a result of the hit—she would have no recourse under the law and would have to cover her own bills. The court does not state whether it would be good or bad for Muniz (P) to cover her own medical bills, but simply applies the rule. *White* also addresses a current rift in the treatment of intent in a battery sense as it addresses the issue of "dual intent." The Court writes: "More recently, some courts around the nation have abandoned this dual intent requirement in an intentional tort setting, that being an intent to contact and an intent that the contact be harmful or offensive, and have required only that the tortfeasor intend a contact with another that results in a harmful or offensive touching. Under this view, a victim need only prove that a voluntary movement by the tortfeasor resulted in a contact which a reasonable person would find offensive or to which the victim did not consent." Thus there are two ways of looking at intent and battery. The Colorado Supreme Court disapproves of abandonment of the dual intent requirement, and gives the following example of the possibility of problems that might arise when there is no dual intent requirement. It wrote: "These [abandoning] courts would find intent in contact to the back of a friend that results in a severe, unexpected injury even though the actor did not intend the contact to be harmful or offensive. The actor thus could be held liable for battery because a reasonable person would find an injury offensive or harmful, irrespective of the intent of the actor to harm or offend." In the opinion of the Colorado Supreme Court, then, the dual intent requirement is necessary so that a simple slap on the back of a friend will not be considered a battery. Had the Colorado Supreme Court adopted the non-dual intent view, the jury would not even have considered whether Everly had intent to harm, but only whether she made contact with Muniz (P) and whether a reasonable person would find the contact and the result unreasonable. Thus, a good argument can be made that under this different rule, the result in the case would have been different, for Everly's intent would be irrelevant and most people would find a blow to the jaw offensive.

■ CASE VOCABULARY

DUAL-INTENT REQUIREMENT: A requirement that, in order for a battery to be established, there must be both intent to contact and an intent to cause harmful or offensive results.

INTENTIONAL TORT: A tort that can only be committed when there exists intent, general or specific, to act. Examples of intentional torts include assault, battery, trespass, and false imprisonment.

Cullison v. Medley

(Assault Victim) v. *(Father)*
570 N.E.2d 27 (Ind.1991)

THE JURY DETERMINES WHETHER THE APPREHENSION OF HARMFUL CONDUCT WAS REASONABLE

■ **INSTANT FACTS** Cullison (P) sued the Medleys (D) for assault after they intimidated him while Mr. Medley was armed.

■ **BLACK LETTER RULE** Assault occurs when one acts intending to cause a harmful or offensive contact with the person of the other or an imminent apprehension of such contact.

■ **PROCEDURAL BASIS**

On appeal to review a decision of the Indiana Court of Appeals affirming summary judgment for the defendants.

■ **FACTS**

Cullison (P) met Sandy Medley (D) in a grocery store parking lot. After exchanging pleasantries, Cullison (P) invited Sandy to come back to his home to talk. Cullison (P) returned home alone and was later awakened by a knock at the door. After getting dressed, Cullison (P) found Medley's (D) father, mother, and other family members standing in his living room with Medley (D). Medley's (D) father had a pistol strapped to his thigh, while her mother kept her hand in her pocket as she spoke to him, convincing Cullison (P) that she, too, was carrying a gun. The presence of the others intimidated Cullison (P). While Medley's (D) father never withdrew the gun from its holster, he grabbed at it several times while making threatening remarks. Cullison (P) was never touched, but feared he would be shot. After the Medleys (D) left his house, Cullison (P) experienced chest pains and had a heart attack. Shortly thereafter, Cullison (P) learned that Medley's (D) father had shot a man in the past. Several months later, Medley's (D) father, again armed with a pistol, glared at Cullison (P) in a restaurant while standing with the pistol one foot from Cullison's (P) face. As a result of these experiences, Cullison (P) sought psychiatric help. Cullison (P) sued the Medleys (D) for assault. The trial court granted the defendants' motion for summary judgment and the Indiana Court of Appeals affirmed. Cullison (P) appealed to the state supreme court.

■ **ISSUE**

Did the court err in granting summary judgment to the defendants on the plaintiff's assault claim?

■ **DECISION AND RATIONALE**

(Krahulik, J.) Yes. "[A]ssault, unlike battery, is effectuated when one acts intending to cause a harmful or offensive contact with the person of the other or an imminent apprehension of such contact." No physical contact is required to establish assault, so long as a reasonable person would fear that harmful or offensive contact is imminent. Here, the court of appeals determined that because the father never removed the gun from its holster, his threats were conditional and did not express an intent to harm Cullison (P). Further, having alleged only emotional distress, Cullison (P) failed to establish the necessary damages to sustain an assault claim. Because assault is an injury to the mind rather than the body, however, mental anguish and emotional distress are recoverable damages. Similarly, Cullison (P) has presented sufficient facts to allow a reasonable juror to find that, by surrounding him in his home while armed and grabbing at the pistol, the Medleys (D) intended to frighten Cullison (P). It is for the jury to decide whether Cullison (P) had a reasonable apprehension of harmful or offensive contact. Reversed and remanded.

Analysis:

The court's conclusion creates an interesting situation. If an action for assault can be sustained by establishing emotional damages, it would be difficult to imagine an assault claim without a companion claim for intentional infliction of emotional distress. But not all intentional infliction of emotional distress claims will constitute assault, for emotional distress may arise without an apprehension of harmful contact.

■ CASE VOCABULARY

ASSAULT: The threat or use of force on another that causes that person to have a reasonable apprehension of imminent harmful or offensive contact; the act of putting another in reasonable fear or apprehension of an immediate battery by means of an act amounting to an attempt or threat to commit a battery.

APPREHENSION: Fear; anxiety.

EMOTIONAL DISTRESS: A highly unpleasant mental reaction (such as anguish, grief, fright, humiliation, or fury) that results from another person's conduct; emotional pain and suffering.

Koffman v. Garnett

(Football Player) v. *(Football Coach)*

265 Va. 12, 574 S.E.2d 258 (2003)

AN APPREHENSION OF FEAR MUST EXIST BEFORE THE HARMFUL CONTACT TO SUPPORT AN ASSAULT CLAIM

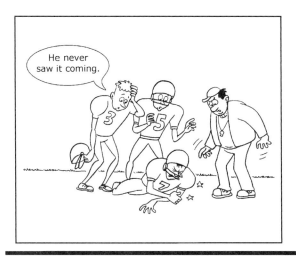

■ INSTANT FACTS Garnett (D), an adult football coach, lifted Koffman (P) and threw him to the ground to demonstrate proper tackling technique.

■ BLACK LETTER RULE Assault consists of an act intended to cause either harmful or offensive contact with another person or apprehension of such contact, and that creates in that other person's mind a reasonable apprehension of an imminent battery.

■ PROCEDURAL BASIS

On appeal to review the dismissal of the plaintiff's assault and battery claims.

■ FACTS

Koffman (P), in his first year of organized football, was placed on the defensive team under the defensive coach, Garnett (D). To demonstrate the proper tackling technique, Garnett (D), without warning, thrust himself into Koffman (P), picking him up and throwing him to the ground, thereby breaking Koffman's (P) arm. Koffman (P) sued Garnett (D) for assault. After the trial court dismissed the assault and battery claims, Koffman (P) appealed.

■ ISSUE

Did Koffman (P) have a reasonable apprehension of imminent harmful contact to establish an assault claim?

■ DECISION AND RATIONALE

(Lacy, J.) No. "[A]ssault consists of an act intended to cause either harmful or offensive contact with another person or apprehension of such contact, and that creates in that other person's mind a reasonable apprehension of an imminent battery." Dismissal was appropriate because Koffman (P) alleged no apprehension of an imminent battery. Any inference of apprehension is negated by the fact that Koffman (P) had no prior warning of Garnett's (D) actions. Any apprehension that occurred before Koffman (P) hit the ground occurred after Garnett's (D) battery and does not amount to assault. Koffman's (P) claims for battery, however, were properly supported. In his pleading, Koffman (P) alleged only that he consented to contact with other players. Whether he consented to Garnett's (D) contact is a question of fact for the jury. Reversed.

Analysis:

Assault and battery are often used interchangeably by laypersons and, to some extent, legal professionals. This is so because often one will not exist without the other. Under many circumstances, a victim of

---

battery also has a reasonable apprehension that the battery is imminent. However, when the battery occurs without prior warning, the victim's apprehension does not exist, and an assault claim fails.

McCann v. Wal-Mart Stores, Inc.

(Store Patron) v. *(Store Owner)*

210 F.3d 51 (1st Cir.2000)

FALSE IMPRISONMENT CAN OCCUR DESPITE AN ABSENCE OF PHYSICAL BARRIERS OR PHYSICAL FORCE

■ **INSTANT FACTS** Three store patrons sued Wal-Mart for false imprisonment when two store employees backed them into a corner and held them there for over an hour while waiting for a store security guard to arrive.

■ **BLACK LETTER RULE** The tort of false imprisonment occurs when conduct by one party serves to confine another within certain boundaries fixed by the actor and the victim is conscious of the confinement or harmed by it.

■ **PROCEDURAL BASIS**

Certification to the United States Court of Appeals for the First Circuit of an appeal of a jury verdict granting $20,000 in damages to a victim of false imprisonment.

■ **FACTS**

On December 11, 1996, Debra McCann (P) and two of her children went shopping at the Bangor, Maine, Wal-Mart (D). The McCanns (P) paid for their purchases at 10:10 p.m. As they were leaving the store, two Wal-Mart (D) employees stepped in front of their cart, blocking their exit from the store. They then told McCann (P) that her children were not allowed in the store because they had been caught stealing on a prior occasion. The two employees were mistaken. Despite McCann's (P) protestations, one employee told McCann (P) that they had the records to prove their allegations, that the police were being called, and that the McCanns (P) "had to go with her." The employees never called the police, but instead contacted a store security officer who would be able to identify the earlier shoplifter. Eventually the officer arrived at the store and informed the two employees that the McCanns (P) were not the family whose son had been caught shoplifting. The McCanns (P) left the store at 11:15 p.m. They brought suit and the jury awarded them $20,000 on their claim of false imprisonment. Wal-Mart (D) appealed.

■ **ISSUE**

Can false imprisonment be found when there is no actual physical force exerted against the person confined?

■ **DECISION AND RATIONALE**

(Authoring Judge Not Stated) Yes. The gist of the common law tort of false imprisonment is conduct by the actor which is intended to, and does in fact, confine another within boundaries fixed by the actor and, in addition, the victim is either conscious of the confinement or is harmed by it. While confinement can be imposed by physical barriers or physical force, much less will do. It is generally settled that mere threats of physical force can suffice, and it is also settled that the threats may be implicit as well as explicit, and that confinement can also be based on a false assertion of legal authority to confine. In this case, the direction to the McCann's (P) to follow the employee, the reference to the police, and the continued presence of the employees were enough to induce reasonable people to believe either that they would be restrained physically if they sought to leave, or that the store was claiming lawful authority to confine them until the police arrived, or both. Wal-Mart (D) asserts that under Maine law, the jury had to find "actual, physical restraint," a phrase taken from *Knowlton v. Ross,* 95 A. 281 (1915). This is a good example of taking language out of context. In *Knowlton,* the wife of a man who owed a hotel for past bills entered a hotel office and was told that she would go to jail if the bills were not paid. The hotel did not ask her into the room, did not touch her, and did not tell her that she could not leave. The threat of jail was also just "evidence of an intention to imprison at some future time." In context, the reference to the necessity of "actual, physical restraint" is best understood as a reminder that a plaintiff must actually be confined, which Ms. Knowlton was not. Taking too literally the phrase "actual, physical restraint" would put Maine law broadly at odds with both the Restatement and a practically uniform body of common law in other states that accepts the mere threat of physical force, or a claim of lawful authority to restrain, as enough to satisfy the confinement requirement for false imprisonment. Affirmed.

Analysis:

McCann teaches the basics of the tort of false imprisonment, one of the common law intentional torts. As one court wrote, "False imprisonment occurs when a person confines another intentionally without lawful privilege and against his consent within a limited area for any appreciable time, however short." *Bennett v. Ohio Dept. of Rehab. and Correction,* 573 N.E.2d 633 (1991). Further, as *McCann* points out, the victim must "either [be] conscious of the confinement or . . . harmed by it." Evil motive is not a necessary element of a false imprisonment claim. In this case, false imprisonment was found because the McCanns were confined without their consent and were aware of the confinement. It did not matter that the confinement lasted merely one hour—that was enough time to constitute false imprisonment. Nor did it matter that the McCanns were not harmed in any way, as false imprisonment is a trespassory tort and therefore no harm needs to be shown to collect damages (so long as the plaintiff is aware of the confinement). In most cases, exclusion from a place, as opposed to confinement to a place, will not be grounds for a suit for false imprisonment. Thus, a refusal to allow a person to enter a certain premises will not be the grounds for an action for false imprisonment. Depending on the individual circumstances of a case, false imprisonment may occur by means of duress, assertion of authority, or threats, in place of physical force.

■ CASE VOCABULARY

FALSE IMPRISONMENT: An intentional tort involving the confinement of a person to a physically limited area without lawful justification or consent.

Brown v. Muhlenberg Township

(*Dog Owner*) v. (*Local Government*)
269 F.3d 205 (3d Cir.2001)

KILLING A STRAY DOG MAY BE AN UNREASONABLE SEIZURE

■ **INSTANT FACTS** A Muhlenberg Township (D) police officer shot and killed Brown's (P) dog when it escaped from its fenced yard.

■ **BLACK LETTER RULE** Under the Fourth Amendment, all people have the right to be secure in their persons, houses, papers, and effects against unreasonable searches and seizures.

■ **PROCEDURAL BASIS**

On appeal to the Third Circuit Court of Appeals to review a trial court order for the defendant.

■ **FACTS**

Brown's (P) pet Rottweiler escaped from his backyard. Eberly, a police officer for Muhlenberg Township (D), was passing by in his police car when he saw the Rottweiler loose in an adjacent parking lot. When Eberly clapped his hands together and called for the dog, the dog withdrew behind a parked car. When Eberly approached the dog, the dog did not bark, growl, or show any aggression. At this point, Brown (P) observed Eberly drawing his gun on the dog. Despite Brown's screams, the officer shot the dog. After the dog fell and was attempting to crawl back to its yard, Eberly fired four more shots, killing the dog. The Browns (P) sued Muhlenberg Township (D) under 42 U.S.C. § 1983, alleging that Eberly's actions deprived them of their right to be free of unreasonable governmental seizures of their property.

■ **ISSUE**

Could Eberly's destruction of Brown's (D) dog be an unreasonable governmental seizure of his property?

■ **DECISION AND RATIONALE**

(Stapleton, J.) Yes. Under the Fourth Amendment, all people have the right "to be secure in their persons, houses, papers, and effects, against unreasonable searches and seizures." A seizure occurs when there is a "meaningful interference with an individual's possessory interests in that property," and destruction of property constitutes a seizure. Because Brown (P) had a possessory interest in the dog, Eberly's killing of the dog was a seizure under the Fourth Amendment.

For a seizure to be constitutionally protected, it must be reasonable. While reasonable seizures ordinarily are effected pursuant to a court order, such as a warrant, where the governmental interest justifying the seizure is compelling and not disproportionately intrusive upon the person's possessory interest in the property, a seizure is reasonable. Certainly a state has a compelling interest in detaining animals found at large to protect the life and safety of the public. When the animal poses no imminent danger to the public, however, the Fourth Amendment does not necessarily sanction destroying the animal, especially when the owner is available to regain custody and control. Under the facts, Eberly's destruction of Brown's (P) dog could be considered an unreasonable seizure in violation of the Fourth Amendment. Reversed and remanded.

Analysis:

Despite the emotional connection pet owners have to companion animals, the law generally treats pets as personal property. Accordingly, the amount of recovery from one who injures, kills, or otherwise deprives the owner of possession of the pet is limited to the value of the pet itself. Often this monetary value is insignificant compared to the emotional loss the owners endure. When a police officer unjustifiably injures or kills a pet, however, the damages exceed the value of the animal because the owners can recover for the deprivation of their constitutional rights as well.

■ CASE VOCABULARY

FOURTH AMENDMENT: The constitutional amendment, ratified with the Bill of Rights of 1791, prohibiting unreasonable searches and seizures and the issuance of warrants without probable cause.

POSSESSORY INTEREST: The present right to control property, including the right to exclude others, by a person who is not necessarily the owner. A present or future right to the exclusive use and possession of property.

SEIZURE: The act or an instance of taking possession of a person or property by legal right or process; especially, in constitutional law, a confiscation or arrest that may interfere with a person's reasonable expectation of privacy.

CHAPTER FOUR

Defenses to Intentional Torts—Privileges

Great Atlantic & Pacific Tea Co. v. Paul

Instant Facts: A store employee detained a customer who he thought was going to steal a can of tick spray.

Black Letter Rule: Under the common law, a storekeeper may detain a customer only to recover stolen property, not to investigate the facts.

Katko v. Briney

Instant Facts: The Brineys (D) set up a spring gun in their unoccupied farm house. The spring gun went off and injured Katko (P) when he broke into the house.

Black Letter Rule: A landowner may not use a spring gun to defend an unoccupied farm house.

Brown v. Martinez

Instant Facts: Martinez (D) shot and injured Brown (P) when Brown (P) and some other boys trespassed on Martinez's (D) land to steal watermelons.

Black Letter Rule: A landowner may not use force calculated to cause death or serious bodily injury to prevent a trespass or an unlawful act not amounting to a felony.

Surocco v. Geary

Instant Facts: Geary (D), the mayor of San Francisco, authorized Surocco's (P) house to be blown up in order to stop the progress of a raging fire.

Black Letter Rule: A person is not liable for destroying another's property if it is necessary to prevent an imminent public disaster.

Wegner v. Milwaukee Mutual Ins. Co.

Instant Facts: A homeowner whose house was damaged when police apprehended a suspect in the house sued the city for damages.

Black Letter Rule: Despite a public necessity, a city must compensate a homeowner whose property is damaged by police.

Vincent v. Lake Erie Transportation Co.

Instant Facts: During a fierce storm, a steamship was repeatedly thrown against a dock, causing damage to the dock.

Black Letter Rule: Damage caused to another's property due to necessity requires compensation for the actual harm caused.

Great Atlantic & Pacific Tea Co. v. Paul

(Supermarket) v. *(Customer)*
256 Md. 643, 261 A.2d 731 (1970)

UNDER COMMON LAW, STOREKEEPER MAY NOT DETAIN CUSTOMER SUSPECTED OF STEALING MERCHANDISE TO INVESTIGATE FACTS, ONLY TO RECOVER STOLEN PROPERTY

■ **INSTANT FACTS** A store employee detained a customer who he thought was going to steal a can of tick spray.

■ **BLACK LETTER RULE** Under the common law, a storekeeper may detain a customer only to recover stolen property, not to investigate the facts.

■ **PROCEDURAL BASIS**

Appeal of damages action for false imprisonment.

■ **FACTS**

Paul (P) went to the Great Atlantic & Pacific Tea Co. (the "A&P") (D) soon after recovering from a heart attack. Parker, an assistant manager at the A&P (D), believed that Paul (P) had put a can of tick spray in his coat and intended to steal it. Parker confronted Paul (P) and forced him to go to the manager's office. Parker searched Paul (P), but did not find any tick spray. Paul (P) sued the A&P (D) for false imprisonment. The jury awarded Paul (P) compensatory and punitive damages. The A&P (D) appealed, claiming the trial court failed to instruct the jury properly. The A&P (D) claimed the trial court failed to instruct the jury regarding the storekeeper's privilege under the Restatement (Second) of Torts, Section 120 A [storekeeper has a privilege to detain customer suspected of stealing for the time necessary to reasonably investigate the facts].

■ **ISSUE**

Under the common law, may a storekeeper detain a customer suspected of stealing to reasonably investigate the facts?

■ **DECISION AND RATIONALE**

(Digges, J.) No. Maryland follows the common law, not the Restatement (Second) of Torts, Section 120 A. Under the common law, a storekeeper may detain a person who he believes has stolen property. However, a storekeeper may do so only to prevent theft or recapture property. If the detained person does not unlawfully possess the storekeeper's property, the storekeeper is liable for false imprisonment. Here, Paul (P) did not unlawfully possess the A&P's (D) property. Therefore, the A&P (D) is liable for false imprisonment. Even if we applied Section 120 A, the A&P (D) would be liable. Under Section 120 A, the storekeeper invoking the privilege must reasonably believe that the customer tortiously took the property. As a matter of law, no reasonable belief exists until the customer actually attempts to leave the store without paying, unless the customer unequivocally manifests his intent to steal. Here, Parker did not see Paul (P) put the tick spray in his coat. In addition, Parker stopped Paul (P) before Paul (P) indicated that he was leaving the store without paying. Thus, Parker's belief that Paul (P) stole the tick spray was not reasonable. Affirmed.

Analysis:

The Maryland court refused to apply the Restatement Section 120 A privilege. The court states that the Maryland legislature had enacted a statute similar to Section 120 A, but it was found unconstitutional due to titling defects. The legislature did not reenact the statute, so here the court refused to rewrite the law. When a storekeeper claims the privilege to detain a customer under either the common law or under Section 120 A, two issues may arise. First, the privilege does not apply unless the storekeeper had probable cause, or a reasonable belief, that the customer stole something. Here, since Parker did not actually see Paul (P) take the tick spray, the court held that the A&P (D) did not have probable cause to believe that Paul (P) stole it. Second, the privilege does not apply if the storekeeper's actions in detaining the customer are unreasonable. Although the court never reached this issue, here too, the A&P (D) probably would have lost. The jury found that Parker grabbed Paul (P) and forced him to the manager's office. Paul (P) testified that the incident aggravated his heart condition and caused him pain, suffering, and humiliation. These actions would probably be considered unreasonable.

■ CASE VOCABULARY

FALSE IMPRISONMENT: A willful detention without consent and without legal authority.

PRIVILEGE: Circumstances that justify conduct that would otherwise constitute a tort.

Katko v. Briney

(Intruder) v. *(Landowner)*
183 N.W.2d 657 (Iowa 1971)

OWNER MAY NOT USE A SPRING GUN TO DEFEND UNOCCUPIED FARM HOUSE

■ **INSTANT FACTS** The Brineys (D) set up a spring gun in their unoccupied farm house. The spring gun went off and injured Katko (P) when he broke into the house.

■ **BLACK LETTER RULE** A landowner may not use a spring gun to defend an unoccupied farm house.

■ **PROCEDURAL BASIS**

Appeal of a tort action for damages.

■ **FACTS**

After suffering years of break-ins, the Brineys (D) set up a spring gun in an unoccupied farm house they owned. The spring gun was rigged with a wire from the bedroom doorknob to the gun's trigger and was aimed to hit an intruder's legs. There was no sign warning intruders about the gun. Katko (P) and a friend broke into the house to steal bottles and fruit jars. When Katko (P) entered the bedroom, the shotgun went off and blew away much of his right leg. Katko (P) was fined and sentenced to jail for larceny. The jury awarded Katko (P) actual and punitive damages. The Brineys (P) appealed, claiming that the law permits using a spring gun to prevent unlawful entry into a dwelling.

■ **ISSUE**

May a landowner use a spring gun to defend an unoccupied farm house?

■ **DECISION AND RATIONALE**

(Moore, C.J.) No. The value of human life and health outweighs a landowner's interest in protecting property. Therefore, a landowner may not use force intended or likely to cause death or serious harm to defend property against an intruder, unless the intruder threatens the property's occupants with death or serious harm. Here, the farm house was unoccupied, and Katko (P) did not threaten anyone with death or serious harm. The Brineys (P) could not use more force when they were not present than they could have used if they were present. Accordingly, the Brineys (D) were not justified in using a spring gun to protect their property. Affirmed.

■ **CONCURRENCE**

Someone who possesses land is privileged to use reasonable force to defend the possession against intrusion or harm. However, the possessor must limit the force to meet the apparent need for it. Reasonable force is usually the least force that is reasonably likely to be effective to defend the property. Deadly force or force likely to cause grave bodily harm may not be used against a peaceable intruder. Deadly force may be used only if the intruder appears to threaten a person with deadly force. Special rules apply to spring guns, as the Brineys (D) used here. Indeed, this is the most famous American case dealing with spring guns. Under the Restatement, a spring gun is allowed, but only when the homeowner could have used such force in person. This rule is often difficult to apply, but courts have generally held that homeowners may protect a dwelling place by spring guns against intruders who are entering or attempting to enter in the course of a felony or attempted felony. A homeowner has no privilege to use spring guns against mere trespassers or those committing minor crimes outside the home.

Analysis:

Katko (P) broke into the farm house to steal bottles and jars. Although he entered the house with the intent to commit a crime, he was allowed to recover. The court based its decision on the Restatement's statement that human life and limb are more important than property interests. This holding seems also influenced by the fact that the Brineys (D) did not live in the farm house and were not present at the time Katko (P) broke in. A home, unlike a warehouse or an office building, is meant to satisfy the fundamental needs for human safety and refuge. Had the Brineys (D) lived there, the court's holding may have been different. Case law is split regarding whether a sign warning intruders that they risk deadly force if they enter a dwelling protects the landowner from liability. The issue then would be whether a mentally competent intruder who is fully informed of the spring gun, but enters anyway, should be compensated for his damages. In that case, the intruder may be held to have assumed the risk of entering the dwelling. Some courts have barred recovery by someone who is injured in the course of his "own wrong." These courts have held that someone who commits a crime "forfeits" his civil rights. However, it is unlikely this rule would apply if a homeowner intentionally and unnecessarily shoots the criminal. While spring guns hold a special place in the law, similar rules would likely apply to other deadly traps such as electrified wire and vicious dogs.

Brown v. Martinez

(Trespasser) v. *(Landowner)*
68 N.M. 271, 361 P.2d 152 (1961)

LANDOWNER MAY NOT USE FORCE CALCULATED TO CAUSE DEATH OR SERIOUS BODILY INJURY TO PROTECT PROPERTY

■ **INSTANT FACTS** Martinez (D) shot and injured Brown (P) when Brown (P) and some other boys trespassed on Martinez's (D) land to steal watermelons.

■ **BLACK LETTER RULE** A landowner may not use force calculated to cause death or serious bodily injury to prevent a trespass or an unlawful act not amounting to a felony.

■ **PROCEDURAL BASIS**

Appeal of dismissal of tort action for damages.

■ **FACTS**

Two boys entered Martinez' (D) land to steal watermelons. Brown (P) was standing outside the property when Martinez (D) came out of his house and fired a rifle away from the boys to scare them away. The bullet hit Brown (P), severely injuring him. The trial court dismissed Brown's (P) claim against Martinez (D).

■ **ISSUE**

May a landowner use force calculated to cause death or serious bodily injury to prevent a trespass or an unlawful act not amounting to a felony on property?

■ **DECISION AND RATIONALE**

(Moise, J.) No. Force used to defend property must be appropriate. The law places a higher value on human safety than on property rights. Here, there is no evidence that Martinez (D) believed that Brown (P) threatened his own safety. Accordingly, he was not privileged to use any force calculated to cause death or serious bodily injury where only his property was threatened. Reversed.

Analysis:

A homeowner may use reasonable force to defend his land or chattels against intrusion or taking. The homeowner must limit the force to meet the apparent need for it. If the homeowner uses more force than is necessary, the homeowner exceeds the privilege and is liable for the harm caused by the excess force. Reasonable force is the least force that would be effective in defending the property. Deadly force and force likely to cause grave bodily harm may not be used against a peaceable intruder. Here, Martinez (D) shot his gun in the opposite direction from the boys stealing his watermelons, intending only to frighten them. That constitutes an assault. Unfortunately, a bullet hit Brown (P), who Martinez (D) may not have known was present. The court did not discuss the possibility that a threat of deadly force might have been a permissible way of defending property. However, the court may have

---

assumed that even a mere threat of deadly force was excessive and could easily backfire, as it did here. Moreover, even just a threat of deadly harm seems out of proportion to the risk of lost watermelons.

Surocco v. Geary

(Homeowner) v. *(Mayor)*

3 Cal. 69 (1853)

PERSON IS NOT LIABLE FOR DESTROYING ANOTHER'S PROPERTY IF NECESSARY TO PREVENT IMMINENT HARM TO THE PUBLIC

■ **INSTANT FACTS** Geary (D), the mayor of San Francisco, authorized Surocco's (P) house to be blown up in order to stop the progress of a raging fire.

■ **BLACK LETTER RULE** A person is not liable for destroying another's property if it is necessary to prevent an imminent public disaster.

■ **PROCEDURAL BASIS**

Appeal of tort action for damages.

■ **FACTS**

Surocco (P) was in the process of removing goods from his home while a fire raged nearby. Geary (D), the mayor of San Francisco, authorized Surocco's (P) house to be blown up to stop the progress of the fire and save adjacent buildings. Surocco (P) sued Geary (D), claiming that he could have recovered more of his goods if the house was not blown up. The trial court held for Surocco (P).

■ **ISSUE**

Is a person liable for destroying another's property if it is necessary to prevent an imminent public disaster?

■ **DECISION AND RATIONALE**

(Murray, C.J.) Yes. This right of necessity is considered a "natural right," independent of society or government. An individual's property rights must give way to the higher law of impending necessity. A house on fire or about to catch fire is a nuisance which is lawful to abate. Otherwise, one stubborn person could ruin an entire city. If property is destroyed without apparent or actual necessity, the destroying person would be liable for trespass. Here, blowing up Surocco's (P) house was necessary to stop the fire. Any delay in blowing up the house to allow Surocco (P) to remove more of his goods would have made blowing up the house too late. Reversed.

Analysis:

This is a classic "public necessity" case. The basic rule provides that a defendant who damages or destroys another's property in the reasonable belief that by doing so he can avoid or minimize an imminent public disaster is protected against all liability. This is in contrast to "private necessity" cases, where the defendant is relieved of liability for trespass, but is still liable for any actual harm caused. In a public necessity case, the defendant must show that public rather than private interests were at stake, that he reasonably believed action was necessary, and that the action he took was indeed reasonable. This rule makes sense from a public policy point of view. The individual is immune from liability to induce him to act to protect the public. It would be unjust to make an individual liable for a loss incurred to protect the public. However, what about the property owner? Why should he be required to bear the cost of protecting the public? In the present case, making Surocco (P) bear the loss may be justified. Surocco's (P) house was about to burn down anyway. The argument could be made that Geary (D) merely hastened a loss that was inevitable. On the other hand, one could argue that because destroying Surocco's (P) house benefitted the public, the public should bear the cost.

■ CASE VOCABULARY

NECESSITAS INDUCIT PRIVILEGIUM QUOD JURA PRIVATA: Necessity gives a preference with regard to private rights.

Wegner v. Milwaukee Mutual Ins. Co.

(Homeowner) v. *(Insurance company)*
479 N.W.2d 38 (Minn.1991)

CITY MUST COMPENSATE A HOMEOWNER WHOSE PROPERTY IS DAMAGED BY POLICE, DESPITE PUBLIC NECESSITY

■ **INSTANT FACTS** A homeowner whose house was damaged when police apprehended a suspect in the house sued the city for damages.

■ **BLACK LETTER RULE** Despite a public necessity, a city must compensate a homeowner whose property is damaged by police.

■ **PROCEDURAL BASIS**

Appeal of tort action for damages.

■ **FACTS**

A suspected felon barricaded himself in Wegner's (P) house. The Minneapolis police and the Emergency Response Unit fired tear gas and grenades into the house, causing extensive damage. Wegner (P) sued the City of Minneapolis (the "City") (D) for trespass. Wegner (P) claimed that the City's (D) actions constituted a "taking" of his private property for public use and that the City (D) was required to compensate him. The City (D) claimed there was no taking because the police action constituted a legitimate exercise of police power. The trial court and the court of appeals held that the City's (D) taking was justified under the doctrine of public necessity and that the City (D) was not required to compensate Wegner (P).

■ **ISSUE**

Must a city compensate a homeowner whose property is damaged by police while apprehending a suspect?

■ **DECISION AND RATIONALE**

(Tomijanovich, J.) Yes. Under Minnesota's constitution, the government must compensate a private landowner for any damage it causes when it takes the landowner's property for public use. The reasonableness of the police action is not relevant. The constitutional provision is not limited to improvements for public use, as the court of appeals held. The doctrine of public necessity does not change our holding. Once a taking is found to exist, compensation is required. If the public necessity doctrine were to apply to a situation like this, no taking would ever be found. Fairness and justice require this result. It would not be fair to allocate to Wagner (P), an innocent homeowner, a loss that was incurred for the public good. Therefore, the City (D) must reimburse Wagner (P) for the loss. In addition, the individual police officers are not personally liable; the public at large must bear the loss. Reversed.

Analysis:

Under the Fifth Amendment to the U.S. Constitution, public entities are required to pay just compensation for property they take. For example, if a city wants to build a freeway or a library, it can take property via eminent domain or condemnation proceedings, and it must pay the landowners just compensation for their land. Destroying property while apprehending a suspect is similar to taking someone's property to build a library. In both situations, the public entity must pay the landowner just compensation. This case rejects the public necessity doctrine that was applied in *Surocco v. Geary* [no liability for destroying another's property if necessary to prevent imminent harm to the public]. Instead, this case is based on the equity of allocating a loss that benefits the public to the public rather than to Wagner (P), an innocent individual. However, in similar cases, other courts have held that compensation is not required, holding that police action that damages private land is either privileged under the public necessity doctrine or protected as an exercise of police power.

■ CASE VOCABULARY

PUBLIC NECESSITY: Doctrine holding that one is privileged to enter another's land if it is, or if the actor reasonably believes it to be, necessary to avert an imminent public disaster.

Vincent v. Lake Erie Transportation Co.

(*Dock owner*) v. (*Ship owner*)

109 Minn. 456, 124 N.W. 221 (1910)

DAMAGE TO ANOTHER'S PROPERTY DUE TO NECESSITY REQUIRES COMPENSATION

■ **INSTANT FACTS** During a fierce storm, a steamship was repeatedly thrown against a dock, causing damage to the dock.

■ **BLACK LETTER RULE** Damage caused to another's property due to necessity requires compensation for the actual harm caused.

■ **PROCEDURAL BASIS**

Appeal of tort action for damages.

■ **FACTS**

The steamship Reynolds, owned by the Lake Erie Transportation Co. ("Lake Erie") (D), was moored to Vincent's (P) dock to unload its cargo. A violent storm developed. During the storm, the Reynolds was unable to safely leave the dock. Lake Erie (D) kept the ship tied tightly to the dock and replaced the ropes used to attach it as they became worn. The fierce wind and waves caused the Reynolds to be thrown against the dock, causing damage to it.

■ **ISSUE**

Does damage to another's property due to a private necessity require compensation?

■ **DECISION AND RATIONALE**

(O'Brien, J.) Yes. Necessity may require one to take or damage another's property, but compensation is still required. If the Reynolds had entered the harbor during the storm and then been thrown against Vincent's (P) dock, Vincent (P) could not have recovered. However, here, Lake Erie (D) deliberately kept the Reynolds in a position that would damage the dock. Although this was the prudent thing to do, Lake Erie (D) is liable for the damage. Affirmed.

■ **DISSENT**

(Lewis, J.) One who constructs a dock and contracts with ship owners for docking assumes the risk of damage caused by storms. Therefore, Vincent (P) assumed the risk of damage and Lake Erie (D) is not liable to him.

Analysis:

This is the leading case on the private necessity privilege. Under this privilege, Lake Erie (D) would not be liable for damages if it did not cause any harm; Lake Erie (D) is not liable for trespassing; Vincent (P) would not have been justified in untying the Reynolds and casting it into the lake; and Lake Erie (D) is still liable for the actual harm it caused. However if the emergency or necessity had been caused by Lake Erie (D), it likely would have lost its immunity from liability for trespass. To invoke the private necessity privilege, a defendant must have been actually threatened or must have reasonably believed that he was threatened with serious and imminent harm. The private necessity privilege differs from the public necessity privilege in that, under the private necessity privilege, the defendant is still liable for any actual harm caused. As was demonstrated in *Surocco v. Geary* [one may destroy another's property if necessary to prevent imminent public disaster], the public necessity doctrine creates total immunity from any liability. The *Vincent* case provokes a lot of discussion among law students because the result may be based on different grounds. For example, the opinion suggests that Lake Erie (D) is liable for restitution, rather than for tort damages, because the captain saved the Reynolds at the expense of Vincent's (P) dock. However, this theory is based on the assumption that the Reynolds was certain to sink or be destroyed if it were cast off into the lake. But because the chance of actual destruction was quite small, the captain protected against only the slight risk of destruction, and, thus, restitution would not be appropriate. The theory that Lake Erie (D) is liable because the captain saved the ship at the expense of the dock also suggests the unlikely result that Lake Erie (D) would not have been liable if, after damaging Vincent's (P) dock, the Reynolds was destroyed anyway. As a practical result, this case may resolve disputes between dock owners and ship owners by clarifying what the parties can and cannot do and who is liable for what. Thus, a dock owner seeing his dock being damaged by a fastened ship might be tempted to cast the ship out, while the captain tries to tie the ship even tighter to the dock. This case makes clear that each party is liable for any actual damage it causes to the other party. Thus, the dock owner can feel confident that the ship owner will pay to repair any damage to the dock, and the ship owner can feel confident that the ship will not be destroyed at sea.

CHAPTER FIVE

The Prima Facie Case for Negligence

Stewart v. Motts

Instant Facts: Stewart (P) suffered burns from an explosion which occurred when he poured gasoline into a car's carburetor and Motts (D) turned the key.

Black Letter Rule: There is one standard of care for negligence actions, the standard of reasonable care under the circumstances, which requires a person to exercise care in proportion to the danger of his activity.

Wilson v. Sibert

Instant Facts: To avoid a collision with a vehicle backing into Sibert's (D) car, Sibert (D) moved his vehicle in reverse without looking, striking Wilson's (P) car.

Black Letter Rule: When a sudden emergency exists, the standard of care required of a defendant is that of a reasonable person in a similar situation.

Robinson v. Lindsay

Instant Facts: Anderson, age thirteen, had an accident while driving a snowmobile which caused Robinson (P) to lose the full use of her thumb.

Black Letter Rule: When a child engages in an inherently dangerous activity, or an activity which is normally one for adults only, courts will hold the child to an adult standard of care.

Creasy v. Rusk

Instant Facts: Rusk (D), an Alzheimer's patient, kicked Creasy (P), his nurse, while she was trying to put him to bed, injuring her knee and lower back.

Black Letter Rule: In general, the standard of care for adults with mental disabilities is the same standard of reasonable care that governs adults without mental disabilities, with no allowance for their capacity to control or understand the consequences of their actions.

Roman v. Estate of Gobbo

Instant Facts: After undergoing heart bypass surgery, Gobbo (D) suffered a heart attack while driving, causing a multi-car accident.

Black Letter Rule: An operator of a motor vehicle who, while driving, becomes suddenly stricken by a fainting spell or loses consciousness from an unforeseen cause and is unable to control the vehicle, is not chargeable with negligence or gross negligence.

Chaffin v. Brame

Instant Facts: Blinded by undimmed oncoming headlights, Chaffin (P) collided with an unlighted truck left blocking the entire right lane.

Black Letter Rule: A driver's ultimate duty is to exercise reasonable care under the circumstances, which may not always include a duty to be able to stop his vehicle within the range of its lights.

Rains v. Bend of the River

Instant Facts: After Aaron Rains purchased ammunition for a handgun from Bend of the River (D) in violation of the federal Gun Control Act, Aaron committed suicide.

Black Letter Rule: Violation of a penal statute is negligence as a matter of law.

Wright v. Brown

Instant Facts: Prior to the expiration of the 14 days required by statute, the dog warden (D) released Brown's (D) dog from quarantine and the dog attacked Wright (P).

Black Letter Rule: To maintain a negligence action based on a statutory standard of care, a person must (1) be within the class of persons the statute is intended to protect, and (2) suffer the type of injury the statute is intended to prevent.

Impson v. Structural Metals, Inc.

Instant Facts: A truck driver attempted to pass a car within 100 feet of an intersection in violation of a statute, but hit the car when the car turned left.

Black Letter Rule: When there is evidence that a party has violated a statutory standard of care, the court has no duty to submit the issue of negligence to the jury where there is no evidence of a legally acceptable excuse or justification.

Stewart v. Motts

(Mechanic-Helper) v. *(Repair Shop Owner)*
539 Pa. 596, 654 A.2d 535 (1995)

THE STANDARD OF CARE FOR NEGLIGENCE ACTIONS IS ALWAYS REASONABLE CARE, BUT THE AMOUNT OF CARE WHICH IS REASONABLE VARIES

■ **INSTANT FACTS** Stewart (P) suffered burns from an explosion which occurred when he poured gasoline into a car's carburetor and Motts (D) turned the key.

■ **BLACK LETTER RULE** There is one standard of care for negligence actions, the standard of reasonable care under the circumstances, which requires a person to exercise care in proportion to the danger of his activity.

■ **PROCEDURAL BASIS**

Appeal after jury trial of personal injury action for damages.

■ **FACTS**

Stewart (P) stopped at Motts' (D) auto repair shop and offered to help Motts (D) repair a car's fuel tank. In order to start and move the car with the gas tank unattached, Stewart (P) suggested that he pour gasoline into the carburetor and that Motts (D) turn the ignition key at a given moment. When they did so, the car backfired and caused an explosion which caused Stewart (P) to suffer severe burns. At trial, Stewart (P) asked the judge to instruct the jury that a person must exercise a high degree of care around gasoline because it is a dangerous substance. The judge refused this request, and the jury returned a verdict for Motts (D).

■ **ISSUE**

Does a heightened standard of "extraordinary care" apply to negligence cases that involve dangerous instrumentalities rather than the standard of reasonable care?

■ **DECISION AND RATIONALE**

(Montemuro) No. We reaffirm the principle that there is only one standard of care for negligence actions that involve dangerous instrumentalities. This is the standard of reasonable care. As stated in Comment b to the *Restatement (Second) of Torts § 298* [defines reasonable care], "[t]he care required is always reasonable care. The standard never varies, but the care which it is reasonable to require of the actor varies with the danger involved in his act and is proportionate to it. The greater the danger, the greater the care which must be exercised." Our cases have stated that a reasonably prudent person must exercise a higher degree of care when their activity involves a dangerous substance such as gasoline. However, taken in context, these cases only reaffirm the principle that a reasonable man must use an amount of care which is proportionate to the danger of his activity. When we referred to a "higher degree of care," we were not creating a second tier of "extraordinary care." Rather, this language merely stated the common sense conclusion that the use of a dangerous agency requires a reasonably prudent person to exercise more care. Thus, we recognize only one standard of care in negligence actions involving dangerous instrumentalities, the standard of reasonable care under the circumstances. A reasonable man must exercise care in proportion to the danger involved in his act.

The trial judge properly instructed the jury that the proper standard of care was reasonable or ordinary care under the circumstances, and that the amount of care this standard requires varies with the circumstances and must be proportionate to the level of danger involved. Affirmed.

Analysis:

A person must establish five elements in a negligence action: (1) a legal duty of care; (2) breach of that duty; (3) actual damages; (4) actual causation; and (5) proximate causation. The standard of care defines the scope of the duty of care. This case discusses the general standard of care for negligence cases, the standard of reasonable care, which is the care that a reasonably prudent person would exercise under the circumstances. In *Stewart* the court adopts the orthodox view that the standard of reasonable care applies to all negligence actions and never varies, although the amount of care which is reasonable does vary with the danger involved and is proportionate to it. As § 298, Comment b of the Restatement explains, the greater the danger, the greater the care which a person must exercise to avoid being negligent. For example, acts which involve a risk of death or serious bodily harm require the highest amount of care. Thus, while the standard of care is an invariable, non-contextual, question of law, the amount of care required by this standard is a variable, contextual, question of fact. It is the amount of care the standard requires, not the standard itself, that changes. In *Stewart* the court finds that while the standard of care remains that of reasonable care even in cases involving dangerous instrumentalities such as gasoline, the dangerousness of the gasoline requires a reasonably prudent person to exercise more care. The court explains that there is no hierarchy of standards such that "reasonable care" would apply in most circumstances and "extraordinary care" would apply in circumstances involving dangerous instrumentalities. Rather, the court affirms that when a case involves a dangerous instrumentality, extraordinary care *is* reasonable care.

■ CASE VOCABULARY

CARE: Attention, caution and prudence to perceive and avoid harm to oneself and others.

NEGLIGENCE: Failure to exercise the amount of care that a reasonably prudent person would exercise under the circumstances.

REASONABLE CARE: The care which a reasonably prudent person with similar information and competence would exercise under the circumstances, sometimes referred to as ordinary care or due care.

REASONABLY PRUDENT PERSON: A fictitious person who exercises those qualities of attention, knowledge, intelligence, and judgment which society requires for the protection of his own interests and the interests of others.

Wilson v. Sibert

(Motorist) v. *(Motorist)*

535 P.2d 1034 (Alaska 1975)

A SUPERFLUOUS JURY INSTRUCTION IS NOT AN ABUSE OF DISCRETION WHEN THE JURY IS NOT IMPROPERLY INFLUENCED

■ **INSTANT FACTS** To avoid a collision with a vehicle backing into Sibert's (D) car, Sibert (D) moved his vehicle in reverse without looking, striking Wilson's (P) car.

■ **BLACK LETTER RULE** When a sudden emergency exists, the standard of care required of a defendant is that of a reasonable person in a similar situation.

■ **PROCEDURAL BASIS**

On appeal to review a decision of the Alaska Court of Appeals affirming judgment for the defendant.

■ **FACTS**

Sibert (D) was stopped in line at a drive-through window at the bank. Wilson (P) was in the car immediately behind him. When the car in front of Sibert (D) began to move backwards, Sibert (D) put his car in gear and, without looking back, drove in reverse to avoid the collision. In the process, Sibert (D) struck Wilson's (P) vehicle. At trial, the court gave the jury two separate instructions over Wilson's (P) objection. The first instruction defined negligence in general, and the second set forth the sudden emergency doctrine. After the court denied Wilson's (P) motion for a directed verdict, the jury returned a verdict for Sibert (D). Wilson appealed, challenging the court's sudden emergency instruction and its denial of her motion for a directed verdict.

■ **ISSUE**

When a general negligence jury instruction accurately informs the jury of the proper standard of care, is giving a separate instruction on the sudden emergency doctrine an abuse of discretion?

■ **DECISION AND RATIONALE**

(Rabinowitz, C.J.) No. The law of negligence requires the jury to consider the actions of a defendant against the actions of a reasonable person in the same circumstances. When those circumstances include an emergency situation, the person's actions may be acceptable although unreasonable in other circumstances. Because reasonable minds could differ on the actions required to avoid an impending collision with another vehicle, a directed verdict was inappropriate.

Similarly, although the general negligence instruction accurately informs the jury of the standard of care in emergency situations, the appropriateness of a separate sudden emergency instruction is within the discretion of the court. Despite any potential effect on the jury by emphasis on the circumstances constituting an emergency, the trial court could issue a separate instruction when an emergency situation exists, and the jury should not be improperly influenced by the instruction. Because there was no abuse of discretion, the instruction was appropriate. Affirmed.

Analysis:

For some, application of the sudden emergency doctrine results in grossly inequitable results. For instance, assume that Sibert's (D) rear bumper was strong enough to withstand any damage to his vehicle, causing only damage to Wilson's (P) vehicle. By operation of the sudden emergency doctrine, Sibert (D) effectively transferred the damage that would have been caused to his vehicle, had he not moved, to Wilson's (P) vehicle, because he chose to avoid his own damages. Wilson (P) is left to bear the financial burden of the damage to her vehicle.

■ **CASE VOCABULARY**

EMERGENCY DOCTRINE: A legal principle exempting a person from the ordinary standard of reasonable care if that person acted instinctively to meet a sudden and urgent need for aid.

NEGLIGENCE: The failure to exercise the standard of care that a reasonably prudent person would have exercised in a similar situation; any conduct that falls below the legal standard established to protect others against unreasonable risk of harm, except for conduct that is intentionally, wantonly, or willfully disregardful of others' rights.

STANDARD OF CARE: In the law of negligence, the degree of prudence that a reasonable person should exercise.

Robinson v. Lindsay

(Accident Victim) v. *(Not Stated)*
92 Wn.2d 410, 598 P.2d 392 (1979)

THE REASONABLE CARE STANDARD TAKES ACCOUNT OF A CHILD'S ABILITIES EXCEPT WHEN THE CHILD ENGAGES IN ADULT ACTIVITIES

■ **INSTANT FACTS** Anderson, age thirteen, had an accident while driving a snowmobile which caused Robinson (P) to lose the full use of her thumb.

■ **BLACK LETTER RULE** When a child engages in an inherently dangerous activity, or an activity which is normally one for adults only, courts will hold the child to an adult standard of care.

■ **PROCEDURAL BASIS**

Appeal of order granting new trial in personal injury action for damages.

■ **FACTS**

Anderson, thirteen years old, had an accident while driving a snowmobile which caused Robinson (P), eleven years old, to lose the full use of her thumb. The trial court instructed the jury that a child's duty is to exercise the same care that a reasonably careful child of the same age, intelligence, maturity, training and experience would exercise under the circumstances. Robinson (P) objected to the court's instructing the jury on this standard rather than the adult standard of care. After a jury verdict in favor of Anderson, the trial court ordered a new trial because it believed it should have instructed the jury as to the adult standard of care.

■ **ISSUE**

Must a child who participates in an inherently dangerous activity conform to the adult standard of care?

■ **DECISION AND RATIONALE**

(Utter) Yes. The jury instruction the trial court used fairly reflects current state law. In the past we have always compared a child's conduct to that expected of a reasonably careful child of the same age, intelligence, maturity, training and experience. Here we consider for the first time a child's liability for injuries that result from his or her operation of a motor vehicle or participation in an inherently dangerous activity. Because of the apparent injustice that would occur if a child engaged in such activity could escape liability by arguing that other similarly situated children would not have been more careful, courts in other jurisdictions have created an exception to the special child standard of care. Some courts have couched this exception in terms of children engaging in activities which are normally only for adults. We believe the better rationale is to hold a child to an adult standard of care whenever the child engages in inherently dangerous activity, such as operating a powerful mechanical vehicle. This rule allows children to be children, but discourages immature individuals from engaging in inherently dangerous activities. [Are "immature people" generally concerned about potential legal liability?] Children would not be held to an adult standard of care for traditional childhood activities, which generally do not cause grave danger to the child or others when a child exercises less than the amount of care expected of an adult. Other courts have emphasized the hazard to the public without this exception, particularly with respect to the operation of motor vehicles. Courts have applied the adult standard in cases in which children operated motor vehicles including motor boats, tractors, motorcycles, minibikes and automobiles. Operating a snowmobile likewise requires adult care and competence. Studies show that snowmobile accidents claim hundreds of casualties each year, and that these accidents occur more frequently among inexperienced operators. Because Anderson was operating a powerful motor vehicle, we hold him to the adult standard of care. Affirmed.

Analysis:

This case discusses both the ordinary standard of care for children and the exception to that rule, under which children who engage in adult activities are held to the adult standard of care. The standard of care for children, set forth in the *Restatement (Second) of Torts § 283A* is that of a reasonable person of like age, intelligence, and experience under like circumstances. The law recognizes that the immaturity of children, particularly very young children, may make them incapable of exercising the judgment, intelligence, knowledge, experience, and prudence which the reasonable care standard requires of adults, and thus holds them to a standard of care proportionate to their capacity. This standard takes into account whether a child is mentally retarded or unusually bright, as well as the experiences and education the child has had. Very young children may be utterly incapable of exercising any of the qualities necessary for avoiding a particular danger, while older children may be just as capable as adults. This accommodation for children reflects society's interest in their welfare and protection, as well as the wide basis of experience which makes it practical to determine what society expects of them. Like physical disabilities and unlike mental disabilities, childhood is a circumstance that plainly makes certain precautions impossible. Also unlike mental disabilities, there is little need for concern about faking childhood to avoid tort liability.

■ CASE VOCABULARY

EXCEPT: To make a formal objection during trial to a judge's ruling to show a higher court on appeal that the lawyer disagreed with it.

Creasy v. Rusk

(Nurse) v. *(Alzheimer's Patient)*
730 N.E.2d 659 (Ind.2000)

THE LAW GENERALLY HOLDS INSANE PEOPLE TO THE STANDARD OF A REASONABLE PERSON

■ **INSTANT FACTS** Rusk (D), an Alzheimer's patient, kicked Creasy (P), his nurse, while she was trying to put him to bed, injuring her knee and lower back.

■ **BLACK LETTER RULE** In general, the standard of care for adults with mental disabilities is the same standard of reasonable care that governs adults without mental disabilities, with no allowance for their capacity to control or understand the consequences of their actions.

■ **PROCEDURAL BASIS**

Appeal after Court of Appeals reversed summary judgment granted in a negligence action for damages.

■ **FACTS**

Rusk (D) was an Alzheimer's patient at a healthcare center for three years, during which time he experienced periods of anxiousness, confusion, and agitation. Rusk (D) was often combative and aggressive and would hit staff members when they tried to care for him. On one occasion when Creasy (P) and another nurse tried to put Rusk (D) to bed, he was very agitated and combative, and was hitting and kicking wildly. Creasy (P) alleged that Rusk (D) kicked her several times and injured her knee and lower back. Rusk (D) moved for summary judgment, and the trial court granted the motion. Creasy (P) appealed and the Court of Appeals reversed, holding that a person's mental capacity must be factored into the determination of whether a legal duty exists.

■ **ISSUE**

Does the general duty of care for adults with mental disabilities take those mental disabilities into account?

■ **DECISION AND RATIONALE**

(Sullivan) No. The generally accepted rule, set forth in the *Restatement (Second) of Torts § 283B* [standard of care for the mentally disabled], is that a mental disability does not excuse a person from liability for conduct which does not conform to the standard of reasonable care under the circumstances. Courts commonly hold the mentally disabled liable for their intentional and negligent torts, with no allowance for their level of intelligence, exciteability, proneness to accident, or other mental or emotional disabilities. Legal scholars recognize that it is impossible to ascribe any level of fault to a person who is unable to control his or her own actions through any exercise of reason. However, they nonetheless hold the mentally disabled to the general standard of care for several policy reasons: (1) to allocate losses between two innocent parties to the party who caused the loss; (2) to encourage those responsible for the mentally disabled to prevent harm; (3) to discourage faking a mental disability to avoid liability; (4) to avoid difficulties in assessing the significance of a person's mental disability; and (5) to force the mentally disabled to pay for any damage they cause if they "are to live in the world" rather than in an institution. While the Restatement rule may be based on a policy of institutionalizing the mentally disabled, modern policy now favors community treatment and integration into the least

---

restrictive environment, and reflects a determination to treat the mentally disabled the same way as non-disabled persons.   However, both of these policies yield to the same common law rule that holds adults with mental disabilities to the same duty of care that the law requires of those without mental disabilities. Thus, the law generally holds a person with mental disabilities to the standard of a reasonable person under the circumstances, regardless of the person's capacity to control or understand the consequences of his or her actions.   Notwithstanding this general rule, an Alzheimer's patient owes no duty of care to a person who is employed to care for him and who knows of the combativeness his disease causes.   Rusk (D), therefore, is not liable in this case.   The Court of Appeals opinion is vacated and the trial court's order granting summary judgment is affirmed.

Analysis:

In this case the court adopts the prevailing rule, expressed in § 283B of the Restatement, that the general duty of care for adults with mental deficiencies is the same as that for adults without mental deficiencies.   Mentally disabled adults must conform to the general standard of reasonable care under the circumstances, and their incapacity to control or understand their actions or to conform to this standard is not a circumstance that affects the amount of care this standard requires of them.   The rule that mentally disabled adults are liable for their torts originated in an English trespass case decided in 1616, when strict liability still controlled.   When fault-based liability replaced strict liability, courts kept the rule on public policy grounds.   The Restatement and *Creasy* both list public policy reasons for holding the mentally disabled to the general standard of reasonable care.   First, the rule allocates losses between two innocent parties to the one who caused the loss, at least as long as the person who experienced the loss did not assume risks with respect to its cause.   Second, the rule encourages those responsible for mentally disabled people to prevent them from harming others and to restrain those who are potentially dangerous.   In this respect, the rule encourages institutionalizing the mentally disabled, contrary to the modern trend of integrating them into society.   Third, the rule discourages people from faking a mental disability to escape liability for their negligence.   Fourth, the rule lets courts and juries avoid the difficulty of distinguishing mental disabilities from other variations of temperament, intellect, and emotional balance which cannot affect the amount of care required of a person.   Finally, the rule reflects the policy that if mentally disabled people do "live in the world," they should pay for any damage they cause.   Again, this may reflect an assumption that the mentally disabled should live in institutions rather than "in the world," but it is also consistent with the modern integrationist trend in that it treats mentally disabled people the same way as non-disabled people.   In addition to describing the general rule for the mentally disabled, *Creasy* also provides an example of an exception to that rule: a person who is institutionalized with a mental disability and who does not have the capacity to control or appreciate his actions cannot be liable in negligence for injuries to caretakers employed by that institution.   As the dissent in the appellate court concluded, "no duty to refrain from violent conduct arises on the part of a person who has no capacity to control it to one who is specifically employed to do just that."   Thus although Rusk (D), as a mentally disabled person, had a general duty to conform to the standard of reasonable care, he did not owe a duty of care to Creasy (P), an employee of the institution which he entered precisely because of his incapacity to control himself.   Because Rusk (D) owed no duty of care to Creasy (P), he was not liable for his substandard conduct which caused her injury.

Roman v. Estate of Gobbo

(Injured Motorist) v. *(Estate of Deceased Motorist)*
99 Ohio St.3d 260, 791 N.E.2d 422 (2003)

AN UNFORESEEN MEDICAL EMERGENCY RELIEVES ONE FROM LIABILITY

Well, no one ever told me I shouldn't be driving.

■ **INSTANT FACTS** After undergoing heart by-pass surgery, Gobbo (D) suffered a heart attack while driving, causing a multi-car accident.

■ **BLACK LETTER RULE** An operator of a motor vehicle who, while driving, becomes suddenly stricken by a fainting spell or loses consciousness from an unforeseen cause and is unable to control the vehicle, is not chargeable with negligence or gross negligence.

■ PROCEDURAL BASIS

On appeal to review a decision of the Ohio Court of Appeals affirming a trial court judgment for the defendant.

■ FACTS

Despite his having had heart bypass surgery, Gobbo's (D) doctors did not foresee an imminent threat of heart attack and did not advise him not to drive. While operating a vehicle, however, Gobbo (D) suffered a heart attack and died, and his vehicle struck a passing vehicle, causing a multi-car accident. The occupants of the other vehicles sued Gobbo's (D) estate. After the closing arguments, the trial court instructed the jury on the sudden medical emergency doctrine, which excuses negligence if Gobbo (D) could not have reasonably foreseen the heart attack and could not have controlled his vehicle after suffering the heart attack. Although the jury concluded that Gobbo (D) violated a state statute forbidding the crossing of the centerline without reasonable control, it determined that Gobbo (D) could not have reasonably foreseen the heart attack. The jury therefore returned a verdict for the estate (D).

■ ISSUE

Can a defendant motorist be negligent although he could not reasonably foresee a medical situation that caused his unconsciousness and led to a collision?

■ DECISION AND RATIONALE

(Resnick, J.) No. "[A]n operator of a motor vehicle, who, while driving, becomes suddenly stricken by a fainting spell or loses consciousness from an unforeseen cause, and is unable to control the vehicle, is not chargeable with negligence or gross negligence." Unlike mental illness, which is not a defense to negligence, a sudden medical emergency is less susceptible of being feigned and is an acceptable defense. The fact that Gobbo (D) ceases to be a tortfeasor by operation of the doctrine, thus depriving the plaintiffs of the right to collect against his or their own insurance policies, is immaterial to tort law, as the issue concerns the insurance contracts. Likewise, the reasonableness of a defendant's actions is not determined by his knowledge of any prior medical condition, for then any driver with slightly imperfect health would be unable to succeed on the sudden medical emergency defense. Instead, the law sufficiently ensures the appropriateness of the defense by placing the burden on the defendant to prove that unconsciousness was unforeseeable. If a defendant succeeds in his burden, his actions are not unreasonable, and unreasonableness is required for negligence to attach. Without unreasonable conduct, the defendant is not at fault, and judgment should be entered in his favor. Affirmed.

■ CONCURRENCE

(Pfeifer, J.) Although Gobbo (D) may be blameless for the consequences of his medical condition, the plaintiffs too are blameless. The application of the sudden medical emergency doctrine in this case deprives them of the ability to vindicate their losses and collect against the one who caused their injuries. Moreover, the strict application of the doctrine prevents them from collecting on their own insurance policies, which they purchased to protect themselves in situations such as this.

Analysis:

In some respects, the sudden medical emergency defense is a legal fiction. At its center, the defense relieves actors from liability because the resulting damages are not foreseeable from the defendant's actions. Under the reasonable person standard, all that is required of a defendant is that he act as a reasonable person would under the circumstances. If the defendant's sudden medical emergency is not foreseeable and he has no means of knowing his actions may injure others, he has not acted unreasonably under the general standard of care.

■ CASE VOCABULARY

FORESEEABILITY: The quality of being reasonably anticipatable. Foreseeability, along with actual causation, is an element of proximate cause in tort law.

Chaffin v. Brame

(Night Driver) v. *(Truck Owner)*
233 N.C. 377, 64 S.E.2d 276 (1951)

COURT DECLINES TO USE THE "RANGE OF LIGHTS" RULE TO FIND NEGLIGENCE AS A MATTER OF LAW

■ **INSTANT FACTS** Blinded by undimmed oncoming headlights, Chaffin (P) collided with an unlighted truck left blocking the entire right lane.

■ **BLACK LETTER RULE** A driver's ultimate duty is to exercise reasonable care under the circumstances, which may not always include a duty to be able to stop his vehicle within the range of its lights.

■ **PROCEDURAL BASIS**

Appeal after jury trial of negligence action for damages.

■ **FACTS**

Chaffin (P) was driving along a highway at night when another car approached without dimming his headlights. Blinded by the lights, Chaffin (P) ran into Brame's (D) truck, which was unlighted and blocking the entire right lane. Brame (D) argued that Chaffin (P) was guilty of contributory negligence as a matter of law, but the trial court let the case go to the jury, and the jury returned a verdict for Chaffin (P). Citing *Marshall v. Southern Railway Co.* [driver must keep his vehicle under such control at night as to be able to stop within the range of its lights], Brame (D) argues that it is negligence as a matter of law to drive an automobile on a public highway in the dark at such a speed that the driver cannot stop the automobile within the distance that objects are visible ahead of it.

■ **ISSUE**

Does a driver have a duty to always keep his vehicle under such control at night as to be able to stop within the range of its lights?

■ **DECISION AND RATIONALE**

(Ervin) No. The application of *Marshall's* rule to particular cases is one of the most difficult tasks of trial law. Enhancing this difficulty, judges and attorneys tend to regard this rule as a rule of thumb, and not as a formula for applying to a recurring factual situation the principle. The purpose of this rule was to enforce the concept that courts should not permit an injured person to shift his loss to another when his loss results in part from his own failure to see the obvious. However, the rule does not require night drivers to be infallible, and it does not prevent them from recovering compensation for injuries caused by collisions with unlighted obstructions in the highway. Courts must decide each case on its own facts because the true and ultimate test is what a reasonably prudent person would do in those circumstances. The *Marshall* line of cases simply enforces the legal duty every person has to exercise ordinary care for his own safety. Viewing the evidence in the light most favorable to Chaffin (P), we may reasonably infer that Chaffin (P) was keeping a proper lookout and driving at a reasonable speed. We may also infer that when he was partially and temporarily blinded by oncoming headlights, Chaffin (P) exercised due care in reducing his speed and proceeding with extreme caution rather than stopping his car because he reasonably assumed that the oncoming driver would obey the law and dim his

---

lights, and thus restore his normal vision. Chaffin (P) had no reason to expect a truck to be standing on the highway with no warning lights, and did all he could to avoid the truck once it became visible. Therefore, we cannot hold Chaffin (P) guilty of contributory negligence as a matter of law. No error.

Analysis:

This case discusses negligence as a matter of law. For a judge to be able to hold a party negligent as a matter of law and thus to withdraw the issue of negligence from the jury, the facts must be such that reasonable jurors could not find otherwise. In *Chaffin* the court refused to apply *Marshall's* "range of lights" rule as a rule of law, which would have required a directed verdict. Instead, the court construed it as a rule of thumb to guide application of the reasonable care standard in similar factual situations. In *Marshall,* a driver who was blinded by oncoming high beams ran into a railroad trestle, and the court held him negligent as a matter of law. The court stated that it was a general rule of law that a driver must exercise ordinary care, and that this duty includes a duty to keep his vehicle under such control at night as to be able to stop within the range of its lights. Similarly, Chaffin (P), also facing blinding oncoming lights, ran into Brame's (D) unlighted truck which he left parked on the highway. The jury returned a verdict for Chaffin (P). Relying on *Marshall's* "range of lights" rule, Brame (D) argued that the case should not have gone to the jury because Chaffin (P) was contributorily negligent as a matter of law. The court explained that the "range of lights" rule only enforces a driver's duty of reasonable care, and that ultimately each case must be decided on its own facts. Because the court found that on the facts of this case it was reasonable to infer that Chaffin (P) exercised due care, reasonable jurors might find that he was not negligent, and the court thus could not hold him contributorily negligent as a matter of law.

■ CASE VOCABULARY

CONTRIBUTORY NEGLIGENCE: The now largely abolished doctrine that if a person's negligence was a partial cause of his injury, it bars his recovery of damages from another whose negligence also was a partial cause of his injury, regardless of the relative fault of the parties.

NEGLIGENCE AS A MATTER OF LAW: A judge's determination of negligence based on evidence of conduct that is so clearly below the level of care a reasonable person would exercise that a jury could not reasonably find otherwise.

SHIBBOLETH: A saying which those who hold a particular belief use, but which others usually regard as empty of real meaning.

Rains v. Bend of the River

(Teenager) v. *(Firearms Seller)*
124 S.W.3d 580 (Tenn.Ct.App.2003)

THE SALE OF AMMUNITION IN VIOLATION OF FEDERAL LAW IS NEGLIGENCE PER SE

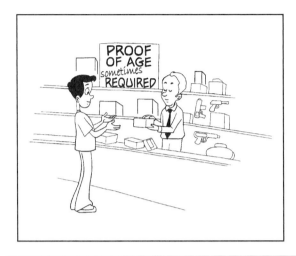

■ **INSTANT FACTS** After Aaron Rains purchased ammunition for a handgun from Bend of the River (D) in violation of the federal Gun Control Act, Aaron committed suicide.

■ **BLACK LETTER RULE** Violation of a penal statute is negligence as a matter of law.

■ **PROCEDURAL BASIS**

On appeal to review a decision of the trial court denying the defendant's motion for summary judgment.

■ **FACTS**

Eighteen-year-old Aaron Rains found a key to his father's gun lockbox and stole a handgun. Aaron then purchased ammunition from Bend of the River (D), which violated the federal Gun Control Act by selling ammunition to a person under age twenty-one. A couple of hours later, Aaron killed himself. Aaron's family (P) sued Bend of the River (D) for Aaron's death. After the court denied the defendant's motion for summary judgment, the defendant appealed.

■ **ISSUE**

Is the sale of ammunition to a minor in violation of the federal Gun Control Act negligence per se?

■ **DECISION AND RATIONALE**

(Koch, J.) Yes. Although under common law, a person is negligent if his conduct does not conform to that of a "reasonable person under the circumstances," the legislature may establish a more specific standard of conduct by statute in one of two ways. First, the legislature may create a legal duty and provide a civil cause of action for any breach. Second, the legislature may enact a penal statute and allow affected individuals a civil remedy for its violation through the doctrine of negligence per se. When negligence per se applies, a violation of the penal statute gives rise to negligence as a matter of law, and liability attaches if the plaintiff proves the conduct was the cause of his injuries. Negligence per se is not created, however, unless the penal statute specifically establishes the required standard of conduct above ordinary reasonableness and the court in its discretion adopts the statutory standard as the reasonable standard under the circumstances. Courts must consider whether the plaintiff belongs to the class of persons to be protected by the penal statute and whether the resulting injury is of a kind the statute intended to prevent. Further, the court must determine whether the statute is the sole source of the defendant's duty, whether the statute clearly defines the prohibited conduct, whether the statute would impose liability without fault, whether negligence per se would impose damages disproportionate to the statutory violation, and whether the plaintiff's injury is a direct or indirect result of the violation.

Here, the statute did not create a private civil cause of action for its violation, nor does it clearly define the standard of conduct with regard to minors who may intend to use firearms for suicide. However, courts have interpreted the statute as designed for public protection, making the sale of ammunition in violation of the statute negligence per se. Because the sale was not the legal or proximate cause of Aaron's death, however, summary judgment for the defendant was appropriate. Reversed.

Analysis:

The requirements of causation and damages in negligence per se cases distinguish that theory from strict liability. Under strict liability, a violation of a statutory directive conclusively establishes the actor's liability. Strict liability generally applies only to those activities that are ultrahazardous and inherently dangerous so as to justify strict enforcement of public safety provisions.

■ **CASE VOCABULARY**

PROXIMATE CAUSE: A cause that is legally sufficient to result in liability. A cause that directly produces an event and without which the event would not have occurred.

NEGLIGENCE PER SE: Negligence established as a matter of law, so that the breach of the duty is not a jury question. Negligence per se usually arises from a statutory violation.

Wright v. Brown

(Dog Attack Victim) v. *(Dog Owner)*
167 Conn. 464, 356 A.2d 176 (1975)

COURTS CAN AVOID THE NEGLIGENCE PER SE DOCTRINE IF A PLAINTIFF DOES NOT SATISFY BOTH PRONGS OF THE CLASS OF PERSONS/TYPE OF HARM TEST

■ **INSTANT FACTS** Prior to the expiration of the 14 days required by statute, the dog warden (D) released Brown's (D) dog from quarantine and the dog attacked Wright (P).

■ **BLACK LETTER RULE** To maintain a negligence action based on a statutory standard of care, a person must (1) be within the class of persons the statute is intended to protect, and (2) suffer the type of injury the statute is intended to prevent.

■ **PROCEDURAL BASIS**

Appeal from sustaining of demurrer in negligence action for damages.

■ **FACTS**

The complaint alleged that Brown's (D) dog attacked someone, and that the dog warden (D) then quarantined the dog. The complaint further alleged that before the 14-day quarantine period required by statute had expired, the warden (D) released the dog, and the dog then attacked and injured Wright (P). Wright (P) brought a negligence action against Brown (D), the town (D), and the dog warden (D) alleging that they failed to comply with the statutory standard of conduct. The dog warden (D) and town (D) demurred, arguing that violation of the statute would not constitute negligence because Wright (P) was not within the class of persons the statute was designed to protect. The trial court found that the statute was designed to quarantine a dog for a period necessary to determine whether a person bitten by the dog needed a rabies vaccine and to protect the community from being bitten by diseased dogs. Because Wright (P) did not allege that she was bitten by a diseased dog, the trial court concluded that she was not within the class of persons protected by the statute and thus dismissed her case against the dog warden (D) and the town (D).

■ **ISSUE**

Must a person be within the class of persons a statute is intended to protect to maintain a negligence claim based on a violation of that statute?

■ **DECISION AND RATIONALE**

(Bogdanski) Yes. The purpose of the quarantine requirement is clear from the meaning of that word. "Quarantine" means to isolate in order to protect others from exposure to contagious disease. While the legislature may have specifically intended to protect dog bite victims from rabies, it did not expressly restrict its purpose in the statute. Because the intent expressed in the statute controls, the trial court correctly concluded that the legislature intended this statute not only to protect dog bite victims from rabies, but also to protect the general public from diseased dogs. To maintain an action for statutory negligence, a person must (1) be within the class of persons the statute is intended to protect, and (2) suffer the type of injury the statute is intended to prevent. This statute does not limit the class of persons it protects. Rather, the legislature intended this statute to protect the general public. The town (D) and dog warden (D) addressed their demurrer only to the class of persons protected by this statute. Because Wright (P), as a member of the general public, is within that class, the trial court should not have sustained the demurrer on that ground. However, because Wright (P) alleges only that she was attacked and injured by a dog that was prematurely released from quarantine, she does not allege injuries of the type the statute was intended to prevent. Reversed and remanded.

Analysis:

If a court finds that a statute or regulation is clearly intended to provide for tort liability, then the court must apply it as the standard of care in a negligence action unless it is unconstitutional. This case illustrates the generally accepted two-pronged test courts use to guide their determination of whether it would be proper to apply such a statute or regulation in a particular case. Under this two-pronged test, the court asks (1) whether the plaintiff belongs to the class of persons the statute or regulation was intended to protect, and (2) whether the plaintiff's injury is of the type the statute was intended to prevent. In this case Wright (P) incurred injuries when a dog attacked her after the warden released it from quarantine early. The court found that the class of persons protected by a dog-quarantine statute was not limited, and that Wright (P), as a member of the general public, was entitled to its protection. However, a court's determination of whether to apply a statute in a negligence per se action depends not only on the plaintiff being within the class of persons the legislature intended to protect, but also on the harm suffered being of the type the legislature intended to prevent. Because the purpose of the statute was to protect against the threat of rabies and against contact with diseased dogs, and because Wright (P) was not bitten but attacked by a diseased dog, her injury was not of the type the legislature intended to prevent.

■ CASE VOCABULARY

DEMURRER: A request to dismiss a lawsuit because the alleged facts, even if true, do not support a legal claim, now often referred to as a motion to dismiss for failure to state a claim.

Impson v. Structural Metals, Inc.

(*Car Driver*) v. (*Truck Driver*)
487 S.W.2d 694 (Tex.1972)

A LEGALLY SUFFICIENT EXCUSE MAY ALSO PERMIT A PARTY TO AVOID THE NEGLIGENCE PER SE DOCTRINE

■ **INSTANT FACTS** A truck driver attempted to pass a car within 100 feet of an intersection in violation of a statute, but hit the car when the car turned left.

■ **BLACK LETTER RULE** When there is evidence that a party has violated a statutory standard of care, the court has no duty to submit the issue of negligence to the jury where there is no evidence of a legally acceptable excuse or justification.

■ **PROCEDURAL BASIS**

Appeal after judgment in personal injury and wrongful death actions for damages.

■ **FACTS**

The driver of Structural Metals, Inc.'s (Structural Metals) (D) truck attempted to pass Impson's (P) car within 100 feet of an intersection, but the car turned left and the truck hit the car. Because a statute prohibits passing within 100 feet of an intersection, the trial judge found negligence as a matter of law and entered judgment for Impson (P). Structural Metals (D) argued that the court should excuse its driver's violation because he forgot the existence of the intersection; the sign marking it was small; there were no "no passing" lines on the road; and the driver was watching the car, which was partly off the road on the right, rather than looking for intersection signs. The Court of Appeals held that a jury must decide the negligence issue because Structural Metals (D) offered some excuses.

■ **ISSUE**

When there is evidence that a party has violated a statutory standard of care, but the party offers evidence of some excuse, must the court submit the issue of negligence to the jury?

■ **DECISION AND RATIONALE**

(Greenhill) No. Not all excuses or justifications are legally acceptable. In other cases we have accepted excuses including a tire blowout, unavoidable skidding on wet streets, and the impossibility of stopping a truck within the prescribed distance from a railroad track. However, we did not address the legal sufficiency of the excuse in any of these cases. The *Restatement of Torts (Second) § 288A* [lists some categories of excuses for statutory violations] states that an excused violation of a statute is not negligence. Although not exclusive, this section lists some excusable situations, including: (a) incapacity, such as blindness, a heart attack, or young age; (b) reasonable lack of knowledge of the need for compliance, such as when a tail light unexpectedly goes out without the driver's knowledge; (c) inability after reasonable diligence to comply, such as when it is impossible to stop a truck within a certain distance; (d) an emergency not due to the person's own misconduct, such as an unexpected tire blowout or brake failure; and (e) a greater risk of harm from compliance, such as when a law requires pedestrians to walk on one side of the road, but circumstances make this more dangerous than walking on the other side. We approve the Restatement's general treatment of legally acceptable excuses. However, the excuses Structural Metals (D) offered for its driver's violation all fell within the realm of ordinary care. The driver acted deliberately, with knowledge of the law and at least notice of the presence of the intersection. There was no impossibility, emergency, incapacity, or greater risk of harm from compliance with the law to excuse the driver's violation. Because there was no evidence offered of any legally acceptable excuse or justification, this was, in law, an unexcused violation which, when coupled with the jury's finding of proximate cause, entitled Impson (P) to judgment. Court of Appeals judgment reversed, trial court judgment affirmed.

Analysis:

This case illustrates another method of avoiding the doctrine of negligence per se. Under this doctrine, if a statute defines the standard of care for a negligence case, then an unexcused violation of that statute conclusively establishes negligence. However, the court may find that the violation was excused, as long as the statute does not indicate that no excuses are permissible. This case discusses some of the categories of situations which courts usually find legally sufficient to excuse the violation of a standard-setting statute. In *Impson*, Structural Metals' (D) driver violated a statute that prohibited passing within 100 feet of an intersection and collided with a car turning left into the intersection. The trial court did not submit the issue of negligence to the jury. The Court of Appeals agreed with the trial court that the statutory violation constituted negligence per se, but held that because Structural Metals (D) offered evidence of justification or excuse, the trial court had a duty to submit the issue of negligence to the jury. The Supreme Court of Texas disagreed. Because it found that none of the excuses Structural Metals (D) offered were legally acceptable, it held that the trial court was correct in deciding that the violation was unexcused as a matter of law, and that the issue of negligence therefore did not require submission to the jury. In *Impson*, the court explained that mere ordinary care does not necessarily constitute a legally acceptable excuse. If it did, the doctrine of negligence per se would be meaningless, because a violation would only constitute negligence per se when it would also constitute a failure to exercise ordinary care, or ordinary negligence. Because the excuses offered by Structural Metals (D) only fell within the realm of ordinary care and were not legally acceptable, the violation of the statute was, in law, unexcused and therefore constituted negligence per se.

■ CASE VOCABULARY

EXCUSE: A reason for exemption from a duty of care.

INCAPACITY: A lack of physical or mental abilities that makes a person unable to exercise ordinary care.

JUSTIFICATION: A legally sufficient reason for conduct that frees a person from liability where his conduct would otherwise be tortious.

CHAPTER SIX

Negligence: The Breach or Negligence Element of the Negligence Case

Indiana Consolidated Insurance Co. v. Mathew

Instant Facts: Mr. Mathew (D) started his brother's lawnmower to cut his brother's lawn and the lawnmower caught fire damaging his brother's garage.

Black Letter Rule: The standard of care to adjudge negligent conduct is whether a person exercised the duty to use care that an ordinary prudent person would exercise under the same or similar circumstances.

Stinnett v. Buchele

Instant Facts: Employee hired to paint a barn roof falls from the roof while painting it and injuries himself.

Black Letter Rule: An employer does not breach a duty to its employee to provide a reasonably safe place to work and reasonably safe tools for doing the work when the employee injures himself during the scope of his employment and the employee's knowledge of the dangers to be incurred while working is equal to or exceeds the knowledge of the employer.

Bernier v. Boston Edison Co.

Instant Facts: Mr. Bernier (P) was injured when an electric light pole fell on him after it was struck by an automobile that was involved in a minor traffic accident.

Black Letter Rule: Failure to take reasonable steps to prevent unreasonable risk of injury from reasonably foreseeable accidents is negligence.

United States v. Carroll Towing Co.

Instant Facts: A barge, without a bargee on broad broke adrift, was carried by wind into a tanker whose propeller broke a hole in barge's bottom, and barge lost its cargo and sank.

Black Letter Rule: Absence a reasonable excuse, barge owner's failure to take reasonable steps to prevent unreasonable risk of barge breaking away in busy wartime harbor by manning barge with bargee is negligence.

Santiago v. First Student, Inc.

Instant Facts: Santiago (P) was injured while riding a bus operated by First Student, Inc. (D).

Black Letter Rule: A plaintiff bears the burden of proving a defendant's actions were the proximate cause of her injuries.

Upchurch v. Rotenberry

Instant Facts: Automobile passenger is injured when automobile strikes a tree after automobile driver attempts to avoid an animal on the roadway.

Black Letter Rule: It is the duty of the jury to determine whether a defendant in a negligence case exercised reasonable care under the circumstances.

Thoma v. Cracker Barrel Old Country Store, Inc.

Instant Facts: Restaurant patron sustains injuries from a fall in a restaurant.

Black Letter Rule: Proof of negligent conduct in a slip and fall case requires a finding by the jury that the owner of or employees at the premises either created a dangerous condition or had knowledge of the dangerous condition that lead to the fall and resulting injuries.

Wal–Mart Stores, Inc. v. Wright

Instant Facts: Wright (P) slipped in a puddle of water at a Wal–Mart (D) store.

Black Letter Rule: A violation of subjectively established policies and procedures does not establish negligence.

The T. J. Hooper

Instant Facts: Large barge filled with coal and the tugboat which was its tow were lost at see during heavy weather.

Black Letter Rule: Notwithstanding a custom of usage or the lack thereof, there are precautions so imperative that even their universal disregard will not excuse their omission.

Byrne v. Boadle

Instant Facts: Barrel of flour falls on a man as he passes a flour shop.

Black Letter Rule: Under certain circumstances, the fact that an accident occurred can support an inference or presumption of negligence.

Giles v. City of New Haven

Instant Facts: Elevator operator is injured when chain of elevator she was operating became hooked on the rail bracket in the elevator shaft.

Black Letter Rule: Use by the plaintiff of the instrumentality that caused her injury does not preclude a finding that the defendant had control of the instrumentality.

Warren v. Jeffries

Instant Facts: Six-year old boy jumped out of a car when it begins to roll backward. When the boy jumped he fell, and the front wheel of the car rolled over his chest, killing him.

Black Letter Rule: Pure speculation is not a basis for applying the doctrine of res ipsa loquitur.

Widmyer v. Southeast Skyways, Inc.

Instant Facts: Airplane encounters a heavy snow squall and crashes killing pilot and passengers.

Black Letter Rule: Plaintiff's introduction of specific evidence of negligence does not preclude the use of the doctrine of res ipsa loquitur, unless the evidence furnishes a complete explanation of the accident.

Indiana Consolidated Insurance Co. v. Mathew

(Insurance Co. Seeking Damages) v. *(Non-Negligent Defendant)*

402 N.E.2d 1000 (Ind.App.1980)

INDIANA APPEALS COURT FINDS THAT APPELLEEE'S CONDUCT WHILE OPERATING A LAWNMOW-ER WAS NOT NEGLIGENT

■ **INSTANT FACTS** Mr. Mathew (D) started his brother's lawnmower to cut his brother's lawn and the lawnmower caught fire damaging his brother's garage.

■ **BLACK LETTER RULE** The standard of care to adjudge negligent conduct is whether a person exercised the duty to use care that an ordinary prudent person would exercise under the same or similar circumstances.

■ **PROCEDURAL BASIS**

Appeal from trial court finding that Mr. Mathew (D) did not act negligently.

■ **FACTS**

Mr. Mathew (D) and his brother took turns mowing their lawns. When Mr. Mathew's (D) brother was out of town, Mr. Mathew (D) decided to mow his brother's lawn. Mr. Mathew (D) went to his brother's garage to retrieve a twelve-horsepower Toro riding lawnmower to mow the lawn. The lawnmower was in good working condition. Noticing that the lawnmower was low on fuel, Mr. Mathew (D) filled the lawnmower's fuel tank to three-fourths of its capacity. Twenty minutes later, Mr. Mathew (D) returned to the garage and started the lawnmower. Upon starting the lawnmower, Mr. Mathew (D) noticed a flame in the engine area, and he immediately shut the engine off. When Mr. Mathew (D) opened the hood of the lawnmower to investigate, he observed a flame four to five inches tall under the fuel tank. Mr. Mathew (D) then attempted to extinguish the flame with a towel; however, he was unsuccessful. Failing to find a means to extinguish the flame and realizing the lawnmower was spewing fuel, Mr. Mathew (D) left the garage to call the fire department. When he returned, he found the garage engulfed in flames. Indiana Consolidated Insurance Co. (Consolidated) (P), the insurer of Mr. Mathew's (D) brother's garage, brought suit against Mr. Mathew (D) alleging that Mr. Mathew (D) breached a duty owed to his brother to exercise due care in starting the lawnmower. The trial court found that Mr. Mathew (D) had not acted negligently, and Consolidated (P) appealed.

■ **ISSUE**

Is the standard of care to adjudge negligent conduct whether a person exercised the duty to use care that an ordinary prudent person would exercise under the same or similar circumstances?

■ **DECISION AND RATIONALE**

(Hoffman) Yes. The standard of care to adjudge negligent conduct is whether a person exercised the duty to use care that an ordinary prudent person would exercise under the same or similar circumstances. The trial court record shows that Mr. Mathew (D) added fuel to the lawnmower's fuel tank in a careful manner. He did not fill the fuel tank to its capacity, nor did he spill any fuel while inserting it into the tank. Under the circumstances, Mr. Mathew (D) did not breach a duty to exercise care that an ordinary prudent person would exercise. Consolidated's (P) contention that Mr. Mathew's (D) conduct of starting the lawnmower in the garage is negligent conduct is without merit. Garages are designed to permit the starting of motorized vehicles and are commonly used for such purposes. It was not reasonably foreseeable that a lawnmower in good working condition would catch fire. Therefore, Mr. Mathew (D) was not negligent when he started the lawnmower in the garage. Consolidated's (P) contention that Mr. Mathew (D) was negligent because he failed to push the flaming lawnmower out of the garage also lacks merit. The flaming lawnmower was spewing fuel, and Mr. Mathew (D) feared for his safety as the fuel tank could explode. Confronted with an emergency, Mr. Mathew (D) chose to call the fire department. Since the law values human life more than it values property, Mr. Mathew's (D) conduct under the circumstance was reasonable. Judgment affirmed.

Analysis:

Negligence is careless conduct under the circumstances. Mr. Mathew (D) did not fill the lawnmower's fuel tank in a careless manner. Since people regularly start lawnmowers in garages, Mr. Mathew (D) was not careless when he started his brother's lawnmower in his brother's garage. Additionally, he was not careless when he called the fire department because he could not extinguish the flames and feared the fuel tank would explode. Under these circumstances, Mr. Mathew (D) did not owe a duty to risk his life to save his brother's garage. Since Mr. Mathew's (D) conduct was not careless under any of the circumstances, he did not act negligently. Notice, simply, that the court analyzed this case by reviewing Mr. Mathew's conduct to determine if he acted reasonably and prudently under the circumstances.

Stinnett v. Buchele

(Painter/Employee) v. *(Employer)*

598 S.W.2d 469 (Ky.App.1980)

EMPLOYEE'S KNOWLEDGE MAY VITIATE CLAIM THAT EMPLOYER BREACHED A DUTY OWED TO THE EMPLOYEE

■ **INSTANT FACTS** Employee hired to paint a barn roof falls from the roof while painting it and injuries himself.

■ **BLACK LETTER RULE** An employer does not breach a duty to its employee to provide a reasonably safe place to work and reasonably safe tools for doing the work when the employee injures himself during the scope of his employment and the employee's knowledge of the dangers to be incurred while working is equal to or exceeds the knowledge of the employer.

■ **PROCEDURAL BASIS**

Negligence plaintiff appeals lower court summary judgment order.

■ **FACTS**

Mr. Buchele (D), a practicing physician, hired Mr. Stinnett (P) to paint his barn roof and nail down its edges. Mr. Stinnett (P) had been in the painting business for two years and had painted numerous barns before his employment with Mr. Buchele (D). Mr. Stinnett (P) fell from the barn roof while painting it and severely injured himself. Mr. Buchele (D) provided the coating for the roof, but he did not provide a safety net. Mr. Stinnett (P) did not supply his own safety net, nor did he request a safety net from Mr. Buchele (D). Mr. Stinnett (P) brought a negligence suit against Mr. Buchele (D). The trial court granted summary judgment for Mr. Buchele (D) as it found that Mr. Buchele (D) had not acted in a negligent manner. Mr. Stinnett (P) appealed.

■ **ISSUE**

Does an employer breach a duty to its employee to provide a reasonably safe place to work and reasonably safe tools for doing the work when the employee injures himself during the scope of his employment and the employee's knowledge of the dangers to be incurred while working is equal to or exceeds the knowledge of the employer?

■ **DECISION AND RATIONALE**

(Oakes) No. An employer does not breach a duty to its employee to provide a reasonably safe place to work and reasonably safe tools for doing the work when the employee injures himself during the scope of his employment and the employee's knowledge of the dangers to be incurred while working is equal to or exceeds the knowledge of the employer. Mr. Stinnett (P) filed a workmen's compensation claim for his injuries, and the Workmen's Compensation Board denied that claim. He now contends that Mr. Buchele (D) was negligent for failing to comply with occupational and health regulations and for failure to provide a safe place to work. This Court does not find any evidence that Mr. Buchele (D) was negligent in failing to provide to Mr. Stinnett (P) a safe place to work. While an employer has a duty to provide a reasonably safe place to work and reasonably safe tools with which to work, that duty does not extend to the impossible duty of providing an absolutely safe workplace and tools. Even though painting a barn may be dangerous, this Court does not find that Mr. Buchele (D) is liable for negligence because he asked Mr. Stinnett (P) to paint his barn roof. Further, an employer's duty to provide safety devices rests upon the assumption that the employer has more knowledge than the employee. Liability ceases to exist when the employee's knowledge of the dangers to be incurred is equal to the knowledge of the employer. Since Mr. Stinnett (P) is an experienced barn painter, this court does not find that Mr. Buchele (D), as an employer, breached a duty owed to Mr. Stinnett (P). As there is no evidence of negligence to submit to the jury, this Court affirms the trial court's judgment.

Analysis:

This case illustrates the central principle of negligence cases. Negligence is careless conduct under the circumstances. The circumstances in the instant case do not support a finding of negligence, because Mr. Stinnett (P) is an experienced painter. He knows the danger involved with painting a barn. On the other hand, Mr. Buchele (D) is a physician. There is no evidence that Mr. Buchele's (D) barn painting knowledge equals or exceeds Mr. Stinnett's (P) knowledge. Therefore, Mr. Buchele (D) was not careless under the circumstances. Contributory negligence on the part of the plaintiff and lack of negligence on the part of the defendant are easily confused in these circumstances. The issue often arises in "open and obvious danger" cases, when the defendant creates a condition that will be dangerous to anyone who ignores it but that is safe enough when people pay reasonable attention. Also, an express assumed risk ordinarily will relieve the defendant of the duty that otherwise existed. Alternatively, it will establish a standard of care that shows he has breached no duty.

Bernier v. Boston Edison Co.

(Person Injured When A Utility Pole Fell On Him) v. *(Designer/Maintainer Of Utility Pole)*
380 Mass. 372, 403 N.E.2d 391 (1980)

SUPREME JUDICIAL COURT OF MASSACHUSETTS FINDS THAT PERSONS HAVE A DUTY TO REASONABLY FORESEE ACCIDENTS THAT CREATE AN UNREASONABLE RISK OF HARM

■ **INSTANT FACTS** Mr. Bernier (P) was injured when an electric light pole fell on him after it was struck by an automobile that was involved in a minor traffic accident.

■ **BLACK LETTER RULE** Failure to take reasonable steps to prevent unreasonable risk of injury from reasonably foreseeable accidents is negligence.

■ FACTS

Mr. Bernier (P) was injured when Ms. Ramsdell (D1) lost control of her automobile after she was involved in a minor traffic collision with Mr. Boireau's (D2) automobile. Following the collision between the two vehicles, a collision that resulted from the drivers of the two vehicles failure to correctly negotiate a right turn, Ms. Ramsdell (D1) lost control of her vehicle. Her vehicle then entered and traveled down a sidewalk. While on the sidewalk, Ms. Ramsdell's (D1) vehicle struck and knocked down an electric light pole that Boston Edison Co. (D3) owned. The pole fell on Mr. Bernier's (P) legs. The impact of the pole broke Mr. Bernier's (P) thighs and left shin bone. The break to Mr. Bernier's (P) left shin bone caused a permanent shorting of his left leg. Mr. Bernier (P) and a female friend who was injured after Ms. Ramsdell (D1) lost control of her car brought a negligence cause of action against Ms. Ramsdell (D1), Mr. Boireau (D2), and Edison (D3). The trial court jury rendered an adverse verdict against Ms. Ramsdell (D1) and Edison (D3), and Edison (D3) appealed.

■ ISSUE

Does a person or a corporation have a duty to reasonably foresee accidents that create an unreasonable risk of injury and take reasonable steps to mitigate the risk of injury?

■ DECISION AND RATIONALE

(Kaplan) Yes. A person or a corporation has a duty to reasonably foresee accidents that create an unreasonable risk of injury and take reasonable steps to mitigate the risk of injury. Edison (D3) designed the electric light pole that is the focus of this case. A designer or co-designer and maintainer of such a pole must anticipate the environment in which the pole is used. Further, it must design against reasonably foreseeable risks associated with the use of electric light poles under the circumstances. Trial court evidence shows that there was a risk of automobiles colliding with Edison (D3) poles and that Edison (D3) was aware of this risk. Edison (D3) was aware of the risk because 100 to 120 Edison poles a year are knocked down by automobiles. Therefore, Edison (D3) has a duty to foresee collisions with its poles and the risks that such collisions pose to pedestrians. Trial evidence fails to show that Edison (D3) appreciated the risks. Rather, the evidence shows that Edison (D3) was more concerned with the cost of constructing and maintaining poles than with the risk of harm to pedestrians. When the potential for serious injury exists, consideration of safety measures is warranted, even if the likelihood of accidents is not great. Expert testimony from Mr. Bernier's (P) expert witness revealed that the pole in question in the instant case would collapse when struck by an automobile traveling six m.p.h. Further, the expert testified that Edison (D3) could increase the stability of the pole at low costs. Even Edison (D3) employees offered testimony that suggests that more stable types of poles were known to and available to Edison (D3). Edison (D3) has a duty to reasonably foresee injuries to pedestrians that result from automobile collisions with its electric light poles. The trial jury found that Edison (D3) was negligent in the design and maintenance of the pole that is at issue in the instant case. Since the pole in question will topple when struck by a vehicle traveling at an extremely low speed, the pole creates an unreasonable risk of injury to pedestrians. Judgment affirmed.

Analysis:

Again, negligence is careless conduct under the circumstances. In the instant case, Edison (D3) designed its electric light poles. It was aware of the existing pole technology and its cost. Further, it was aware that many of its poles are struck by automobiles and then topple to the ground. A reasonable person would realize that a falling electric light pole poses a serious risk of injury to pedestrians. Edison (D3) was aware of this risk but chose to ignore it. Ignoring a known serious risk of injury to others, a risk that one can reasonably make an effort to mitigate, is careless conduct under the circumstances. Note the balancing that the court had to do in this case. If the pole gives way and falls on impact, the passengers in the car are safer than if they had collided with an immovable object. On the other hand, falling poles may strike pedestrians or others. To make things safer for pedestrians is to make them riskier for car passengers and vice versa. So if the telephone company installs stronger poles to protect the pedestrian, part of the cost of doing so will be borne by car passengers who suffer injury as a result. Note also that an expert testified that the defendant's pole would fall when struck by an automobile driving at only six miles per hour. This kind of testimony is admissible to help the jury estimate how risky the defendant's pole really was. Sometimes studies about the riskiniess of a given activity or product design are admissible, too, if for nothing else than to show that harm was foreseeable.

United States v. Carroll Towing Co.

(Party in Admiralty) v. *(Tug Boat Towing Co.)*

159 F.2d 169 (C.C.A.2, 1947)

UNITED STATES COURT OF APPEALS FINDS THAT BARGE OWNER AND ITS EMPLOYEES WERE NEGLIGENT WHEN BARGEE WAS ABSENT WHEN BARGE BROKE ADRIFT, LOST HER CARGO, AND SANK

■ **INSTANT FACTS** A barge, without a bargee on broad broke adrift, was carried by wind into a tanker whose propeller broke a hole in barge's bottom, and barge lost its cargo and sank.

■ **BLACK LETTER RULE** Absence a reasonable excuse, barge owner's failure to take reasonable steps to prevent unreasonable risk of barge breaking away in busy wartime harbor by manning barge with bargee is negligence.

■ **PROCEDURAL BASIS**

Proceedings in admiralty.

■ **FACTS**

A barge broke adrift from a tugboat that the Carroll Towing Co. (Carroll) (D) operated. Upon breaking adrift, the wind and tide carried the barge against a tanker. The tanker's propeller broke a hole in the barge. As a result, the barge lost its cargo of flour and sank. The trial court found that the owners and operators of the tugboat assigned to the barge were liable for the damages to the barge and then considered if the absence of a bargee on board the barge at the time of the incident reduced the recovery of the owner of the barge.

■ **ISSUE**

Whether absence a reasonable excuse, barge owner's failure to take reasonable steps to prevent unreasonable risk of barge breaking away in busy wartime harbor by manning barge with bargee is negligence?

■ **DECISION AND RATIONALE**

(Hand) Yes. Absence a reasonable excuse, barge owner's failure to take reasonable steps to prevent the unreasonable risk of the barge breaking away in the harbor by manning a barge with a bargee is negligence. There is no general rule to determine when the absence of a bargee will make the owner of a barge liable for damages to other vessels. Under certain circumstances, any vessel may break free from her mooring and become a menace to other vessels. Therefore, the duty of a vessel's owner depends upon the probability (P) that the vessel will break free, the gravity of the resulting injury (L) if she does break free, and the burden (B) of adequate precautions to prevent her from breaking free or mitigating damages if she does break free. If the burden of adequate precautions is less than the product of the probability that a vessel will break free and the gravity of the resulting injury if she does (B < PL), liability would attach under the appropriate circumstances. Whether a barge will break from her fast and cause damage depends on circumstances such as stormy weather and busy harbor conditions. However, a barge is not a bargee's prison. In the instant case, the bargee left the barge at 5:00 PM on January 3rd. The barge broke away at 2:00 PM on the following day. The bargee was absent, without excuse, from 5:00 PM on January 3rd to 2:00 PM the following day. The bargee's absence occurred in January when the days are short. Further, the incident of the instant case occurred in the full tide of war activity when barges are constantly drilled in an out. Given the weather conditions and the busy nature of the harbor, this court holds that it is reasonable to require a barge owner to have a bargee on board during the working hours of daylight, unless there is a reasonable excuse for the bargee's absence.

Analysis:

Courts routinely apply some form of risk-utility weighing as a means of determining whether conduct was negligent. The structured or rigorous model is usually traced to this opinion. Judge Hand recognized the traditional idea that a weighing of risks and utilities was necessary. The burden of precaution in Judge Hand's formula includes any cost the defendant might have to incur to make things safe enough, but it also includes costs that would be inflicted upon others or upon society at large. More, the burden or precaution was simple: the increased or marginal cost to the defendant of keeping a bargee on board 24 hours a day. Thinking about costs and benefits in terms of the *Carroll Towing* formula, a judge or juror can compare benefits with costs because they have now been put on a common scale. One of the most important functions of the formula may be to direct lawyers to helpful kinds of evidence. Plaintiffs' lawyers may be led by the formula to claim that the defendant failed to use a cheaper means of achieving safety. For instance, a plaintiff's lawyer might try to prove that the defendant could have avoided the breakaway in *Carroll Towing* by making a one-time capital investment in better tie-down technology that would be far less costly than either the full-time bargee or the potential harm from breakaways. Although probability is used to discount the damage when the point is to determine the defendant's negligence, probability is not used to reduce the plaintiff's actual recovery. If the defendant is found to be negligent by application of these rules, he is liable for all of the plaintiff's injury, whether it is $50, $100, or many times those amounts. The discount applies only as a way of determining the total risk imposed by the defendant's conduct. Averaging, or the use of the probability discount, is important if the defendant is to estimate the appropriate overall amount to invest in safety. Any particular injured individual might suffer damages much less than the defendant's cost to avoid the harm but still recover because the average harm would exceed that cost. And vice versa: the injured individual might suffer much greater harm than the defendant's cost of avoidance and yet be denied recovery because the cost of avoidance was too high compared to the average or probable overall harms. Indeed, one of the criticisms of the formula, at least as it might be rigorously applied, is that it may do social good without doing individual justice.

Santiago v. First Student, Inc.

(Student) v. *(Bus Company)*
839 A.2d 550 (R.I.2004)

A PLAINTIFF'S INABILITY TO RECALL DETAILS IS FATAL TO HER CASE

■ **INSTANT FACTS** Santiago (P) was injured while riding a bus operated by First Student, Inc. (D).

■ **BLACK LETTER RULE** A plaintiff bears the burden of proving a defendant's actions were the proximate cause of her injuries.

■ **PROCEDURAL BASIS**

On appeal to review a decision of the Rhode Island Court of Appeals, affirming summary judgment for the defendant.

■ **FACTS**

First Student, Inc. (D) operates a school bus that allegedly collided with a car at an intersection that Santiago (P), an injured school-age passenger, could not identify. During her deposition, Santiago (P) testified that she could not remember at which intersection the accident occurred, but she said that she saw an unidentified vehicle approaching the intersection, after which it collided with the bus, causing her face to strike the seatback in front of her. She could not testify as to whether there was a stop sign at the intersection or to the extent of damage to the other vehicle. Because the police did not respond, no report was prepared. The trial court granted First Student's (D) motion for summary judgment.

■ **ISSUE**

Without evidence of causation, is summary judgment for the defendant appropriate?

■ **DECISION AND RATIONALE**

(Per curiam.) Yes. While the evidence supports that Santiago (P) was injured in an accident, holding the defendant liable for the accident based on the evidence provided would be pure speculation. The plaintiff has provided no evidence that the bus driver failed to stop at a stop sign or was otherwise negligent. The plaintiff bears the burden of proving the defendant's actions caused her injuries, and her burden cannot be relieved because the nature of the incident renders liability difficult to prove. Affirmed.

Analysis:

In an ordinary negligence case, the plaintiff always bears the burden of proving that the defendant's negligence caused her injuries. Under a special class of negligence cases, however, causation can be inferred under the doctrine of res ipsa loquitor. This doctrine applies when an accident occurs under circumstances that would not otherwise occur absent a defendant's negligence. The doctrine does not apply in this case, because the injuries here could have resulted without any negligence by the defendant.

■ **CASE VOCABULARY**

BURDEN OF PROOF: A party's duty to prove a disputed assertion or charge.

CAUSATION: The causing or producing of an effect.

PROXIMATE CAUSE: A cause that is legally sufficient to result in liability.

Upchurch v. Rotenberry

(*Parent of Deceased Son*) v. (*Driver of Automobile*)

761 So.2d 199 (Miss.2000)

IT IS THE ROLE OF THE JURY TO DETERMINE IF THE DEFENDANT IS NEGLIGENT

■ **INSTANT FACTS** Automobile passenger is injured when automobile strikes a tree after automobile driver attempts to avoid an animal on the roadway.

■ **BLACK LETTER RULE** It is the duty of the jury to determine whether a defendant in a negligence case exercised reasonable care under the circumstances.

■ PROCEDURAL BASIS

Appeal from an adverse jury verdict and denial of motion for judgment notwithstanding the verdict.

■ FACTS

Timothy Adam Upchurch (Adam) was a passenger in Ms. Rotenberry's (D) car. While Adam was a passenger in the car, Ms. Rotenberry (D) lost control of her car and struck a tree. The collision with the tree caused Adam to receive injuries that lead to his death, and Adam's mother, Ms. Upchurch (P) brought a wrongful death action against Ms. Rotenberry (D). Only Ms. Rotenberry (D) witnessed the accident. During the trial, there was conflicting testimony about the speed at which Ms. Rotenberry's car was traveling when it struck the tree and the manner in which the car left the road. Additionally, there was conflicting testimony about whether Ms. Rotenberry (D) was intoxicated at the time of the accident. During the trial, Ms. Rotenberry (D) testified that she did not remember the events leading up to the accident. However, five weeks after the accident, she signed a document that stated a large animal such as a dog or deer ran across the road causing her to swerve to the right to avoid the animal and then leave the road. The jury returned a verdict in favor of Ms. Rotenberry (D), and Ms. Upchurch (P) moved the court for a judgment notwithstanding the verdict. The trial court denied the motion, and Ms. Upchurch (P) appealed.

■ ISSUE

Does a jury have a duty to determine whether a defendant in a negligence case exercised reasonable care under the circumstances?

■ DECISION AND RATIONALE

(Pittman) Yes. It is the duty of the jury to determine whether a defendant in a negligence case exercised reasonable care under the circumstances. This Court will not second-guess a jury's findings regarding the credibility of witnesses, nor will it second-guess its findings of fact; for the jury is the judge of the weight of the evidence and the credibility of witnesses. The jury, in accord with its duty, determined that Ms. Rotenberry (D) acted reasonably in maneuvering her car to avoid an animal. Further, it found that she did not have time to avoid the tree after her car left the road. Absent some clear evidence of juror misconduct, this Court will not interfere with the jury's findings.

Analysis:

Upon first reading the facts, one wonders how this accident could have been caused by anyone other than the defendant [unless the tree miraculously jumped in front of the defendant's car]. But, some other evidence was presented. The defendant had earlier made a statement that an animal had run in front of her car. If this were true, a reasonably prudent person would swerve the car to avoid the collision. Thus, the cause of the accident may have been the unexpected appearance of the animal and not the negligence of the defendant. Ultimately, the question of negligence is for the jury. In this case, apparently the jury believed that the cause of the accident was the sudden appearance of the large animal. Accordingly, there was no basis for the appellate court to overturn the jury verdict.

Thoma v. Cracker Barrel Old Country Store, Inc.

(Person Who Fell in Restaurant) v. *(Restaurant Owner)*
649 So.2d 277 (Fla.Dist.Ct.App.1995)

IN A SLIP AND FALL CASE, A PLAINTIFF MUST PROVE THAT THE DEFENDANT CREATED A DANGEROUS CONDITION OR HAD KNOWLEDGE OF SUCH A CONDITION

■ **INSTANT FACTS** Restaurant patron sustains injuries from a fall in a restaurant.

■ **BLACK LETTER RULE** Proof of negligent conduct in a slip and fall case requires a finding by the jury that the owner of—or employees at—the premises either created a dangerous condition or had knowledge of the dangerous condition that lead to the fall and resulting injuries.

■ **PROCEDURAL BASIS**

Appeal from summary judgment.

■ **FACTS**

Ms. Thoma (P) slipped and fell in the Cracker Barrel Restaurant (Cracker Barrel) (D) after eating her breakfast. When Ms. Thoma (P) arose to her feet, she noticed drops of clear liquid in a one foot by two feet area. Ms. Thoma (P) claims she slipped on the liquid. Before the fall, Ms. Thoma (P) did not see anyone drop anything on the restaurant floor. A witness to the fall described the area in which Ms. Thoma (P) fell as an area where waitresses would frequently go in and out of the kitchen door. The witness saw waitresses carry beverage pitchers in the area. He did not see customers carrying beverages in the area, nor did he see anyone spill anything in the area. After the fall, the manager of the restaurant inspected the area, and he did not discover any foreign object on the floor. The trial court granted Cracker Barrel (D) summary judgment and Ms. Thoma (P) appealed.

■ **ISSUE**

Does proof of negligent conduct in a slip and fall case require a finding by the jury that the premises owner or his employees either created a dangerous condition or had knowledge of the dangerous condition that lead to the fall and resulting injuries?

■ **DECISION AND RATIONALE**

(Kahn) Yes. Proof of negligent conduct in a slip and fall case requires a finding by the jury that the owner of the premises or his employees either created a dangerous condition or had knowledge of the dangerous condition that lead to the fall and resulting injuries. In this case, there is no evidence that Ms. Thoma (P) or the witness to her fall saw anyone drop or spill anything in the area in which Ms. Thoma (P) fell. Since Cracker Barrel (D) waitresses regularly traversed the area to enter and exit the kitchen, the area in which the fall occurred was in their clear view. Further, no one saw anybody, except restaurant employees, carrying beverages in the area of the fall. If a jury had the opportunity to hear the evidence in this case, it could find that there was a liquid in the area in which Ms. Thoma (P) fell and Cracker Barrel (D) employees, through the exercise of due diligence, should have noticed the liquid before the fall. It is the duty of the jury to determine by the preponderance of the evidence whether Cracker Barrel exercised due diligence in the maintenance of its restaurant floor. Therefore, summary judgment is reversed and this case is remanded to the trial court.

Analysis:

Slip and fall cases and their variants are quite common. The duty of reasonable care is routinely played out in three ways: First, if the defendant negligently creates the dangerous condition, as where a grocery clerk spills a slippery substance on the floor, or the defendant negligently waxes the floor, the defendant will be subject to liability for injuries suffered in the invitee's fall. Second, if the landowner negligently markets goods in such a way that they are likely to be dislodged by other customers with resulting injury to the plaintiff, the trier can find negligence. Finally, as in the situation in this case, if some unknown person creates a condition of danger, by dropping a substance on the floor, for example, the defendant is not negligent in creating the danger but may be negligent in failing to inspect periodically for such mishaps. Courts often say that the defendant must have actual or constructive knowledge of the danger. This expression is merely another way of alluding to the negligence standard: the plaintiff must prove that the defendant either knew or should have known of the danger Courts tend to say that if the dangerous substance has been present for a long period of time, the trier can infer that the store was negligent in failing to inspect or discover. Courts refuse to apply *res ipsa loquitur* to slip and fall cases, and if no evidence supports an inference that the condition has been present for a substantial period, the jury has no basis for concluding that the defendant was negligent.

Wal-Mart Stores, Inc. v. Wright

(Retail Store Chain) v. *(Customer)*
774 N.E.2d 891 (Ind.2002)

NEGLIGENCE REQUIRES THE BREACH OF AN OBJECTIVE STANDARD OF CARE

■ **INSTANT FACTS** Wright (P) slipped in a puddle of water at a Wal-Mart (D) store.

■ **BLACK LETTER RULE** A violation of subjectively established policies and procedures does not establish negligence.

■ **PROCEDURAL BASIS**

On appeal to review a decision of the Indiana Court of Appeals affirming a trial court judgment for the plaintiff.

■ **FACTS**

Wright (P) slipped in a puddle of water at the outdoor lawn and garden area of a Wal-Mart store. Wright (P) sued Wal-Mart Stores, Inc. (D), alleging negligent maintenance, care, and inspection of the premises. Wal-Mart (D) introduced into evidence its store manual, given to all employees, detailing its procedures for dealing with spills. At the close of evidence, the trial court instructed the jury that it may consider any violation of the provisions of the store manual in determining whether Wal-Mart (D) was negligent, explaining that any violation was evidence of the degree of care taken by Wal-Mart (D). The jury returned a verdict for Wright (P) and Wal-Mart (D) appealed, claiming the jury instruction was erroneous. The court of appeals affirmed.

■ **ISSUE**

Does a violation of the provisions of a store's employee manual establish negligence?

■ **DECISION AND RATIONALE**

(Boehm, J.) No. "[F]ailure to follow a party's precautionary steps or procedures is not necessarily failure to exercise ordinary care." A party may establish procedures that exceed ordinary care such that a failure to follow those procedures does not amount to a breach of the duty of ordinary care. Likewise, even if Wal-Mart (D), by establishing its procedures, subjectively viewed those procedures as ordinary care, the standard of conduct against which Wal-Mart's (D) conduct must be measured is an objective one. Regardless of whether Wal-Mart's (D) employees breached its subjectively reasonable policies, negligence requires a breach of the duty of objectively reasonable care. Accordingly, the jury instruction was error. Reversed and remanded.

Analysis:

A party may voluntarily assume a higher standard of care than is required by the law. When the party does so, a breach of that voluntary duty does not establish negligence unless the care demonstrated also falls below an objectively reasonable standard of care required under the law of negligence. In

---

some circumstances, the outcome may seem unfair if a person comes to rely on the higher standard of care and suffers an injury. Under such circumstances, the injured party may have other legal recourse.

■ **CASE VOCABULARY**

OBJECTIVE STANDARD: A legal standard based on conduct and perceptions external to a particular person. In tort law, for example, the reasonable-person standard is considered an objective standard because it does not require a determination of what the defendant was thinking.

SUBJECTIVE STANDARD: A legal standard peculiar to a particular person and based on the person's individual views and experiences.

The T. J. Hooper
(Unseaworthy Tugboat)
60 F.2d 737 (C.C.A.2, 1932)

EVEN IF A DEFENDANT ACTS ACCORDING TO THE CUSTOM OF HIS INDUSTRY, HE MAY STILL BE LIABLE

■ **INSTANT FACTS** Large barge filled with coal and the tugboat which was its tow were lost at see during heavy weather.

■ **BLACK LETTER RULE** Notwithstanding a custom of usage or the lack thereof, there are precautions so imperative that even their universal disregard will not excuse their omission.

■ **PROCEDURAL BASIS**

Appeal from finding that tugboat owner was liable for damages to cargo and barge owners.

■ **FACTS**

A barge filled with a cargo of coal was lost at sea in heavy weather. The tugboat Hooper (D), the barge's tow, was also lost at sea. The cargo owner brought suit against the owners of the barge and tugboat. The trial court found that all vessels were unseaworthy. The Hooper (D) was found to be unseaworthy because she did not have a radio receiving set on board that was capable of receiving weather forecasts. Tugs do not usually carry such radios. Additionally, the trial court found the tug and the barge jointly liable to the cargo owner. Further, it found that the tug was liable for half of the damages for the loss of the barge. The owner of the Hooper (D) and the barge owner appealed.

■ **ISSUE**

Is the custom of usage the proper standard to apply in a negligence action?

■ **DECISION AND RATIONALE**

(Hand) No. Notwithstanding a custom of usage or the lack thereof, there are precautions so imperative that even their universal disregard will not excuse their omission. The Hooper (D) was lost in heavy weather. A radio receiving set was on board the Hooper (D), but this set was her master's personal property. Further, the set was not in working order. Since the radio receiving set was not functioning, the Hooper's (D) master failed to receive radio broadcasts of coming heavy weather. Had he received the broadcasts, he could have sought shelter and save the Hooper (D) and her tow. Radio receiving sets are inexpensive and reliable if maintained properly. However, there is no custom as to the use of radio receiving sets on tugboats. Some tugs have them; others do not. Notwithstanding, there are precautions so imperative that their disregard will not excuse their omission. If the Hooper (D) had a functioning radio receiving set, she would have received the weather forecast and taken appropriate action. Since she did not have such a set, she was unseaworthy and liable for the damages that she caused. Decree affirmed.

Analysis:

Violation of, or compliance with, custom is relevant and admissible but not conclusive on the negligence issue; custom merely provides evidence that may or may not persuade the jury on the negligence issue. In this case, the general practice of the tug industry was not the standard of care. It was admissible as evidence but not conclusive, so the tug could properly be held responsible in spite of the fact that it had operated in line with industry practice. Evidence of a custom may be used either as a sword or a shield. As a sword, the plaintiff can show the defendant's violation of a safety custom as some evidence that the defendant failed to act as a reasonable person under the circumstances. As a shield, the defendant can show his compliance with custom as evidence that his conduct was that of a reasonable person. Similarly, the plaintiff who is charged with contributory fault is permitted to show that what he did was in accordance with custom and hence arguably, but not conclusively, evidence that he exercised due care.

Byrne v. Boadle

(Man Injured By Falling Barrel of Flour) v. *(Flour Shop Owner)*
2 H. & C. 722 (1863)

RES IPSA LOQUITUR: THE THING SPEAKS FOR ITSELF

■ **INSTANT FACTS** Barrel of flour falls on a man as he passes a flour shop.

■ **BLACK LETTER RULE** Under certain circumstances, the fact that an accident occurred can support an inference or presumption of negligence.

■ **PROCEDURAL BASIS**

Appeal from nonsuit judgment in a negligence suit.

■ **FACTS**

Mr. Byrne (P) was walking in the road and then became unconscious. He then filed a negligence suit. At Mr. Byrne's (P) trial, a witness testified that a barrel of flour fell on Mr. Byrne (P). Mr. Boadle's (D) shop was adjacent to Mr. Byrne (P), and the barrel appeared to have fallen from Mr. Boadle's (D) shop. At his trial, Mr. Byrne (P) failed to produce any direct evidence of negligent conduct, and the trial judge enter judgment of nonsuit for Mr. Boadle (D). Mr. Byrne (P) appealed.

■ **ISSUE**

Under certain circumstances, can the fact that an accident occurred support an inference or presumption of negligence?

■ **DECISION AND RATIONALE**

(Pollock) Yes. Under certain circumstances, the fact that an accident occurred can support an inference or presumption of negligence. At trial, Mr. Boadle's (D) attorney argued that Mr. Byrne (P) failed to introduce any direct evidence that connects Mr. Boadle (D) or his employees with the accident. Even if the facts alleged by Mr. Byrne (P) are true, the attorney argued that Mr. Byrne (P) should not prevail as he failed to present affirmative proof of Mr. Boadle's (D) negligent conduct. This is a case of *res ipsa loquitur.* Some courts have held that in certain cases the fact that an accident occurred is evidence of negligent conduct. Other courts have held that a plaintiff is not entitled to a jury verdict unless he presents some affirmative evidence that the defendant engaged in negligent conduct. It would be incorrect for this Court to hold that a presumption of negligence can never arise from the fact that an accident occurred. It would also be incorrect for this court to hold that a presumption of negligence does not arise in the instant case. Persons who store barrels in a warehouse have a duty to keep the barrel secure in the warehouse. If a barrel escapes, its escape is prima facie evidence of negligence. To require a plaintiff in such a case to call as witnesses the defendant's warehouse employees to present affirmative evidence of negligent conduct is preposterous.

Analysis:

Res ipsa loquitur is a rebuttable presumption or inference that the defendant was negligent, which arises upon proof that the instrumentality causing injury was in the defendant's exclusive control, the accident was one which ordinarily does not happen in the absence of negligence, and the plaintiff did not contribute to his own injuries. The barrel of flour was under the control of Mr. Boadle (D) and his employees. Since barrels of flour do not fly out of windows or doors on their own accord, it is appropriate to presume that negligent conduct caused one of Mr. Boadle's (D) barrels to escape and injure Mr. Byrne (P). Although it was a fair inference that the barrel had come from the defendant's shop, the plaintiff was unable to show that the defendant had been negligent in any particular way. Nevertheless, the court thought the happening spoke for itself and that the jury would be permitted to find that the defendant was negligent, albeit in unspecified ways. *Res ipsa loquitur* cases permit the jury to infer negligence without knowing any particular misconduct at all. For instance, in *Byrne*, the plaintiff did not prove, either circumstantially or otherwise, that the barrel had been stored on its side instead of standing up, or that a rope holding the barrel had frayed and broken or any other particular acts that could be counted as negligence. The claim was only that the circumstances warranted the belief that the defendant was negligent in a wholly mysterious way. Res ipsa loquitur allows the plaintiff to establish negligence circumstantially without establishing the particular acts of the defendant that caused the harm. The doctrine does permit an inference of both negligence and causation.

■ CASE VOCABULARY

RES IPSA LOQUITUR: Literally, "The thing speaks for itself." Rebuttable presumption or inference that the defendant was negligent, which arises upon proof that the instrumentality causing injury was in the defendant's exclusive control, the accident was one which ordinarily does not happen in the absence of negligence, and the plaintiff did not contribute to his own injuries.

Giles v. City of New Haven

(*Lady Injured in Elevator*) v. (*Representative for Otis Elevator Co.*)
228 Conn. 441, 636 A.2d 1335 (1994)

RES IPSA LOQUITUR: THE DIMINISHING ROLE OF EXCLUSIVE CONTROL

■ **INSTANT FACTS** Elevator operator is injured when chain of elevator she was operating became hooked on the rail bracket in the elevator shaft.

■ **BLACK LETTER RULE** Use by the plaintiff of the instrumentality that caused her injury does not preclude a finding that the defendant had control of the instrumentality.

■ **PROCEDURAL BASIS**

Appeal from an appellate court decision holding that the trial court should not have granted the defendant a directed verdict.

■ **FACTS**

Otis Elevator Company (Otis) (D) installed and maintained an elevator that Ms. Giles (P) had operated for fourteen years. One day while ascending in her elevator, Ms. Giles (P) was injured when the elevator's chain became entangled with a bracket on the wall of the elevator shaft. The chain then tightened and broke, and the elevator cab began to shake and shudder. Fearing for her safety, Ms. Giles (P) reversed the direction of the elevator and directed it to the nearest floor so she could escape. Ms. Giles (P) brought suit, and the trial court entered a directed verdict for Otis (D). Ms. Giles (P) appealed and the appellate court reversed the trial court's decision. Otis (D) appealed the appellate court's decision.

■ **ISSUE**

Does use by the plaintiff of the instrumentality that caused her injury preclude a finding that the defendant had control of the instrumentality?

■ **DECISION AND RATIONALE**

(Katz) No. Use by the plaintiff of the instrumentality that caused her injury does not preclude a finding that the defendant had control of the instrumentality. During the appellate court's proceedings, the parties agreed that the accident would not have occurred in the absence of negligence. However, Otis (D) contends that the doctrine of re ipsa loquitur does not apply to this case because Ms. Giles (P) failed to show that Otis (D) had exclusive control over the elevator. It is true that Ms. Giles (P) operated the elevator and controlled the sway of the chain. However, these facts do not automatically preclude the application of the doctrine of res ipsa loquitur. The element of control by the defendant is intended to limit the application of res ipsa loquitur to a situation in which a defendant's negligence was more probably than not the cause of a plaintiff's injuries. Therefore, use of the instrumentality by the plaintiff is not an automatic bar against the application of the doctrine. Rather than a fixed rule, control is a flexible term. Control may exist if a defendant has the right or power of control and the opportunity to exercise it. Many jurisdictions now de-emphasize the role of exclusive control. For example, an inference of negligence may be drawn against a defendant who shares control with another. Otis (D) was in control of the maintenance and repair of the elevator and its parts, and operation of the elevator by Ms. Giles (P) was tantamount to the elevator's use. To avoid liability, Otis (D) argues that even though it controlled the elevator chain, Ms. Giles (P) controlled its sway. Ms. Giles (P) operation of the elevator may diminish the exclusivity of Otis's (D) control; however, a jury could find that her operation of the elevator did not vitiate Otis's (D) control of the chain and its condition, which resulted in excessive sway. Appellate court judgment affirmed.

Analysis:

Res ipsa loquitur is a rebuttable presumption or inference that the defendant was negligent, which arises upon proof that the instrumentality causing injury was in the defendant's exclusive control, the accident was one which ordinarily does not happen in the absence of negligence, and the plaintiff did not contribute to his own injuries. This case demonstrates the word exclusive does not mean exclusive. For *res ipsa loquitur* to apply, a defendant need only have a degree of control or responsibility such that his negligence was more probably than not the cause of plaintiff's injuries. In the instant case, Otis (D) had control of the maintenance of the elevator and its parts. Ms. Giles (P) operated the elevator and its chain. The Court reasoned that if Otis (D) had maintained the elevator and the chain properly, the chain would not have hooked on a shaft wall bracket. This assessment appears reasonable since Ms. Giles (P) had operated the elevator for fourteen years without incident. Although there are still decisions that apply the control rule to reject *res ipsa loquitur,* courts have generally reformulated the rule in one or more ways. They say the control required is control at the time of the negligence rather than the time of the injury, or that it is the right or authority to control, not actual physical control that counts, or that the test ultimately is not so much control per se but "management" or "responsibility." Other courts continue to state the exclusive control test, but determine "control" on the basis of an estimate of probabilities that the defendant rather than another person had control at the relevant time. Overall, it seems safe to say more simply that the plaintiff can point to the defendant as the negligent person by evidence that excludes the possibility that others were negligent or by showing that the defendant was responsible for all of the probable causes of the injury.

Warren v. Jeffries

(Plaintiff in Wrongful Death Action) v. *(Owner of Car Than Rolled Over Six-Year-Old Boy)*
263 N.C. 531, 139 S.E.2d 718 (1965)

PURE SPECULATION DOES NOT CREATE RES IPSA LOQUITUR

■ **INSTANT FACTS** A six-year old boy jumped out of a car when it begins to roll backward. When the boy jumped he fell, and the front wheel of the car rolled over his chest, killing him.

■ **BLACK LETTER RULE** Pure speculation is not a basis for applying the doctrine of res ipsa loquitur.

■ **PROCEDURAL BASIS**

Appeal from nonsuit judgment.

■ **FACTS**

Mr. Jeffries (D) went to Terry Enoch's home to visit his father. Terry was a six-year-old boy. Terry's father was not at home, and Mr. Jeffries (D) decided to wait for him. Mr. Jeffries (D) parked his car on an incline and went into the house. During this time, there were a dozen children, including Terry, in and around the house. About an hour after Mr. Jeffries (D) arrival, he gave Terry's mother the keys to his car so that she could go to the store and purchase some polish for her children. The mother and five children started towards the car, then Terry's mother returned Terry's eyeglasses to the house. The five children entered the rear seat of the car. Terry was the last person to enter the car. The children did not touch any of the car's controls. When Terry closed the car's door, something clicked in the front of the car, and the car began to roll backwards towards a ditch. One of the children opened the car door and told the other children to jump out of the car. Terry was the first to jump. When he did, he fell, and the front wheel of the car ran over his chest. Later, Terry died. Ms. Warren (P) brought a wrongful death action against Mr. Jeffries (D). The trial court rendered a nonsuit judgment, and Ms. Warren (P) appealed.

■ **ISSUE**

Can pure speculation be a basis for applying the doctrine of res ipsa loquitur?

■ **DECISION AND RATIONALE**

(Per Curiam) No. Pure speculation is not a basis for applying the doctrine of res ipsa loquitur. Ms. Warren (P) alleges that Mr. Jeffries (D) was negligent because he failed to set the hand brake, engage the transmission, and maintain adequate brakes. However, Ms. Warren (P) failed to produce any evidence in support of these allegations. No one examined the car after the accident. This Court can only speculate as to what caused the car to make a clicking sound and roll backwards. Pure speculation does not support the application of the doctrine of res ipsa loquitur. Judgment affirmed.

Analysis:

The Court refused to apply the doctrine of *res ipsa loquitur* in the instant case. The Court states that the cause of the accident is pure speculation; therefore, re ipsa loquitur does not apply. A closer reading of this case reveals that Ms. Warren's (P) attorney may be at fault. The complaint does not allege "the thing speaks for itself." Rather, it alleges three specific negligent acts: failure to set the hand brake, engage the transmission, and maintain adequate brakes. However, Ms Warren (P) failed to produce any evidence in support of her allegations. The nature of Ms. Warren's (P) allegations runs counter to the doctrine of *re ipsa loquitur*. Therefore, the Court found that the doctrine did not apply in this case.

Widmyer v. Southeast Skyways, Inc.

(Plaintiff in Wrongful Death Action Resulting From Airplane Crash) v. *(Air Carrier)*

584 P.2d 1 (Alaska 1978)

EVIDENCE OF NEGLIGENCE DOES NOT PRECLUDE THE USE OF THE DOCTRINE OF RES IPSA LOQUITUR

■ **INSTANT FACTS** An airplane encounters a heavy snow squall and crashes killing pilot and passengers.

■ **BLACK LETTER RULE** Plaintiff's introduction of specific evidence of negligence does not preclude the use of the doctrine of res ipsa loquitur, unless the evidence furnishes a complete explanation of the accident.

■ **FACTS**

A Southeast Skyways, Inc. (Skyways) (D) airplane crashed after encountering a heavy snow squall, killing its pilot and all passengers. The plane crashed in a vertical nose-down position. Widmyer (P) brought a wrongful death suit. During trial, experts offered conflicting opinions about the cause of the crash. Widmyer's (P) expert attributed the crash to pilot error. Skyways' (D) expert attributed the crash to the snow squall. Widmyer (P) asked the trial judge to give a res ipsa loquitur jury instruction. The trial judge denied the request, and the jury returned a verdict that was adverse to Widmyer (P). Widmyer (P) then appealed.

■ **ISSUE**

Does plaintiff's introduction of specific evidence of negligence preclude the use of the doctrine of res ipsa loquitur when the evidence fails to furnish a complete explanation of the accident?

■ **DECISION AND RATIONALE**

(Boochever) No. Plaintiff's introduction of specific evidence of negligence does not preclude the use of the doctrine of res ipsa loquitur, unless the evidence furnishes a complete explanation of the accident. When a plaintiff introduces specific evidence of negligence, Alaska courts do not preclude the use of the doctrine of res ipsa loquitur, unless the evidence furnishes a complete explanation of the accident. If the evidence discloses the circumstances of an accident to the extent that there is nothing to infer, res ipsa loquitur is not applicable. In the instant case, the parties' reliance on inferences provided by expert testimony precludes a finding that Widmyer (P) furnished a complete explanation of the accident. When there are no survivors of an accident and no direct evidence of the cause of the accident, a plaintiff should not be precluded from utilizing the doctrine of res ipsa loquitur simply because he or she offered a possible explanation of the cause of the accident to the jury. Skyways (D) contends that res ipsa loquitur does not apply, as it does not have superior knowledge about the cause of the crash. There is case law that holds that when a plaintiff's knowledge about an accident is equal or superior to a defendant's knowledge, res ipsa loquitur does not apply. However, this authority is not on point as Widmyer (P) and Skyways (D) are equally ignorant of the cause of the crash. Further, Skyways failed to cite any Alaska law requiring a defendant to have superior knowledge about the cause of an accident before a court can apply res ipsa loquitur. The foundation that a plaintiff must lay to invoke res ipsa loquitur is that the accident at issue normally does not happen absent negligent conduct, the defendant had exclusive control over the instrumentality that caused the accident, and the plaintiff did not contribute to his or her injuries. The applicability of the doctrine depends on the facts and circumstances of each case. If courts strictly apply the requirement of no contribution by the plaintiff to his or her injuries, they would never give a res ipsa loquitur instruction when plaintiffs lack evidence to prove a negative. This Court holds that there must exist some evidence upon which a jury could find that a plaintiff contributed to his injury before denying a request to give the re ipsa loquitur jury instruction. When the record is silent about a plaintiff's conduct, it is reasonable to infer that a plaintiff did not contribute to his injury. By analogy, a plaintiff need not prove that a crash was not caused by bad weather in order to receive a res ipsa loquitur jury instruction. After reviewing, the present state of air technology and safety, this Court finds that air crashes do not normally occur absent negligence even in inclement weather. Therefore, the trial court erred when it refused to give a res ipsa loquitur jury instruction.

Analysis:

A *res ipsa loquitur* plaintiff need only lay a proper foundation to invoke the doctrine. This case holds that a plaintiff's evidence about the cause of an accident that does not furnish a complete explanation of the accident does not preclude the application of the doctrine of *res ipsa loquitur*. In the instant case, the Court found that conflicting testimony failed to provide a complete explanation of the cause of the crash. Since there were no survivors or eyewitnesses of the crash, it held that Widmyer (P) need not prove a negative by proving that passengers of the plane did not cause the crash. Since there was not a complete explanation about the cause of the crash and airplanes do not normally crash absent negligent conduct, this Court found that the doctrine of *res ipsa loquitur* applied to the instant case. When you read this case, you may have decided that the rule of law is that the doctrine is applicable when there is not a complete explanation for the cause of an accident. You may be correct, but remember pure speculation is not a basis for the invocation of the doctrine.

CHAPTER SEVEN

Harm and Causation in Fact

Preston v. Cestaro

Instant Facts: Preston (P) claimed a back injury after Cestaro's (D) vehicle slightly struck the bus on which Preston (P) was riding.

Black Letter Rule: Without proof of an actual injury caused by the defendant's breach of duty, legal recovery is unavailable.

Salinetro v. Nystrom

Instant Facts: Dr. Nystrom (D) took x-rays of Salinetro (P) when, unbeknownst to her, she was pregnant, and as a result she chose to have an abortion.

Black Letter Rule: If the injury would not have occurred but-for the defendant's negligence, causation exists.

Landers v. East Texas Salt Water Disposal Co.

Instant Facts: Two independent companies caused salt and oil to flow into Lander's (P) lake killing the fish, and both were jointly and severally liable.

Black Letter Rule: Where the independent tortious acts of two or more wrongdoers join to produce an indivisible injury, which from its nature cannot be apportioned with reasonable certainty to the individual wrongdoers, all of the wrongdoers are jointly and severally liable for the entire damages.

Anderson v. Minneapolis, St. Paul & Sault Ste. Marie Railway

Instant Facts: Fire from smoldering engine and another fire from unknown origins combined to burn Anderson's (P) property.

Black Letter Rule: If two or more causes concur to bring about harm, a tortfeasor is liable if its wrongdoing was a material or substantial element in causing the harm.

Dillon v. Twin State Gas & Electric Co.

Instant Facts: Young boy on bridge loses balance, grabs electrical wire and is electrocuted.

Black Letter Rule: When determining liability and damages for negligence, the probable future of the victim but for the negligence must be considered.

Summers v. Tice

Instant Facts: Two hunters, acting independently of each, negligently fired guns, only one of which hit Summers (P).

Black Letter Rule: Where two or more tortfeasors are negligent, but only one could have caused the harm to an injured third party, the tortfeasors are jointly and severally liable even absent proof as to which one actually caused the injury.

Lord v. Lovett

Instant Facts: After Lovett (D) and others allegedly misdiagnosed Lord's (P) neck injury, Lord (P) sued for the lost opportunity for a better recovery.

Black Letter Rule: A plaintiff may recover for a loss-of-opportunity injury in medical malpractice cases when the defendant's alleged negligence aggravates the plaintiff's preexisting injury such that it deprives the plaintiff of a substantially better outcome.

Preston v. Cestaro

(Passenger) v. *(Motorist)*
28 Conn. L. Rptr. 711, 2001 WL 254343 (Conn.Super.2001)

NOMINAL DAMAGES ARE UNAVAILABLE IN A NEGLIGENCE ACTION

Now if I could only be in a bus accident, I could collect some money!

■ **INSTANT FACTS** Preston (P) claimed a back injury after Cestaro's (D) vehicle slightly struck the bus on which Preston (P) was riding.

■ **BLACK LETTER RULE** Without proof of an actual injury caused by the defendant's breach of duty, legal recovery is unavailable.

■ PROCEDURAL BASIS

Trial court consideration of the sufficiency of the plaintiff's claim.

■ FACTS

Preston (P) was a passenger on a public bus when it was slightly contacted by a vehicle driven by Cestaro (D). Preston (P) allegedly suffered a back injury in the accident, sued, and moved for summary judgment. The court granted Preston's (P) motion as to liability for negligence, but concluded that Preston's (P) back injury was caused by a fall from a bunk bed weeks earlier. The court determined that the slight force of the accident was insufficient to cause Preston's (P) injury.

■ ISSUE

Can a plaintiff recover nominal damages from a defendant merely because of his breach of duty?

■ DECISION AND RATIONALE

(Pittman, J.) No. Negligence requires proof of a defendant's duty and breach of duty, causation, and injury. Without proving each element, a plaintiff may not have his claim considered by a jury. Without actual injury caused by a defendant's breach of duty, a plaintiff is entitled to no compensation. While some claims, such as those for common law assault, may not require actual injury in order for the plaintiff to recover against a wrongful defendant, nominal damages for breach of duty are unavailable in a negligence action. Judgment for the defendant.

Analysis:

People breach duties owed to other people every day. Whenever a person unwillingly bumps into another on a sidewalk due to inattentiveness, that person breaches his duty owed to the other person. However, unless the person suffers injury from the physical contact, she has no cause of action for negligence.

■ CASE VOCABULARY

NOMINAL DAMAGES: A trifling sum awarded when a legal injury is suffered but when there is no substantial loss or injury to be compensated.

PROXIMATE CAUSE: A cause that is legally sufficient to result in liability. A cause that directly produces an event without which the event would not have occurred.

Salinetro v. Nystrom

(*Pregnant Patient*) v. (*Negligent Doctor*)

341 So.2d 1059 (Fla.Dist.Ct.App.1977)

BUT-FOR CAUSATION TEST IS NOT ALWAYS HELPFUL

■ **INSTANT FACTS** Dr. Nystrom (D) took x-rays of Salinetro (P) when, unbeknownst to her, she was pregnant, and as a result she chose to have an abortion.

■ **BLACK LETTER RULE** If the injury would not have occurred but-for the defendant's negligence, causation exists.

■ **PROCEDURAL BASIS**

Appeal from judgment following directed verdict in medical malpractice action seeking damages.

■ **FACTS**

Salinetro (P) was in an auto accident and underwent a medical examination in connection with back injuries sustained. Dr. Nystrom (D) took x-rays of her lower back and abdominal areas. Unknown to Salinetro (P), at the time the x-rays were administered, she was approximately four to six weeks pregnant. Dr. Nystrom (D), his receptionist and his x-ray technician failed to inquire whether or not Salinetro (P) was pregnant or the date of her last menstrual period. After the pregnancy was confirmed, Salinetro's (P) gynecologist advised her to terminate her pregnancy because of the possible damage to the fetus by the x-rays. Salinetro (P) underwent a therapeutic abortion and the pathology report stated that the fetus was dead at the time of the abortion. Salinetro (P) sued Dr. Nystrom (D) for medical malpractice. At the close of all evidence, Dr. Nystrom (D) moved for a directed verdict on the ground that Salinetro (P) failed to make a prima facie case of medical malpractice. The trial judge granted the motion, and judgment was entered for Dr. Nystrom (D).

■ **ISSUE**

If the injury would not have occurred but-for the defendant's negligence, does causation exist?

■ **DECISION AND RATIONALE**

(Per Curiam) Yes. The but-for causation test provides that if the injury would not have occurred but-for the defendant's negligence, causation exists. Even if we were to assume that Dr. Nystrom's (D) conduct fell below the standard of care in the medical community, the failure to inquire about pregnancy or last menstrual period was not the cause of the injury. Salinetro (P) testified that even if she had been asked about being pregnant, she would have answered in the negative. She also testified that being a few days late with her menstrual period was not unusual and did not indicate to her that she may have been pregnant. Six days prior to her visit to Dr. Nystrom (D), Salinetro (P) had seen her gynecologist and he had found no evidence that she was pregnant. Simply because Salinetro (P) was late with her period would not in and of itself mean that she was pregnant because further tests were required to ascertain if she was pregnant. Thus, this point is without merit.

Analysis:

Without using the words, this case examines the *but-for test* of causation. The court believed that since Salinetro (D) did not know that she was pregnant at the time of the x-rays, had the doctor acted in a non-negligent manner and asked her if she was pregnant, her response would have been "no". Thus, in the court's view, the result would have been the same. Asking the question *but-for* the negligent act of the doctor would Salinetro (D) been injured, the answer theoretically would be yes. Thus, no liability. However, the court's analysis is somewhat flawed. Perhaps if the doctor had asked the question, it would have caused Salinetro (D) to inquire about the risk of x-rays if she was pregnant. If the doctor said that x-rays could cause serious consequences, it may have prompted her to have a pregnancy test, or forego the x-rays. The court's opinion is really based on speculation about whether the injury could have been avoided if the doctor had not been negligent. In law, speculation should be avoided if possible. If anything, this case is an example of why certain scholars have urged abandoning the but-for test.

■ CASE VOCABULARY

ARGUENDO: For sake of argument, but without admitting the truth of the statement.

DIRECTED VERDICT: Judge entering judgment for one party before return of jury verdict.

PER CURIAM: An opinion by the whole court, rather than one judge.

PRIMA FACIE CASE: When the evidence is sufficient to prove the case, unless contrary evidence is presented by the other side.

Landers v. East Texas Salt Water Disposal Co.

(Lake Owner) v. *(Salt Polluter)*

151 Tex. 251, 248 S.W.2d 731 (1952)

WRONGDOERS CAN BE LIABLE JOINTLY AND SEVERALLY FOR SAME INJURY

■ **INSTANT FACTS** Two independent companies caused salt and oil to flow into Lander's (P) lake killing the fish, and both were jointly and severally liable.

■ **BLACK LETTER RULE** Where the independent tortious acts of two or more wrongdoers join to produce an indivisible injury, which from its nature cannot be apportioned with reasonable certainty to the individual wrongdoers, all of the wrongdoers are jointly and severally liable for the entire damages.

■ PROCEDURAL BASIS

Appeal from lower court ruling regarding sufficiency of pleading for negligence and damages.

■ FACTS

Landers (P) owned a small lake and stocked it with fish at considerable expense. He sued East Texas Salt Water Disposal Co. (Salt Water) (D1) alleging that its pipe lines broke and thousands of barrels of salt water flowed into the lake, killing the fish. Landers (P) also sued Sun Oil Company (Oil Co.) (D2) alleging that on or about the same day it caused large quantities of salt water and oil to flow into the lake, killing the fish. [This was not a good day to be fishing.] He alleged that both Salt Water (D1) and Oil Co. (D2) were negligent and liable for the damages resulting from the loss of the fish.

■ ISSUE

Where the independent tortious acts of two or more wrongdoers join to produce an indivisible injury, which from its nature cannot be apportioned with reasonable certainty to the individual wrongdoers, are all of the wrongdoers jointly and severally liable for the entire damages?

■ DECISION AND RATIONALE

(Calvert) Yes. We hold that where the independent tortious acts of two or more wrongdoers join to produce an indivisible injury, which from its nature cannot be apportioned with reasonable certainty to the individual wrongdoers, all of the wrongdoers are jointly and severally liable for the entire damages. We overrule the holding of *Sun Oil Co. v. Robicheaux*, which stated that an action cannot be maintained against several defendants jointly, where each acts independently of the other and there is no concert or unity of design between them, and a defendant is liable only for the damages from his own act. This rule has made it impossible for gravely injured plaintiffs to obtain damages through joint and several judgments against all wrongdoers whose independent tortious acts have joined in producing an injury. The plaintiffs in these suits were denied relief because they were unable to apportion the injury attributable to each defendant. From the pleadings in this case, it appears that there was neither concert of action nor unity of design between Salt Water (D1) and Oil Co. (D2) in the commission of their alleged tortious acts. [Strange coincidence that two separate companies polluted the lake with salt on the same day.] However, their alleged wrongful acts produced the death of the fish, which is an indivisible injury that cannot be apportioned among the wrongdoers. Therefore, Salt Water (D1) and Oil Co. (D2), if established by the evidence, can be held jointly and severally liable for Landers' (P) damages.

Analysis:

Joint and several liability is the topic of this case. However, the case also demonstrates a problem with the *but-for* test. Applying the but-for test separately to both Salt Water (D1) and Oil Co. (D2), it is clear that two sets of negligence *caused* a single injury. Since either negligent act alone could have killed the fish, a strict interpretation of the but-for test would prohibit liability against either wrongdoer. In this situation, most courts apply a substantial factor test, so that all defendants who are substantial factors in the harm are causes in fact. If both wrongdoers may be held liable, the issue becomes whether to apply joint and several liability, or proportionate fault liability. Since the death of the fish cannot be apportioned, both wrongdoers will be held liable. Note that if there was evidence the Oil Co. (D2) only released oil into the lake and it killed a certain type of fish and Salt Water's (D1) release of salt killed plant life, then the damages to Landers (P) could be apportioned among both wrongdoers.

■ CASE VOCABULARY

JOINTLY AND SEVERALLY LIABLE: A form of liability where the injured party may sue one or more wrongdoers separately, or all together, and enforce the judgment obtained against one or all.

Anderson v. Minneapolis, St. Paul & Sault Ste. Marie Railway

(*Land Owner*) v. (*Smoldering Engine*)
146 Minn. 430, 179 N.W. 45 (1920)

SUBSTANTIAL FACTOR TEST MAY BE USED IN PLACE OF BUT-FOR CAUSATION TEST

■ **INSTANT FACTS** Fire from smoldering engine and another fire from unknown origins combined to burn Anderson's (P) property.

■ **BLACK LETTER RULE** If two or more causes concur to bring about harm, a tortfeasor is liable if its wrongdoing was a material or substantial element in causing the harm.

■ **PROCEDURAL BASIS**

Appeal from judgment following jury verdict in action for negligence seeking damages.

■ **FACTS**

In the month of October, Anderson's (P) property was burned by fire that was started by an engine owned by Minneapolis, St. Paul & Sault Ste. Marie Railway (Railway) (D). The fire started in August and smoldered until October, when it swept east and burned Anderson's (P) property. [Why wasn't someone checking on the engine for two months?] Railway (D) offered proof tending to show that there were other fires sweeping east towards Anderson's (P) property and that these fires might have originated from other and perhaps non-negligent causes. The jury found for Anderson (P). Railway (D) appealed contending that it should not be liable since the unknown origin fire could have damaged Anderson's (P) property regardless of the fire started by its engine.

■ **ISSUE**

If two or more causes concur to bring about harm, is a tortfeasor liable if its wrongdoing was a material or substantial element in causing the harm?

■ **DECISION AND RATIONALE**

(Less) Yes. We hold that if two or more causes concur to bring about harm, a tortfeasor is liable if its wrongdoing was a material or substantial element in causing the harm. The jury in this case was instructed that if they found that "other fires not set by one of the defendant's [Railway's (D)] engines mingled with one that was set by one of the defendant's [Railway's (D)] engines, there may be difficulty in determining whether you should find that the fire set by the engine was a material or substantial element in causing plaintiff's [Anderson's (P)] damage. If it was, the defendant [Railway (D)] is liable; otherwise it is not. . . ." Railway (D) argued that the jury should have been instructed that if there were a number of fires combining that would have caused the damage to Anderson's (P) property regardless of Railway's (D) engine fire, then it is not liable. We do not agree. If this were the law, then if one of the fires were of an unknown origin and united with Railway's (D) fire, either fire of which could have destroyed the property, there would be no liability. We are not prepared to adopt this as the law of this state. Since Railway's (D) fire was found to be a material or substantial element in causing Anderson's (P) damage, it should be held liable. [In other words, if the but-for rule does not work, find another way to hold 'em liable.] Therefore, the trial court did not err in refusing to so instruct the jury.

Analysis:

This case examines the *substantial factor* test as an alternative to the but-for test. Although the facts are not clear, it appears that the two fires combined and caused the damage to Anderson's (P) property. However, each fire was sufficient standing alone to cause the damage. As discussed earlier, if a strict but-for interpretation were applied, Railway (D) would not be found liable since but-for its engine fire, the fire of unknown origins would still have burned Anderson's property. However, under the substantial factor test, if two fires both cause the damage, and either one alone was sufficient to cause the damage, the wrongdoer, i.e., Railway (D) is liable for all the damage since its fire was "a material or substantial element" in causing the damage. One legal scholar has devised a "duplicative" and "preempted" causation test as a modification of the but-for test. In this case, since each fire could have done the harm alone, they are "duplicative" causes. Where duplicative causes exist and the but-for test produces the wrong result, the substantial factor test is favored.

■ **CASE VOCABULARY**

CHARGE THE JURY: Where the judge instructs the jury on the law.

Dillon v. Twin State Gas & Electric Co.

(Estate of Deceased Child) v. *(Electric Co.)*

85 N.H. 449, 163 A. 111 (1932)

PRESENT VALUE APPORTIONMENT IS USED WHERE NEGLIGENCE CAUSES THE DEATH OF ONE IMMEDIATELY THREATENED WITH PROBABLE HARM OR DEATH

■ **INSTANT FACTS** Young boy on bridge loses balance, grabs electrical wire and is electrocuted.

■ **BLACK LETTER RULE** When determining liability and damages for negligence, the probable future of the victim but for the negligence must be considered.

■ **PROCEDURAL BASIS**

Appeal from denial of directed verdict following trial on claim of negligence for wrongful death.

■ **FACTS**

Twin State Gas & Electric Co. (Electric Co.) (D) was a utility company that maintained uninsulated wires across a bridge that boys habitually climbed and sat atop near the wires. The decedent, a 14-year old boy, was sitting atop the bridge, lost his balance, and grabbed the wire to save himself from falling. The wire carried high voltage current and the boy was electrocuted. Electric Co. (D) moved for a directed verdict which was denied. The jury could not agree on a verdict. It was probable that had he not grabbed the wire, he would have fallen to his death or been severely injured. The trial judge transferred the case to the State's Supreme Court on Electric Co.'s (D) exception to the denial of its motion for directed verdict.

■ **ISSUE**

When determining liability and damages for negligence, should the probable future of the victim but for the negligence be considered?

■ **DECISION AND RATIONALE**

(Allen) Yes. When determining liability and damages for negligence, the probable future of the victim but for the negligence must be considered. But for the current in the wire, the decedent would have fallen to the floor of the bridge or into the river and have been killed or seriously injured. Because of the loss of balance, he was bound to fall and did not have long to live or was to be maimed. If it were found that he would have fallen with death probably resulting, Electric Co. (D) would not be liable unless there was conscious suffering from the shock. If it were found that but for the current he would have fallen with serious injury, then the loss of life or earning capacity resulting from the electrocution would be measured by its value in such injured condition. Evidence that he would be permanently injured would be taken into account in the same manner as though he had already been permanently injured. The future of the decedent, but for the current, bears on liability as well as damages. Whether the shock from the current threw him back on the girder or whether he would have recovered his balance, with or without the aid of the wire, or if it had not been charged, are issues of fact, which may lead to different conclusions. [Who knows what would have happened?] The exception is overruled.

Analysis:

The application of the but-for test to the facts of this case creates problems. The uninsulated wires caused harm to a boy who was already endangered and about to fall from the bridge. There are various unknown scenarios that could have occurred if the wire had been insulated and the child not electrocuted. For example, but-for the current the child may still have fallen to his death or sustained serious injury. However, but-for the current, the child may have used the wire to regain his balance and not have been injured. The court held that there were issues of fact that were properly presented to the jury. With the different scenarios, one may wish to structure the negligence claim in such a fashion as to establish causation. Asserting negligence based upon certain hypothetical scenarios can resolve causation problems created by the application of the but-for test. The court held that the future of the decedent must be considered for purposes of liability and damages.

■ CASE VOCABULARY

EXCEPTION: Noting an objection to the decision of the court, which will be reserved for later review or appeal.

Summers v. Tice

(Shot in the Face Victim) v. *(Negligent Hunter)*
33 Cal.2d 80, 199 P.2d 1 (1948)

ALTERNATIVE CAUSATION RULE ESTABLISHED WHEN TWO PEOPLE ARE NEGLIGENT BUT ONLY ONE COULD HAVE CAUSED THE INJURY

■ **INSTANT FACTS** Two hunters, acting independently of each, negligently fired guns, only one of which hit Summers (P).

■ **BLACK LETTER RULE** Where two or more tortfeasors are negligent, but only one could have caused the harm to an injured third party, the tortfeasors are jointly and severally liable even absent proof as to which one actually caused the injury.

■ **PROCEDURAL BASIS**

Appeal from judgments entered following court trial in action for negligence seeking personal injury damages.

■ **FACTS**

Summers (P), Tice (D1) and another hunter (D2) were quail hunting on an open range when Summers (P) was struck by birdshot discharged from a shotgun. Summers (P) sued Tice (D1) and the other hunter (D2) for negligence for personal injuries to his right eye and face. The trial judge found that both Tice (D1) and the other hunter (D2) were using the same type of shotgun and shells. They both shot at a quail in a negligent manner. [Why were they negligent you ask? The bird was only 10 feet off the ground between them and Summers (P), and they knew Summers (P) was only 75 yards away.] Summers (P) was struck in his right eye and in his upper lip, but the shot to the eye caused the most damage. The shot to the eye could only have come from one gun, not both. Judgment was entered against both Tice (D1) and the other hunter (D2). They both appealed [trying to make Summers (P) prove who fired the damaging shot].

■ **ISSUE**

Where two or more tortfeasors are negligent, but only one could have caused the harm to an injured third party, are the tortfeasors jointly and severally liable absent proof as to which one actually caused the injury?

■ **DECISION AND RATIONALE**

(Carter) Yes. We hold that where two or more tortfeasors are negligent, but only one could have caused the harm to an injured third party, the tortfeasors are jointly and severally liable even absent proof as to which one actually caused the injury. Other cases have held that where two defendants negligently act in concert and cause injury to a third person, both are liable, even though only one of them could have caused the injury and the injured party is unable to prove which one caused the injury. If this were not the case, both tortfeasors would be exonerated from liability even though each was negligent and the injury resulted from such negligence. It is clear that the burden of proof on the subject should be shifted to the negligent wrongdoers. They are the negligent ones who brought about the injury, and hence it should rest with them each to absolve himself if he can. It would be unfair to require the injured party to point to who caused the harm. Thus, we affirm the decision of the lower court holding both Tice (D1) and the other hunter (D2) liable for Summers' (P) injuries. Summers (P) is not required to prove which hunter shot him in the eye. The burden shifts to Tice (D1) and the other hunter (D2) to try to absolve one or the other from liability.   Affirmed.

Analysis:

This famous case created the *alternative causation rule*. The rule extends joint and several liability so that where both tortfeasors are negligent, but only one of them causes the injury, both will be held liable. In such situations, the burden of proof shifts to the defendants to exculpate themselves, if possible, from liability. The rationale is that the negligent defendants should bear the loss rather than the innocent plaintiff. It should be noted, however, that virtually all courts reject the alternative causation rule in products liability cases with numerous defendants.

■ **CASE VOCABULARY**

CONSOLIDATED: Combing two different cases for trial at the same time before the same judge.

REMEDILESS: Being without redress or ability to enforce a right.

TRIER OF FACT: Either the judge or a jury who decides the disputed factual matters at trial.

Lord v. Lovett

(Patient) v. *(Physician)*
146 N.H. 232, 770 A.2d 1103 (2001)

THE LOST OPPORTUNITY FOR A BETTER OUTCOME IS A RECOVERABLE LOSS

■ **INSTANT FACTS** After Lovett (D) and others allegedly misdiagnosed Lord's (P) neck injury, Lord (P) sued for the lost opportunity for a better recovery.

■ **BLACK LETTER RULE** A plaintiff may recover for a loss-of-opportunity injury in medical malpractice cases when the defendant's alleged negligence aggravates the plaintiff's preexisting injury such that it deprives the plaintiff of a substantially better outcome.

■ **PROCEDURAL BASIS**

On appeal to review the lower court's decision.

■ **FACTS**

After Lord (P) suffered a broken neck in an automobile accident, she was treated by Lovett (D) and others at the hospital. Lord (P) sued the defendants, claiming that by failing to properly diagnose her spinal cord injury, properly immobilize her, and administer appropriate therapy, she lost the opportunity for a better recovery. After learning that the defendants intended to file a motion to dismiss, the trial court permitted Lord (P) to make an offer of proof. Lord (P) offered that her expert would testify that the defendants' negligence caused her loss of opportunity, but could not determine the degree to which her recovery would have improved.

■ **ISSUE**

May the plaintiff recover in a medical malpractice action for the loss of opportunity for a substantially better recovery?

■ **DECISION AND RATIONALE**

(Nadeau, J.) Yes. The loss-of-opportunity doctrine allows a medical malpractice plaintiff whose preexisting injury is aggravated by a physician's negligence to recover for her lost opportunity to obtain a better recovery. Three approaches to this doctrine have been proposed. First, a minority of jurisdictions allows recovery if the plaintiff was deprived of at least a fifty-one-percent chance of a better recovery. Under this approach, a plaintiff who can establish such proof is entitled to full recovery, while she is denied all recovery if the necessary burden of proof is not met. Second, a plaintiff is entitled to recover if the defendant's negligence "more likely than not increased the harm to the plaintiff." Under this standard, the plaintiff need not quantify the degree to which her recovery would have improved, but rather must only establish that the defendant's negligence increased the harm of a preexisting injury to some degree, which varies by jurisdiction. The final approach treats the loss of opportunity as an injury itself, for which the plaintiff may recover. Under this approach, the plaintiff need not establish a particular degree of loss to recover, but her recovery is limited by the degree of loss proven. Thus, "if the plaintiff can establish the causal link between the defendant's negligence and the lost opportunity, the plaintiff may recover that portion of damages actually attributable to the defendant's negligence." The third approach is the most sound, for it acknowledges the loss of opportunity as a compensable injury, but insists on proper valuation of the injury. Accordingly, "a plaintiff may recover for a loss of opportunity injury in medical malpractice cases when the defendant's alleged negligence aggravates a plaintiff's preexisting injury such that it deprives the plaintiff a substantially better outcome." The fact that such an injury is intangible and often difficult to calculate does not relieve a defendant of liability, because the difficulty is caused by the defendant himself and many other injuries are compensable although difficult to quantify. When expert testimony establishes the measure of the plaintiff's loss, she may recover. Reversed and remanded.

Analysis:

The approach adopted by the court harmonizes a patient's loss with the degree of the physician's liability. Analogous to comparative negligence, the patient may recover only for those injuries she has sustained due to the physician's negligence. Unlike the other approaches, here the court's adopted rationale compensates the patient for even the mildest loss of opportunity, while protecting the physician from paying more than the patient is due.

■ CASE VOCABULARY

OFFER OF PROOF: A presentation of evidence for the record (but outside the jury's presence) usually made after the judge has sustained an objection to the admissibility of that evidence, so that the evidence can be preserved on the record for an appeal of the judge's ruling.

CHAPTER EIGHT

Negligence: The Scope of Risk or "Proximate Cause" Requirement

Medcalf v. Washington Heights Condominium Ass'n, Inc.

Instant Facts: A visitor who was attacked outside a condominium sued the owners' association on the ground that the electronic buzzer system was kept in disrepair, which allowed her attacker to injure her while she waited to be admitted to the building.

Black Letter Rule: For a defendant to be held liable for negligence, the harm or injury caused must be within the foreseeable scope of risk created by the defendant's negligence.

Palsgraf v. Long Island Railroad Co.

Instant Facts: A passenger waiting for a train was injured on a railroad platform after railway employees dislodged from the arm of another passenger who they were negligently helping jump onto a moving train, a package of fireworks that exploded when it fell on the tracks, the shock from which caused scales to fall on the plaintiff.

Black Letter Rule: The risk reasonably to be perceived defines the duty to be obeyed.

Hughes v. Lord Advocate

Instant Facts: While playing in and around an unguarded open manhole, two young boys accidentally knocked a kerosene lantern into the manhole, breaking the lantern and causing an unforeseeable explosion.

Black Letter Rule: The fact that the defendant's negligence causes a known harm in an unforeseeable manner does not relieve him of liability.

Derdiarian v. Felix Contracting Corp.

Instant Facts: A road worker was injured after a man negligently drove his car through the work site and struck a boiling cauldron of enamel that was negligently left unguarded from traffic, causing the enamel to splatter and burn the worker.

Black Letter Rule: An intervening act may not serve as a superseding cause, and relieve an actor of responsibility, where the risk of the intervening act occurring is the very same risk which renders the actor negligent.

Sheehan v. City of New York

Instant Facts: While stopped at an intersection, a city bus that negligently failed to pull over to the curb to pick-up and drop-off passengers was rear-ended by a sanitation truck.

Black Letter Rule: An actor has not proximately caused an accident if he merely furnishes the condition or occasion for the occurrence of an event.

Ventricelli v. Kinney System Rent A Car, Inc.

Instant Facts: A man was struck by a moving vehicle while trying to shut the defective trunk lid on the vehicle he rented.

Black Letter Rule: A rental car company could not have foreseen that a driver would strike its client while the client was attempting to shut the trunk lid negligently left in disrepair by the company.

Marshall v. Nugent

Instant Facts: A man that was struck while attempting to warn oncoming traffic of an obstruction in the road, sued the truck driver that caused the obstruction.

Black Letter Rule: In a traffic mix-up due to negligence, before the waters have become placid and normal again, the unfolding of events between the culpable act and the plaintiff's eventual injury may be bizarre indeed; yet the defendant may be liable for the result.

Medcalf v. Washington Heights Condominium Ass'n, Inc.

(*Injured Tenant Visitor*) v. (*Unit Owners Association*)

57 Conn.App. 12, 747 A.2d 532 (2000)

PROXIMATE CAUSE LIMITS A DEFENDANT'S LIABILITY FOR NEGLIGENCE TO THOSE RISKS THAT ARE FORESEEABLE

■ **INSTANT FACTS** A visitor who was attacked outside a condominium sued the owners' association on the ground that the electronic buzzer system was kept in disrepair, which allowed her attacker to injure her while she waited to be admitted to the building.

■ **BLACK LETTER RULE** For a defendant to be held liable for negligence, the harm or injury caused must be within the foreseeable scope of risk created by the defendant's negligence.

■ **PROCEDURAL BASIS**

Decision of Appellate Court of Connecticut reversing the trial court's denial of the defendant's motion for a directed verdict.

■ **FACTS**

While visiting a friend, Tracy Skiades, at the Washington Heights Condominium, Ms. Medcalf (P) used the intercom system outside the lobby doors to telephone Skiades for admittance to the building. Skiades attempted to buzz Medcalf (P) in, but the system failed to work. While waiting for Skiades to come down and let her in, Medcalf (P) was attacked by a man. Medcalf sued Washington Heights Condominium Association (D) (Association) and the property manager, Professional Property Management Company, Inc., (Management) (D) for failure to maintain the intercom system in working order. The Association and Management moved for a directed verdict, but the motion was denied.

■ **ISSUE**

In order to be liable for negligence, must the harm caused by an individual's negligence be within the foreseeable scope of risk?

■ **DECISION AND RATIONALE**

(Mihalakos, J.) Yes. For a defendant to be held liable for negligence, the harm or injury caused must be within the foreseeable scope of risk created by the defendant's negligence. Proximate cause establishes a reasonable connection between an act or omission of a defendant and the harm caused by the plaintiff. Proximate cause is an actual cause that is a substantial factor in the resulting harm. A factor is substantial if the harm which occurred was of the same general nature as the foreseeable risk created by the defendant's negligence. Although proximate cause is a question of fact, it becomes a question of law when the mind of a fair and reasonable person could reach only one conclusion. Accordingly, we find, as a matter of law, that the jury could not reasonably have found that the assault on Ms. Medcalf (P) and the resultant injury were within the foreseeable scope of risk created by Management's (D) failure to maintain the intercom system. Reversed.

Analysis:

To prevail in a negligence action the plaintiff must prove that the defendant "proximately caused" his injury. While the issue of *cause in fact* is often settled by a "but for" inquiry, the issue of proximate cause is more complex. Proximate cause is not really a causation issue, rather, the inquiry focuses on the scope of responsibility. This case emphasizes the importance foreseeability plays in determining that scope. The court states that the fundamental inquiry is whether the harm which occurred was one within the scope of foreseeable risks. In a way, the inquiry requires a trier of fact to place a block in the right square. The rule assumes that a certain negligent act has certain foreseeable risks. It is up to the trier of fact to determine whether the harm that occurred in a particular case was one of the risks that was a foreseeable result of the defendant's negligence. The court here determined that the attack on Ms. Medcalf (P) was not a foreseeable risk of maintaining a buzzer system in disrepair. Do you agree? The court's ruling as a matter of law illustrates another important, but more subtle point. Courts often use the issue of proximate cause to trump a jury verdict.

Palsgraf v. Long Island Railroad Co.

(Injured Bystander) v. *(Railway Company)*

248 N.Y. 339, 162 N.E. 99 (1928)

A DEFENDANT IS NOT LIABLE FOR UNFORESEEABLE HARMS

■ **INSTANT FACTS** A passenger waiting for a train was injured on a railroad platform after railway employees dislodged—from the arm of another passenger whom they were negligently helping to jump onto a moving train—a package of fireworks. The fireworks exploded when it fell on the tracks, and the shock from the explosion caused scales to fall on the plaintiff.

■ **BLACK LETTER RULE** The risk reasonably to be perceived defines the duty to be obeyed.

■ PROCEDURAL BASIS

Appeal to the New York Court of Appeals, challenging the decision of the Appellate Division upholding a jury verdict for the plaintiff.

■ FACTS

Ms. Palsgraf (P) was standing on a platform waiting for her train to arrive. While waiting, another train was disembarking. A man carrying a package of unidentified contents jumped onto the moving train, but seemed unsteady, as if about to fall. Two railway officials, one on the train the other on the platform, helped the man regain balance, but in the process dislodged the package from the man's arm. The package was filled with fireworks, which began to explode when they fell. The shock of the explosion threw some scales down. The scales fell on Ms. Palsgraf (P) and caused her injuries, for which she sued. The jury found for Mrs. Palsgraf (P) and the Appellate Division affirmed.

■ ISSUE

Does a defendant owe a duty of care to a plaintiff whose injury was the result of an unforeseeable risk?

■ DECISION AND RATIONALE

(Cardozo, J.) No. The risk reasonably to be perceived defines the duty to be obeyed. Negligence is not actionable unless it involves the invasion of a legally protected interest, the violation of a right. The conduct of the railway official may have been a wrong to the man carrying the package, but was not a wrong in relation to Mrs. Palsgraf (P), standing far away. Nothing gave notice that the falling package had the ability to injure those standing at such a distance. This case does not turn on the issue of proximate cause, for that question arises only after it has been established that the defendant violated a duty to the plaintiff. We can assume that negligence in relation to the plaintiff would entail liability for any and all consequences, no matter how extraordinary. But the issue of consequences is rooted in a wrong, which we do not find in this case. Reversed.

■ DISSENT

(Andrew, J.) This case turns not on the issue of negligence, but on whether the Long Island Railway Co.'s agent proximately caused Ms. Palsgraf's (P) injury. The majority holds too narrow a view of negligence. It is true that negligence is relational. That relationship, however, is not merely, as the majority holds, between a man and those whom he might reasonably expect his act would injure.

Rather, the relationship is between a man and those to whom he does in fact injure. Simply stated, every one owes to the world at large the duty to refrain from those acts that may unreasonably threaten the safety of others. But liability is not endless, for it is limited by proximate cause, which is determined by several factors. Probable cause is a line arbitrarily drawn by the law so as to conveniently determine the point at which liability for negligence will cease. In deciding proximate cause the court must ask itself several questions. Was there a natural and continuous sequence between cause and effect? Was the act a substantial factor in producing the harm? Was there a direct connection between them, without too many intervening causes? Is the cause likely to produce the result? Could the result have reasonably been foreseen? Is the cause too remote in space and time? Applying these factors to the present case leads me to conclude that the act of knocking a package onto the ground proximately caused Ms. Palsgraf's injury. The explosion was a substantial factor in causing the injury. The events were the result of a natural and continuous sequence. There was no remoteness of time, and very little remoteness of space. It is also obvious that the explosion would foreseeably cause injury to anyone on the platform.

Analysis:

This is one of those few cases where both majority and dissenting opinions are often cited for their propositions. This is due to the fact that Justices Cardozo and Andrews framed the issue presented differently. Justice Cardozo's opinion focused on the duty owed to the plaintiff. As you may have learned in previous chapters, one of the elements of a negligence action is the existence of a duty owed to the plaintiff by the defendant. Justice Cardozo's opinion essentially ties the scope of this duty to the foreseeability of the harm caused and the injured plaintiff. If the harm caused was not a foreseeable risk of the defendant's action, then no duty was owed to the plaintiff. Consequently, there can be no negligence if there is no duty. Similarly, if an injury occurs to a person whom no one could have foreseen being injured, the defendant is not liable because there is no duty owed to unforeseeable plaintiffs. Justice Andrews, however, saw the issue in terms of proximate cause. In rejecting the majority's narrow view of negligence and the duty owed. Justice Andrews states that everyone owed to the world at large a duty to refrain from acts that unreasonably threaten the safety of others. Most courts have rejected this view, choosing to adopt Justice Cardozo's foreseeability inquiry. But Justice Andrews dissent is still valid for its elucidation on proximate cause. Andrews refused to limit the issue of proximate cause to an inquiry of foreseeability alone. Instead, he lists several factors that are essential to determining whether proximate cause exists. Factors such as the continuity of space and time, whether the negligent act was a substantial factor in the injury, and the foreseeability of the result among others are all used by courts today in reaching the issue of proximate cause.

Hughes v. Lord Advocate

(Injured Child) v. *(Government Tortfeasor)*

A.C. 837 (H.L.) (1963)

A HARM IS NOT OUTSIDE THE SCOPE OF RISK SIMPLY BECAUSE IT OCCURS IN AN UNEXPECTED MANNER

■ **INSTANT FACTS** While playing in and around an unguarded open manhole, two young boys accidentally knocked a kerosene lantern into the manhole, breaking the lantern and causing an unforeseeable explosion.

■ **BLACK LETTER RULE** The fact that the defendant's negligence causes a known harm in an unforeseeable manner does not relieve him of liability.

■ **PROCEDURAL BASIS**

Not provided.

■ **FACTS**

While on break, Post Office employees working on a telephone cable left unguarded an open manhole, covered with a tent and kerosene lamps. Two boys found the unguarded site and descended into the hole, tying one of the lamps to a rope. The boys climbed out with no problem, but once out of the whole, they knocked a kerosene lamp into the hole, breaking the lamp. Some of the kerosene unforeseeably vaporized and came into contact with the open flame, causing an explosion. The Hughes (P) boy fell into the hole as a result of the shock created by the explosion and suffered severe burns.

■ **ISSUE**

May a defendant escape liability on the ground that the harm caused, while foreseeable, occurred in an unforeseeable manner?

■ **DECISION AND RATIONALE**

(Lord Reid) No. The fact that the defendant's negligence causes a foreseeable harm in an unforeseeable manner does not relieve him of liability. It is agreed that the accident was so unlikely as to be unforeseeable. But the mere fact that the way in which an accident happened could not be anticipated is not enough to relieve the defendant of liability. The cause of this accident was a known source of danger, the lamp, but it behaved in an unpredictable way. In my judgment that affords no defense.

■ **CONCURRENCE**

(Lord Guest) I find unacceptable the argument that liability should not be had because although the burns suffered were a foreseeable risk from the lamps, the explosion which caused the burns was unforeseeable. An explosion is nothing more than one way which burning might be caused by a potentially dangerous lamp.

■ **CONCURRENCE**

(Lord Pearce) The explosion did not create an accident and damage of a different type from the misadventure and damage that was foreseeable. The accident was but a variant of the foreseeable. The harm which resulted was neither greater than nor different in kind from that which was foreseeable.

Analysis:

This case illustrates the "manner of injury" rule. The rule identifies the "foreseeability" that should be applicable to the proximate cause analysis adopted in *Medcalf v. Washington Heights Condominium Ass'n, Inc.* [Appellate Court of Connecticut holds that a woman that was attacked while visiting a friend could not sue the property manager for keeping the buzzer system in disrepair, because the attack was not a foreseeable harm] and *Palsgraf v. Long Island Railroad Co.* [New York Court of Appeals holds that the foreseeability of a harm defines the scope of the duty owed to the plaintiff by the defendant]. The law, essentially, does not require that a defendant have foreseen the manner in which an injury occurred. Rather, for proximate cause, the foreseeability that is controlling is the foreseeability of the particular type of harm or injury that occurred. The fact that the foreseeable harm occurs as the result of an unforeseeable sequence of events does not absolve the negligent actor of liability. Therefore, the court here held that because burns were a foreseeable harm of leaving kerosene lamps unattended, it did not matter that the burns to Hughes (P) were caused by an unforeseeable explosion caused by the kerosene lamps.

Derdiarian v. Felix Contracting Corp.

(Injured Road Worker) v. *(General Contractor)*

51 N.Y.2d 308, 434 N.Y.S.2d 166, 414 N.E.2d 666 (1980)

THE FACT THAT A THIRD PARTY NEGLIGENTLY TRIGGERED THE HARM CREATED BY THE DEFENDANT'S NEGLIGENCE DOES NOT AUTOMATICALLY PRECLUDE RECOVERY FROM THE DEFENDANT

■ **INSTANT FACTS** A road worker was injured after a man negligently drove his car through the work site and struck a boiling cauldron of enamel that was negligently left unguarded from traffic, causing the enamel to splatter and burn the worker.

■ **BLACK LETTER RULE** An intervening act may not serve as a superseding cause, and relieve an actor of responsibility, where the risk of the intervening act occurring is the very same risk which renders the actor negligent.

■ **PROCEDURAL BASIS**

Appeal to the New York Court of Appeals, challenging the decision of the Appellate Division to uphold a jury verdict for the plaintiff.

■ **FACTS**

Felix Contracting Corp. (Felix) (D) was installing an underground gas main along side a road. Mr. Derdiarian (P) was in charge of a kettle filled with liquid enamel, boiling to 400 degrees at the job site. Felix (D) insisted that the kettle be set on the west side of the excavation, facing oncoming traffic. The work site, including the kettle, was protected only by a single wooden horse. Testimony established that the work site was improperly protected. While driving eastbound, Mr. Dickens (D) lost control of his vehicle when he suffered a epileptic seizure brought on by his failure to take medication at the proper time. Mr. Dickens' (D) vehicle crashed into Mr. Derdiarian (P) and the kettle, causing the latter to splatter over the former's face and body.

■ **ISSUE**

Does a third party intervening act invariably break the causual link between the defendant's negligence and the harm caused?

■ **DECISION AND RATIONALE**

(Cooke, C.J.) No. An intervening act may not serve as a superseding cause, and relieve an actor of responsibility, where the risk of the intervening act occurring is the very same risk which renders the actor negligent. It is well settled that a plaintiff need not show that the precise manner in which an accident occurred was foreseeable. Where the acts of a third party intervene between the defendant's conduct and the plaintiff's injury, the question of liability turns upon whether the intervening act is a normal or foreseeable consequence of the situation created by the defendant's negligence. Although foreseeability can often be a question of law, especially where only one conclusion could be reached, the question is often left to the trier of fact. We cannot say as a matter of law that Dickens' (D) negligence was a superseding cause which interrupted the link between Felix's (D) negligence and Mr.

Derdiarian's (P) injury. A prime hazard associated with failing to secure a roadwork site is that a driver will negligently enter the site and cause injury. The finder of fact could have concluded that the foreseeable result of the risk created by Felix (D) was the injury of a worker caused by a driver negligently entering the work site.

Analysis:

This case serves as an example of the prototypical intervening cause case. In these cases a first actor will negligently create the risk of harm, which the second actor will negligently trigger. Courts often use the term "superseding cause" when the negligence of a second actor renders the first actor not liable. This case illustrates that the existence of an intervening actor does not always serve to supersede the negligence of the first actor. As with most issues related to proximate cause, foreseeability is the crucial factor in determining the extent of liability. If foreseeable, the intervening act will not supersede the negligence of the first actor. In this case the intervening act, Mr. Dickens (D) negligently crashing into the work site, was the exact risk created by Felix' (D) negligence. The court here holds of no consequence the fact that the negligence was caused by a failure to take medicine and not an inability to drive safely. The exact harm that was foreseeable—injury to workers—was the harm that occurred. In many cases, such as this one, the sequence of events leading to the harm is largely irrelevant because the negligence is broad enough to cover a variety of events.

Sheehan v. City of New York

(Bus Driver) v. *(Owner of Sanitation Truck)*
40 N.Y.2d 496, 387 N.Y.S.2d 92, 354 N.E.2d 832 (1976)

PROXIMATE CAUSE IS A SUBJECTIVE INQUIRY BASED UPON MIXED CONSIDERATIONS OF LOGIC, COMMON SENSE, JUSTICE, POLICY, AND PRECEDENT

■ **INSTANT FACTS** While stopped at an intersection, a city bus that negligently failed to pull over to the curb to pick up and drop off passengers was rear-ended by a sanitation truck.

■ **BLACK LETTER RULE** An actor has not proximately caused an accident if he merely furnishes the condition or occasion for the occurrence of an event.

■ **PROCEDURAL BASIS**

Appeal to the Court of Appeals of New York, challenging the decision of the Appellate Division reversing the trial judge's order setting aside the jury verdict against the city.

■ **FACTS**

Mr. Sheehan (D) was operating a city bus in Manhattan when he stopped at an intersection to permit passengers to board and alight. Contrary to traffic regulations, Sheehan (D) failed to pull over to the curb. While stopped, the bus was rear-ended by a sanitation truck that had lost its brakes. Mr. Novak (P), an injured bus passenger, sued the City (D), as owner of the sanitation truck, and the Transit Authority (D), as owner of the bus. A jury found against both, but the trial judge set aside the verdict against the Transit Authority (D). The Appellate Division reversed and reinstated the verdicts.

■ **ISSUE**

Is a rear-end accident within the scope of risk created by a bus' failure to pull over to the curb to allow passengers to board and alight?

■ **DECISION AND RATIONALE**

(Fuchsberg, J.) No. An actor has not proximately caused an accident if he merely furnishes the condition or occasion for the occurrence of an event. The bus at the time of the accident was at one point in the street where it had a right to be - the traveling lane - rather than another point where it had a right to be - the bus stop. The result of the brake failure would have been no different if a pedestrian or other vehicle had been using the street at that same point in time. Unlike those cases where a defendant's active obstruction of a street compelled the injured party to detour to a place of danger, no act of the bus in the case before us caused the sanitation truck to be any place other than where it was. We conclude, therefore, as a matter of law, that the negligence of the sanitation truck was the sole proximate cause of the injuries and that the continued presence of the bus merely furnished the condition or occasion for the occurrence of the event. Furthermore, it appears that, if the bus' presence could be regarded as a proximate cause of the accident, the failure of the truck's brakes might have been an independent, supervening cause. When such an intervening cause interrupts the natural sequence of events, it will prevent a recovery on account of the act or omission of the original wrongdoer.

Analysis:

This case should serve as a perfect example of the illusory nature of proximate cause. Notice that the court does not mention foreseeability, substantial factor, remoteness of time and space or any other of the considerations that go into the proximate cause analysis. The opinion can be seen as the court's subjective belief that proximate cause did not exist. Although the court reaches the correct result, its reasoning is somewhat faulty. The court states that the Transit Authority (P) was not liable because the bus did not cause the "sanitation truck to be an place other than where it was." But proximate cause is not about "causing" a party to do anything. This case is really about the scope of risk, and should have been decided on that basis. Traffic regulations required the driver to pull up to the curb to let passengers on and off the bus. In all likelihood, the harm sought to be avoided by this traffic regulation was that of passengers being struck by oncoming vehicles attempting to pass the bus, or some other risk of that nature. In any case, it is highly unlikely that the regulation was passed to prevent the bus from being rear-ended. This conclusion is bolstered by the fact that, as the court points out, the bus has the right to be in the travel lane when there are no passengers boarding or alighting. In an effort to bolster the strength of its holding, the court compounds its error by stating that even if Sheehan's (D) failure to pull to the curb were a proximate cause of the accident, the brake failure was a superseding cause. Foreseeability is the critical factor in determining whether an intervening cause will supersede the original tortfeasor's negligence. Thus, the court's conclusion with respect to that issue is questionable at best, for it is obviously foreseeable that a rear-end accident would be caused by faulty breaks.

Ventricelli v. Kinney System Rent A Car, Inc.

(Injured Lessee) v. *(Rental Car Company)*
45 N.Y.2d 950, 411 N.Y.S.2d 555, 383 N.E.2d 1149 (1978)

THE FORESEEABILITY OF AN INTERVENING ACT CAN BE A QUESTION OF LAW OR FACT, DEPENDING ON THE CIRCUMSTANCES

■ **INSTANT FACTS** A man was struck by a moving vehicle while trying to shut the defective trunk lid on the vehicle he rented.

■ **BLACK LETTER RULE** A rental car company could not have foreseen that a driver would strike its client while the client was attempting to shut the trunk lid negligently left in disrepair by the company.

■ **PROCEDURAL BASIS**

Appeal to the Court of Appeal of New York, challenging the decision of the Appellate Division reversing and dismissing the verdict against the rental car company.

■ **FACTS**

Mr. Ventricelli (P) rented from Kinney System Rent A Car, Inc. (Kinney) (D) a vehicle that had a defective trunk lid that did not close properly. While he and a passenger were attempting to shut the trunk, Ventricelli was struck by a car driven by Mr. Maldonado (D). At the time of the accident, Ventricelli (P) was "safely" in a parking space.

■ **ISSUE**

Could Kinney (D) have foreseen that a driver would negligently strike its client while the latter was attempting to shut the trunk negligently maintained by Kinney?

■ **DECISION AND RATIONALE**

(Memorandum) No. The immediately effective cause of Ventricelli's (P) injuries was the negligence of Maldonado (D). It was certainly foreseeable that Kinney's (D) negligence would lead to Ventricelli's repeated attempts to close the lid. What was not foreseeable was the collision between vehicles both parked a brief interval before the accident. Ventricelli (P) was in a relatively safe parking space, not in an actively traveled lane. He might have been in that situation independent of any negligence on the part of Kinney (D). Under these circumstances, to hold the accident a foreseeable consequence of Kinney's (D) negligence is to stretch the concept of foreseeability beyond acceptable limits. Affirmed.

■ **DISSENT**

(Fuchsberg, J) Not only was it foreseeable, but it was a reasonable expectation that a driver confronted with a trunk lid with a penchant for flying open would alight and promptly proceed to the rear of the car to attempt to secure the lid manually so that he might continue on his way without further danger. Kinney's (P) negligence thrust upon Ventricelli (P) a choice between the danger from the defective lid and the danger of being struck while attempting to close the trunk.

Analysis:

The court simply states that the accident was not a foreseeable consequence of Kinney's (P) failure to properly maintain the trunk lid. The court decides the issue as a matter of law, even though the issue is not cut and dry, as evidenced by the dissent. This case could be seen as an application of the rule, eventually adopted by this court in *Sheehan v. City of New York* [Court of Appeals of New York held that a bus driver's failure to pull up to the curb was not the proximate cause of an accident in which the bus was rear-ended], that an actor has not proximately caused an accident if his negligence merely furnishes the condition or occasion for the occurrence of an event. In support of this reading of the case are the facts that the court considered it important that Ventricelli (P) was "safely" parked, and that Ventricelli (P) could have been in that same position for any number of reasons, e.g. loading and unloading the trunk. The court could have reached the exact opposite result under the "manner of harm" rule. The court could have held immaterial the fact that Mr. Ventricelli (D) was struck while the car was parked, because a car accident is a foreseeable result of a faulty trunk lid. Regardless, this case, more than any other in this chapter, illustrates the arbitrary line that is "proximate cause."

Marshall v. Nugent

(Injured Pedestrian/Passenger) v. *(Intervening Negligent Driver)*

222 F.2d 604 (1st Cir. 1955)

THE SCOPE OF RISK FROM A DEFENDANT'S NEGLIGENCE CAN BE EXTENDED TEMPORALLY AND GEOGRAPHICALLY, DEPENDING ON THE CIRCUMSTANCES

■ **INSTANT FACTS** A man that was struck while attempting to warn oncoming traffic of an obstruction in the road, sued the truck driver that caused the obstruction.

■ **BLACK LETTER RULE** In a traffic mix-up due to negligence, before the waters have become placid and normal again, the unfolding of events between the culpable act and the plaintiff's eventual injury may be bizarre indeed; yet the defendant may be liable for the result.

■ **PROCEDURAL BASIS**

Appeal to the Second Circuit, challenging the decision of the district court denying the defendant's motion for a directed verdict.

■ **FACTS**

Marshall (P) was a passenger in a vehicle that was forced off the road by a truck that was partly in both lanes. The truck stopped to help pull the vehicle back onto the road, an effort that partly blocked the road. In an effort to warn oncoming vehicles, Marshall (P) walked toward the top of a hill, but was struck by Nugent's (D) vehicle before reaching the top. Marshall (P) sued Nugent (D) and the truck driver, Prince (D). The jury found against the truck driver, who appealed arguing that he was not the proximate cause.

■ **ISSUE**

Must a defendant's negligence immediately precede the harm to the plaintiff?

■ **DECISION AND RATIONALE**

(Magruder, J.) No. In a traffic mix-up due to negligence, before the waters have become placid and normal again, the unfolding of events between the culpable act and the plaintiff's eventual injury may be bizarre indeed; yet the defendant may be liable for the result. We find semantic the argument that Prince's (D) negligence was "merely a condition" to the accident and not the proximate cause thereof. The issue of proximate cause requires a flexible approach in defining the risk, or risks, narrowly, or more broadly, as seems appropriate to an individual case. With regard to motor vehicle accidents, the possibilities are endless. It is often impossible for a defendant to predict how his negligent act will work out. When the issue of proximate cause arises in a borderline case, we leave it to the jury to decide. Consequently, the district court did not err in refusing to direct a verdict for Prince (D). Marshall (P) was a passenger in the vehicle Prince (D) ran off the road. Prince's negligence was a breach of duty to Marshall; and although the act of negligence was over and done with, its consequences were still attendant.

Analysis:

This case serves as an example that the temporal scope of risk attendant to a negligent act is often broad, which, of course, increases the possibility of an intervening cause. The court refused to accept the "merely a condition" argument that was adopted in *Sheehan v. City of New York* [Court of Appeals of New York held that a bus driver's failure to pull up to the curb was not the proximate cause of an accident in which the bus was rear-ended], holding that the conclusion that an act is merely a condition to an event is simply another way of stating there was no proximate cause. Instead, the court adopts what it deems a flexible approach that broadens or narrows the scope of risk depending on the circumstances. The court gives lip service to the idea that proximate cause is an effort to define foreseeability. But the opinion fails to mention the foreseeability of Nugent's (D) negligent driving. Rather, the court holds that the possibilities for harm arising from a traffic mishap are too numerous to be foreseeable. Which brings up the question: Can the scope of risk be so broad as to render foreseeability irrelevant? Probably not, but some negligent acts are broad enough to cover a wide variety of harms. Regardless of the court's rationale, the point to be taken from this case is that scope of harm can be stretched both temporally and geographically depending on the circumstances.

CHAPTER NINE

Contributory/Comparative Fault

Butterfield v. Forrester

Instant Facts: Butterfield (P) was thrown from his horse and was injured after encountering an obstruction which Forrester (D) had placed in the road.

Black Letter Rule: When a plaintiff's lack of ordinary care contributes to an accident, he cannot recover for injuries sustained.

Sollin v. Wangler

Instant Facts: Wangler (D) dropped a bale of hay on Sollin (P), who was working on the grinder in which Wangler (D) was loading the hay.

Black Letter Rule: A jury should be instructed on the effect of its apportionment of comparative fault on the ultimate outcome of the plaintiff's recovery.

Wassell v. Adams

Instant Facts: Susan (P) sued motel owners for negligence and failure to warn after she opened her motel door to a stranger who ended up raping her.

Black Letter Rule: An appellate court is authorized to upset the jury's apportionment of negligence only if persuaded that the trial judge abused his discretion in determining that the jury's verdict was not against the clear weight of the evidence.

Mercer v. Vanderbilt University

Instant Facts: Mercer (P), as conservator, sued Vanderbilt University (D) for malpractice after her brother suffered brain damage during a CT scan.

Black Letter Rule: A patient's negligence that provides only the occasion for medical treatment may not be compared to that of a negligent physician such that the physician's liability is reduced by the patient's original negligence.

Bexiga v. Havir Manufacturing Corp.

Instant Facts: A machine operator sued the manufacturer of the machine after his hand was crushed, resulting in the loss of fingers and deformity of his hand.

Black Letter Rule: In negligence cases the defense of contributory negligence has been held to be unavailable where considerations of policy and justice dictate.

Leroy Fibre Co. v. Chicago, M. & St. P. Ry.

Instant Facts: A manufacturing business sued a railroad after sparks from the nearby railroad ignited stacks of flax which were on the business' land abutting the railroad.

Black Letter Rule: One's uses of his property are not subject to the servitude of the wrongful use by another of his property; thus the contributory negligence defense presents no question for the jury.

Butterfield v. Forrester

(Horseback Rider) v. *(House Repairman)*
11 East. 59, 103 Eng. Rep. 926 (1809)

A PLAINTIFF CANNOT RECOVER FOR INJURY FROM AN ACCIDENT WHEREIN HE DID NOT USE ORDINARY CARE

■ **INSTANT FACTS** Butterfield (P) was thrown from his horse and was injured after encountering an obstruction which Forrester (D) had placed in the road.

■ **BLACK LETTER RULE** When a plaintiff's lack of ordinary care contributes to an accident, he cannot recover for injuries sustained.

■ **PROCEDURAL BASIS**

Plaintiff appeals from the jury's judgment for the defendant.

■ **FACTS**

Forrester (D), while making repairs to his house, put a pole across the part of the road which was close to his home. Free passage was left by another road, however. Butterfield (P), who had just left a tavern [drunk riding?], was riding his horse very fast down the road and did not see the obstruction. He was thrown by his horse and was injured [but did he spill his beer?]. A witness testified that, although darkness was approaching, there was enough light left to see the obstruction from 100 yards away, and if Butterfield (P) had not been riding so fast he might have observed and avoided it. There was no evidence that Butterfield (P) was intoxicated at the time [didn't have breathalyzers back then!]. The jury found for Forrester (D), and this appeal followed.

■ **ISSUE**

Can a plaintiff recover for personal injury when his lack of ordinary care contributed to the accident?

■ **DECISION AND RATIONALE**

(Bayley, J. and Ellenborough, C.J.) No. When a plaintiff's lack of ordinary care contributes to an accident, he cannot recover for injuries sustained. Butterfield (P) was riding his horse as fast as he could go through the streets. If he had used ordinary care he would have seen the obstruction and been able to avoid it. One person being in fault will not dispense with another's using ordinary care for himself. Application for a new trial is denied.

Analysis:

This case demonstrates the defense of contributory negligence. Contributory negligence is an affirmative defense which must be raised and proved by the defendant in a case. In general, the same rules and tests apply to determine whether conduct is contributorily negligent as are used to determine if conduct is negligent. However, conduct which is negligent is not ipso facto contributory negligence as well. The prima facie case for contributory negligence is similar to the prima facie case for negligence, except that the duty here is not owed to any other person; rather, it is a duty to exercise ordinary care in the circumstances to avoid one's own injury at the hands of another. Also, there is no requirement of an "act"—the duty of self-protection always exists and is often violated by unreasonable inaction in the face of danger. At common law, the plaintiff's contributory negligence is an absolute and complete bar to any recovery for the negligence of the defendant. Additionally, this is true no matter how slight the negligence of the plaintiff as compared to the negligence of the defendant. However, contributory negligence is a defense only to negligence; it is no defense at all to an intentional tort. Neither is contributory negligence generally recognized as a defense to liability based on statutory concepts of "reckless" or "willful" misconduct.

■ CASE VOCABULARY

CONTRIBUTORY NEGLIGENCE: Conduct on the part of the plaintiff that is a contributing cause to his own injuries.

INTENTIONAL TORT: A wrong or injury caused by the purposeful actions of the defendant.

IPSO FACTO: In and of itself.

ORDINARY CARE: Care which is reasonably commensurate with a known danger.

PRIMA FACIE: Not requiring further support to establish existence, validity or credibility.

Sollin v. Wangler

(Farmhand) v. *(Farmhand)*

627 N.W.2d 159 (N.D.2001)

THE ULTIMATE OUTCOME RULE REQUIRES A JURY INSTRUCTION ON APPORTIONMENT OF LIABILITY

■ **INSTANT FACTS** Wangler (D) dropped a bale of hay on Sollin (P), who was working on the grinder in which Wangler (D) was loading the hay.

■ **BLACK LETTER RULE** A jury should be instructed on the effect of its apportionment of comparative fault on the ultimate outcome of the plaintiff's recovery.

■ **PROCEDURAL BASIS**

On appeal to review a decision of the North Dakota Court of Appeals.

■ **FACTS**

Wangler (D) dropped a heavy bale of straw on Sollin (P) while Wangler (D) was attempting to load it into a grinder. Wangler (D) alleged that Sollin (P) was contributorily negligent by working on the grinder while it was operating. Under state law, Sollin (P) would not have been able to recover if his fault was "as great as the combined fault of all other persons." At trial, Sollin (P) did not request a jury instruction on how his comparative fault would affect his damages. Instead, Sollin (P) requested that the jury be instructed to determine the percentage of fault of all parties who proximately caused the damages. The jury returned a verdict apportioning fifty percent of the fault to Wangler (D) and fifty percent to Sollin (P), but it awarded Sollin (P) $108,000 in damages. Because Sollin's (P) fault was as great as Wangler's (D), however, the claims were dismissed with prejudice. After the court denied Sollin's (P) request for a new trial because the court should have advised the jury on how apportionment affected recovery, Sollin (P) appealed.

■ **ISSUE**

Must a jury be instructed on the effect of its apportionment of fault on the plaintiff's recovery?

■ **DECISION AND RATIONALE**

(VandeWalle, C.J.) Yes. Generally, a jury should be instructed of the consequences of its verdict, because lack of knowledge will likely result in a verdict produced out of ignorance and potentially contrary to its intended outcome. This "ultimate outcome" instruction contemplates that the jurors, having heard and considered the evidence, will issue a verdict according to their sense of fairness and justice. A rule depriving the jury of an understanding of the consequences of its decision may lead to incorrect speculation and undermine the purpose of the judicial process. Further, a "blindfold rule" places defense counsel at an advantage by raising equitable concerns and convincing jurors that the parties should equally bear responsibility, only to result in a defense verdict by operation of the statute. Accordingly, the jury should be instructed on the effect of its apportionment on a plaintiff's eventual recovery. However, because the plaintiff failed to request such an instruction before the trial court, the decision denying the plaintiff's motion for a new trial must be affirmed.

Analysis:

The concern over the ultimate outcome instruction is that jurors will determine how a case should be decided before considering the factual findings necessary to reach that outcome. A jury that, for instance, is sympathetic to a plaintiff's injuries may answer questions posed in a special interrogatory in a way that leads to a verdict for the plaintiff rather than allowing the factual findings to determine the proper outcome as a matter of law.

■ CASE VOCABULARY

CONTRIBUTORY NEGLIGENCE: A plaintiff's own negligence that played a part in causing the plaintiff's injury and that is significant enough (in a few jurisdictions) to bar the plaintiff from recovering damages.

COMPARATIVE NEGLIGENCE: A plaintiff's own negligence that proportionally reduces the damages recoverable from a defendant.

Wassell v. Adams

(Rape Victim) v. *(Motel Owner)*
865 F.2d 849 (7th Cir.1989)

IN COMPARATIVE NEGLIGENCE, THE REQUIRED COMPARISON IS BETWEEN THE RESPECTIVE COSTS TO THE PLAINTIFF AND TO THE DEFENDANT OF AVOIDING THE INJURY

■ **INSTANT FACTS** Susan (P) sued motel owners for negligence and failure to warn after she opened her motel door to a stranger who ended up raping her.

■ **BLACK LETTER RULE** An appellate court is authorized to upset the jury's apportionment of negligence only if persuaded that the trial judge abused his discretion in determining that the jury's verdict was not against the clear weight of the evidence.

■ **PROCEDURAL BASIS**

Plaintiff appeals the trial judge's refusal to set aside the jury's verdict.

■ **FACTS**

Susan Wassell (P) brought this diversity suit charging the Adamses (D) with negligence in failing to warn Susan (P) or take other precautions to protect her against an assault which occurred in a motel owned by the Adamses (D). Before Susan was married, she traveled with her fiancée's (Michael) parents to Chicago for Michael's graduation from basic training. The three checked into a motel owned by Wilbur and Florena Adams (D). Four blocks to the west of the motel is a high-crime area [nice choice!]. The Adamses (D) occasionally warned women guests not to walk alone in the neighborhood at night. They did not warn the Wassells or Susan (P). After the graduation, Susan (P) stayed on at the hotel after the Wassells left; she was to find an apartment as Michael was to be stationed there permanently. One evening, after returning to the motel, Susan (P) locked the door, fastened the chain, and went to bed. She fell into a deep sleep, from which she was awakened by a knock on the door. She noted it was 1:00 a.m. as she went to the door. She looked through the peephole but saw no one. She unlocked the door (two locks plus the chain) and opened it wide [always a great idea!], thinking that Michael had come from the base. A respectably dressed black man was standing there, and he asked for Cindy. She told him there was no Cindy there, and he then asked for a glass of water. She went to the bathroom to get him the water [sure, why not?]. When she came out of the bathroom, the man was sitting at the table in the room [are *no* bells ringing yet?]. He told her the water wasn't cold enough, and that he had no money. Susan (P) told him she had $20 in her car. He then got up and went into the bathroom. Susan (P) began to get nervous [ya think?]. She hid her purse, which had $800 in it, and her car keys. There was no telephone in the room, however the television had an alarm attached to it which would go off if someone tried to remove it. Susan (P) was not told of the alarm, although there was a notice about it posted next to the television set. The parking lot on which the motel rooms opened was brightly lit by floodlights. A few minutes passed while the man was in the bathroom. He asked Susan (P) to join him, which she refused. The man then came out of the bathroom naked from the waist down. Susan (P) fled the room and beat on the door of the adjacent room, but no one answered. The man grabbed her and dragged her back into her room. She screamed but no one appeared. The motel had no security guard and the Adamses (D) did not hear the screams. The man raped Susan (P) at least twice for over an hour. Eventually Susan (P) persuaded the rapist to take a shower with her. After the shower, she managed to get out of the room and escape in her car. The rapist was never prosecuted. A suspect was caught, but Susan (P) was too upset to identify him [she only had a couple of hours to get a good look at him!]. Susan (P) married Michael, but the rape has induced post-traumatic stress that has blighted her life. A jury found that the Adamses (D) were indeed negligent and that their negligence was a proximate cause of the assault. The jury assessed Susan's damages at $850,000, however the jury also found that Susan (P) had been negligent too. The jury found Susan (P) to be 97% to blame for the attack and the Adamses (D) only 3%. Thus Susan (P) was awarded only $25,500 in damages.

■ ISSUE

Did the trial judge abuse his discretion in determining that the jury's apportionment was not against the weight of the evidence?

■ DECISION AND RATIONALE

(Posner, C.J.) No. Susan's (P) counsel insists that Susan (P) was not negligent at all but that, if she was, she was at most 5% responsible for the catastrophe which, he argues, could have been averted without cost by a simple warning from the Adamses (D). To this the Adamses' (D) counsel replied that a warning would have been costly as it might have scared guests away. We think that absurd, for the loss of business from telling the truth is not a social loss, it is a social gain. We have suggested in previous cases that one way to make sense of comparative negligence is to assume that the required comparison is between the respective costs to the plaintiff and to the defendant of avoiding the injury. If each could have avoided it at the same cost, they are each 50% responsible for it. According to this method of comparing negligence, the jury found that Susan could have avoided the attack at a cost of one thirty-second the cost to the Adamses (D). Is this possible? Giving the jury every benefit of the doubt, we must assume that it did not believe the Adamses' (D) negligence consisted in failing to give a futile warning. Rather, we must assume that the jury thought the Adamses' (D) negligence consisted in failing to have a security guard, or telephones in each room, or alarms designed to protect the motel's patrons rather than just the owners' television sets. The cost of these omitted precautions might be much greater than the monetary equivalent of the greater vigilance on the part of Susan (P) that would have averted the attack. If we were the trier of fact, we would assess the Adamses' (D) share at more than 3%. But we are not the trier of fact, and are to upset the jury's apportionment only if persuaded that the trial judge abused his discretion in determining that the jury's verdict was not against the clear weight of the evidence. We are not so persuaded. It seems probably wrong to us, but we have suggested an interpretation of the evidence under which the verdict was consistent with the evidence and the law. That is enough to require us to uphold the district judge's refusal to set aside the verdict. Affirmed.

Analysis:

The old common law rule barring the contributorily negligent plaintiff from recovering any damages came eventually to seem too harsh. That is why it has been changed in most jurisdictions. It was harsh, all right, at least if one focuses most narrowly on the plight of individual plaintiffs, but it was also simple and therefore cheap to administer. The same cannot be said for comparative negligence, which is far from being simple. It requires a formless, unguided inquiry, because there is no methodology for comparing the causal contributions of the plaintiff's and of the defendant's negligence to the plaintiff's injury. In this case, either Susan (P) or the Adamses (D) could have avoided the injury. It is hard to say more, but the statute requires more (yet without giving the finder of facts any guidance as to how to make the apportionment). It is careless to open a motel door in the middle of the night without trying to find out who is knocking. But surely a warning to Susan (P) would not have cost the Adamses (D) 32 times the cost to her of schooling herself to greater vigilance. However, it is unlikely that a warning would have averted the attack. Susan (P) testified that she thought it was her fiancée at the door. Thinking this, she would have opened the door no matter how dangerous she believed the neighborhood to be. It is absurd to think that the hotel managers are required to give such an obvious warning as to tell guests to not open their doors in the middle of the night under any circumstances without ascertaining who it was. Everyone, or at least the average person, knows better than to open his or her door to a stranger in the middle of the night. Thus, it seems correct that Susan (P) should lose a percentage of the total damages because of her unreasonable behavior.

■ **CASE VOCABULARY**

COMPARATIVE NEGLIGENCE: Approach which attempts to individualize accident recoveries by placing the economic "sting" on the parties in proportion to their fault.

DIVERSITY SUIT: Federal jurisdiction over the case due to the controversy being between citizens of different states.

NEGLIGENCE: Failure to exercise the degree of care a reasonable person would exercise under the same circumstances.

PROXIMATE CAUSE: An event without which the injury would not have occurred.

Mercer v. Vanderbilt University

(Conservator) v. *(Medical Facility)*

134 S.W.3d 121 (Tenn.2004)

A PATIENT'S DRINKING DOES NOT AFFECT A PHYSICIAN'S MALPRACTICE LIABILITY

■ **INSTANT FACTS** Mercer (P), as conservator, sued Vanderbilt University (D) for malpractice after her brother suffered brain damage during a CT scan.

■ **BLACK LETTER RULE** A patient's negligence that provides only the occasion for medical treatment may not be compared to that of a negligent physician such that the physician's liability is reduced by the patient's original negligence.

■ **PROCEDURAL BASIS**

On appeal to review a decision of the Tennessee Court of Appeals reversing a judgment for the plaintiff.

■ **FACTS**

After Qualls was injured in an automobile accident, he was brought to the Vanderbilt University Medical Center (D) for treatment. While there, tests suggested that at the time of the accident, Qualls had been highly intoxicated. Several days later, Qualls was transferred to a CT suite for reconstructive facial surgery. In preparation for the transfer, Qualls was connected to a ventilator, which was attached to three oxygen tanks, two of which were only half-full. While in the CT monitor, none of the defendant's staff members recorded the ventilator's settings or Qualls's vital signs. Shortly after the CT exam, Qualls turned gray and stopped breathing, which resulted in severe and permanent brain damage. Mercer (P), Qualls's sister and conservator, sued Vanderbilt University (D) for malpractice by virtue of its failure to ensure all oxygen tanks were full and monitor Qualls's vital signs during the procedure. Vanderbilt (D) contended that although the nurses were negligent in these areas, the cause of Qualls's injuries was a seizure or heart arrhythmia brought on by his alcohol withdrawal. After evidence was presented, the plaintiff moved for a directed verdict on the issue of comparative fault, which was denied. The jury returned a verdict for the plaintiff, but attributed thirty percent of the liability to Qualls. Nonetheless, the court ordered judgment on the full amount of damages found by the jury. On appeal, the Tennessee Court of Appeals reversed the judgment.

■ **ISSUE**

May a patient's negligence in causing his own injuries be compared to a physician's negligence in treating those injuries to reduce the physician's liability for malpractice?

■ **DECISION AND RATIONALE**

(Holder, J.) No. Under Tennessee law, when a patient suffers a single indivisible injury proximately caused by the separate, independent acts of the patient and the physician, comparative fault applies in a medical malpractice action. However, no other American jurisdiction acknowledges the indivisible/separate injury distinction. Instead, most jurisdictions reason that "a patient's negligence that provides only the occasion for medical treatment may not be compared to that of a negligent physician" so that a physician's liability is reduced by the patient's original negligence. To the extent that Tennessee cases permit a physician to avoid liability for a breach of the standard of care because the

---

patient's initial injuries were caused by his own negligence, they are overruled. Because Qualls's negligence may not be compared to Vanderbilt's (D) negligence, the trial court did not err in entering judgment for the full damages awarded by the jury. Reversed.

Analysis:

Taken to its dangerous extreme, if a patient's negligence could be considered in cases like this, medical malpractice claims would be considerably restricted. There appears to be no reasonable distinction between the plaintiff's own negligence and that of a third party (such as in a car accident case), for both created the opportunity for medical malpractice to occur. The result of allowing such consideration would be a complicated review of all negligence that may have led to the medical treatment, which could enable medical professionals to escape liability for their negligence.

Bexiga v. Havir Manufacturing Corp.

(Machine Operator) v. *(Machine Manufacturer)*

60 N.J. 402, 290 A.2d 281 (1972)

WHERE CONSIDERATIONS OF JUSTICE AND POLICY DICTATE, CONTRIBUTORY NEGLIGENCE IS UNAVAILABLE AS A DEFENSE TO EITHER NEGLIGENCE OR STRICT LIABILITY CLAIMS

■ **INSTANT FACTS** A machine operator sued the manufacturer of the machine after his hand was crushed, resulting in the loss of fingers and deformity of his hand.

■ **BLACK LETTER RULE** In negligence cases the defense of contributory negligence has been held to be unavailable where considerations of policy and justice dictate.

■ **PROCEDURAL BASIS**

Appeal from the Appellate Division's affirmance of the trial court's dismissal of the action at the close of the plaintiff's case.

■ **FACTS**

This is a products liability case. Bexiga (P), a minor, was operating a power punch press for his employer when his right hand was crushed by the machine, resulting in the loss of fingers and deformity of his hand. Bexiga (P) mistakenly placed his hand under the ram at the same time the foot pedal was depressed, and no safety devices were in place to prevent this action. His father brought this suit on behalf of Bexiga (P) against Havir Manufacturing Corp. (D), the manufacturer of the machine. Bexiga's (P) expert, Andrew Gass, a mechanical engineer, testified that the machine amounted to a "booby trap" because there were no safety devices in its basic design and none were installed prior to the accident. Gass described two "basic types" of protective safety devices, both of which were known in the industry at the time of the manufacture and sale. These and other safety devices were available from companies specializing in safety equipment. The trial court dismissed the action at the close of Bexiga's (P) case. The Appellate Division affirmed and this appeal followed.

■ **ISSUE**

Can contributory negligence be used as a defense in a case where the injury was the very eventuality the duty owed was designed to protect against?

■ **DECISION AND RATIONALE**

(Proctor, J.) No. In negligence cases the defense of contributory negligence has been held to be unavailable where considerations of policy and justice dictate. We think this case presents a situation where the interests of justice dictate that contributory negligence be unavailable as a defense to either the negligence or strict liability claims. The asserted negligence of Bexiga (P)—placing his hand under the ram while at the same time depressing the foot pedal—was the very eventuality the safety devices were designed to guard against. It would be anomalous to hold that Havir (D) has a duty to install safety devices but a breach of that duty results in no liability for the very injury the duty was meant to protect against. We hold that under the facts presented to us in this case the defense of contributory negligence is unavailable. The judgment of the Appellate Division is reversed and the cause is remanded for a new trial.

Analysis:

This case can be understood as holding that when a defendant undertakes to protect a plaintiff from his own fault, or when the law imposes such a duty, the entire responsibility for care by definition falls upon the defendant, and the plaintiff's fault cannot be held against him. That is logical enough, but when should the law impose such a duty if it is not one voluntarily undertaken by the defendant? A reasonable rule would be that such a duty is imposed when the defendant imposes a risk upon the plaintiff, but that plaintiff's fault imposes no similar risk upon the defendant. In other words, the risks are not reciprocal or mutual. Perhaps, additionally, the plaintiff's vulnerability might play a part in determining responsibility, such as when the defendant knows of a plaintiff's disability which prevents or inhibits the plaintiff's care for himself, or when the plaintiff's risky conduct endangers himself but not others.

■ **CASE VOCABULARY**

PRODUCTS LIABILITY: A doctrine holding a manufacturer liable when an article is placed into the market with a defect which causes an injury.

STRICT LIABILITY: Liability imposed without regard to fault.

LeRoy Fibre Co. v. Chicago, M. & St. P. Ry.

(Manufacturing Business) v. *(Railroad)*
232 U.S. 340, 34 S.Ct. 415, 58 L.Ed. 631 (1914)

PLAINTIFFS MAY BE ENTITLED TO USE THEIR PROPERTY EVEN IF IN DOING SO THEY ARE IN DANGER OF HARM BY THE DEFENDANT'S NEGLIGENCE

■ **INSTANT FACTS** A manufacturing business sued a railroad after sparks from the nearby railroad ignited stacks of flax which were on the business' land abutting the railroad.

■ **BLACK LETTER RULE** One's uses of his property are not subject to the servitude of the wrongful use by another of his property; thus the contributory negligence defense presents no question for the jury.

■ PROCEDURAL BASIS

Appeal from the jury's finding for the defendant after being charged on the contributory negligence defense.

■ FACTS

LeRoy Fibre Co. (P) stacked flax about 75 feet from Chicago, Minneapolis & St. Paul Railway's (D) railroad tracks which were abutting his land. LeRoy (P) alleged that the Railway (D) negligently emitted sparks and coals which set fire to and destroyed the flax. The Railway (D) argued that LeRoy (P) was contributorily negligent in stacking the combustible flax so near the railroad.

■ ISSUE

Can the Railroad's (D) liability for negligence be relieved by LeRoy Fibre's (P) contributory negligence in the use of its property?

■ DECISION AND RATIONALE

(McKenna, J.) No. That one's use of his property may be subject to the servitude of the wrongful use by another of his property seems an anomaly. It upsets the presumptions of law, and takes from him the assumption, and the freedom which comes from the assumption, that the other will obey the law, not violate it. It casts upon him the duty of not only using his own property so as not to injure another, but so to use his own property that it may not be injured by the wrongs of another. This would cause an unjust result, and as such we hold that the contributory negligence defense presented no question for the jury.

■ CONCURRENCE

(Holmes, J.) As a general proposition, people are entitled to assume that their neighbors will conform to the law and will not be negligent.

Analysis:

The legal conception of property is of rights. When you attempt to limit them by wrongs, and declare that a right is subject to a wrong, you confound the meaning of both. There are some principles that have a self-evident character. The tangibility of property is in its uses, and that the uses by one owner of his property may be limited by the wrongful use of another owner of his is a contradiction. This case is best discussed in terms of LeRoy's (P) entitlements. Plaintiffs in general may be entitled to use their property even if in doing so they are in danger of harm by the defendant's negligence. Thus, the plaintiff is under no duty to protect himself by the use of reasonable care, and, as such, cannot be charged with contributory negligence for failing to do so. This is not to say that if a man stacked his flax so near the railroad tracks that it obviously was likely to be set fire to by a well-managed train that he could put the loss on the railroad. But that issue is not addressed here, and the Court chooses not to answer that question until required. Suffice it to say that property law, emphasizing the owner's right to use property as he pleases, is sometimes at odds with negligence law, which emphasizes the safety of conduct and judges safety case by case after the event has occurred.

■ CASE VOCABULARY

ENTITLEMENT: A right or privilege.

CHAPTER TEN

Assumption of the Risk

Moore v. Hartley Motors

Instant Facts: After Moore (P) signed a release to participate in an ATV safety course, she was injured when thrown from an ATV.

Black Letter Rule: A court may invalidate a release as against public policy upon consideration of such factors as the type of service performed and whether the party seeking exculpation has a decisive advantage in bargaining strength because of the essential nature of the service.

Crews v. Hollenbach

Instant Facts: Crews (P) was severely injured when a gas leak, made when Hollenbach (D) struck a buried gas line, ignited and exploded.

Black Letter Rule: A plaintiff who voluntarily consents, either expressly or impliedly, to exposure to a known risk cannot later sue for damages incurred from exposure to that risk.

Turcotte v. Fell

Instant Facts: Turcotte (P) sued another jockey for negligence and "foul riding" after he was thrown from his horse during a race and paralyzed.

Black Letter Rule: While a participant's consent to join in a sporting activity is not a waiver of all rules infractions, a professional's clear understanding and acceptance of the usual incidents of competition which result from the customarily accepted method of playing the sport relieves other participants of any duty of reasonable care with respect to known dangers.

Moore v. Hartley Motors

(Safety Course Participant) v. *(Landowner)*

36 P.3d 628 (Alaska 2001)

THE SCOPE OF A RELEASE IS DETERMINED BY THE PARTIES' INTENT

■ **INSTANT FACTS** After Moore (P) signed a release to participate in an ATV safety course, she was injured when thrown from an ATV.

■ **BLACK LETTER RULE** A court may invalidate a release as against public policy upon consideration of such factors as the type of service performed and whether the party seeking exculpation has a decisive advantage in bargaining strength because of the essential nature of the service.

■ **PROCEDURAL BASIS**

On appeal to review summary judgment for the defendants.

■ **FACTS**

When Moore (P) purchased a four-wheel ATV, the seller offered a rebate if Moore (P) would complete a safety course conducted on the property of Hartley Motors (D). Before the course, Moore (P) executed a consent form and release. During the course, Moore (P) was thrown from the ATV and was injured on a rock concealed by grass. Moore (P) sued Hartley Motors (D), the seller, and the course instructor, alleging they failed to provide a safe training course and location. After the court granted the defendants' motion for summary judgment, Moore (P) appealed.

■ **ISSUE**

Did a genuine issue of material fact exist concerning whether the plaintiff executed a valid release of the defendants' negligence?

■ **DECISION AND RATIONALE**

(Fabe, C.J.) Yes. While releases are usually upheld as valid, a court may invalidate a release as against public policy upon consideration of such factors as the type of service performed and whether the party seeking exculpation has a decisive advantage in bargaining strength because of the essential nature of the service. Because the ATV course is not an essential service, the defendants did not have a bargaining advantage over Moore (P) because she had a choice as to whether to take the class. Accordingly, the release does not violate public policy. However, the court failed to consider the scope of the release. The contract released the defendants from liability for bodily injuries and property damage arising out of Moore's (P) participation in the course, but did not mention a release of negligence generally. A reasonable reading of the release demonstrates Moore's (P) intent to release claims for negligence related to the inherent risks of ATV riding, but not for injuries caused by unreasonably dangerous defects on the property. Because the release does not address these claims, a genuine issue of material fact exists concerning the danger associated with the ATV course and the application of the release. Reversed and remanded.

Analysis:

The key to the court's decision that the release does not violate public policy was Moore's (P) meaningful choice whether to accept the terms of release. Because the ATV course was not required of her by law, public policy does not forbid the release. If the course were required by law, such as in the case of motorcycle training in certain states, public policy may forbid a waiver.

■ CASE VOCABULARY

ASSUMPTION OF THE RISK: The act or an instance of a prospective plaintiff's taking on the risk of loss, injury, or damage.

RELEASE: Liberation from an obligation, duty, or demand; the act of giving up a right or claim to the person against whom it could have been enforced.

Crews v. Hollenbach

(Burned Gas Man) v. *(Excavator)*

358 Md. 627, 751 A.2d 481 (2000)

INTENTIONAL AND VOLUNTARY EXPOSURE TO A KNOWN DANGER INDICATES CONSENT ON THE PART OF THE PLAINTIFF TO RELIEVE THE DEFENDANT OF AN OBLIGATION OF CONDUCT TOWARD HIM AND TO TAKE HIS CHANCES FROM HARM FROM A PARTICULAR RISK

■ **INSTANT FACTS** Crews (P) was severely injured when a gas leak, made when Hollenbach (D) struck a buried gas line, ignited and exploded.

■ **BLACK LETTER RULE** A plaintiff who voluntarily consents, either expressly or impliedly, to exposure to a known risk cannot later sue for damages incurred from exposure to that risk.

■ **PROCEDURAL BASIS**

Appeal from the intermediate court's affirmance of the trial court's grant of summary judgment in favor of the defendants.

■ **FACTS**

Hollenbach (D) was excavating land that had been marked to indicate the location of gas lines. Despite the markers, Hollenbach (D) struck a buried natural gas line, creating a leak in the line. Neither Hollenbach (D) nor anyone at the scene contacted anyone about the leak [that's responsiblel], and natural gas released freely into the air and ground. Two hours later, a resident, located approximately one mile from the leak, recognized the smell of gas in the air and notified the fire department. The neighborhood and surrounding area were evacuated and the gas company dispatched a repair crew to the scene of the leak. Crews (P), the foreman in charge of the gas company crew, began to dissipate the gas that had permeated the ground. The gas ignited and exploded, and Crews (P) was injured severely. The cause of the spark which ignited the gas was unknown, and no allegation was made that Hollenbach (D) was the cause of the ignition source. Crews (P) sued Hollenbach (D) and his employer and others engaged in the project [someone else is always to blame]. The trial court granted summary judgment for Hollenbach (D) on the ground that Crews (P) had assumed the risk.

■ **ISSUE**

Can a plaintiff recover for injuries caused by exposure to a known danger?

■ **DECISION AND RATIONALE**

(Harrell, J.) No. In defining the defense of assumption of the risk, we have stated that the defense rests upon an intentional and voluntary exposure to a known danger and, therefore, consent on the part of the plaintiff to relieve the defendant of an obligation of conduct toward him and to take his chances from harm from a particular risk. In deciding whether a plaintiff had knowledge and appreciation of a particular risk, we apply an objective standard. We will not be swayed by a plaintiff's subjective denial that he or she did not comprehend the extent of a clearly obvious danger. The question of whether a plaintiff knew and understood the risk in a case is generally one for the trier of fact, but if a person of normal intelligence, in the same position as the plaintiff, would clearly have comprehended the danger, the question is one for the court. A plaintiff who voluntarily consents, either expressly or impliedly, to exposure to a known risk cannot later sue for damages incurred from exposure to that risk. The danger Crews (P) encountered the day in issue is the very danger that he accepted the risk of confronting when he became an employee of the gas company twenty years earlier. In his own words, he accepted that responsibility when he was hired. Thus, the aspect of his job duties that involved fixing gas leaks, a clearly dangerous endeavor, and which he continued to confront for more than twenty years, constitutes a voluntary assumption of those risks which might reasonably be expected to exist on the day of the explosion. It seems to us, on this record, that the risk that led to Crews' (P) injuries was reasonably identifiable and inherent in his job both when he was first hired as well as on the day of the explosion. Accordingly, we find no error of law in the Circuit Court's grant of summary judgment, on this record, in favor of Hollenbach (D).

Analysis:

Assumption of the risk serves as a complete bar to a plaintiff's recovery. The defense is grounded on the theory that a plaintiff who voluntarily consents, either expressly or impliedly, to exposure to a known risk cannot later sue for damages incurred from exposure to that risk. The task in a conventional assumption of the risk analysis is to determine whether the plaintiff (1) had knowledge of the risk of danger; (2) appreciated the risk; and (3) voluntarily exposed himself or herself to that risk. Crews (P) plainly knew of the risks inherent in working on a gas leak. He had been an employee of the gas company for over twenty years. He stated in his deposition that he had been taught that "any type of gas leak or odor is always dangerous." Additionally, this was the field and career which Crews (P) chose and continued to work in. Thus, he cannot say that he was forced to act in this regard; it was his chosen occupation. There was no evidence introduced into the record to determine what any implications may have been had he not acted. The Court correctly ruled that the risk which led to Crews' (P) injuries was assumed voluntarily, thus relieving Hollenbach (D) of any liability.

■ CASE VOCABULARY

ASSUMPTION OF RISK: An affirmative defense claiming that the plaintiff had knowledge of a danger or risk, yet voluntarily exposed himself to the hazard, thereby relieving the defendant of any liability for any resulting injury.

EXPRESS CONSENT: Consent which is made known explicitly and in declared terms.

IMPLIED CONSENT: Consent manifested by signs, actions or facts, or by inaction or silence, which raises a presumption that consent has been given.

SUMMARY JUDGMENT: A preverdict judgment rendered by the court in response to a motion by one of the parties who claims that there is no dispute as to material facts or questions of law.

Turcotte v. Fell

(*Injured Jockey*) v. (*Jockey*)

68 N.Y.2d 432, 502 N.E.2d 964, 510 N.Y.S.2d 49 (1986)

KNOWN, APPARENT AND FORESEEABLE DANGERS OF A SPORT ARE NOT ACTIONABLE AGAINST PARTICIPANTS

■ **INSTANT FACTS** Turcotte (P) sued another jockey for negligence and "foul riding" after he was thrown from his horse during a race and paralyzed.

■ **BLACK LETTER RULE** While a participant's consent to join in a sporting activity is not a waiver of all rules infractions, a professional's clear understanding and acceptance of the usual incidents of competition which result from the customarily accepted method of playing the sport relieves other participants of any duty of reasonable care with respect to known dangers.

■ PROCEDURAL BASIS

Appeal from the Appellate Divisions affirmance of the trial court's grant of summary judgment in favor of the defendant.

■ FACTS

Turcotte (P) was a renowned jockey who was thrown from his horse when it tripped on the heels of another horse. Turcotte (P) was severely injured and rendered a paraplegic. He sued Fell (D), the jockey on another horse, claiming he was negligent and also violated rules which regulate foul riding [horses aren't fowl!]. Turcotte (P) alleged that Fell (D) rode his horse so as to impede Turcotte (P) [isn't that the objective?], and further, that Fell (D) caused his horse to jostle and strike Turcotte's (P) horse without any fault on Turcotte's (P) part. The trial court granted Fell's (D) motion for summary judgment, and the Appellate Division affirmed the grant.

■ ISSUE

Can a sporting professional be held liable for negligently causing injury to another during a competition?

■ DECISION AND RATIONALE

(Name of Judge Not Stated) No. The trial court, in granting summary judgment for Fell (D), held that Turcotte (P), by engaging in the sport of horse racing, relieved other participants of any duty of reasonable care with respect to known dangers. While the determination of the existence of a duty and the concomitant scope of that duty involve a consideration not only of the wrongfulness of the defendant's action or inaction, they also necessitate an examination of the plaintiff's reasonable expectations of the care owed him by others. This is particularly true in professional sporting contests, which by their nature involve an elevated degree of danger. If a participant makes an informed estimate of the risks involved in the activity and willingly undertakes them, then there can be no liability if he is injured as a result of those risks. It would be a rare thing, indeed, if the election of a professional athlete to participate in a sport at which he makes his living could be said to be involuntary. Turcotte's (P) participation certainly was not involuntary in this case and thus we are concerned only with the scope of his consent. Some of the restraints of civilization must accompany every athlete onto the playing field, and, as such, our rule is qualified to the extent that participants do not consent to acts which are reckless or intentional. The question of whether the consent was an informed one includes consideration of the participant's knowledge and experience in the activity generally. Manifestly a professional athlete is more aware of the dangers of the activity, and presumably more willing to accept them in exchange for a salary, than is an amateur. Turcotte (P) conceded that there is a fine line between what is lawful and unlawful in the movement of a horse on the track during a race and that when and where a horse can lawfully change its position is a matter of judgment. Such dangers are inherent in the sport. Because they are recognized as such by Turcotte (P), the courts below properly held that he consented to relieve Fell (D) of the legal duty to use reasonable care to avoid crossing into his lane of travel. Turcotte (P) nonetheless contends that Fell's (D) violation of the rule which prohibits foul riding is sufficient to sustain their complaint. The rules of the sport, however, do not necessarily limit the scope of the professional's consent. As the rule recognizes, bumping and jostling are normal incidents of the sport. They are not flagrant infractions unrelated to the normal method of playing the game and done without any competitive purpose. Turcotte (P) does not claim that Fell (D) intentionally or recklessly bumped him, he claims only that as a result of carelessness, Fell (D) failed to control his mount as the horses raced for the lead and a preferred position on the track. While a participant's consent to join in a sporting activity is not a waiver of all rules infractions, a professional's clear understanding and acceptance of the usual incidents of competition which result from the customarily accepted method of playing the sport relieves other participants of any duty of reasonable care with respect to known dangers. Thus the motion for summary judgment in favor of Fell (D) was properly sustained.

Analysis:

Traditionally, a participant's conduct was conveniently analyzed in terms of the defensive doctrine of assumption of risk. With the enactment of the comparative negligence statute, however, assumption of risk is no longer an absolute defense. Thus, it has become necessary, and quite proper, when measuring a defendant's duty to a plaintiff to consider the risks assumed by the plaintiff. The shift in the analysis is proper because the doctrine of assumption of risk deserves no separate existence (except for express assumption of risk) and is simply a confusing way of stating certain no-duty rules. Accordingly, the analysis of care owed to Turcotte (P) in the professional sporting even by a co-participant and by the proprietor of the facility in which it takes place must be evaluated by considering the risks Turcotte (P) assumed when he elected to participate in the event and how those assumed risks qualified Fell's (D) duty to him. The risk assumed has been defined a number of ways, but in its most basic sense it means that the plaintiff, in advance, has given his consent to relieve the defendant of an obligation of conduct toward him, and to take his chances of injury from a known risk arising from what the defendant is to do or leave undone. The situation is then the same as where the plaintiff consents to the infliction of what would otherwise be an intentional tort, except that the consent is to run the risk of unintended injury. The result is that the defendant is relieved of his legal duty to the plaintiff; and being under no duty, he cannot be charged with negligence. The defendant's duty, under such circumstances, is a duty to exercise care to make the conditions as safe as they appear to be. If the risks of the activity are fully comprehended or perfectly obvious, the plaintiff has consented to them and the defendant has performed its duty.

■ CASE VOCABULARY

CONSTRUCTIVE CONSENT: Not actual consent, but accepted in law as a substitute for whatever is otherwise required.

CHAPTER ELEVEN

Defenses Not on the Merits

Crumpton v. Humana, Inc.

Instant Facts: A woman was injured when her nurse improperly attempted to lower her hospital bed after surgery.

Black Letter Rule: The statute of imitations commences running from the date of injury, and there is no authority to suggest that the statute of limitations should be tolled during the time when the parties were negotiating a settlement.

Schiele v. Hobart Corp.

Instant Facts: Schiele (P), a meat wrapper, developed serious lung problems allegedly from using Hobart Corp.'s (D) machine in the course of her employment.

Black Letter Rule: The statute of limitations begins to run when a reasonably prudent person associates his symptoms with a serious or permanent condition and at the same time perceives the role which the defendant has played in inducing that condition.

Doe v. Maskell

Instant Facts: Two girls sued a priest from their high school after they recovered repressed memories of his sexually abusing them when they were students twenty years earlier.

Black Letter Rule: The mental process of repression of memories of past sexual abuse does not activate the discovery rule to lost memory cases such as to toll the running of the statute of limitations.

Hoery v. United States

Instant Facts: Hoery (P) sued the United States (D) for groundwater contamination caused by the defendant's dumping of toxic chemicals.

Black Letter Rule: If a tort is permanent, the claim accrues when the plaintiff learned or should have learned of the injury, but if the tort is continuing, the claim continues to accrue as long as the defendant fails to rectify the condition causing the injury.

Crumpton v. Humana, Inc.

(*Injured Hospital Patient*) v. (*Hospital's Insurance Co.*)

99 N.M. 562, 661 P.2d 54 (1983)

THE STATUTE OF LIMITATIONS COMMENCES RUNNING FROM THE DATE OF INJURY, AND IS NOT TOLLED DURING SETTLEMENT NEGOTIATIONS

■ **INSTANT FACTS** A woman was injured when her nurse improperly attempted to lower her hospital bed after surgery.

■ **BLACK LETTER RULE** The statute of imitations commences running from the date of injury, and there is no authority to suggest that the statute of limitations should be tolled during the time when the parties were negotiating a settlement.

■ **PROCEDURAL BASIS**

Appeal from the trial court's grant of summary judgment in favor of the defendant.

■ **FACTS**

On February 8, 1979, Wanda Crumpton (P) underwent surgery at a Medical Center. Three days later, when a nurse attempted to lower her hospital bed, she alleged that she sustained injuries to her neck and legs. Her suit was filed more than three years later [oops!] on February 15, 1982. The trial court granted a motion for summary judgment on the ground that the suit was barred by the three year statute of limitations.

■ **ISSUE**

Is a statute of limitations tolled during a time of negotiations between the parties?

■ **DECISION AND RATIONALE**

(H. Vern Payne, C.J.) No. Crumpton (P) argues that her injury was not ascertainable until some time after the accident occurred [delayed reaction?]. Further, she contends that the statute of limitations should have been tolled during the time the parties were negotiating. These arguments are entirely without merit. Crumpton (P) plainly testified in her deposition that her injuries occurred on February 11, 1979. She also testified that the problems she continues to have are attributable to the February 11, 1979 accident. In our view, the fact that she had continuing treatments and hospitalizations after the injury does not necessarily make the date of the injury unascertainable. The statute of limitations commences running from the date of injury. Crumpton (P) cites no authority for her argument that the statute should be tolled during the time the parties were negotiating a settlement. Humana (D) did not fraudulently lead Crumpton (P) to believe that the case would be settled at some future date; in fact, in May, 1981, Humana (D) sent Crumpton a letter making a final offer for a compromise settlement of the case. Accordingly, we affirm the trial court's grant of summary judgment against Crumpton (P). Because we determine this appeal to be frivolous and entirely without merit, costs and attorneys fees are to be borne by Crumpton (P) [take that!].

Analysis:

Statutes of limitation are not limited to torts cases. Almost every type of claim must be brought within a period of time specified by the applicable statute of limitations. Otherwise legitimate claims are barred by the statute if not brought within the required time period. The time limit imposed may vary depending upon the tort, and once the action is properly brought, the statute of limitations has no other function. It merely requires commencement of the action within a certain period of time; it does not impose requirements on the actual commencement of the trial. The cause of action generally accrues when an injury results in cases of negligence, thus the statute of limitations was properly deemed to have begun to "run" at the time Crumpton (P) was injured.

■ CASE VOCABULARY

DEPOSITION: A pre-trial witness statement made under oath taken in question and answer form.

FRIVOLOUS APPEAL: Clearly lacking in substance, and insufficient as a matter of law.

MERITLESS ARGUMENT: No validity or credibility of a cause.

STATUTE OF LIMITATIONS: A statutorily set period of time beyond which an action may not be brought.

TOLL: To stop the running of the statute of limitations.

Schiele v. Hobart Corp.

(Injured Worker) v. *(Machine Manufacturer)*
284 Or. 483, 587 P.2d 1010 (1978)

THE STATUTE OF LIMITATIONS BEGINS TO RUN WITH THE PLAINTIFF'S ASSOCIATION OF SYMPTOMS WITH A SERIOUS OR PERMANENT CONDITION POSSIBLY INDUCED BY THE DEFENDANT

■ **INSTANT FACTS** Schiele (P), a meat wrapper, developed serious lung problems allegedly from using Hobart Corp.'s (D) machine in the course of her employment.

■ **BLACK LETTER RULE** The statute of limitations begins to run when a reasonably prudent person associates his symptoms with a serious or permanent condition and at the same time perceives the role which the defendant has played in inducing that condition.

■ **PROCEDURAL BASIS**

Appeal from the trial court's grant of summary judgment in favor of the defendant.

■ **FACTS**

Schiele (P) worked as a meat wrapper at Fred Meyer [any relation to Oscar?] from 1948 through March of 1974. In May or June of 1972, Fred Meyer purchased and installed Hobart Corp.'s (D) meat wrapping machine. The machine used a hot wire to cut the polyvinyl chloride meat wrapping film. In December 1972, Schiele (P) began using the machine during a considerable part of her work day. Prior to this time, Schiele (P) had been in good health. Soon after beginning the use of the machine, she began to experience a variety of health problems such as nausea, dizziness, choking, coughing, and difficulty catching her breath. Almost from the outset, Schiele (P) associated these problems with the fumes which the machine generated as its hot wire cut the polyvinyl chloride meat wrapping film. Over time, Schiele's (P) condition worsened. While at work she experienced coughing spells six to eight times a day which forced her to walk outside to get air. She complained to her employer's manager but nothing was done. Schiele's (P) condition continued to deteriorate, and she began to experience fatigue, shortness of breath, and a burning sensation in her eyes, in addition to the symptoms previously described. To facilitate breathing at night, Schiele (P) elevated her head with two or three pillows. In January of 1974, Schiele (P) noted that her lungs were more sore than usual. During the latter part of January and the first part of February 1974, the pain became almost constant, and on March 12, 1974, Schiele (P) left her job. Almost immediately thereafter she was hospitalized for pulmonary pneumonia. After testing and x-rays, Schiele's (P) doctors informed her on or about April 15, 1974, that her illness was possibly due to her exposure to polyvinyl chloride fumes on the job. Schiele (P) filed her complaint in this action on March 8, 1976, and the trial court gave summary judgment for Hobart Corp. (D) on the ground that the two-year statute of limitations had run.

■ **ISSUE**

Is Schiele's (P) cause of action time barred because the statute of limitations began to run more than two years earlier, when she first became aware of her symptoms and their cause?

■ **DECISION AND RATIONALE**

(Holman, J.) No. Schiele (P) contends that the statute of limitations did not begin to run until she was informed by a physician of the nature of her disease or injury and its possible cause. Since this did not occur until April of 1974 she argues that her March 8, 1976 filing fell within the limitation period. Hobart (D) argues that the limitation period began to run when Schiele (P) first became aware of her symptoms and their cause. Since she first associated her symptoms with the fumes prior to March 8, 1974, Hobart (D) believes the two-year limitation period had expired by the time Schiele (P) initiated her action. The statute of limitations begins to run when a reasonably prudent person associates his symptoms with a serious or permanent condition and at the same time perceives the role which the defendant has played in inducing that condition. Of course, one's condition may deteriorate to the point where a delay in seeking medical attention is no longer reasonable and to further such delay would be to charge the individual with any knowledge which a medical examination would otherwise have disclosed. If knowledge of the occupational disease, its symptoms, and its causes is widespread among persons similarly situated to Schiele (P), then we hold that Schiele (P), as a reasonable person, should have recognized her condition for what it was and brought the action within the applicable period of limitation following the onset of the symptoms. However, Hobart (D) has made no showing that there was any prevalent knowledge concerning the dangers of the fumes from polyvinyl chloride. This is an extremely close case, but we believe we cannot say as a matter of law that a reasonably prudent person would have apprehended more than two years prior to the commencement of Schiele's (P) action that she was being seriously or permanently injured. Many persons would probably have realized the seriousness of their condition and have gone to a doctor with the same degree of alacrity. We cannot, therefore, say as a matter of law that anyone who is optimistic about his condition's taking a turn for the better is unreasonable. The trial court's grant of summary judgment is reversed and the case is remanded for trial.

Analysis:

This case stands for the proposition that the statute of limitations on claims involving negligent infliction of an occupational disease does not begin to run until the plaintiff knows, or as a reasonably prudent person should know, that he has the condition for which his action is brought and that the defendant has caused it. Schiele's (P) actionable condition in this case is alleged to be her permanent injuries. However, it still remains to be determined exactly what type of knowledge she must have before it should be said that she knew or should have known of her condition. Schiele (P) argued that the statute of limitations did not begin to run until her physician diagnosed her disease and identified its source. The Court agreed that the acquisition of such information from a physician would undoubtedly start the period running. However, the Court correctly rejected Schiele's (P) contention that nothing short of a positive diagnosis by a physician will have this effect. A plaintiff whose condition has not yet been diagnosed by a physician can have or, in the exercise of reasonable care, could have access to information which requires or would require a reasonable person to conclude she is being seriously or permanently injured. On the other hand, the Court also correctly rejected Hobart's (D) claim that knowledge of symptoms and their causal relationship to Hobart's (D) actions in and of itself initiates the running of the statute. It is simply not believable that the legislature intended that the statute be applied in a manner which would require one to file an action for temporary sickness or discomfort or risk the loss of a right of action for permanent injury.

■ CASE VOCABULARY

ACTIONABLE: Wrongful conduct which may form the basis of a cause of action.

Doe v. Maskell

(Sexually Abused Girls) v. *(School Chaplain)*

342 Md. 684, 679 A.2d 1087 (1996)

THE TWO PROCESSES OF REPRESSION AND FORGETTING ARE INDISTINGUISHABLE SCIENTIFICALLY, THUS IT FOLLOWS THAT THEY SHOULD BE TREATED THE SAME LEGALLY

■ **INSTANT FACTS** Two girls sued a priest from their high school after they recovered repressed memories of his sexually abusing them when they were students twenty years earlier.

■ **BLACK LETTER RULE** The mental process of repression of memories of past sexual abuse does not activate the discovery rule to lost memory cases such as to toll the running of the statute of limitations.

■ **PROCEDURAL BASIS**

Appeal from the trial judge's grant of summary judgment for the defendant.

■ **FACTS**

Jane Roe and Jane Doe (P) were high school students at a parochial school. Both girls were individually referred for counseling to the school chaplain, Father Maskell (D). Maskell (D) subjected the girls to repeated sexual, physical, and psychological abuse. Both girls were allegedly threatened with extreme punishments if they informed anyone of the abuse, which continued until the girls graduated and left the high school. At some point, both of the girls claim they ceased to recall the abuse suffered at the hands of Father Maskell (D), due to repression. Both plaintiffs began to recover their memories of this abuse nearly twenty years later. Roe and Doe (P) sued Father Maskell (D), various superiors, a doctor, and the school. On the basis of the three year statute of limitations, the trial judge gave summary judgment for Maskell (D).

■ **ISSUE**

Does the mental process of repression of memories of past sexual abuse activate the discovery rule to lost memory cases such as to toll the running of the statute of limitations?

■ **DECISION AND RATIONALE**

(Karwacki, J.) No. Because we are evaluating the grant of summary judgment, all factual inferences must be resolved in the non-moving party's favor. Thus we must accept that the repression occurred in a serial fashion. Alternatively, however, if the repression happened in a collective fashion, after the girls (P) achieved majority, and the girls (P) were under no disability, the statute of limitations immediately begins to run. Under traditional Maryland law, once the statute of limitations begins to run against a plaintiff, ordinarily no subsequent event will arrest it. Therefore, if Roe or Doe (P) had not yet repressed the memories of the sexual assault by Maskell (D) by even the day after their attaining majority, the statute of limitations barred these claims three years after their eighteenth birthdays. We find that the critical question to the determination of the applicability of the discovery rule to lost memory cases is whether there is a difference between forgetting and repression. It is crystal clear that in a suit in which a plaintiff forgot and later remembered, the existence of a cause of action beyond the three-year limitations period, that suit would be time-barred. Roe and Doe (P), however, claim that in order to avoid the pain associated with recalling the abuse they suffered, their memories were "repressed," not merely "forgotten," and later "recovered," rather than "remembered." They argue that this difference renders them blamelessly ignorant and excuses their failure to file suit in a timely manner. We have reviewed the expert testimony provided at the summary judgment hearing, and reviewed numerous scientific journals submitted by the parties. As a result, we are unconvinced that repression exists as a phenomenon separate and apart from the normal process of forgetting. Because we find these two processes to be indistinguishable scientifically, it follows that they should be treated the same legally. Therefore we hold that the mental process of repression of memories of past sexual abuse does not activate the discovery rule to lost memory cases such as to toll the running of the statute of limitations. The suits are thus barred by the statute of limitations and the judgment of the trial court is affirmed.

Analysis:

Strict application of the statute of limitations can be especially harsh in certain cases where the plaintiff justifiably failed to discover that he even had a cause of action until after the limitation period had expired. In response to this problem, courts, and sometimes legislatures, have created a discovery rule whereby the statute is tolled and does not commence to run until the plaintiff discovers (or by the exercise of reasonable care should have discovered) that (1) he is injured, and (2) the injury is the result of someone's tortious conduct. This discovery rule was first applied in medical malpractice cases, and is often extended to others such as product liability and other professional negligence cases. Whether the plaintiff meets the requirements for the discovery rule is normally a question of fact for the jury. Additionally, a statute of limitations normally does not begin to run if the plaintiff is a minor or person under some other legal disability when the cause of action accrues. It commences when the plaintiff is no longer under any disability. That is why the Court spoke of the statute of limitations expiring three years after the girls (P) reached the age of eighteen. As to the Court's refusal to recognize a difference between "repression" and mere "forgetting," the Court was more persuaded by the extensive arguments discrediting the concept of repression.

■ CASE VOCABULARY

ACHIEVED MAJORITY: Having reached the age of eighteen.

COLLECTIVE REPRESSION: The distressing memories are all repressed until some time later, after the abuse stopped.

NON-MOVING PARTY: The party to the lawsuit who did not bring the motion.

REPRESSION: An involuntary, selective storing of painful memories in the unconscious.

SERIAL REPRESSION: The distressing memories are repressed immediately following each separate event.

Hoery v. United States

(*Landowner*) v. (*Federal Government*)
64 P.3d 214 (Colo.2003)

THE DUMPING OF TOXIC CHEMICALS IS A CONTINUING TORT

Don't worry, we stopped dumping the toxic chemicals a long time ago.

■ **INSTANT FACTS** Hoery (P) sued the United States (D) for groundwater contamination caused by the defendant's dumping of toxic chemicals.

■ **BLACK LETTER RULE** If a tort is permanent, the claim accrues when the plaintiff learned or should have learned of the injury, but if the tort is continuing, the claim continues to accrue as long as the defendant fails to rectify the condition causing the injury.

■ **PROCEDURAL BASIS**

Consideration of a certified question from the Tenth Circuit Court of Appeals.

■ **FACTS**

In 1993, Hoery (P) purchased a property in Colorado with a groundwater well located near the Lowry Air Force Base. The United States (D) had been using the base to dump toxic substances, which migrated under Hoery's (P) property even after the United States (D) ceased dumping in 1994. When Hoery (P) brought suit in federal district court in 1998, the court dismissed the complaint on the basis of the statute of limitations. On appeal, the Tenth Circuit certified a question to the Colorado Supreme Court.

■ **ISSUE**

Is contamination from the dumping of toxic chemicals a continuing tort, so that a new cause of action arises each day the condition persists?

■ **DECISION AND RATIONALE**

(Bender, J.) Yes. "If the tort was 'permanent' the claim accrues when the plaintiff learned or should have learned of the injury, but if the tort is 'continuing' the claim continues to accrue." Generally, when a trespass or nuisance is committed it is complete and the statute of limitation begins to run. When the trespass involves something placed on or beneath a plaintiff's property, however, the invasion continues if the defendant fails to stop the invasion and remove the harmful condition, thus constituting a continuing tort. When the tort is continuing, each subsequent invasion constitutes a new tort and a new cause of action is created, renewing the statute of limitations each time until the conduct ceases. Here, the seepage from the base constitutes a continuing tort. Unlike irrigation ditches, which are enterprises vital to the development of the state, the contamination is not permanent and can be abated. Nor is the contamination vital to the development of the state such that public policy can support the Government's (D) actions as a permanent invasion. "Under Colorado law, a tortfeasor's liability for continuing trespass and nuisance creates a new cause of action each day the property invasion continues."

Analysis:

In the context of toxic torts, the continuing tort doctrine encourages one who contaminates to cease the contamination upon discovery. If the continual contamination of groundwater or land were treated as a permanent property invasion, once the statute of limitations had run on a claim for trespass, the defendant would be exposed to no liability and would have no incentive to cease further contamination.

Clearly, public policy encourages remedial action to abate contamination of the country's land and groundwater.

■ CASE VOCABULARY

STATUTE OF LIMITATIONS: A statute establishing a time limit for suing in a civil case, based on the date when the claim accrued (as when the injury occurred or was discovered).

CERTIFIED QUESTION: A point of law on which a federal appellate court seeks guidance from either the U.S. Supreme Court or the highest state court by the procedure of certification.

DISCOVERY RULE: The rule that a limitations period does not begin to run until the plaintiff discovers (or reasonably should have discovered) the injury giving rise to the claim.

CHAPTER TWELVE

Carriers, Host–Drivers and Landowners

Gladon v. Greater Cleveland Regional Transit Authority

Instant Facts: A man sued a transit authority for negligence for failing to exercise care when the train ran him over after he was forced onto the tracks by his assailants.

Black Letter Rule: Once an invitee goes outside the area of invitation, his status becomes one of a licensee or trespasser, depending on the circumstances.

Bennett v. Stanley

Instant Facts: Bennett's (P) wife and son drowned when the son was playing with frogs near Stanley's (D) unenclosed pool.

Black Letter Rule: Under the attractive-nuisance doctrine, a landowner is liable for injuries to an unknowing child trespasser caused by an artificial condition if (1) the landowner knows or has reason to know that children are likely to trespass on his land and that the condition is reasonably likely to cause injury or death to child trespassers, (2) the child trespasser does not discover or appreciate the danger of the condition, (3) the landowner's burden of safeguarding the condition is not outweighed by the degree of risk to the child, and (4) the landowner fails to reasonably eliminate the danger.

O'Sullivan v. Shaw

Instant Facts: Plaintiff sued after suffering an injury when he dove into the shallow end of defendants' swimming pool.

Black Letter Rule: The statutory abolition of the assumption of risk defense did not implicitly abolish the defense that a landowner has no duty to warn of an open and obvious danger.

Minnich v. Med–Waste, Inc.

Instant Facts: Minnich (P) was injured on the job while attempting to stop a truck from rolling into a public street.

Black Letter Rule: The firefighter's rule bars tort recovery by a firefighter or police officer for on-the-job injuries sustained during the discharge of his or her duties.

Rowland v. Christian

Instant Facts: A guest in an apartment sued his host after the guest sliced his hand on a broken faucet.

Black Letter Rule: A landowner owes a duty of reasonable care to all who enter upon his land.

Pagelsdorf v. Safeco Insurance Co. of America

Instant Facts: A tenant's guest sued the owner of the building after the guest fell off the second story balcony due to a faulty railing.

Black Letter Rule: A landlord is under a duty to exercise ordinary care in the maintenance of the premises.

Gladon v. Greater Cleveland Regional Transit Authority

(Injured Passenger) v. *(Metro Operator)*

75 Ohio St.3d 312, 662 N.E.2d 287 (1996)

THE STATUS OF THE PERSON WHO ENTERS UPON THE LAND DEFINES THE SCOPE OF THE DUTY THAT THE LANDOWNER OWES TO THE ENTRANT

■ **INSTANT FACTS** A man sued a transit authority for negligence for failing to exercise care when the train ran him over after he was forced onto the tracks by his assailants.

■ **BLACK LETTER RULE** Once an invitee goes outside the area of invitation, his status becomes one of a licensee or trespasser, depending on the circumstances.

■ **PROCEDURAL BASIS**

Appeal challenging the trial court's instruction to the jury that the plaintiff was an invitee as a matter of law, and the trial court's denial of the defendant's motion for a directed verdict.

■ **FACTS**

After mistakenly exiting a Greater Cleveland Regional Transit Authority (RTA) (D) at the wrong station, Robert Gladon (P) was assaulted on the platform, ending up on the train tracks either by force or in an effort to evade his assailants. While Gladon (P) lay on the tracks, an RTA (D) train approached the station. Mary Bell (D), the train's operator, first observed a tennis shoe and then Gladon's (P) leg on the tracks. Bell (D) pulled the control handle and then hit the emergency brake. Gladon (P) sued RTA (D) and Bell (D) alleging negligence in operation of the train; specifically, that Bell (D) negligently failed to bring the train to a stop after the point she perceived or should have perceived Gladon's (D) peril. The trial court overruled RTA's (D) motion for a directed verdict. The court also instructed the jury that Gladon was an invitee as a matter of law, which required RTA (D) to use ordinary care to discover and to avoid danger.

■ **ISSUE**

Is the status of an invitee absolute?

■ **DECISION AND RATIONALE**

(Cook, J.) No. Once an invitee goes outside the area of invitation, his status becomes one of a licensee or trespasser, depending on the circumstances. If he goes outside the area with consent, he becomes an invitee, otherwise he becomes a trespasser for purposes of determining the liability of the landowner. RTA's (D) invitation to Gladon (P) did not extend to the area on or around the tracks, as evidenced by the rule disallowing the public in that very area. Although Gladon (P) argues that he retained his status as an invitee because he did not intentionally enter the restricted area, the Restatement holds that the manner of entry is immaterial, unless entry is privileged. We find it unnecessary to decide whether Gladon (P) became a trespasser or licensee upon entering the tracks because each is owed an identical duty - to refrain from willful, wanton, or reckless conduct which is likely to harm the entrant. There is no duty to anticipate or prevent the presence of licensees or trespassers. However, when a trespasser or licensee is discovered in a position of peril, the landowner is required to use ordinary care to avoid injuring him. This duty arises only after the landowner knows or should know of the licensee or trespasser's presence. Accordingly, we remand for a new trial. Furthermore, we find that, because reasonable minds could differ on the issues of wanton and willful conduct and failure to use reasonable care, the trial court did not err in refusing to direct a verdict. Reversed and remanded.

Analysis:

This case serves to illustrate the somewhat archaic common law rules with regard to a landowner's duty of care toward those who enter upon his land. Under those rules, a landowner's liability was based on the status of the entrant as either an invitee, a licensee, or a trespasser. Essentially, an invitee is a person that is on the land for the benefit of the landowner, or on premises generally held open for the public. The greatest duty of care is owed to invitees, often owed an affirmative duty by the landowner. Licensees include all those who had consent to be on the land, but did not qualify as an invitee. A trespasser is, of course, a person whose entrance was not consented to or unprivileged. Lesser duties of care are owed to both licensees and trespassers. The issue in this case was whether Gladon (P), who held the status of an invitee as a train passenger, lost that status by reason of ending up on the train tracks after his assault. The court notes that an entrant's status as an invitee is subject to change when he ventures away from the area he is entitled to be in. Relying on the Restatement Second of Torts, the court refuses to modify this rule when the invitee ventures off through no fault of his own, in this case by reason of an assault. In such a case the invitee becomes either a licensee or a trespasser, a distinction which was of no import in this case because under Ohio law licensees and trespassers were owed the same duty. As a licensee or trespasser, Gladon (P) was owed only a duty of reasonable care when Bell (D) became aware or should have become aware of the situation. The issue of reasonableness being one for the jury, the court remanded for a new trial.

Bennett v. Stanley

(Father) v. *(Pool Owner)*

92 Ohio St.3d 35, 748 N.E.2d 41 (2001)

THE ATTRACTIVE–NUISANCE DOCTRINE REQUIRES A HIGHER DUTY OF CARE TO CHILD TRESPASSERS

It's great to get rid of this disgusting old fence. It's such an unattractive nuisance.

■ **INSTANT FACTS** Bennett's (P) wife and son drowned when the son was playing with frogs near Stanley's (D) unenclosed pool.

■ **BLACK LETTER RULE** Under the attractive-nuisance doctrine, a landowner is liable for injuries to an unknowing child trespasser caused by an artificial condition if (1) the landowner knows or has reason to know that children are likely to trespass on his land and that the condition is reasonably likely to cause injury or death to child trespassers, (2) the child trespasser does not discover or appreciate the danger of the condition, (3) the landowner's burden of safeguarding the condition is not outweighed by the degree of risk to the child, and (4) the landowner fails to reasonably eliminate the danger.

■ PROCEDURAL BASIS

On appeal to review a decision of the Ohio Court of Appeals affirming summary judgment for the defendant.

■ FACTS

Stanley (D) purchased a home with a swimming pool that had not been used by the previous owners. The pool was enclosed by a fence and a brick wall and covered with a tarp. After moving in, Stanley (D) drained the pool and removed the tarp and fencing around the pool. Over time, the pool filled with rainwater and became pond-like, containing frogs and snakes. Thereafter, Bennett (P) and his family moved in next door. Between Stanley's (D) property and Bennett's (P) property was a fence with an eight-foot gap. Stanley (D) was aware that Bennett (P) had young children, but, having no concern that children would get into the pool, never posted any warnings. One day, Bennett's (P) young son was playing by Stanley's (D) pool and fell in. Attempting to save the child, Bennett's (P) wife drowned, along with the son. Bennett (P) sued Stanley (D) for negligence, arguing that the pool created an unreasonable risk of harm to his children, who could not realize the danger. The court granted summary judgment to Stanley (D), finding that the child was a trespasser to whom Stanley (D) owed only a duty "to refrain from wanton and wilful conduct." On appeal, the Ohio Court of Appeals affirmed.

■ ISSUE

Is a landowner liable for injuries caused by artificial conditions on his land that present a foreseeable risk of danger to unknowing child trespassers?

■ DECISION AND RATIONALE

(Pfeifer, J.) Yes. While ordinarily a landowner owes a trespasser only a duty to refrain from wanton and wilful conduct, children have a special status in tort law. Because of their youth and inexperience, children are owed a higher duty of care to protect them from dangers they may be unable to appreciate. Ohio law has long recognized the dangerous instrumentality exception to a landowner's duty to trespassers, by which the landowner is under a higher duty to a child trespasser when he actively and negligently operates hazardous machinery or other apparatus, the danger of which may not be apparent to a child. The Restatement (Second) of Torts § 339 offers a similar doctrine. Under this attractive-nuisance doctrine, a landowner is liable for injuries to a child trespasser caused by an artificial condition if (1) the landowner knows or has reason to know that children are likely to trespass on his land and that the condition is reasonably likely to cause injury or death to child trespassers, (2) the child trespasser does not discover or appreciate the danger of the condition, (3) the landowner's burden of safeguarding the condition is not outweighed by the degree of risk to the child, and (4) the landowner fails to reasonably eliminate the danger.

The court adopts the attractive-nuisance doctrine. In so doing, the differences between a duty owed by a landowner to different classes of land users are not abandoned, but rather the special duty owed to children is recognized when the condition presents a foreseeable and unreasonable risk of danger or serious bodily harm to children. The doctrine does not automatically impose liability whenever children are injured or killed on another's land, but simply requires a landowner to act with ordinary care to remove any foreseeable dangers on his land to which unknowing children may foreseeably be exposed. By adopting the attractive-nuisance doctrine, a plaintiff need only allege negligence rather than wanton and wilful conduct to establish a cause of action. Reversed and remanded.

Analysis:

Despite the attractive-nuisance doctrine, the outcome of the case may have been different had Stanley (D) taken precautions in advance of the accident to protect children from the pool. Had Stanley (D) maintained the fencing around the pool and repaired the gap in the fence between the neighboring properties, it would be arguable that children's presence on his property was not foreseeable and that he had reasonably eliminated any danger to children. By failing to take such precautions, however, Stanley (D) breached his duty under the attractive-nuisance doctrine.

■ CASE VOCABULARY

ATTRACTIVE–NUISANCE DOCTRINE: The rule that a person who owns property on which there is a dangerous thing or condition that will foreseeably lure children to trespass is under a duty to protect those children from the danger.

DANGEROUS INSTRUMENTALITY: An instrument, substance, or condition so inherently dangerous that it may cause serious bodily injury or death without human use or interference.

TRESPASSER: One who commits a trespass; one who intentionally and without consent or privilege enters another's property.

O'Sullivan v. Shaw

(Injured Swimmer) v. *(Pool Owner)*
431 Mass. 201, 726 N.E.2d 951 (2000)

THE "OPEN AND OBVIOUS DANGER" RULE IS NOT BASED ON ASSUMPTION OF RISK, RATHER, IT CONCERNS THE EXISTENCE OF THE DEFENDANT'S DUTY OF CARE

■ **INSTANT FACTS** Plaintiff sued after suffering an injury when he dove into the shallow end of defendants' swimming pool.

■ **BLACK LETTER RULE** The statutory abolition of the assumption of risk defense did not implicitly abolish the defense that a landowner has no duty to warn of an open and obvious danger.

■ **PROCEDURAL BASIS**

Appeal to the Massachusetts Supreme Court, challenging the trial court's grant of summary judgment to defendants.

■ **FACTS**

Joseph O'Sullivan (P) sued Norman Shaw (D) after O'Sullivan (P) sustained injuries as a result of diving into the shallow end of Shaw's (D) swimming pool. The trial court granted summary judgment to Shaw (D) on the ground that the danger was open and obvious. O'Sullivan (P) appealed on the ground that the open and obvious rule was implicitly abolished by the statute that expressly abolished the assumption of risk defense.

■ **ISSUE**

Did the legislature's abolition of the assumption of risk defense implicitly abolish the open and obvious danger rule?

■ **DECISION AND RATIONALE**

(Lynch, J.) No. The statutory abolition of the assumption of risk defense did not implicitly abolish the defense that a landowner has no duty to warn of an open and obvious danger. The open and obvious danger rule holds that where a danger would be obvious to a person of ordinary perception and judgment, a landowner may reasonably assume that a visitor has knowledge of it, and therefore, any further warning is unnecessary to reduce the risk of harm. O'Sullivan (P) argues that this rule was implicitly abolished by the comparative negligence statute, which expressly abolishes the assumption of risk defense. We reject this argument. The assumption of risk was an affirmative defense that focused on the plaintiff's own carelessness and negligence. The open and obvious rule, however, is a defense in connection with the defendant's duty to protect others from dangerous conditions which the defendant is aware of or should be aware of. Thus, the open an obvious rule concerns the duty owed to the plaintiff by the defendant, whereas the assumption of risk defense goes to the plaintiff's failure to exercise due care for his own safety. Therefore, because each rule is based on different policy considerations, we find that the express abolition of one could not imply the rejection of the other. Affirmed.

Analysis:

With the coming of comparative fault systems courts found it necessary to define the theory behind the open an obvious rule. In this case, the Massachusetts Court adopts the mainstream position that the open and obvious rule is a "no duty" rule. In other words, because the danger is readily apparent, the landowner owes the entrant no duty to warn. In contrast to the Massachusetts Court, those courts that see the issue as one of contributory negligence or assumed risk have rejected the open and obvious rule under a comparative fault scheme. Some courts have espoused an intermediate position, arguing that the rule is not one of duty or contributory negligence, but rather goes to the defendant's negligence. Under this theory, the argument is that the landowner owes the entrant a duty of care, but because the danger is open and obvious, it is not foreseeable that harm will occur. The intermediate position seems to allow the jury to hear some cases where, although the danger is open and obvious, it is still foreseeable that someone will be harmed.

Minnich v. Med–Waste, Inc.

(Public Safety Officer) v. *(Medical Waste Hauler)*
319 S.C. 567, 564 S.E.2d 98 (2002)

THE SOUTH CAROLINA SUPREME COURT REFUSES TO ADOPT THE FIREFIGHTER'S RULE

■ **INSTANT FACTS** Minnich (P) was injured on the job while attempting to stop a truck from rolling into a public street.

■ **BLACK LETTER RULE** The firefighter's rule bars tort recovery by a firefighter or police officer for on-the-job injuries sustained during the discharge of his or her duties.

■ **PROCEDURAL BASIS**

Consideration of a certified question from a federal district court.

■ **FACTS**

Minnich (P) was working as a public safety officer for the Medical University of South Carolina when he was called upon to assist in loading medical waste onto a truck owned by Med–Waste, Inc. (D). When the truck began to roll toward a public street, Minnich (P) ran to the truck and stopped it. In the process, Minnich (P) suffered injuries allegedly due to the acts and omissions of the defendant's employees. Minnich (P) sued Med–Waste (D) in federal court. The defendants contended that Minnich's (P) claims were barred by the firefighter's rule, which precludes firefighters and certain other public employees from recovering against a negligent defendant for injuries sustained in the course of their employment. The federal court certified to the South Carolina Supreme Court the question of the application of the firefighter's rule to emergency professionals.

■ **ISSUE**

Does the firefighter's rule bar an emergency professional's claim for injuries sustained in the course of his duties as a result of a defendant's negligence?

■ **DECISION AND RATIONALE**

(Pleicones, J.) No. Historically, the firefighter's rule was adopted to bar a firefighter's claims for injuries sustained while controlling a fire that was caused by a homeowner's negligence. The firefighter's rule has been justified by firefighters' and police officers' assumption of the known and inherent risks associated with their duties. Public policy also supports the firefighter's rule, in that any on-the-job injuries are compensable by workers' compensation, and firefighters and police officers often enter private property unannounced such that the level of care owed to invitees or licensees would be unreasonable.

Across the country, states vary on the proper application of the firefighter's rule. Some courts permit recovery for injuries caused by a defendant's wanton and wilful conduct resulting in the injuries, while others permit recovery for negligence unrelated to the specific reason the firefighter was originally called to the scene. Some states have enacted legislation to abolish the firefighter's rule altogether. South Carolina has never recognized the firefighter's rule in any situation, much less applied it to emergency professionals. South Carolina tort law adequately addresses negligence claims brought against third parties arising out of the discharge of a firefighter's duties, and it applies equally to other emergency professionals.

Analysis:

In theory, the firefighter's rule is largely based on public policy. Because firefighters and police officers have a duty to protect the public from danger, often placing themselves in harm's way to save others, it would be inequitable to permit such public servants to recover for injuries sustained while knowingly performing their duties. In some circumstances, the threat of civil liability may even prompt individuals not to seek needed assistance.

Rowland v. Christian

(Injured Guest) v. *(Homeowner)*
69 Cal.2d 108, 70 Cal.Rptr. 97, 443 P.2d 561 (1968)

A LANDOWNER OWES A GENERAL DUTY OF CARE TO ALL THOSE WHO ENTER UPON HIS LAND

■ **INSTANT FACTS** A guest in an apartment sued his host after the guest sliced his hand on a broken faucet.

■ **BLACK LETTER RULE** A landowner owes a duty of reasonable care to all who enter upon his land.

■ **PROCEDURAL BASIS**

Appeal from the trial court's grant of summary judgment for the defendant.

■ **FACTS**

James Rowland (P), a social guest at Nancy Christian's (D) apartment, severed his hand on the porcelain handle of a bathroom faucet. Christian (D) knew the faucet was broken, but failed to warn Rowland (P).

■ **ISSUE**

Does liability for negligence of a possessor of land depend on whether the plaintiff is classified as a trespasser, licensee or invitee?

■ **DECISION AND RATIONALE**

(Peters, J.) No. A landowner owes a duty of reasonable care to all who enter upon his land. With regard to the liability of a possessor of land for injuries to persons who have entered upon that land, courts have often departed from the fundamental rule of liability for negligence by classifying the plaintiff as a trespasser, licensee or invitee, and then adopting special rules as to the duty owed to each. Whatever the their historical justifications, these distinctions are not justified in light of our modem society. Although the rules are simple, complexity and confusion have been caused by attempts to apply this ancient terminology in our modern society. The classifications, with their corresponding immunities and exceptions, are often irrelevant to the factors that determine liability. These factors include the connection between the defendant's conduct and the injury, the defendant's culpability, the policy of preventing future harm, and the availability of insurance. A man's life or limb does not become less worthy under the law simply because he has come upon land without permission, or with permission but no business purpose. Reasonable people do not ordinarily vary their conduct upon such matters. The common law rules obscure rather than illuminate the proper considerations which should be govern the question of duty. Reversed.

■ **DISSENT**

(Burke, J.) I find that the common law rules supply a workable approach to the problems involved, one which provides the degree of stability and predictability so highly prized in the law. The majority's approach has left the question to a case by case analysis, with no principles to guide.

Analysis:

With this case, the activist California Supreme Court of the 1960s was the first to abolish the common law categories upon which landowner liability was based. At the time this case was decided, in most jurisdictions, the trial court would have found for Rowland (P) on the ground that his status as a licensee required Christian (D) to warn him of all concealed dangers, the broken faucet being one such danger. Under the rules in place in California, however, a licensee was owed the same duty as a trespasser—to refrain from wanton and willful injury. Thus, the question came before the court: Should premises liability be based on common law distinctions? The court here answers no, basing its decision on modern social mores and humanitarian values, and the fact that the distinctions between trespassers, licensees and invitees is often arbitrary. In place of these distinctions, the court lists several factors which should determine liability, such as foreseeability, the connection between the injury and the defendant's conduct, and the availability of insurance.

Pagelsdorf v. Safeco Insurance Co. of America

(Injured Tenant Guest) v. *(Landlord's Insurer)*

91 Wis.2d 734, 284 N.W.2d 55 (1979)

ALTHOUGH THE COMMON LAW RELIEVES LANDLORDS FROM LIABILITY FOR INJURIES TO HIS TENANTS AND THEIR VISITORS RESULTING FROM DEFECTS IN THE PREMISES, THE MODERN TREND IS TO APPLY GENERAL PRINCIPLES OF NEGLIGENCE

■ **INSTANT FACTS** A tenant's guest sued the owner of the building after the guest fell off the second story balcony due to a faulty railing.

■ **BLACK LETTER RULE** A landlord is under a duty to exercise ordinary care in the maintenance of the premises.

■ **PROCEDURAL BASIS**

Not provided.

■ **FACTS**

While James Pagelsdorf (P) was helping the Blattners move from their home in a two-story duplex, he fell off the second-story balcony after the railing gave way. Pagelsdorf (P) sued Mahnke (D), the owner of the duplex. An inspection showed that the wood which formed the railing suffered from dry rot, a defect that was not apparent to the eye. Although Mahnke (D) had contracted to keep the premises in repair, that duty was limited to known or reported defects.

■ **ISSUE**

Is a landlord liable for injuries suffered by tenants and their guests as a result of the landlord's negligence in keeping the premises in disrepair?

■ **DECISION AND RATIONALE**

(Callow, J.) Yes. A landlord is under a duty to exercise ordinary care in the maintenance of the premises. Under the traditional rule, a landlord is not liable for injuries to his tenants and their visitors resulting from defects in the premises. This rule is based on the notion that a lease is a conveyance of property under which the landlord transfers possession and control of the premises. There are, however, exceptions to the rule of nonliability. A landlord is liable if he contracts to repair defects, or if knowing of a defect at the time of the lease, the landlord conceals it from a tenant who could not reasonably be expected to discover it. There are further exceptions where the premises are leased for public use, or are retained by the landlord, or where the landlord negligently makes repairs. It does not appear as if any of these exceptions are applicable in this case. Under the traditional rule, Mahnke (D) would be held not liable as a matter of law. But we reject this approach, and instead adopt a rule requiring a landlord to exercise ordinary care in the maintenance of the premises. Reversed.

Analysis:

This case illustrates just one avenue courts have taken to avoid applying the common law rule that relieved landlords from liability for injuries that occur on the premises while the tenant is in possession.

The court here simply imposes upon landlords a duty to exercise reasonable care to the tenant and his guests. The opinion, however, discusses some of the traditional exceptions to the general rule of nonliability. Take a second look at these exceptions, for they have enlarged to the point of swallowing the "rule." In addition, some courts have imposed an implied warranty of habitability, which requires a landlord to keep the premises in certain conditions. However, these implied warranties usually form the basis of actions for breach of contract, not actions in tort. Legislatures have also added to the mix by enacting statutes that impose certain affirmative duties on landlords. In total, the rule of nonliability still remains, but the exceptions have become so numerous that it would be a mistake to term it the "general" rule of nonliability.

CHAPTER THIRTEEN

Duties of Medical and Other Professionals

Walski v. Tiesenga

Instant Facts: A patient who suffered vocal paralysis during surgery sought to establish the negligence of her surgeon through the use of an expert's testimony, the thrust of which was that the expert would have performed the surgery differently.

Black Letter Rule: It is insufficient for a plaintiff to establish a prima facie case of medical malpractice merely to present testimony of another physician that he would have acted differently from the defendant.

Vergara v. Doan

Instant Facts: The parents of a newborn injured during delivery sued the small town doctor who performed the delivery, claiming that he failed to meet the medical standard of care.

Black Letter Rule: A physician must exercise that degree of care, skill, and proficiency exercised by reasonably careful, skillful, and prudent practitioners in the same class to which he belongs, acting under the same or similar circumstances.

Velazquez v. Jiminez

Instant Facts: Velazquez (P) sued Drs. Jiminez (D) and Ranzini (D) when her baby was delivered with severe brain damage and ultimately died.

Black Letter Rule: Good Samaritan immunity encompasses only those situations in which a physician (or other volunteer) comes, by chance, upon a victim who requires immediate emergency medical care, at a location lacking adequate facilities, equipment, expertise, sanitation, and staff.

Smith v. Knowles

Instant Facts: The husband of a woman who died of from complications from pregnancy sued the woman's doctor for failure to diagnose the woman's condition and failure to treat it properly.

Black Letter Rule: Where in a medical malpractice case against a physician there is a lack of sufficient expert testimony to show that the doctor departed from the proper standard of care or that his action or inaction was a direct cause of the injury, a jury should not be allowed to speculate.

States v. Lourdes Hospital

Instant Facts: While undergoing surgery for the removal of an ovarian cyst, States' (P) arm was injured, allegedly due to Lourdes Hospital's (D) negligence in administering anesthesia.

Black Letter Rule: The doctrine of res ipsa loquitur permits a factfinder to find negligence simply from the fact that an injury occurred, when the injury is of a kind that ordinarily does not occur absent negligence.

Ybarra v. Spangard

Instant Facts: A patient that suffered minor paralysis during an appendectomy sought to recover against every doctor and nurse in whose care he was placed during the surgery, arguing that the doctrine of res ipsa loquitur allowed an inference against of negligence against each defendant.

Black Letter Rule: Where a plaintiff receives unusual injuries while unconscious and in the course of medical treatment, the doctrine of res ipsa loquitur may be used to infer negligent conduct on the part of all those defendants that had control over him or the instrumentalities which might have caused the injuries.

Harnish v. Children's Hospital Medical Center

Instant Facts: After undergoing a procedure that resulted in the total loss of tongue function, a patient sued her doctor and the hospital for negligently failing to inform her before surgery of the risk of loss of tongue function.

Black Letter Rule: A physician owes to his patient the duty to disclose in a reasonable manner all significant medical information that the physician possesses or reasonably should possess that is material to an intelligent decision by the patient whether to undergo a proposed procedure.

Arrington v. Wong

Instant Facts: After receiving a call from emergency personnel announcing its imminent arrival, Wong (D) redirected an ambulance to a different hospital.

Black Letter Rule: Under the Emergency Medical Treatment and Active Labor Act, a hospital may not divert a patient en route to the hospital for emergency medical care unless it is in diversionary status.

Horizon/CMS Healthcare Corp. v. Auld

Instant Facts: The administratrix of nursing home's former patient brought suit against the home, claiming that the decedent was subjected to negligent medical care.

Black Letter Rule: Investigation reports written by state officials may be used as evidence of a defendant's subjective knowledge of the peril his conduct creates.

Walski v. Tiesenga

(Injured Patient) v. *(Surgeon)*

72 Ill.2d 249, 21 Ill.Dec. 201, 381 N.E.2d 279 (1978)

ONE ELEMENT OF A CAUSE OF ACTION FOR MEDICAL MALPRACTICE IS PROOF OF THE STANDARD OF CARE, ESTABLISHED THROUGH EXPERT TESTIMONY, BY WHICH THE DEFENDANT PHYSICIAN'S CONDUCT IS TO BE MEASURED

■ **INSTANT FACTS** A patient who suffered vocal paralysis during surgery sought to establish the negligence of her surgeon through the use of an expert's testimony, the thrust of which was that the expert would have performed the surgery differently.

■ **BLACK LETTER RULE** It is insufficient for a plaintiff to establish a prima facie case of medical malpractice merely to present testimony of another physician that he would have acted differently from the defendant.

■ **PROCEDURAL BASIS**

Appeal to the Illinois Supreme Court, challenging the decision of the appellate court affirming the directed verdict issue by the trial court in favor of the defendant.

■ **FACTS**

Dr. Marvin Tiensenga (D) operated to perform a thyroidectomy on Ms. Harriet Walski (P). The procedure carried with it the risk of damaging the laryngeal nerves, resulting in a loss of voice. Although Dr. Teinsenga (D) made a cut wide enough to avoid the area where the nerves were thought to be, he in fact severed the nerves, paralyzing Ms. Walski's (P) vocal chords. As part of her case against Dr. Tiensenga (D), Ms. Walski (P) offered expert testimony from Dr. Berger, who stated that he was taught to perform, and would have in fact performed the surgery in a different manner than that chosen by Dr. Tiensenga (D). When confronted with a quotation from a medical textbook that indicated there existed a certain amount of controversy concerning the procedures available, Dr. Berger testified that he did not agree. At the conclusion of the trial, the court directed a verdict for Dr. Tiensenga (D). The appellate court affirmed.

■ **ISSUE**

May a plaintiff establish a prima facie case of medical malpractice merely by offering testimony from an expert who states that he would have acted differently?

■ **DECISION AND RATIONALE**

(Kluczynski, J.) No. It is insufficient for a plaintiff to establish a prima facie case of medical malpractice merely to present testimony of another physician that he would have acted differently from the defendant. A plaintiff in a cause of action for medical malpractice must first establish, through expert testimony, the standard of care owed by the defendant doctor. Once the standard has been established, the plaintiff must prove that the defendant doctor departed from that standard. Ms Walski (P) has failed to establish the proper standard of care. Dr. Berger testified only concerning his own personal preference in performing a thyroidectomy. He in no way testified that such a preference was the generally accepted medical standard of care. In contrast, Dr. Tiensenga (D) testified that although a medical treatise advised using a different procedure, his course of action was based on the fact that Ms. Walski (P) had previous surgeries which necessitated a departure from the procedure indicated in the treatise. Differences in opinions are consistent with the exercise of due care. Affirmed.

Analysis:

In any negligence action, a plaintiff must establish that the defendant owed him some duty of care. In the context of medical malpractice, the duty owed to a patient is expressed as the "standard of care." A physician normally must possess the skill and ability of other physicians. Exactly what that skill entails must be established by expert testimony. In this case the court holds that Dr. Berger's testimony did not establish the standard of care, but rather merely expressed his opinion. This court held, as have most courts, that a mere disagreement with the defendant's conduct does not establish the standard of care. There is a subtle difference between an expert's opinion on what constitutes the standard of care, and his opinion on what should have been done. To illustrate, notice the difference between what Dr. Bereger testified and what courts generally require. In effect, Dr. Berger's testimony can be summarized in one sentence: "I would have done things differently." But what courts require is a statement to the effect of, "under the established medical practice, things should have been done differently." The difference between these two hypothetical statements is the focus of the court's opinion. The expert's opinion should go to the standard of care, not necessarily the care he would provide.

Vergara v. Doan

(Parent's of Injured Newborn) v. *(Doctor)*
593 N.E.2d 185 (Ind.1992)

THE STANDARD OF CARE OWED BY A PHYSICIAN DOES NOT NECESSARILY DEPEND ON THE SIZE OF THE COMMUNITY THE PHYSICIAN PRACTICES IN

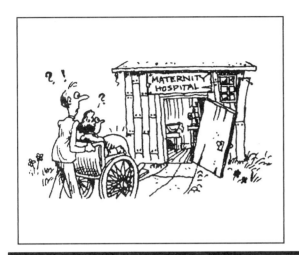

■ **INSTANT FACTS** The parents of a newborn injured during delivery sued the small town doctor who performed the delivery, claiming that he failed to meet the medical standard of care.

■ **BLACK LETTER RULE** A physician must exercise that degree of care, skill, and proficiency exercised by reasonably careful, skillful, and prudent practitioners in the same class to which he belongs, acting under the same or similar circumstances.

■ **PROCEDURAL BASIS**

Appeal to the Supreme Court of Indiana, challenging the decision of the Court of Appeals affirming the jury verdict in favor of the defendant.

■ **FACTS**

During birth, Javier Vergara (P) suffered severe and permanent injuries. His parents sued Dr. John Doan (D), the doctor who delivered Javier (P), for medical malpractice. At trial, Dr. Doan's (D) conduct was measured against the standard of care given in similar localities. The jury found for Dr. Doan (D), and the Court of Appeals affirmed.

■ **ISSUE**

Is the standard of care owed by a doctor to a patient dependent on the locality where the medical services are rendered?

■ **DECISION AND RATIONALE**

(Shepard, C.J.) No. A physician must exercise that degree of care, skill, and proficiency exercised by reasonably careful, skillful, and prudent practitioners in the same class to which he belongs, acting under the same or similar circumstances. The strict locality rule measured a doctor's conduct against that of other doctors in the same community. Under modified locality rule, heretofore adhered to by this Court, the standard of care was that degree of care, skill, and proficiency which is commonly exercised by ordinarily careful, skillful, and prudent physicians, at the time of the operation and in similar localities. We believe the modified rule is no longer applicable in today's society. The reasons for the locality rule, in either of its forms, was that there was a great disparity between rural and urban areas with respect to medical opportunities, equipment, facilities, and training. Travel and communication were also difficult. Thus the locality rule was intended to prevent the inequity that would result from holding rural doctors to the same standard as doctors in large cities. However, with advances in communication, travel, and medical education, those disparities have significantly diminished. Moreover, the modified locality rule has a major drawback. It permits a lower standard of care to be exercised in smaller communities because other communities are likely to have the same care. Under the rule we adopt today, locality is only one factor to be considered in determining whether a doctor acted reasonably. Other factors include advances in the profession, availability of facilities, and

---

whether the doctor is a specialist or general practitioner. Applied to the present case, we find that the new rule would not have changed the way the case was tried. The Vergaras (P) medical expert, a doctor from Pittsburgh, offered testimony that the standard of care in small communities required Dr. Doan (D) to perform a cesarean section, and required the presence of a anesthesiologist, or like professional. Evidently the jury disagreed and found Dr. Doan's (D) conduct reasonable. Affirmed.

Analysis:

This case illustrates the trend to move away from locality rules that measure the standard of care with reference to the geographical community. As the court points out, the rationale for the locality rule was that doctors in small town communities might not have the latest equipment, facilities, or training. This justification is questionable at best. A doctor who lacks the necessary equipment or facilities need only refer the patient elsewhere. Furthermore, the availability of equipment, facilities and training is no reason to lower the standard of care. Instead, because a doctor's negligence is always judged in the particular circumstances, these factors should be used to determined whether the doctor departed from the standard. Regardless, the locality rule persisted for years. But with today's advances in transportation, communications and medical training, the rule has become difficult to justify. The rule adopted by this court alleviates the locality rule's major drawback: doctors in small communities are given an incentive to refrain from becoming acquainted with the latest medical techniques if they are held to the standards of similar communities. Nevertheless, the court's disposition of the case is not entirely reasonable. The court notes that the application of the modified locality rule did not prejudice the Vergara's (P). It reasoned that, because the Vergara's (P) expert, a doctor from a big city, testified that the standards of the smaller community required Dr. Doan (D) to perform a cesarean section, the verdict merely reflected the jury's disagreement with the Vergara's (P) expert. But it is just as reasonable to think that the verdict reflected the jury's opinion that Dr. Doan (D), being an urban doctor, was unfamiliar with the standards of a small community. If that indeed was the case, then the Vergara's (P) were prejudiced by the application of the modified locality rule, because the standards of a small community are irrelevant under the generally applicable standard adopted by the court.

Velazquez v. Jiminez

(Mother) v. *(Doctor)*

172 N.J. 240, 798 A.2d 51 (2002)

GOOD SAMARITAN IMMUNITY DOES NOT APPLY TO PHYSICIANS PROVIDING EMERGENCY CARE IN A HOSPITAL

■ **INSTANT FACTS** Velazquez (P) sued Drs. Jiminez (D) and Ranzini (D) when her baby was delivered with severe brain damage and ultimately died.

■ **BLACK LETTER RULE** Good Samaritan immunity encompasses only those situations in which a physician (or other volunteer) comes, by chance, upon a victim who requires immediate emergency medical care, at a location lacking adequate facilities, equipment, expertise, sanitation, and staff.

■ PROCEDURAL BASIS

On appeal to review a jury verdict against the defendant.

■ FACTS

During delivery of Velazquez's (P) baby, Dr. Jiminez (D) encountered complications that threatened the baby's life. After delivering the baby's head, Jiminez (D) was unable to complete the delivery because the baby's shoulders had become lodged against Velazquez's (P) pubic bone. He requested the assistance of Dr. Ranzini (D), who had not previously treated Velazquez (P). After attempting to delivery the baby naturally, Ranzini (D) prepared Velazquez (P) and the baby for a Caesarian section delivery. The baby was born with severe brain damage due to a lack of oxygen. The baby died of pneumonia before reaching his third birthday. Velazquez (P) sued Jimenez (D) and Ranzini (D) for medical malpractice. A jury returned a verdict for the plaintiff and apportioned three percent of the liability to Ranzini (D). Ranzini appealed, claiming immunity under the New Jersey Good Samaritan Act.

■ ISSUE

Is a physician with no prior duty to a patient immune from liability under the Good Samaritan Act for malpractice committed in a hospital setting?

■ DECISION AND RATIONALE

(Long, J.) No. New Jersey's Good Samaritan Act provides that any person with specialized medical training who in good faith renders emergency care "at the scene of an accident or emergency" is not liable for any damages resulting from any acts or omissions while rendering such emergency care. Good Samaritan laws encourage those qualified to assist others in emergency situations to do so without threat of liability. Every state has enacted Good Samaritan laws in some form. Some states immunize physicians from liability for care rendered within a medical facility, while others afford immunity only when the care is rendered without the equipment and environment required to afford reasonably competent medical care. In New Jersey, the statute does not establish which version applies.

When construing an immunity statute, the court must do so narrowly to avoid substantial restrictions on a plaintiff's right to recover for injuries she has sustained. While the legislature did not define whether the "scene of an accident or emergency" exists within the hospital setting, a narrow reading of the statute demonstrates a legislative intent to limit immunity to those settings outside a medical facility. If the legislature had intended to afford immunity regardless of the setting, it could have done so. This narrow reading harmonizes an injured plaintiff's right of recovery with the goal of encouraging medical assistance to those in settings in which they may be unlikely to receive necessary medical care. When a patient is submitted to a hospital, she is there for the purpose of receiving medical care and would ordinarily not be deprived of needed care without Good Samaritan immunity. Good Samaritan immunity is not created because the physician had no prior duty to the patient, but rather by the existing circumstances that may otherwise result in a lack of medical care. Accordingly, "Good Samaritan immunity ... encompasses only those situations in which a physician (or other volunteer) comes, by chance, upon a victim who requires immediate emergency medical care, at a location compromised by lack of adequate facilities, equipment, expertise, sanitation and staff." Importantly, however, the lack of Good Samaritan immunity does not establish a physician's liability, for the plaintiff must still demonstrate the physician's breach of the standard of care under the emergency circumstances to establish liability. Affirmed.

Analysis:

Good Samaritan Acts have been enacted in many jurisdictions to encourage those who can assist others in danger to do so. At common law, there is no legal duty to rescue or aid another in danger. The common law rule has been changed by statute in some states to require those persons who come upon another in danger to provide any reasonable assistance under the circumstances. Without immunity, persons who come upon an emergency situation place themselves at risk of liability if they voluntarily offer assistance.

■ CASE VOCABULARY

RESCUE: The act or an instance of saving or freeing another from danger or captivity.

GOOD SAMARITAN LAW: A statute that exempts from liability a person (such as an off-duty physician) who voluntarily renders aid to another in imminent danger but negligently causes injury while rendering the aid.

IMMUNITY: Any exemption from a duty, liability, or service of process; especially, such an exemption granted to a public official.

Smith v. Knowles

(Trustee for the Heirs of Deceased Patients) v. *(Doctor)*

281 N.W.2d 653 (Minn.1979)

A PLAINTIFF IN A CAUSE OF ACTION FOR MEDICAL MALPRACTICE MUST ESTABLISH BY EXPERT TESTIMONY THAT THE DEFENDANT DEPARTED FROM THE STANDARD OF CARE AND THAT THE DEPARTURE CAUSED THE PLAINTIFF'S INJURY

■ **INSTANT FACTS** The husband of a woman who died of from complications from pregnancy sued the woman's doctor for failure to diagnose the woman's condition and failure to treat it properly.

■ **BLACK LETTER RULE** Where in a medical malpractice case against a physician there is a lack of sufficient expert testimony to show that the doctor departed from the proper standard of care or that his action or inaction was a direct cause of the injury, a jury should not be allowed to speculate.

■ **PROCEDURAL BASIS**

Appeal to the Supreme Court of Minnesota, challenging the decision of the trial court to dismiss the plaintiff's action on the ground that there lacked sufficient expert evidence for the jury to consider the claim of negligence.

■ **FACTS**

Dr. Knowles (D) was a general practitioner caring for Diane Smith, Clinton Smith's (P) pregnant wife. Diane Smith and her unborn child died as a result of eclampsia, a serious complication of pregnancy. In the weeks preceding her death, Diane Smith complained of nausea, blurred vision, headaches, and other symptoms of pre-eclampsia. As a result of his examination of Mrs. Smith, Dr. Knowles (D) discovered that there were no danger signals and that blood pressure and urine were normal. The week before her death, Diane Smith awoke sick and went to Dr. Knowles' (D) office. His examination there revealed that she had pre-eclampsia, and he admitted her to the hospital. Due to some confusion, Mrs. Smith did not receive the necessary medication until 4 hours after her admittance to the hospital. Later that evening, Mrs. Smith lost consciousness and her child was delivered stillborn. A week later Mrs. Smith died. In his cause of action, Mr. Smith (P) offered no independent expert medical testimony. Instead, he chose to prove his case through his cross-examination of Dr. Knowles (D) and the use of several medical treatises. The trail court reviewed the evidence and found it insufficient.

■ **ISSUE**

May a plaintiff establish a prima facie case of medical malpractice without expert testimony by using medical treatises?

■ **DECISION AND RATIONALE**

(Scott, J.) No. Where in a medical malpractice case against a physician there is a lack of sufficient expert testimony to show that the doctor departed from the proper standard of care or that his action or inaction was a direct cause of the injury, a jury should not be allowed to speculate. Expert testimony is necessary to establish the standard of care, and the defendant's departure therefrom. Expert testimony must also establish that the defendant's negligence caused the plaintiff's injury. Mr. Smith's (P) evidence was, at best, minimally sufficient to establish the requisite standard of care. No expert testimony was offered showing that Dr. Knowles (D) departed from that standard. Even more troubling was the lack of any expert testimony as to causation. Affirmed.

Analysis:

As was seen in *Walski v. Tiensenga* [Illinois Supreme Court holds that a doctor's opinion regarding what he would have done is insufficient to establish the standard of medical care] expert testimony is essential to a plaintiff's cause of action for medical malpractice. Not only must it be used to establish the standard of care, but expert testimony must also establish that the doctor failed to meet that standard and that his negligence caused the injury. In essence, expert medical testimony must establish all the elements of a prima facie case for medical malpractice, save for damages. In the court's view, Mr. Smith's (P) use of a medical treatise as evidence went only to establishing the standard of care, not the breach of that standard or causation. Mr. Smith's (P) effort to establish his case through the use of a medical treatise brings up one other point. Under the common law, a medical treatise was considered hearsay and could not be used to establish the plaintiff's case. Although this rule is still applicable in some states, the Federal Rules of Evidence, which have been adopted by many states, expressly permit treatises to be admitted into evidence.

States v. Lourdes Hospital

(Patient) v. (Hospital)

100 N.Y.2d 208, 792 N.E.2d 151, 762 N.Y.S.2d 1 (2003)

EXPERT MEDICAL TESTIMONY MAY CLARIFY THE APPLICATION OF RES IPSA LOQUITUR

■ **INSTANT FACTS** While undergoing surgery for the removal of an ovarian cyst, States' (P) arm was injured, allegedly due to Lourdes Hospital's (D) negligence in administering anesthesia.

■ **BLACK LETTER RULE** The doctrine of res ipsa loquitur permits a factfinder to find negligence simply from the fact that an injury occurred, when the injury is of a kind that ordinarily does not occur absent negligence.

■ **PROCEDURAL BASIS**

On appeal to review a decision of the New York Appellate Division reversing a trial court denial of summary judgment.

■ **FACTS**

States (P) successfully underwent surgery at Lourdes Hospital (D) to remove an ovarian cyst. Before the procedure, States' (P) arm was placed on a board, rotated, and connected to an IV tube. States (P) complained of pain and discomfort, but there were no complications during surgery. Upon awakening from anesthesia, States (P) complained of increasing pain in her arm and shoulder. States (P) sued the hospital for medical malpractice. At the close of discovery, the defendant moved for summary judgment based on a lack of direct evidence of negligence by the anesthesiologist. States (P) responded that, despite the absence of direct evidence, expert medical testimony could establish that her injuries would not have occurred absent negligence, thus invoking res ipsa loquitur. The motion for summary judgment was denied, but the New York Appellate Division reversed, holding that the injury was not of the kind that a jury could draw upon its common experience and knowledge to establish an inference of negligence. States (P) appealed.

■ **ISSUE**

May expert medical testimony be introduced to a jury to establish the likelihood that the injury would not have occurred absent negligence?

■ **DECISION AND RATIONALE**

(Ciparick, J.) Yes. When appropriate, the doctrine of res ipsa loquitur permits a factfinder to draw an inference of negligence by the fact that an injury occurred. To establish res ipsa loquitor, the plaintiff must prove not only that the injury would not occur absent negligence, but also that the injury was caused by an agent or instrumentality exclusively in the defendant's control and that the plaintiff contributed to the injury in no way. Once these three elements are established, a factfinder may infer the defendant's negligence.

Addressing the first element, the defendant here contends that the jury may only rely on its common everyday experiences to determine whether the injury would occur absent negligence. The plaintiff counters that expert medical testimony may be offered to inform the jury's decision. Restatement of Torts § 328D supports the plaintiff's position. Under the Restatement, the jury may consider the issue

---

through not only its common knowledge, but also through evidence offered by the parties, including expert testimony in matters requiring specialized knowledge. Expert testimony reliably establishes the probability that negligence occurred to the same extent that layperson knowledge establishes matters of common understanding. Expert testimony is offered for the purpose of educating and assisting the jury, but the ultimate inference must be drawn by the jury on the basis of its understanding of the case. The burden remains on the plaintiff to establish the elements of res ipsa loquitur and prove the defendant's liability, albeit by reasonable inference. Because the plaintiff is free to offer expert medical testimony in support of its theory, summary judgment was appropriately denied. Reversed.

Analysis:

As the case properly reflects, the doctrine of res ipsa loquitur permits an inference that negligence occurred. Many courts, however, state that res ipsa loquitur creates just a presumption of negligence. Courts often mistakenly interchange the inference of negligence and the presumption of negligence, but the distinction is not subtle. With an inference, a jury is permitted to conclude that negligence occurred, while with a presumption, the jury is compelled to find negligence absent rebuttable evidence offered by the defendant.

■ CASE VOCABULARY

INFERENCE: A conclusion reached by considering other facts and deducing a logical consequence from them.

PRESUMPTION: A legal inference or assumption that a fact exists, based on the known or proven existence of some other fact or group of facts. A presumption shifts the burden of production or persuasion to the opposing party, who can then attempt to overcome the presumption.

RES IPSA LOQUITUR: The doctrine providing that, in some circumstances, the mere fact of an accident's occurrence raises an inference of negligence so as to establish a prima facie case.

Ybarra v. Spangard

(*Injured Patient*) v. (*Head Surgeon*)
25 Cal.2d 486, 154 P.2d 687 (1944)

WHEN A MEDICAL PATIENT SUFFERS AN INJURY WHICH COULD NOT HAVE BEEN CAUSED IN THE ABSENCE OF NEGLIGENCE, BUT WHOSE SOURCE THE PLAINTIFF CANNOT IDENTIFY, AN INFERENCE OF NEGLIGENT CONDUCT MAY BE RAISED AGAINST THOSE CAREGIVERS THAT ASSISTED THE PLAINTIFF

■ **INSTANT FACTS** A patient who suffered minor paralysis during an appendectomy sought to recover against every doctor and nurse in whose care he was placed during the surgery, arguing that the doctrine of *res ipsa loquitur* allowed an inference against of negligence against each defendant.

■ **BLACK LETTER RULE** Where a plaintiff receives unusual injuries while unconscious and in the course of medical treatment, the doctrine of *res ipsa loquitur* may be used to infer negligent conduct on the part of all those defendants that had control over him or the instrumentalities which might have caused the injuries.

■ PROCEDURAL BASIS

Appeal to the Supreme Court of California, challenging the trial court's decision to enter a judgment of nonsuit as to all the defendants.

■ FACTS

Mr. Ybarra (P) was diagnosed with appendicitis by his physician, Dr. Tilley (D), who recommended that he undergo an appendectomy. The surgery was to be performed by Dr. Spangard (D) at a hospital owned and managed by Dr. Swift (D). After Ybarra (P) was wheeled into the operating room by Nurse Gisler (D), Dr. Resser (D), the anesthetist, pulled him toward the head of the operating table, laying him against two hard objects at the top of his shoulders. Shortly thereafter, the surgery was performed, with Ybarra remaining unconscious throughout the procedure. When he awoke, Ybarra, who was being attended in his room by Nurse Thompson (D), complained of a pain between his neck and shoulder. Dr. Tilley (D) gave him appropriate treatment, but the pain persisted. Ybarra (P) eventually developed paralysis and atrophy of the muscles around the shoulder. The medical evidence established that the injury was caused by some trauma, pressure or strain applied between the shoulder and neck. Ybarra (P) sued every doctor and nurse in whose care he was placed, seeking a *res ipsa loquitor* instruction against each. The trial court entered a judgment of nonsuit as to all the defendants.

■ ISSUE

May an inference of negligence be raised against those defendants that had control over a medical patient who suffered unusual injuries during his care?

■ DECISION AND RATIONALE

(Gibson, C.J.) Yes. Where a plaintiff receives unusual injuries while unconscious and in the course of medical treatment, the doctrine of *res ipsa loquitur* may be used to infer negligent conduct on the part of all those defendants that had control over him or the instrumentalities which might have caused the injuries. The present case is one that comes within the reason and spirit of the doctrine of *res ipsa loquitur* perhaps more than any other. It is difficult to see why the doctrine should not apply to a patient, who submits himself to the care and custody of doctors and nurses, is rendered unconscious, and receives an injury from instrumentalities used in his treatment. An opposite rule would restrict a patient who suffered severe injuries from recovering for negligent treatment unless the doctors and nurses volunteered to disclose the identity of the negligent person. It is argued that the doctrine is inapplicable in this case because Ybarra has failed to show which instrumentality caused his injury and which defendant has exclusive control over that instrumentality. First, we believe that, in order to meet the instrumentality requirement, it should be enough that Ybarra (P) can show an injury resulting from an external force applied when he lay unconscious in the hospital. This rule is consistent with those cases that have created an exception to the instrumentality requirement when strict application would defeat the policies behind the doctrine. As to the issue of control, considering that Ybarra (P) was rendered unconscious by Spangard (D) and the others, it is manifestly unreasonable for them to insist that Ybarra (P) identify the person who committed the negligent act. The burden lies upon the defendants to make an initial explanation. It is also argued that the doctrine, if applicable, cannot be applied to all the defendants, for it is unreasonable to believe that each committed the negligent act which caused Ybarra's (P) injury. But every defendant in whose custody the plaintiff was placed for any period was bound to exercise ordinary care to see that no unnecessary harm came to him and each would be liable for failure in this regard. Reversed.

Analysis:

Although disguised as an expansion of the doctrine of *res ipsa loquitur*, this case is really about expanding the duty of care owed to patients, an expansion bordering on strict liability. The doctrine *of res ipsa loquitur* concerns a rational inference of negligence from the facts; but the issue here was not about whether the defendants were negligent, but rather which defendant was negligent. Evidenced by the fact that the court did not suggest that the facts supported a conclusion that the injury would not have occurred in the absence of negligence, a finding that is essential to the application of the doctrine, it is reasonable to say that the court tackled the case by addressing the wrong issue. Instead, the court focused on the duty owed to patients and the patient's lack of information. The court essentially holds each defendant hostage with the threat of liability, until one comes forward with the necessary information. This rule could be justified on the ground that the caregivers are in the best position to provide the necessary information, assuming every caregiver has knowledge of the incident.

Harnish v. Children's Hospital Medical Center

(*Injured Patient*) v. (*Hospital*)
387 Mass. 152, 439 N.E.2d 240 (1982)

DOCTORS OWE THEIR PATIENT A DUTY TO DISCLOSE MATERIAL INFORMATION THAT IS RELEVANT TO THE PATIENT'S DECISION TO UNDERGO TREATMENT

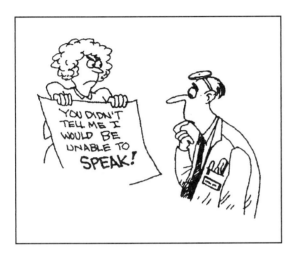

■ **INSTANT FACTS** After undergoing a procedure that resulted in the total loss of tongue function, a patient sued her doctor and the hospital for negligently failing to inform her before surgery of the risk of loss of tongue function.

■ **BLACK LETTER RULE** A physician owes to his patient the duty to disclose in a reasonable manner all significant medical information that the physician possesses or reasonably should possess that is material to an intelligent decision by the patient whether to undergo a proposed procedure.

■ **PROCEDURAL BASIS**

Appeal to the Massachusetts Supreme Court, challenging the decision of the trial court dismissing the action on the grounds of inadequate proof.

■ **FACTS**

Ms. Harnish (P) underwent an operation to remove a tumor in her neck. During the operation, a nerve was severed, causing a permanent and total loss of tongue function. Harnish (P) sued her doctor and the Children's Hospital Medical Center (Hospital) (D) on the ground that they neglected to inform her of the risk of loss of tongue function, which she alleged was a foreseeable and material risk of the operation. There is no claim that the surgery was performed negligently. The trail court dismissed the action for a lack of proof.

■ **ISSUE**

Must a doctor disclose the risks of treatment to a patient?

■ **DECISION AND RATIONALE**

(O'Connor, J.) Yes. A physician owes to his patient the duty to disclose in a reasonable manner all significant medical information that the physician possesses or reasonably should posses that is material to an intelligent decision by the patient whether to undergo a proposed procedure. It is well established that every person has a strong interest in being free from nonconsensual invasion of bodily integrity. Courts have protected this interest by requiring a doctor to obtain his patient's consent before giving treatment or performing a procedure. That consent, however, must be informed. Yet there are limits to what a person can expect from his doctor in this regard. The information a physician should posses is that information possessed by the average qualified physician or, in the case of a specialty, by the average qualified specialist. In either case, what the physician should know must ordinarily be proved by expert testimony. The extent to which the physician must share information depends on what information he should reasonably recognize is material to a reasonable patient's decision. Materiality is an issue that lay persons are qualified to judge upon without expert testimony. The types of information a doctor is expected to disclose include the nature of the patient's condition, the benefits to be expected, the inability to predict results, the irreversibility of the procedure, the likely result of no treatment, and the availability of alternatives, including their risks and benefits. A doctor may, in certain circumstances, withhold otherwise material information. Although we do not find it necessary to discuss the contours of the privilege of nondisclosure, we note that a physician may not withhold information simply because he believes the patient would refuse necessary treatment. Finally, turning to the issue of causation, the plaintiff must show that neither she nor a reasonable person in similar circumstances would have undergone the procedure. Reversed in part, and affirmed in part.

Analysis:

A physician's duty to disclose relevant information is based on informed consent, which embodies the idea that individuals have a right to be free from bodily intrusions and that consent is valid only if it is informed. In adopting a cause of action based on a physician's failure to disclose information, the court provides a thorough elucidation on the requirements of such an action. The rule adopted by the court here creates a cause of action with five elements. First, the plaintiff must prove that the physician failed to disclose required information. A doctor is required to disclose information the he should reasonably believe the patient would find material. Some courts have held that what a doctor should reasonably believe must be established by expert testimony. Second, the plaintiff must prove through expert testimony that the physician knew or should have known the undisclosed information. Third, the plaintiff must prove that the undisclosed information would be materially relevant to a reasonable person in deciding whether to undergo treatment. The court provides a laundry list of the kinds of information that must usually be disclosed. With respect to the materiality and relevance of these kinds of information, the court expressly excludes the need for expert testimony, permitting the jury to decide what is and is not reasonably material. Leaving the materiality issue up to the jury recognizes that it is the patient, not the doctor or medical community, that gets to decide whether to undergo the recommended course of treatment. But the test of materiality is an objective one, for the most part. Materiality is to be judged with reference to the "reasonable patient," and not the plaintiff, unless the physician is aware that the plaintiff attached some special importance to a matter. For example, a physician usually will not need to disclose a risk of loss of voice if it has only a one in ten million chance of occurring; but if the physician knows the patient is a professional opera singer, then he may have a duty to disclose that particular minute risk. The fourth element the court discusses is that of causation, which involves an inquiry that is both, subjective and objective. To prove cause in fact, the plaintiff must show, given the undisclosed information, that a reasonable person would not have undergone the treatment in those particular circumstances. The plaintiff must also show that she herself would not have undergone the treatment. The fifth element, not discussed by the court, is proof of damages, which is essential to any cause of action.

Arrington v. Wong

(Decedent's Estate) v. *(Emergency Room Physician)*
237 F.3d 1066 (9th Cir.2001)

THE EMTALA APPLIES TO ALL PERSONS REQUIRING EMERGENCY MEDICAL TREATMENT

■ **INSTANT FACTS** After receiving a call from emergency personnel announcing its imminent arrival, Wong (D) redirected an ambulance to a different hospital.

■ **BLACK LETTER RULE** Under the Emergency Medical Treatment and Active Labor Act, a hospital may not divert a patient en route to the hospital for emergency medical care unless it is in diversionary status.

■ **PROCEDURAL BASIS**

On appeal to review a trial court dismissal of the plaintiff's complaint.

■ **FACTS**

The plaintiff's complaint alleged that while Arrington was being transported to Queen's Medical Center after suffering a heart attack, the emergency personnel radioed ahead to the hospital to advise of their imminent arrival. Wong (D) redirected the ambulance to a different hospital five miles away. Soon after arrival at the hospital, Arrington died. The plaintiffs sued Wong (D) in federal court under the Emergency Medical Treatment and Active Labor Act (EMTALA), which prevents transfers of unstabilized patients who "come to" an emergency room. The district court dismissed the complaint, ruling that the plaintiff had not stated a claim under the EMTALA.

■ **ISSUE**

Did the plaintiff state a claim under the EMTALA based on the defendant's failure to provide emergency treatment to Arrington?

■ **DECISION AND RATIONALE**

(Reinhardt, J.) Yes. The EMTALA was enacted to prevent hospitals from dumping indigent or uninsured patients by refusing to treat them or transferring them to other hospitals before their condition has stabilized. Because the language of the Act is clear, however, it applies to all patients regardless of financial means. The EMTALA clearly forbids the transfer of a patient who "comes to" the hospital before he has been evaluated and his emergency condition stabilized.

Here, Arrington never arrived at the hospital. Because "comes to" may mean either physical arrival at the hospital or moving toward and approaching the hospital, the statute is ambiguous and its meaning must be determined from other sources. The Act authorizes the U.S. Department of Health and Human Services to promulgate regulations to interpret the statute. Under agency regulation, the Department interprets the phrase broadly to include any hospital property on which a patient receives emergency treatment, including ambulances. However, the ambulance in which Arrington was transported was not owned by Queen's Medical Center. Under the regulations, a hospital may redirect such patients if it receives a call from the ambulance personnel informing the hospital of an imminent arrival and it is in "diversionary status," i.e., without the staff or facilities to accept any additional emergency patients. If the ambulance nonetheless arrives at the hospital, the hospital may not then deny emergency treatment. In this case, the defendant has not contended the hospital was in diversionary status. Therefore, it was obliged to treat Arrington until his emergency condition was stabilized. Reversed and remanded.

Analysis:

In one respect, the court's decision seems illogical. On the one hand, if a hospital is in diversionary status and receives a call of arrival from an ambulance, the hospital may divert the patient to another hospital. On the other hand, if the ambulance driver never calls and simply arrives at the hospital, the hospital must treat the patient even if it is in diversionary status. However, if the hospital has enough staff to treat the patient who arrives unannounced, is there any need to be in diversionary status, and why should an announced patient be diverted? Similarly, if the hospital is truly understaffed, how can it properly treat the unannounced patient without sacrificing the wellbeing of others?

Horizon/CMS Healthcare Corp. v. Auld

(*Nursing Home*) v. (*Administratrix of Deceased Patient's Estate*)
985 S.W.2d 216 (Tex.App.1999)

SUBSTANDARD NURSING CARE AND ELDER ABUSE IS AN OFTEN NEGLECTED PROBLEM

■ **INSTANT FACTS** The administratrix of nursing home's former patient brought suit against the home, claiming that the decedent was subjected to negligent medical care.

■ **BLACK LETTER RULE** Investigation reports written by state officials may be used as evidence of a defendant's subjective knowledge of the peril his conduct creates.

■ **PROCEDURAL BASIS**

Appeal from the jury verdict for the plaintiff, claiming that the trial court mistakenly admitted into evidence written investigation reports made by state officials.

■ **FACTS**

From August 1994 to August 1995, Martha Hary was a resident of Heritage Western Hills Nursing Home, which was owned by Horizon/CMS Healthcare Corp. (Horizon) (D). During that year, Martha's body developed pressure sores, some of which rotted her skin to the point of leaving the bone exposed, and suffered contractures in all extremities. Lexa Auld (P), alleged that Ms. Harry's ailments were the result of Heritage's (D) failure to provide her with medical care and treatment within the acceptable standard of care. The evidence showed that Auld had established that the nursing home failed to: (1) regularly turn and reposition Ms. Hary for a total of 1,680 hours; (2) feed Ms. Harry regularly (she missed 238 total meals); (3) provide incontinent care by not keeping Ms. Hary's skin clean and dry for a total of 1,728 hours; and (4) treat Ms. Harry with passive range of motion exercises. Heritage's own records reflected these deficiencies. The evidence also established that these deficiencies were the cause of Ms. Hary's ailments. At trial, the judge admitted into evidence written investigation reports made by the Texas Department of Human Services to determine compliance with state and federal requirements. A jury found for Ms. Auld (P), awarding $2,371,000 in actual damages, and $90,000,000 in punitive damages, an amount later reduced to just under $9.5 million. Horizon appealed on the ground that the surveys did not establish whether Horizon (D) deviated from the proper standard of care.

■ **ISSUE**

Did the court properly admit into evidence investigation reports written by state officials to determine compliance with state and federal requirements?

■ **DECISION AND RATIONALE**

(Holman, J.) Yes. Investigation reports written by state officials may be used as evidence of a defendant's subjective knowledge of the peril his conduct creates. Because gross negligence was an issue at trial, that subjective knowledge was essential to Ms. Auld's case. The information contained in the reports showed that the state did bring the deficient conditions to Horizon's (D) attention. Thus we conclude that the trial court did not abuse its discretion. Affirmed.

Analysis:

The editors have included this case in the material as an example of the abhorrent conditions that exist in nursing homes and with respect to care for the elderly. Studies indicate that much of the elderly abuse occurs at home. The size of the damages awarded are not surprising, considering that nursing care is a highly profitable business, with some corporate enterprises reporting revenues in the billions. This case just might illustrate how nursing homes manage to make that kind of money, i.e., by cutting corners and providing substandard care. But this case is really an anomaly, for most abuse and neglect goes unreported. Moreover, few causes of action are brought because actual damages are limited by the fact that the elderly have short life expectancy, and bed-ridden patients are not exactly deprived of an active life. The fact that the amount of available damages is low in these types of cases means that lawyers are often unwilling to take them on.

CHAPTER FIFTEEN

Governmental Entities and Officers

Loge v. United States

Instant Facts: Mrs. Loge (P) contracted polio from her son who was given live vaccine, and she sued the government (D) for various forms of negligence.

Black Letter Rule: The United States is not immune from liability if it has negligently violated its own regulations pertaining to safety.

Maas v. United States

Instant Facts: Servicemen exposed to radiation sued United States (D) for its failure to inform them post-discharge of scientific report concerning increased risk of cancer.

Black Letter Rule: The discretionary function exception to the FTCA applies to discretionary acts based on considerations of public policy.

Riss v. City of New York

Instant Facts: Riss (P) sued City (D) for negligence due to the police failing to provide protection from attacker who had previously threatened her on numerous occasions.

Black Letter Rule: A municipality is not liable for failure to provide special police protection to a member of the public who was repeatedly threatened with personal harm and eventually suffered injuries for lack of protection.

Harry Stoller and Co., Inc. v. City of Lowell

Instant Facts: Firefighters negligently failed to use sprinkler system to fight fire, relying only on the fire hoses, and Stoller (P) sued City (D) for destruction of buildings and contents.

Black Letter Rule: In order for the discretionary function exception to apply to governmental acts, the conduct must involve making a policy or planning judgment.

Thompson v. County of Alameda

Instant Facts: Family of small child murdered by temporarily released juvenile offender sued County (D) for wrongful death for failure to warn of known threat of killing a child.

Black Letter Rule: A public entity's failure to warn of the release from custody of a dangerous person does not create liability unless an identifiable victim exists which can be effectively warned.

Vaughn v. Ruoff

Instant Facts: The Vaughns (P) sued Ruoff (P) for due process violations after Mrs. Vaughn underwent tubal ligation in reliance upon Ruoff's (P) assurances that they would regain custody of their children if she did so.

Black Letter Rule: Qualified immunity does not attach when the state deprives an individual of a constitutional right that is clearly established at the time of the deprivation.

Navarro v. Block

Instant Facts: Domestic violence victim called 911 to report that estranged husband was in route to her home to kill her, but operator did not dispatch police, and victim was killed.

Black Letter Rule: A municipality may be liable for civil rights violations if there is proof of the existence of a custom or informal policy with repeated constitutional violations for which municipal officials were not discharged or reprimanded, even if the official policy-makers did not have actual knowledge of the custom and practice.

Loge v. United States

(Polio Victim) v. *(United States)*

662 F.2d 1268 (8th Cir.1981)

THE FEDERAL TORT CLAIMS ACT PERMITS GOVERNMENT TORT LIABILITY BUT WITH CERTAIN LIMITATIONS AND EXCEPTIONS

■ **INSTANT FACTS** Mrs. Loge (P) contracted polio from her son who was given live vaccine, and she sued the government (D) for various forms of negligence.

■ **BLACK LETTER RULE** The United States is not immune from liability if it has negligently violated its own regulations pertaining to safety.

■ **PROCEDURAL BASIS**

Appeal from judgment following ruling that the complaint failed to state a claim for negligence seeking damages.

■ **FACTS**

In 1963, the United States government, by the Secretary of HEW, (D) licensed Lederle Laboratories to manufacture a poliovirus vaccine, composed of three strains of live poliovirus. A characteristic of the vaccines was that not only was the recipient of the vaccine immunized from polio, but unimmunized persons who came into close contact with the recipient were also immunized through a shed virus. However, there was a risk that either a recipient or a contact could develop polio. The United States (D) promulgated regulations pertaining to the safety and potency of the strains to protect susceptible persons from contracting the disease. Before a license can be issued, the manufacturer must prove their product conforms to the regulations. Although there was a risk-free alternative to the live vaccine, the Secretary of HEW promoted the use of the risk-bearing live vaccines. [Hope there was a good reason for doing this.] Mrs. Loge (P) was exposed to the shed virus in 1976 after a doctor inoculated her infant son with the live vaccine, and one month later, she was stricken with a form of polio that left her a paraplegic. She sued the United States (D) and unknown employees of the Department of HEW. Loge (P) alleged two categories of negligence: (1) that the government (D) was negligent in not requiring the drug manufacturer to comply with the government's (D) own regulations pertaining to the safety and potency of the strains, and (2) that the government (D) was negligent in licensing at all, or in licensing without additional safety regulations. The district court held that Loges (P) had failed to state a claim under the Federal Tort Claims Act because there were no allegations that a private person would be liable for activity similar to the government's in this case.

■ **ISSUE**

Is the United States immune from liability if it has violated its own regulations pertaining to safety?

■ **DECISION AND RATIONALE**

(Hanson) No. We hold that the United States is not immune from liability where it is alleged that it has violated its own regulations pertaining to safety. The Federal Tort Claims Act does not waive sovereign immunity for any claim based upon the exercise or performance or the failure to exercise or perform a discretionary function or duty on the part of a federal agency or its employee. Thus, there can be no liability for negligent promulgating or failing to promulgate regulations that would ensure the safety of live vaccines. The district court correctly found that such actions were discretionary functions and therefore the government was immune from suit. However, the district court did find that two causes of action were not barred by the discretionary function exception: the negligent failure to require the mandatory tests when the manufacturer was licensed to manufacture the vaccine and the negligent failure to follow mandatory tests when the lot was approved. The Secretary has no discretion to disregard the mandatory regulatory commands pertaining to criteria a vaccine must meet before licensing its manufacture or releasing a particular lot of vaccine for distribution. Nevertheless, the district court ruled against Loges (P) because no circumstances were alleged where the United States (D), if a private person, would be liable. [This is known as a roller coaster ruling.] However, we find that claims have been stated under any of three alternative grounds for liability. It can be said that the United States (D) increased the risk of harm to Loges (P) by licensing an allegedly untested product and by releasing to the public an untested or negligently tested lot of that vaccine. It can also be said that the government (D) undertook a duty owed by the drug manufacturer to the Loges (P) when it required that proof of the drug's safety be demonstrated before releasing it to the public. Finally, it is alleged that Loges (P) relied on the government's (D) use of due care in approving for release the particular vaccine lot that was eventually administered to the child. [Thus, there are three ways for Loges (P) to show that the government screwed up.]

Analysis:

The Federal Tort Claims Act and its various components are examined in this case. The FTCA provides that the United States shall be liable for tort claims in the same manner and to the same extent as a private individual under like circumstances, except for pre-judgment interest and punitive damages. There are certain procedural rules, and a number of statutory exceptions that permit the government to retain immunity. One such immunity is the discretionary immunity. This case considers these issues. The court mentions that the district court ruled against Loges (P) because there was no allegation that private persons would be liable. The modern approach does not compare the factual similarity to private activities, but rather the principle of tort liability applied to private persons will be the determining factor. Thus, if a private person is responsible if he undertakes to make something safe and negligently fails to do so, then so too will the government be responsible. The subject of discretionary immunity is also considered. Under the FTCA, sovereign immunity exists for a claim based upon a discretionary function. Thus, the court upheld the portion of the lower court's ruling that found actions by the government in failing to promulgate safety regulations to be discretionary functions and immune from suit. Therefore, there can be no claim for failure to adopt regulations that would have prevented Loge's (P) injury. Nevertheless, two causes of action were not barred by the discretionary function exception. The government's violation of its own regulation concerning safety was not discretionary and thus was actionable.

■ CASE VOCABULARY

DISCRETIONARY FUNCTION EXCEPTION: An exception to the Federal Tort Claims Act whereby the government is not liable if performance or nonperformance involves a discretionary function or duty on the part of a federal agency or its employee.

FAILED [FAILURE] TO STATE A CLAIM: Motion is brought before judge to have matter dismissed on ground that allegations in complaint are legally insufficient to state a theory of recovery.

SOVEREIGN IMMUNITY: Exempting the ruling body government from lawsuits and liability.

Maas v. United States

(*Radiation Exposed Servicemen*) v. (*United States*)

94 F.3d 291 (7th Cir.1996)

DISCRETIONARY FUNCTION EXCEPTION BARS VETERANS' CLAIM AGAINST GOVERNMENT FOR FAILURE TO INFORM OF INCREASED CANCER RISK

■ **INSTANT FACTS** Servicemen exposed to radiation sued United States (D) for its failure to inform them post-discharge of scientific report concerning increased risk of cancer.

■ **BLACK LETTER RULE** The discretionary function exception to the FTCA applies to discretionary acts based on considerations of public policy.

■ FACTS

In 1968, an Air Force B-52 bomber carrying nuclear weapons crashed in Greenland, scattering radioactive material over the area. The United States Air Force directed the cleanup project. Maas (P) and three other plaintiffs were among the 300 servicemen and civilian workers who worked on the cleanup project. Two of the plaintiffs allege they suffer from cancer and two contend they are sterile because of radiation exposure during the cleanup. The United States government (D) tested the workers for radiation exposure, but the extreme weather conditions may have compromised the results. Tests were also performed for up to three years after the cleanup project ended, but no tests were performed after Maas (P) and the other plaintiffs left the service. Maas (P) and the other plaintiffs allege that the United States government (D) became aware through a scientific study issued in 1980 that participants in the cleanup project had an increased risk of cancer connected with the radiation exposure, but failed to notify the veterans of this new information. Maas (P) and the other plaintiffs sued the United Sates (D) for damages resulting from radiation exposure. The lower court dismissed the claims of negligence preceding the discharge of Maas (P) and the other plaintiffs as well as the post-discharge negligence claims based on the discretionary function exception.

■ ISSUE

Does the discretionary function exception to the FTCA apply to decisions not to warn veterans after their discharge concerning an increased risk of cancer because of their tour of duty?

■ DECISION AND RATIONALE

(Manion) Yes. The discretionary function exception to the FTCA applies to decisions not to warn veterans after their discharge concerning an increased risk of cancer as a result of their tour of duty. The district court held that the discretionary function immunity exception to the FTCA barred the post-discharge negligence claims of failing to warn the servicemen after their discharge of an increased risk of cancer. This exception covers discretionary acts requiring an element of judgment or choice. It is intended to prevent judicial second-guessing of legislative and administrative decisions. The United States (D) argues that the decision to inform, warn or test veterans based on new studies is purely discretionary because it involves judgment and execution. It argues that such a warning would include resource allocation decisions and involve the weighing of evidence, which would be a matter of discretion. To determine whether such an exception exists, we must consider two factors: (1) whether a discretionary act is involved, that is one which involves an element of judgment or choice; and (2) whether that judgment is of the kind that the exception was designed to shield. The exception protects actions and decisions based on considerations of public policy. We hold that the circumstances of this case satisfy both elements. Since there is no statute or regulation that requires the military to alert veterans of new cancer statistics, the decision to warn is the military's. To provide such notice would require resources and assignment of employees, as well as scientific and administrative determinations. Questions would arise as to how many resources, who should be assigned, how much radiation was too much, how much exposure is enough for notice, which veterans were exposed to how much radiation, which were exposed to too much, and how should the notice be phrased. All of these questions require the exercise of judgment and discretion. Moreover, the exercise of discretion involves policy considerations. The government would have to balance the need for warnings, to whom, and the content with economic concerns. [Why should money be a factor under these circumstances?] Thus, such judgments are based on policy considerations. We therefore hold that the discretionary function exception bars the claims. We also affirm the lower court's dismissal of the claim of negligence preceding discharge of Maas (P) and the other plaintiffs.

Analysis:

The discretionary function exception to the FTCA is examined in this case. The court was required to determine if the alleged negligent conduct was discretionary, and if the decision was one involving policy considerations. The discretionary conduct existed because there was no law or rule that instructed the government to alert veterans of new cancer statistics. Accordingly, the decision whether to do so constituted an act of judgment or choice, which equates to discretion. However, there is an additional requirement that the discretionary actions be based on considerations of public policy. In this case, the weighing of the economic factors with the safety and health of the veterans were held to constitute policy considerations. Although not a significant issue in the case, note that the court of appeals acknowledged the lower court's holding that the *Feres* immunity [servicemen's claims barred where injuries received were "incident to service"] would not protect the government from liability for its negligence in failing to warn Maas (P) and the other plaintiffs after their discharge. Nevertheless, the claims were barred based on the discretionary function exception of the FTCA.

Riss v. City of New York

(Victim of Attack) v. *(City)*

22 N.Y.2d 579, 293 N.Y.S.2d 897, 240 N.E.2d 860 (1968)

CITY IS IMMUNE FROM LIABILITY WHERE POLICE OFFICERS FAILED TO PROVIDE PROTECTION

■ **INSTANT FACTS** Riss (P) sued City (D) for negligence due to the police failing to provide protection from attacker who had previously threatened her on numerous occasions.

■ **BLACK LETTER RULE** A municipality is not liable for failure to provide special police protection to a member of the public who was repeatedly threatened with personal harm and eventually suffered injuries for lack of protection.

■ **PROCEDURAL BASIS**

Appeal following dismissal of action after presentation of the evidence in negligence action seeking damages for personal injuries.

■ **FACTS**

Riss (P) sued the City of New York (D) for negligence alleging that the city police failed to provide police protection. Riss (P) had been terrorized for months by a rejected suitor who threatened to kill or maim her. She repeatedly sought protection from the police. Thereafter, she received a phone call warning that it was her "last chance." She again called the police but nothing was done. The next day, the rejected suitor hired someone to throw lye into Riss' (P) face, causing blindness in one eye, loss of a portion of vision in the other eye, and permanent facial scarring. The trial court [recognizing that the law is not always fair] dismissed Riss' (P) complaint at the end of all the evidence and the appellate division affirmed. Riss (P) appealed.

■ **ISSUE**

Is a municipality liable for failure to provide special police protection to a member of the public who was repeatedly threatened with personal harm and eventually suffered injuries for lack of protection?

■ **DECISION AND RATIONALE**

(Breitel) No. The municipality is not liable for failing to provide police protection to a member of the general public. We first must distinguish certain types of governmental activities where liability may be found. Activities that displace or supplement traditionally private enterprises may lead to liability, such as rapid transit systems, hospitals and places of public assembly. Activities that provide services and facilities for the use of the public may also lead to liability, such as highways, public buildings and the like. The basis for liability is that the services or facilities are for the direct use of members of the public. This case involves governmental protection services from external hazards, such as controlling the activities of criminal wrongdoers. [This is certainly an impossible task.] If we were to permit tort liability for those who seek police protection based on specific hazards, it would cause a determination as to how the limited resources of the community should be allocated and without predictable limits. We should not so dictate the allocation of the resources and it should be left to the legislature to make the determination concerning the scope of public responsibility. Imposing liability in such situations will not cure the problem of crime in cities [and would bankrupt the city]. It is not for the courts, in the absence of legislation, to carve out an area of tort liability for police protection to members of the public. This case is distinguishable from the situation where the police authorities undertake responsibilities to particular members of the public and expose them, without adequate protection, to the risks that then materialize into actual losses. Judgment is affirmed.

Analysis:

This case examines immunities under state, as opposed to federal, law. States have adopted various types of statutes, which abolished sovereign immunity. Accordingly, there are many situations whereby a municipality may be liable under principles of ordinary tort law. However, as with the Federal Tort Claims Act, there are exceptions in certain circumstances, which allow the immunity to remain. This case demonstrates that the police are not liable for failing to provide protection to the public, even if they negligently fail to do so. The court's reasoning is that there is no statutory basis that would provide for such liability, and it was unwilling to judicially create such liability. If it were to do so, the court would be directing the municipality where to put its resources. Note that the court's decision also distinguished the situation of the police undertaking responsibility to particular members of the public, which could lead to liability for negligently failing to act. The difference is that a special relationship has developed with a certain member of the public, as distinguished from the public at large.

Harry Stoller and Co., Inc. v. City of Lowell

(Burned Business) v. *(City)*
412 Mass. 139, 587 N.E.2d 780 (1992)

DISCRETIONARY FUNCTION EXCEPTION DOES NOT APPLY WHEN FIREFIGHTERS USE INADEQUATE METHODS TO FIGHT A FIRE

■ **INSTANT FACTS** Firefighters negligently failed to use sprinkler system to fight fire, relying only on the fire hoses, and Stoller (P) sued City (D) for destruction of buildings and contents.

■ **BLACK LETTER RULE** In order for the discretionary function exception to apply to governmental acts, the conduct must involve making a policy or planning judgment.

■ PROCEDURAL BASIS

Appeal from judgment entered notwithstanding the verdict in negligence action seeking damages.

■ FACTS

Harry Stoller and Co., Inc. (Stoller) (P) sued the City of Lowell (City) (D) for the destruction of its buildings and their contents due to fire. The firefighters, in violation of accepted practice, chose not to use the sprinkler system to fight the fire, relying instead on the fire hoses. [Bad choice.] The jury awarded damages to Stoller (P) but the trial judge granted judgment notwithstanding the verdict for City (D) under the state's statutory discretionary immunity. Stoller (P) appeals contending that the decision by the firefighters to not use the sprinkler system was not a discretionary act involving making a policy or planning judgment.

■ ISSUE

Does the discretionary function exception require that the conduct involve making a policy or planning judgment?

■ DECISION AND RATIONALE

(Wilkins) Yes. In order for the discretionary function exception to apply to governmental acts, the conduct must involve making a policy or planning judgment. In the past, we have declined to apply the discretionary function exception to various governmental acts. Examples include a police officer deciding whether to remove an intoxicated driver from the road, a city physician treating a patient in the emergency room, and failing to provide adequate information to allow the protection of one's property from a client of the mental health department. These acts do not involve discretionary functions that amount to making a policy or planning judgment. With respect to firefighting, certain conduct does have a planning or policy basis. Determining the number and location of fire stations, the amount of equipment to buy, the size of the department, the number and location of hydrants, and the quantity of water supply involve policy considerations, especially the allocation of financial resources. The conduct involved in this case however is different. The negligence of the firefighters in choosing not to use the sprinkler system did not involve planning or policy considerations. Although it may have been discretionary to choose whether to put water through the sprinkler system or through hoses, it was not based on a policy or planning judgment. Thus, the discretionary functions exception does not shield the City (D) from liability. [If it did, everything would be considered discretionary and municipalities would always win.] Reversed.

Analysis:

Recall that if the government acts in a discretionary manner, it will generally be immune from liability. This case concerns the discretionary function exemption as applied to municipalities. It clarifies that in order for the discretionary function exception to apply, the conduct must involve policymaking or planning judgment. The court of appeal held that the conduct did not rise to the level of discretionary function involving policy making or judgment and thus the City (D) could be held liable. Note that the firefighters, in responding to the fire, used inadequate methods to fight the fire. If the fire department had failed to respond to the call, liability may not have resulted. Recall that in *Riss v. City of New York*, the City was not liable for the police refusing to provide protection to a member of the general public. The court in this case concluded that the firefighters exercised discretion in choosing not to use the sprinklers, but such discretion did not involve a choice regarding public policy and planning. Finally, as with the exceptions to the Federal Tort Claims Act, some states have statutes that prevent municipalities from being liable for acts that are discretionary in nature. The state of Massachusetts had such a statute and the court was required to interpret if the conduct involved was "discretionary" within the meaning of the statute.

■ CASE VOCABULARY

JUDGMENT N.O.V.: Latin initials for judgment non obstante veredicto; otherwise known as judgment notwithstanding the verdict, obtained through a motion made post verdict to have judgment rendered in favor of one party notwithstanding a verdict in favor of the other party.

Thompson v. County of Alameda

(*Murdered Child's Family*) v. (*County*)
27 Cal.3d 741, 167 Cal.Rptr. 70, 614 P.2d 728 (1980)

SPECIFIC IMMUNITY STATUTE PROHIBITING LIABILITY FOR RELEASE FROM CUSTODY OF DANGEROUS PERSONS IS NOT A DEFENSE TO FAILURE TO WARN AN IDENTIFIABLE VICTIM WHO IS AT RISK OF A SPECIFIC THREAT OF PERIL

■ **INSTANT FACTS** Family of small child murdered by temporarily released juvenile offender sued County (D) for wrongful death for failure to warn of known threat of killing a child.

■ **BLACK LETTER RULE** A public entity's failure to warn of the release from custody of a dangerous person does not create liability unless an identifiable victim exists which can be effectively warned.

■ PROCEDURAL BASIS

Appeal from judgment dismissing action after sustaining of demurrer in action for damages for wrongful death.

■ FACTS

A juvenile offender [another way to say one of those juvenile delinquent types] in the custody of the County of Alameda (County) (D) was known to have "latent, extremely dangerous and violent propensities regarding young children and that sexual assaults upon young children and violence connected therewith were a likely result of releasing [him] into the community." It was alleged by Thompson (P) that he had said that if released he would kill a child in the neighborhood. The County (D) released him on temporary leave to his mother's custody. No warnings were given to local police or families. [If the authorities lived in the neighborhood, wouldn't they want to be warned?] Within 24 hours of his release, the juvenile offender sexually assaulted and murdered Thompson's (P) 5-year old son. Thompsons (P) sued the County (D) for wrongful death. The trial court sustained the County's (D) demurrer to the complaint. Thompson (P) appealed contending that the County (D) should not be shielded from liability due to the discretionary immunity exception.

■ ISSUE

Is a public entity liable for failure to warn of the release from custody of a dangerous person who causes harm or death to an unidentifiable member of the general public?

■ DECISION AND RATIONALE

(Richardson) No. A public entity's failure to warn of the release from custody of a dangerous person does not create liability unless an identifiable victim exists which can be effectively warned. California has a general discretionary immunity statute and other specific immunity statutes, one of which provides that there is no liability for parole or release of a prisoner. The trial court held that the decision to release the juvenile offender was protected by both these immunities. It also held that discretionary immunity shielded the County (D) from liability for negligent selection of the juvenile's mother as custodian and failure to supervise her. The main issue for consideration by us on appeal is whether the County (D) is liable for its failure to warn the local police and neighborhood parents of the release of the juvenile offender or, alternatively, to warn the juvenile offender's mother of his expressed threat.   In *Johnson,* we held that the state could be sued when a state Youth Authority placement officer placed a minor with homicidal tendencies and a background of violence and cruelty with Mrs. Johnson without warning her of the foreseeable potential peril.   In that situation, there was a relationship between the state and the plaintiff-victim, Mrs. Johnson, which created a duty on the part of the state to inform of any matter that it knew or should have known, might endanger the Johnson family.   In the case now before us, the County (D) bore no special and continuous relationship with the Thompsons (P), nor did the County (D) knowingly place the specific decedent child into a foreseeably dangerous position.   Thus, the holding of the *Johnson* case is not applicable here.   We therefore hold that the duty to warn depends upon and arises from the existence of a prior threat to a specific identifiable victim.   When there is a threat to an identifiable victim or group of victims that can be effectively warned, there may be liability for failure to warn.   Because the decedent victim in this case was not a known, identifiable victim, but rather a member of a large amorphous public group of potential targets, the County (D) had no affirmative duty to warn the Thompsons (P), the police, the mother of the juvenile offender or other neighborhood parents.   [Isn't the threat to a child in the neighborhood a sufficiently identifiable group of targeted victims?   It sounds like the court is saying that the criminal needs to identify his victim by name, rank and serial number] We conclude that the County (D) was either statutorily immunized from liability or, alternatively, bore no affirmative duty that it failed to perform.   Judgment is affirmed.

Analysis:

Generally, public entities will not be held liable for negligently releasing persons from custody, whether they are prisoners, mental patients or others.   Many states, as did the state of California in this case, have specific immunity statutes that prohibit liability for parole or release of a prisoner.   However, the Thompson (P) family also asserted liability against the County (D) for its failure to warn the family, the police or the mother of the juvenile offender.   As the court noted, in the *Johnson* case liability existed for failure to warn of a foster child's homicidal tendencies.   The determining factor, said the court, is whether there is a specific threat to a particular victim that would impose a duty to warn.   If there is no identifiable group targeted there is no duty to warn.   Some legal scholars have suggested that the test should not be whether the victim is identifiable, but whether an effective warning could have been given to someone who would have prevented the harm.   Note that the court held that the County (D) was not liable either because of the immunity statute, or because it had no duty to warn.

■ CASE VOCABULARY

DEMURRER: A challenge to the legal sufficiency of the pleading, such as a complaint.

JUDGMENT OF DISMISSAL: The matter is "thrown out of court" after ruling on the merits but without trial of the issues of the case.

Vaughn v. Ruoff

(Parent) v. *(Social Worker)*
253 F.3d 1124 (8th Cir.2001)

INVOLUNTARY STERILIZATION VIOLATES DUE PROCESS

Your children will be waiting for you.

STERILIZATION

■ **INSTANT FACTS** The Vaughns (P) sued Ruoff (P) for due process violations after Mrs. Vaughn underwent tubal ligation in reliance upon Ruoff's (P) assurances that they would regain custody of their children if she did so.

■ **BLACK LETTER RULE** Qualified immunity does not attach when the state deprives an individual of a constitutional right that is clearly established at the time of the deprivation.

■ **PROCEDURAL BASIS**

On appeal to review a decision of a federal district court denying the defendant qualified immunity.

■ **FACTS**

Margaret and Kevin Vaughn (P) were married. Margaret had been diagnosed as mentally retarded. After Margaret gave birth to the couple's first child, the Missouri Division of Family Services (MDFS) took custody of the child, finding that the plaintiffs had failed to maintain a sanitary home and could not properly care for the child. Ruoff (D), the social worker assigned to the Vaughns' (P) case, counseled Margaret on birth control options, and Margaret agreed to begin using an intravenous contraceptive. Nonetheless, Margaret became pregnant with the couple's second child. After the birth of the second child, the state again took custody, finding that the plaintiffs could not properly care for the child. During the pregnancy, Ruoff (D) had discussed with Margaret the possibility of a tubal ligation to prevent further pregnancies; she told Margaret that if she agreed to the procedure, the Vaughns (P) would regain custody of their children. Margaret agreed to the procedure, but the MDFS nonetheless recommended the termination of the Vaughns' (P) parental rights. The Vaughns (P) sued Ruoff (D) in federal court for violations to their Fourteenth Amendment due process rights. In her defense, Ruoff (D) asserted qualified immunity. The court denied Ruoff's (D) claims of qualified immunity.

■ **ISSUE**

Is involuntary sterilization resulting from the coercion of a public official without notice and an opportunity to be heard a violation the Fourteenth Amendment?

■ **DECISION AND RATIONALE**

(Vietor, J.) Yes. Qualified immunity does not attach when the state deprives an individual of a constitutional right that is clearly established at the time of the deprivation. Under the Fourteenth Amendment, decisions relating to procreation and contraception are protected liberty interests. Before the state may deprive an individual of a protected interest, it must afford the individual certain procedural protections, including notice and an opportunity to be heard. Here, the Vaughns (P) were afforded no procedural protections before undergoing the sterilization procedure. Similarly, the evidence is sufficient to enable a jury to determine that Ruoff (D) deprived the Vaughns (P) of a liberty interest by coercing Margaret's sterilization through her comments. While involuntary sterilization is not unconstitutional if narrowly tailored to achieve a compelling government interest, the state has not established such a compelling interest in this case.

Even if the law had not previously established that Ruoff's (D) actions were unconstitutional at the time they were committed, a constitutional violation can be found when the deprived right is "sufficiently clear and that a reasonable official would understand that what [s]he is doing violates that right." Here, any reasonable person would understand that an involuntary sterilization produced by coercion is compelled and thus unconstitutional. Affirmed.

Analysis:

Qualified immunity attempts to strike a balance between a citizen's right to be free from government intrusion and a government official's need to be free from liability for actions in the normal course of his or her duties. By removing qualified immunity from those actions that unreasonably violate a clearly established right, government officials are charged with being informed of citizens' constitutional rights and acting reasonably in their duties to protect those rights.

■ CASE VOCABULARY

QUALIFIED IMMUNITY: Immunity from civil liability for a public official who is performing a discretionary function, as long as the conduct does not violate clearly established constitutional or statutory rights.

DUE PROCESS CLAUSE: The constitutional provision that prohibits the government from unfairly or arbitrarily depriving a person of life, liberty, or property.

Navarro v. Block

(Family of Murdered Woman) v. *(Sheriff)*

72 F.3d 712 (9th Cir.1995)

A MUNICIPALITY MAY BE LIABLE FOR CIVIL RIGHTS VIOLATIONS IF THERE EXISTS A DISCRIMINATORY CLASSIFICATION THAT AFFECTS PERSONS IN A MANNER NOT RATIONALLY RELATED TO LEGITIMATE GOVERNMENTAL OBJECTIVES

■ **INSTANT FACTS** Domestic violence victim called 911 to report that estranged husband was in route to her home to kill her, but operator did not dispatch police, and victim was killed.

■ **BLACK LETTER RULE** A municipality may be liable for civil rights violations if there is proof of the existence of a custom or informal policy with repeated constitutional violations for which municipal officials were not discharged or reprimanded, even if the official policy-makers did not have actual knowledge of the custom and practice.

■ **PROCEDURAL BASIS**

Appeal from summary judgment entered in action for damages for wrongful death under 42 U.S.C. § 1983.

■ **FACTS**

Maria Navarro received a telephone call one night from the brother of her estranged husband who said that her husband was on his way to her house to kill her and others. Maria called 911 for help and the 911 dispatcher told her to call back if he arrived. [They didn't want the police to sit around just waiting for the killer to arrive.] Fifteen minutes later the estranged husband arrived and shot and killed Maria and others. Maria's family, Navarro (P) filed suit against the County (D1) and the Sheriff, Block, (D2) whose department handled 911 calls. The basis for the claims was that victims of domestic violence were classified as non-emergency calls, thereby being denied equal protection under the law. The trial court granted summary judgment for the County (D1) and Block (D2).

■ **ISSUE**

Can a municipality be held liable for civil rights violations if there is proof of the existence of a custom or informal policy with repeated constitutional violations for which municipal officials were not discharged or reprimanded, even if the official policy-makers did not have actual knowledge of the custom and practice?

■ **DECISION AND RATIONALE**

(Pregerson) Yes. We hold that a municipality may be liable for a custom or policy of civil rights violations even if the official policy-makers did not have actual knowledge of the custom and practice. Under *Monell v. Dept. of Social Services* [municipalities may not be liable under 42 U.S.C. § 1983 unless constitutional violation results from an official municipal policy, custom or official decision], the Supreme Court held that a municipality may also be sued for constitutional deprivations pursuant to governmental custom, even though such custom has not received formal approval through the governmental body's official decision making channels. Thus, if there is proof of the existence of a custom or informal policy with repeated constitutional violations for which municipal officials were not discharged or reprimanded, a municipality may be liable for its custom even if the official policy-makers did not have actual knowledge of the custom and practice. Navarros (P) claim that the County (D1) carried out a policy and practice of not treating 911 domestic violence calls as "emergency" calls. The 911 operator stated that it was the practice of the Sheriff's (D2) department not to classify domestic violence 911 calls as Code 2 or "emergency procedure" calls, although there was no written policy or procedure that precluded sending patrol cars to the scene, or gave them less priority than other calls. We hold that the district court erred in holding that there were no genuine issues of material fact as to whether the County (D1) had a policy or custom of not classifying the domestic violence calls as an emergency. The County (D1) argues that even if there was such a policy or custom, there was no evidence that discrimination against women was a motivating factor behind the alleged policy. The Navarros (P) contend that treating domestic calls differently from non-domestic 911 calls impermissibly discriminates against abused women. Even though such custom may be gender neutral on its face, a discriminatory application of a facially neutral law violates the Constitution. However, there must be proof of discriminatory intent or motive. [Isn't not taking victims of domestic violence seriously a discriminatory intent or motive? The argument is that since males could be victims too, it's not gender based.] In the present case, no such evidence has been offered. There is only a conclusionary allegation to that effect. Nevertheless, even in the absence of evidence of gender discrimination, the equal protection claim survives because the Navarros (P) could prove that the domestic violence/non-domestic violence classification fails the rationality test. The district court did not review the rationality of the County's (D1) domestic violence/non-domestic violence classification and thus the matter should be remanded for a proper determination. We affirm the holding that the Navarros (P) did not offer any evidence to support the claim that the Sheriff's (D2) department failed to train dispatchers properly to avoid an indifference to the equal protection rights of abused women. However, we reverse the granting of summary judgment on the equal protection claim because there are genuine issues of material facts as to whether the County (D1) had a custom of not classifying domestic violence 911 calls as emergencies. If on remand the Navarros (P) prove the existence of a discriminatory custom against victims of domestic violence, the district court must review the rationality of such a custom.

Analysis:

This case looks at the liability of municipalities under 42 U.S.C. § 1983 [depriving one of a right or privilege protected by the federal Constitution or federal law while acting under color of law]. First, we learn that the United States Supreme Court has ruled in *Monell v. Department of Social Services* that a municipality may be liable under a Section 1983 claim only if the constitutional right violated is due to some policy or custom of the municipality. Second, a facially neutral policy that discriminates must have a rational basis. In this case, the district court did not consider the issue of whether there was a rational basis for the County's (D1) objectives. The court of appeals therefore remanded the case so that the district court could determine if there were issues as to whether the County (D1) had a custom of not classifying domestic violence 911 calls as emergencies. It is of interest to note that on remand of the case, the trial judge concluded that the Sheriff's (D2) policy excluded domestic violence cases because they were usually cases of violence not yet in progress, thus, it gave them lower priority than violence in progress calls. A second appeal was filed and the court of appeals held that domestic violence calls could not be equated with not in progress calls because some may involve violence in progress. On remand, the issue was whether there was a policy or custom of giving lower priority to domestic violence calls than to non-domestic violence calls, and if so, whether that policy or custom had a rational basis. Thus, although there was support for Navarro's (P) claim, it is not clear whether they were ultimately able to prevail.

■ **CASE VOCABULARY**

DEPOSITION: Pre-trial discovery method whereby person is questioned, under oath and in the presence of a court reporter, by attorneys for the parties to the action.

GENUINE ISSUES OF MATERIAL FACT: Also referred to as a triable issue of fact or question of fact, which will defeat a motion for summary judgment, so that the matter may proceed to trial.

SUMMARY JUDGMENT: Judgment entered after granting a legal motion for summary judgment in which party requests that the judge enter judgment, before trial, on the grounds that the action has no merit or there is no defense to the action.

CHAPTER SIXTEEN

Nonfeasance

Yania v. Bigan

Instant Facts: Widow and children (P) of Mr. Yania brought wrongful death and survival actions against Bigan (D) for his failure to rescue Mr. Yania from drowning in trench.

Black Letter Rule: There is no duty to rescue or assist one who is in a position of peril.

Wakulich v. Mraz

Instant Facts: Elizabeth Wakulich died after Michael and Brian Mraz (D) bet her she couldn't drink a full bottle of alcohol without losing consciousness or vomiting.

Black Letter Rule: One who voluntarily undertakes to render services to another is liable for bodily harm caused by his failure to perform such services with due care or with such competence and skill as he possesses.

Farwell v. Keaton

Instant Facts: Friend of beating victim failed to seek immediate medical attention for, or inform anyone of, the victim-friend's whereabouts.

Black Letter Rule: Social companions have a duty to aid one another in situations of peril.

Deshaney v. Winnebago County Dept. of Social Services

Instant Facts: Child was severely beaten by his father while in his custody, and social workers monitoring the family following cessation of temporary custody knew of prior abuse but did nothing.

Black Letter Rule: A public entity must have custody of another in order to hold it liable for depriving the person of federal due process rights by failing to prevent harm caused by a third person.

Yania v. Bigan

(Family of Drowning Victim) v. *(Coal Miner Operator)*
397 Pa. 316, 155 A.2d 343 (1959)

THERE IS NO DUTY TO ACT

■ **INSTANT FACTS** Widow and children (P) of Mr. Yania brought wrongful death and survival actions against Bigan (D) for his failure to rescue Mr. Yania from drowning in trench.

■ **BLACK LETTER RULE** There is no duty to rescue or assist one who is in a position of peril.

■ **PROCEDURAL BASIS**

Appeal from dismissal of complaint for wrongful death and survival following sustaining of demurrers.

■ **FACTS**

Bigan (D), an operator of a coal strip-mining operation, had made large cuts or trenches on the property being stripped in order to remove the coal under the earth. One such cut contained 8 to 10 feet of water, with walls or embankments 16 to 18 feet in height. Bigan (D) had installed a pump to remove the water. Joseph Yania, the operator of another coal strip-mining operation, went to see Bigan (D) to discuss business. While on the property, Bigan (D) asked Mr. Yania to help him start the pump. Bigan (D) entered the cut near the pump. Mr. Yania stood at the top of the side walls, jumped into the water and drowned. Mr. Yania's widow, Mrs. Yania and her three children (P), sued Bigan (D) for wrongful death and survival actions. Yania (P) contends that Bigan (D) was responsible for Mr. Yania's death because of Bigan's (D) spoken words and blandishments to Mr. Yania. The inference deductible from the facts alleged in the complaint is that Bigan (D), by the employment of cajolery and inveiglement, caused such a mental impact on Mr. Yania that he was deprived of his volition and freedom of choice and placed under a compulsion to jump into the water. [Sounds like he just acted on a dare to jump!] In addition, it is contended that Bigan (D) failed to take the necessary steps to rescue Mr. Yania from the water. The trial judge sustained Bigan's (D) demurrer to the complaint and Yania (P) appealed.

■ **ISSUE**

Is there a duty to rescue or assist one who is in a position of peril?

■ **DECISION AND RATIONALE**

(Jones) No. There is no duty to rescue or assist one who is in a position of peril. We first reject Yania's (P) contention that the conduct of Bigan (D) caused Mr. Yania to jump into the water. If Mr. Yania had been a young child or a person with a mental deficiency, it is conceivable that taunting and enticement could constitute actionable negligence. However, it is completely without precedent or merit to contend that such conduct directed to an adult in full possession of all his mental faculties constitutes actionable negligence. With respect to Bigan (D) not rescuing Mr. Yania, we must reject this claim as well. There was no legal obligation or duty imposed upon Bigan (D) to rescue Mr. Yania when he saw him in a position of peril in the water. Although there may have been a moral obligation, no facts are alleged which impose upon Bigan (D) a legal duty to rescue. Unless Bigan (D) was legally responsible, in whole or in part, for placing Mr. Yania in the perilous position, no duty exists to rescue. We can only reach the conclusion that Mr. Yania, a reasonable and prudent adult in full possession of his mental faculties, [that's debatable] undertook to perform an act which he knew or should have known was attended with more or less peril and it was the performance of that act, rather than any conduct by Bigan (D), which caused his death. Affirmed.

Analysis:

This case involves the rule of law that *nonfeasance,* or doing nothing, does not create liability. In other words, there is no duty to act in order to protect another from harm. However, if misfeasance negligence is involved, there may be liability for affirmative action. As the other cases in the Chapter will show, there may be more involved than simple nonaction. There are many circumstances where the failure to act is not considered *nonfeasance* and liability will depend upon whether there is a duty to act. Thus, the issue becomes whether conduct is *nonfeasance* or *misfeasance.* Note that the court also rejected Yania's (P) claim that liability should be imposed on Bigan (D) for taunting or enticing Mr. Yania to jump into the water. Since he was an adult in possession of all his mental faculties, there was no basis for such a claim. In other words, Mr. Yania knew or should have known that jumping into the water could have caused him harm.

■ CASE VOCABULARY

SURVIVAL ACTION: Action on behalf of decedent for injuries that survive his death.

WRONGFUL DEATH: Action on behalf of beneficiaries of decedent for damages they sustained because of decedent's death.

Wakulich v. Mraz

(*Decedent's Family*) v. (*Young Men*)
322 Ill.App.3d 768, 751 N.E.2d 1, 255 Ill.Dec. 907 (2001)

ONCE A DUTY IS VOLUNTARILY ASSUMED, IT MUST BE CARRIED OUT IN A REASONABLE MANNER

■ **INSTANT FACTS** Elizabeth Wakulich died after Michael and Brian Mraz (D) bet her she couldn't drink a full bottle of alcohol without losing consciousness or vomiting.

■ **BLACK LETTER RULE** One who voluntarily undertakes to render services to another is liable for bodily harm caused by his failure to perform such services with due care or with such competence and skill as he possesses.

■ PROCEDURAL BASIS

On appeal to review a decision dismissing the plaintiff's complaint for failure to state a claim for relief.

■ FACTS

Sixteen-year-old Elizabeth Wakulich died when Michael and Brian Mraz (D), twenty-one and eighteen years old, respectively, bet her that she could not drink a bottle of Goldschlager without losing consciousness or vomiting. After finishing the bottle, Wakulich began vomiting and lost consciousness. The defendants placed Elizabeth on a couch, provided her with a pillow, and removed her vomit-soaked clothing, but did not seek medical attention and prevented others in the house from calling 911. Wakulich's family (D) sued Michael and Brian Mraz (D) and their father, who was in the house at the time of death. Their complaint was dismissed for failure to state a claim because Illinois law does not recognize social host liability for the provision of alcohol to another. Wakulich (P) appealed.

■ ISSUE

Did the plaintiff sufficiently allege a cause of action for failure to exercise due care for Elizabeth's safety?

■ DECISION AND RATIONALE

(McBride, J.) Yes. "One who voluntarily undertakes to render services to another is liable for bodily harm caused by his failure to perform such services with due care or with such competence and skill as he possesses." Here, when Michael and Brian (D) observed Elizabeth, provided her with a pillow, and removed clothing, they voluntarily assumed a duty to care for her. From the allegations in the complaint, a reasonable jury could determine that the actions taken by the defendants, including their preventing others from calling for medical help, constituted negligence. The plaintiff's complaint states a claim upon with relief may be granted. Reversed and remanded.

Analysis:

The published excerpt focuses on the defendants' conduct after Elizabeth had consumed the alcohol and fallen unconscious. A portion of the case excluded from the published excerpt, however, demonstrates that in some states, one who provides alcohol to a minor may be criminally liable under the state's dram shop act. Here, Michael Mraz (D), an adult, was convicted of a misdemeanor for contributing to the delinquency of a minor. The dram shop act preempted any civil cause of action for social-host liability against the defendants.

■ CASE VOCABULARY

DRAM–SHOP ACT: A statute allowing a plaintiff to recover damages from a commercial seller of alcoholic beverages for personal injury caused by an intoxicated customer.

Farwell v. Keaton

(Heirs of Deceased Teenager) v. *(Not Stated)*
396 Mich. 281, 240 N.W.2d 217 (1976)

SPECIAL RELATIONSHIPS CREATE DUTY TO AID IN TIMES OF PERIL

■ **INSTANT FACTS** Friend of beating victim failed to seek immediate medical attention for, or inform anyone of, the victim-friend's where-abouts.

■ **BLACK LETTER RULE** Social companions have a duty to aid one another in situations of peril.

■ **PROCEDURAL BASIS**

Appeal to state Supreme Court after reversal of judgment following jury trial for wrongful death action.

■ **FACTS**

Farwell's heirs (P) sued for his death resulting from the failure of his friend, Siegrist, to obtain medical assistance for, or to inform of the whereabouts of, Farwell. Farwell and Siegrist, teenaged boys, were friends. While having a few beers, they attempted without success to engage in conversation with some teenaged girls that had walked by. The girls [obviously not interested in the two] complained to friends that they were being followed. Six boys chased Farwell and Siegrist, and Farwell was severely beaten. Siegrist, who escaped injury, put Farwell in the car with ice on his head, and drove around for two hours. Farwell "went to sleep" in the back of the car and later that night Siegrist drove him to his grandparents' home, where he left him in the car after a failed attempt to arouse him. Farwell died three days later from the beating. There was evidence that prompt medical attention could have prevented his death. The jury found for Farwell's heirs (P). The court of appeals reversed on the ground that Siegrist had not assumed any duty to aid his friend Farwell. The matter was appealed to the Michigan Supreme Court.

■ **ISSUE**

Do social companions have a duty to aid one another in situations of peril?

■ **DECISION AND RATIONALE**

(Levin) Yes. Social companions have a duty to aid one another in situations of peril. There is a clearly recognized duty of every person to avoid any affirmative acts that may make a situation worse. If one attempts to aid another and fails to use reasonable care in connection therewith, the person will be held liable. The reason is that the person has voluntarily entered into a relationship by taking charge and control of the situation and such relationship is attended with responsibility. In this case, Farwell and Siegrist were companions on a social venture. Implicit in such a common undertaking is the understanding that one will render assistance to the other when he is in peril, if he can do so without endangering himself. Siegrist knew or should have known when he left Farwell badly beaten and unconscious in the back of the car that no one would find him until morning. [Maybe in thought his friend had just had a few too many beers.] Accordingly, because the two companions were engaged in a common undertaking, a special relationship existed between them. Reversed.

Analysis:

Although there is no general duty to render aid to a person in peril, if a special relationship exists a duty may be created. The Supreme Court of Michigan held in this case that being social companions, *i.e.,* friends, engaged in a common undertaking is sufficient to create such a special relationship. Also, consider whether the conduct of Siegrist put Farwell in a worse condition than he had been in. For example, if Siegrist had left Farwell at the location of the beating, rather than placing him in the car and leaving him unattended overnight, would Farwell have been discovered sooner? Perhaps it is also arguable that Siegrist began to care for Farwell by placing him in his car and transporting him, but failed to act reasonably in that effort. The Restatement of Torts imposes liability on one who discontinues aid only if the defendant has left the victim in a "worse position." The Restatement expressly sets forth five types of relationships that require the use of reasonable care for one's safety, including reasonable affirmative efforts to rescue. They are: 1) carrier-passenger, 2) innkeeper-guest, 3) landowner-invitee, 4) custodian-ward, and 5) employer-employee. There may be other preexisting relationships that impose a duty to act affirmatively when one is in danger. Although the two teenage boys in this case did not have a preexisting recognized status with respect to each other, they did have a special relationship for that evening. As the court noted, to claim that Siegrist had no duty to Farwell under the circumstances would be "'shocking to humanitarian considerations' and fly in the face of the commonly accepted code of social conduct.'"

DeShaney v. Winnebago County Dept. of Social Services

(Abused Child) v. *(Social Services)*

489 U.S. 189, 109 S.Ct. 998, 103 L.Ed.2d 249 (1989)

STATE'S CUSTODY OF ANOTHER WILL CREATE A SPECIAL RELATIONSHIP THAT IMPOSES AN AFFIRMATIVE DUTY TO PREVENT HARM TO THE PERSON

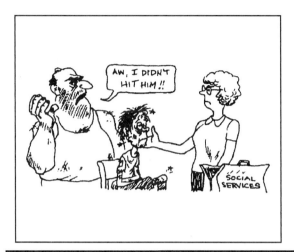

■ **INSTANT FACTS** Child was severely beaten by his father while in his custody, and social workers monitoring the family following cessation of temporary custody knew of prior abuse but did nothing.

■ **BLACK LETTER RULE** A public entity must have custody of another in order to hold it liable for depriving the person of federal due process rights by failing to prevent harm caused by a third person.

■ **PROCEDURAL BASIS**

Appeal to United States Supreme Court following the affirming of summary judgment in action for violation of *42 U.S.C. § 1983.*

■ **FACTS**

A brain-damaged child and his mother, DeShaney (P), sued Winnebago County Dept. of Social Services (Social Services) (D) claiming that their failure to act deprived the DeShaney (P) boy of his liberty in violation of the Due Process Clause of the Fourteenth Amendment to the U.S. Constitution. Social Services (D) received complaints that the DeShaney (P) boy was being abused by his father, with whom he lived, following his parents' divorce. Social Services (D) took temporary custody of the boy, but returned him to his father after an agreement was reached with the father in which he promised to cooperate in accomplishing certain measures designed to protect the boy. Social Services (D) continued to monitor the boy at his father's home. Evidence of further abuse and noncompliance with the agreement was noted, but Social Services (D) did not act to remove the boy from the father's custody. Thereafter, the boy was so severely beaten by his father that he suffered severe and permanent brain damage rendering him profoundly retarded. The boy and his mother, DeShaney (P), filed suit under *42 U.S.C. § 1983* [depriving one of a right or privilege protected by the federal Constitution or federal law while acting under color of law] contending that Social Services (D) denied the boy due process. The trial court [having the awful job of correctly interpreting the law against DeShaney (P)] granted summary judgment for Social Services (D), the court of appeal affirmed, and an appeal was taken to the United States Supreme Court.

■ **ISSUE**

Must a public entity have custody of another in order to hold it liable for depriving the person of federal due process rights by failing to prevent harm caused by a third person?

■ **DECISION AND RATIONALE**

(Rehnquist) Yes. We hold that a public entity must have custody of another in order to hold it liable for depriving the person of federal due process rights by failing to prevent harm caused by a third person. The Due Process Clause of the Fourteenth Amendment provides that "[n]o State shall deprive any person of life, liberty, or property, without due process of law." DeShaney (P) contends that Social

Services (D) is liable for failing to provide the boy with adequate protection against his father's violence. However, the Due Process Clause does not impose affirmative duties on the State to protect the life, liberty, and property of its citizens against invasion by private actors. Although the Clause forbids the State itself from depriving individuals of life, liberty, and property without due process of law, its language cannot be extended to impose any affirmative duty to ensure that those interests are not harmed through other means. Thus, a State's failure to protect an individual against private violence does not constitute a violation of the Due Process Clause. The DeShaneys (P) also contend that a "special relationship" existed between the boy and the State because it knew that the boy faced special danger of abuse by his father and it proclaimed its intention to protect him against that danger. We reject this contention. In limited circumstances, the State has an affirmative duty to care and protect particular individuals. See, *Estelle v. Gamble* [State is required to provide adequate medical care to incarcerated prisoners] and *Youngberg v. Romeo* [State is required to provide involuntarily committed mental patients with such services as are necessary to ensure reasonable safety from themselves and others]. However, such affirmative duty arises when the State takes a person into its custody and holds him there against his will. In these circumstances, the Constitution imposes upon the State a duty to assume some responsibility for the person's safety and general well being. These cases have no application to the case at bar. Although the State took temporary custody of the boy, when it returned him to his father's custody it placed him in no worse position than that in which he would have been had it not acted at all. [But shortly thereafter, the boy was in a much worse condition.] We note that it may well be that in voluntarily undertaking to protect the boy, the State acquired a duty under *state tort law* to provide him with adequate protection against that danger. However, the claim before us is one based on the Due Process Clause of the Fourteenth Amendment. The conduct involved does not constitute a violation of the Due Process Clause. Affirmed.

■ DISSENT

(Brennan) I would recognize that the State's knowledge of an individual's predicament and its expressions of intent to help can amount to a limitation of his freedom to act on his own or to obtain help from others. I would read the holdings of *Youngberg* and *Estelle* to stand for the proposition that if a State cuts off private sources of aid and then refuses aid itself, it should be held responsible. Members of the public, other than those working for Social Services (D), would feel that their job was done as soon as they reported the suspicions of child abuse. If Social Services (D) then ignores or dismisses these suspicions, it has thus effectively confined the boy within the walls of the father's violent home. Conceivably, children in this situation are made worse off when the social service entities fail to do their jobs. I disagree with the Majority for its failure to see that inaction can be every bit as abusive of power as action, that oppression can result when a State undertakes a vital duty and then ignores it.

■ DISSENT

(Blackmun) The facts in this case involve not mere passivity, but active state intervention in the life of the boy. This intervention triggered a fundamental duty to aid the boy once the State learned of the severe danger to which he was exposed.

Analysis:

The United States Supreme Court's decision in this famous case stands for the proposition that in order for a civil rights violation to exist that will impose liability upon the State, the State must have *custody* of the victim. The Court distinguished this case from two other cases where constitutional violations resulted in liability. Depriving one of life, liberty or property under the Due Process Clause requires that the person deprived be in custody before such deprivation will result in liability. In order for an exception to "the no duty to act" rule to apply, there must be a special relationship. The special relationship necessary for a constitutional claim is the public entity's *custody* of the victim. Note however that this case concerns violations of federal constitutional rights. Liability may exist under state tort law in non-custodial situations. For example, a medical doctor may be under a duty to report child abuse, and some state statutes create a special relationship or direct duty of reasonable care by the protective agency to an abused child. The majority concluded that Social Services (D) placed the boy in no worse position than that in which he would have been had it not acted at all. However,

Justice Brennan's dissent stated that he believed that the inaction by Social Services (D) amounted to taking away further possible aid by the public, and then ignoring it. This, he said, makes children in this situation worse off. Justice Blackmun concluded that there was active state intervention in the life of the boy. Thus, the Court was divided as to whether nonfeasance or misfeasance existed.

CHAPTER SEVENTEEN

Contract and Duty

Thorne v. Deas

Instant Facts: The Thornes (P) and Deas (D) owned a ship together. Deas (D) promised to get insurance for the ship but did not. The ship wrecked.

Black Letter Rule: When one person promises to do something for another, and that promise is gratuitous, that person is not liable under tort law if they take no action to fulfill the promise.

Mobil Oil Corp. v. Thorn

Instant Facts: A tenant sued its landlord for personal injuries sustained after the landlord had notice to make repairs but failed to, in violation of the lease.

Black Letter Rule: A lessor is liable for the personal injuries of a tenant which occurred after the lessor breached an agreement to make repairs.

H.R. Moch Co. v. Rensselaer Water Co.

Instant Facts: The Water Co. (D) contracted with the city to provide water for city fire hydrants. A building caught fire and Rensselaer (D) failed to provide enough water to the fire-hydrant which resulted in the fire spreading to a warehouse owned by Moch (P).

Black Letter Rule: A party can not maintain an action in torts based on a contract to which they are neither a party nor an intended third party beneficiary.

Paz v. State of California

Instant Facts: A motorcyclist was injured in an accident at an unmarked intersection, and he is suing the defendants for failing to timely install traffic signals.

Black Letter Rule: When the defendant does nothing to increase the risk of physical harm to a plaintiff beyond that which already existed at the intersection, a defendant will not be held liable for simply failing to complete before the plaintiff's accident a project that might have reduced the preexisting hazard.

Florence v. Goldberg

Instant Facts: A six-year-old child was severely injured after being struck by a car at an unguarded street crossing while walking to school alone.

Black Letter Rule: A police department, having assumed a duty to a special class of persons, and having gone forward with performance of that duty in the past, has an obligation to continue its performance.

Thorne v. Deas

(*Promisor*) v. (*Promisee*)
4 Johns. (N.Y.) 84 (1809)

THE COMPLETE FAILURE TO PERFORM A GRATUITOUSLY PROMISED ACTION DOES NOT CREATE LIABILITY

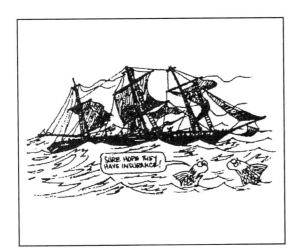

■ **INSTANT FACTS** The Thornes (P) and Deas (D) owned a ship together. Deas (D) promised to get insurance for the ship but did not. The ship wrecked.

■ **BLACK LETTER RULE** When one person promises to do something for another, and that promise is gratuitous, that person is not liable under tort law if they take no action to fulfill the promise.

■ **PROCEDURAL BASIS**

Interlocutory appeal to decide if recovery was possible?

■ **FACTS**

The Thornes (P) owned a half-interest in a vessel called the Sea Nymph. Deas (D) owned the other half-interest. The Sea Nymph was scheduled to sail from New York to North Carolina. Deas (D) promised, in two separate conversations with one of the Thornes (P) that he would procure insurance for the ship. This promise was gratuitous. Deas (D) did not procure the insurance. The vessel wrecked. The Thornes (P) sued Deas (D) for nonfeasance in failing to get the insurance. The trail court issued a verdict for the Thornes (P) equal to one half the value of the vessel, subject to the opinion of this court as to whether recovery was proper.

■ **ISSUE**

Is a person who makes a gratuitous promise liable for the losses caused by failure to act in performance of that promise?

■ **DECISION AND RATIONALE**

(Kent) No. If a party promises to do something and then through negligence does it improperly, resulting in damage to the other party, this would give rise to an action against the first party for negligence. However under common law a party who makes a gratuitous promise is only responsible when he undertakes to fulfill the promise and does it incorrectly, he is not responsible for failing to do it altogether. This is one of the many moral obligations that are not enforced by the law, but are left to the individual's conscience. Therefore because Deas' (D) promise to get the insurance was completely gratuitous, and because Deas (D) took no steps to perform his promise, Deas (D) is not liable. Judgment for the defendant. [The moral of this story being: Don't trust the other guy to get the insurance.]

Analysis:

The outcome in this case could easily be seen as unfair. Deas (D) promised in two separate conversations to get insurance on the ship. The fact that this came up on two separate occasions suggests that the Thornes (P) were concerned about insurance, and that but for the promise made by Deas (D) they would have procured it themselves. Thus, it seems clear that Deas (D) caused the financial loss that the Thornes (P) suffered as a result of his failure to fulfill his promise. It seems then that the Thornes (P) should then have a right to recover. To understand why they do not recover, one must look at the nature of the duty involved. Generally speaking the law does not require that one person take affirmative action to help another. Deas (D) was not required to get insurance for the benefit of the Thornes (P). His mere failure to get the insurance would not create a cause of action because he had no duty to do so. What creates a situation where it seems that Deas (D) has a duty here is the fact that Deas (D) made a promise to get the insurance. The question then is whether this promise creates a duty that would serve as a basis for a claim? The courts have found that a promise, which is gratuitous, does not create a duty to perform an affirmative action. One explanation for this is that the enforcement of promises is usually left to contract law rather than torts, and a gratuitous promise would not normally be enforceable under contract law. The courts have not wanted to provide a remedy for a broken promise in torts where there is not one under contract law.

■ **CASE VOCABULARY**

GRATUITOUS: An adjective that describes something given or undertaken without consideration or payment.

MISFEASANCE: The improper or incompetent performance of an action that is otherwise legal.

NONFEASANCE: The complete failure to do an act. Usually carries the meaning of failure to do something, which is that person's duty or responsibility.

Mobil Oil Corp. v. Thorn

(*Landlord Oil Company*) v. (*Tenant Service Station Operator*)
401 Mich. 306, 258 N.W.2d 30 (1977)

TWENTY-SIX STATES HAVE REJECTED THE RULE THAT A LESSOR IS NOT RESPONSIBLE FOR PERSONAL INJURIES OF ITS TENANTS DUE TO THE LESSOR'S FAILURE TO MAKE REPAIRS

■ **INSTANT FACTS** A tenant sued its landlord for personal injuries sustained after the landlord had notice to make repairs but failed to, in violation of the lease.

■ **BLACK LETTER RULE** A lessor is liable for the personal injuries of a tenant which occurred after the lessor breached an agreement to make repairs.

■ **PROCEDURAL BASIS**

Appeal from the Court of Appeals' affirmance of the trial court's judgment for the plaintiff.

■ **FACTS**

Mobil Oil (P) sued its lessee, Thorn (D), for monies due from the sale of petroleum products. Thorn (D) counterclaimed for injury on the leased premises, alleging that the roof leaked, and Mobil (P) had notice to repair but it failed to do so, and that as a result the floor was slippery and the lessee was injured in a fall. A provision of the lease obligated Mobil (P) to make repairs after notice, but the trial court and the Court of Appeals held this could be no basis for liability.

■ **ISSUE**

Is a lessor liable for the personal injuries of a tenant which occurred after the lessor breached an agreement to make repairs?

■ **DECISION AND RATIONALE**

(Fitzgerald, J.) Yes. It is apparent that the trial court correctly found that Thorn's (D) claim was unenforceable under existing law, as it has been a well-settled rule in this state that "an action in tort cannot be predicated, by a tenant, upon a breach by the lessor of an agreement to make repairs." While this common law rule has been abrogated in its applicability to leases for residential dwellings, the rule has been left unchanged in its applicability to leases for commercial premises. The question before this Court, then, is whether to retain the rule or to reject it in its entirety. At present, 26 states have rejected the rule that a lessor is not liable for personal injuries under such circumstances. The American Law Institute (ALI) has adopted the modern rule which provides that a lessor is subject to liability for physical harm caused to his lessee and others by a condition of disrepair if the lessee had contracted to keep the land in repair, the disrepair creates an unreasonable risk, or the lessor fails to exercise reasonable care to perform his contract. The rule does not distinguish between "residential" and "commercial" leases, and we believe that had the ALI intended to limit the rule to residential leases, it would have done so with clear language to that effect. As such, we reject the common law rule that a lessor is not liable for personal injuries to its tenant under circumstances such as in this case, and remand the matter to the trial court for further proceedings.

Analysis:

The landlord's common law tort liability for conditions of the leased premises that cause injury is now often affected by statutes and ordinances. Liability is also affected by the recognition that the modern lease is not analogous to the medieval lease from which the no-duty rule developed, but instead represents a combination of property and services usually provided as a part of the landlord's business. The landlord's undertaking, express or implied, as a term of the lease or otherwise, is often a basis for the duty to protect the tenant. Apart from the landlord's voluntary undertaking or assumption of a duty, however, the usual claim depends in part on the foreseeability of harm, and if harm is not foreseeable, no precaution is required. When the landlord has superior knowledge of danger, other cases may require him to warn the tenant. Although the general trend is to bring the landlord within the normal rules of negligence law by imposing a duty to provide reasonable protection against foreseeable harms, almost every decision for liability has a counterpart somewhere that rejects liability.

■ CASE VOCABULARY

ABROGATE: To repeal a former law by legislative act, or by usage.

COUNTERCLAIM: A claim presented by a defendant in opposition to or deduction from the claim of the plaintiff.

FORESEEABILITY: The reasonable anticipation that harm or injury is a likely result from certain acts or omissions. lessor is not liable for personal injuries

H.R. Moch Co. v. Rensselaer Water Co.

(*Warehouse Owner/Third Party*) v. (*Water Company/Contractor*)
247 N.Y. 160, 159 N.E. 896 (1928)

A CONTRACTUAL PROMISE DOES NOT CREATE LIABILITY TO THIRD PARTY NON-INTENDED BENEFICIARIES

■ **INSTANT FACTS** The Water Co. (D) contracted with the city to provide water for city fire hydrants. A building caught fire and Rensselaer (D) failed to provide enough water to the fire-hydrant which resulted in the fire spreading to a warehouse owned by Moch (P).

■ **BLACK LETTER RULE** A party can not maintain an action in torts based on a contract to which they are neither a party nor an intended third party beneficiary.

■ **PROCEDURAL BASIS**

Appeal to the Court of Appeals of New York after the Appellate Division reversed the decision by the trial court to deny the motion to dismiss the complaint.

■ **FACTS**

The Rensselaer Water Company (the Water Co.) (D) contracted with the City of Rensselaer (city) to supply water for the city's needs and also to private customers at an agreed upon rate. Included in this contract was the requirement that the Water Co. (D) provide water to the city's fire hydrants at a rate of $42.50 each per year. While the contract was in force a building caught fire. The Water Co. (D) was notified of the fire but failed to provide adequate water to allow it to be extinguished before the fire spread. H.R. Moch Co. (Moch) (P) owned a warehouse that was totally destroyed by the fire after it spread. Moch (P) brought suit against the Water Co. alleging a cause of action based on a breach of contract, and a cause of action under common-law tort. The Water Co. (D) brought a motion to dismiss the complaint. This was denied by the trial court, but this denial was then reversed by the Appellate Division.

■ **ISSUE**

Can an action in tort be maintained based on a contract to which the injured party is neither a party nor an intended third party beneficiary?

■ **DECISION AND RATIONALE**

(Cardozo) No. The city has no general duty to protect its citizens from fire. [That's news.] That being so the Water Co. (D) when it contracted to supply water to the hydrants did not contract to assume a duty owed by the city to its citizens. It is true that every city contract should properly be entered into for the benefit of the public. But to maintain an action based on the breach of contract a more specific intent to benefit Moch (P) would have to be shown. It would be necessary to show a benefit that was so immediate and clear that the Water Co. (D) could be said to have assumed the risk of such a duty. That is not the case here. If all those who contracted with the city were to be assumed to have assumed such general risks the cost of city services would become astronomical. Thus there is no liability here for breach of contract. There is also no liability here under tort. It is true that once a party assumes to act they have undertaken a duty to act with care. Moch (P) argues that there should be liability in this case under that principle. But the key question here is whether the Water Co. (D) has actually undertaken to act, such that any relationship of duty exists between them. Moch (P) argues that the Water Co (D) entered into such a relationship with them, and any other who might have benefited by the supply of water when it entered into its contract with the city. We believe that this would again create too great an extension of liability. Under this logic any wholesaler would be liable to any retail customer who claimed injury from its failure to provide the retailer with goods. Everyone making a promise having the quality of a contract would be liable not only to the party promised but to an infinite number of potential beneficiaries once the performance of that promise had begun. Thus we find no tort liability for the failure to provide water to the city in this case. (What is the intended purpose of supplying water to fire hydrants if not to allow the city to put out fires?)

Analysis:

One way to look at this case is that it is simply a nonfeasance case and that as the Water Company (D) never started to provide water to the hydrant, it never took any affirmative action which would make it liable for negligence in not providing adequate water. However, this case is not really that simple. Supplying the water to the hydrant at adequate pressure seems to be very closely linked to the bigger action of correctly running a water company. It is clear that the Water Co. (P) did undertake to run a water company, and even undertook to provide water to some hydrants, having taken this action isn't it reasonable to say that it was negligent in not doing this in a way that was adequate to prevent Moch's (P) warehouse from burning down? What the court seems to be really arguing is that there must be a limit to the liability assumed by entering into a contract so that the burden of potential liability does not bring commerce to a halt. Thus, the case is apparently more a question of the scope of duty than the difference between misfeasance and nonfeasance.

■ CASE VOCABULARY

ASSUMPTION OF A DUTY: The agreement to take upon oneself a duty that primarily belongs to someone else.

MAINTAIN AN ACTION: The act of continuing or pursuing an action or suit at law. When a suit survives a motion to dismiss it has been maintained, though it has not yet been won.

NON-INTENDED THIRD-PARTY BENEFICIARY: A person who derives benefit from a contract, though not a party to the contract, when the parties to the contract did not directly intended him to benefit.

Paz v. State of California

(Injured Motorist) v. *(Signal Light Installers)*

22 Cal.4th 550, 93 Cal.Rptr.2d 703, 994 P.2d 975 (2000)

THE NEGLIGENT UNDERTAKING THEORY OF LIABILITY REQUIRES MORE THAN SIMPLY ESTABLISHING A DEFENDANT'S UNDERTAKING TO ANOTHER

■ **INSTANT FACTS** A motorcyclist was injured in an accident at an unmarked intersection, and he is suing the defendants for failing to timely install traffic signals.

■ **BLACK LETTER RULE** When the defendant does nothing to increase the risk of physical harm to a plaintiff beyond that which already existed at the intersection, a defendant will not be held liable for simply failing to complete— before the plaintiff's accident—a project that might have reduced the preexisting hazard.

■ **PROCEDURAL BASIS**

Appeal From the Court of Appeals' reversal of the trial court's grant of summary judgment in favor of the defendants.

■ **FACTS**

Stoneman Corp. (D) was developing condos and other residential projects near an unmarked intersection. As a condition of granting a permit for the development, the city (D) required Stoneman (D) to install traffic signals and road markings at the intersection [anything to get out of doing it themselves]. Stoneman hired an engineer, who hired KOA (D) to design and install the signals. Two years later, the signals still had not been installed, in part due to KOA's (D) delay in seeking permits from the state. The intersection was already dangerous, and there had been a number of accidents there, when Paz (P) crashed his motorcycle into a car in the intersection. Paz (P) sued the state, the city, Stoneman (D) and KOA (D), alleging that they were negligent in failing to get the traffic signals installed. The trial court granted summary judgment in favor of the defendants, the Court of Appeals reversed, and this appeal followed.

■ **ISSUE**

Can a defendant be held liable for negligent failure to timely install traffic signals at an intersection where there was a subsequent accident resulting in injuries to a plaintiff?

■ **DECISION AND RATIONALE**

(Chin, J.) No. Paz (P) asserts that a timely installation of the traffic signals would have alleviated the allegedly dangerous conditions at the intersection and hence prevented his collision with the car. Thus his claim necessarily is grounded in the negligent undertaking theory of liability articulated in section 324A. This section provides that one who undertakes to render services to another, for the protection of a third person, is subject to liability to that third person for physical harm resulting from his failure to exercise reasonable care to perform his undertaking, if (1) his failure to exercise reasonable care increases the risk of such harm, or (2) he has undertaken to perform a duty owed by the other to the third person, or (3) the harm is suffered because of reliance of the other or the third person upon the undertaking. However, the negligent undertaking theory of liability requires more than simply establishing the defendant's undertaking to another, and in this case, none of these three conditions for section 324A liability are present. The evidence fails to support an inference that the conduct of Stoneman (D) and KOA (D) increased the risk of physical harm to Paz beyond that which allegedly existed at the intersection. Instead, Stoneman (D) and KOA (D) simply did not succeed in completing—before Paz's (P) collision—a project that might have reduced the preexisting hazard at the intersection. In this instance, where the record shows that nothing changed but the passage of time, a failure to alleviate a risk cannot be regarded as tantamount to increasing that risk. Neither the record nor the law shows any basis for satisfying the second alternative condition required for section 324A liability. In agreeing to the traffic signal installation condition, Stoneman (D) and KOA (D) did not undertake to perform a duty that the City (D) owed to Paz (P), for cities generally have no affirmative duty to install traffic control signals. Finally, there is no evidence that Paz (P) was harmed because either he or the City (D) relied on Stoneman's (D) and KOA's (D) timely installation of traffic control signals. The City (D) did not make a contract to install the signals; it was merely made a condition of Stoneman's (D) condo project. If Stoneman (D) had abandoned the project, the obligation to install the signals would not have continued. Thus, there could be no reliance on the installation being completed before the development project's completion. The cause is remanded with instruction to enter judgment for KOA (D) and Stoneman (D).

■ CONCURRENCE

(Mosk, J.) I do not understand or agree with the majority's foreclosing liability for negligent delay when a developer has breached a legal obligation to install a traffic improvement by a certain time or under a certain condition. There are circumstances when a municipality could be said to rely upon such installation, and the developer could accordingly be held liable for the harm resulting from its negligent delay based on that reliance.

■ DISSENT

(George, C.J.) Once a developer has made a commitment to install a needed safety measure as a condition of obtaining a development permit, the local entity and the public reasonably anticipate that the safety measure in question will be provided by the developer within a reasonable period of time. Thus I believe the developer owed a duty to the users of the intersections under the third condition of section 324A.

Analysis:

When the defendant's undertaking or contract with A is clearly made to protect B from physical harm, every reason supports a duty of care to B, both in contract and in tort. Under the Restatement's rules, even if the defendant's promise is not enforceable as a contract, the contract may still furnish the source of a tort duty to protect against physical harm when failure to perform increases the risk to the plaintiff and when the plaintiff reasonably relies upon performance. Consistent with the Restatement rules, the defendant is of course subject to liability if he assumes a duty by making a safety promise, and then negligently performs it, causing injury. That is a simple case of misfeasance and neither privity nor nonfeasance rules apply. However, to eliminate the privity and nonfeasance rules is not necessarily to impose liability for breach of all contracts when nonperformance leads to harm. As always, the courts' sense of policy and justice bear on the decision to recognize a duty. If negligent nonperformance causes harm, but the harm caused is not the result of any increased risk (as was ruled in this case), liability is inappropriate.

■ CASE VOCABULARY

AFFIRMATIVE DUTY: An obligation to perform in order to protect others against unreasonable risks.

ENCROACHMENT PERMIT: A permit allowing a fixture to invade a street, so as to impose restrictions.

NEGLIGENCE: The failure to use such care as a reasonably prudent and careful person would use under similar circumstances.

PRIVITY: That connection or relationship which exists between two or more contracting parties.

REMANDED: The act of an appellate court when it sends a case back to the trial court and orders the trial court to take some further action.

SUMMARY JUDGMENT: Procedural device available for prompt and expeditious disposition of controversy without trial when there is no dispute as to material facts, or if only a question of law is involved.

Florence v. Goldberg

(*Run-Over Child*) v. (*Car Driver and City*)
44 N.Y.2d 189, 404 N.Y.S.2d 583, 375 N.E.2d 763 (1978)

A PARTY WILL BE LIABLE FOR THE FAILURE TO PERFORM A DUTY, WHICH WAS VOLUNTARILY AND REGULARLY ASSUMED, IF THAT FAILURE RESULTS IN INJURY TO ANOTHER

WHY WAS THIS CHILD ALONE IN THE STREET? AND, WHERE WAS THE CROSSING GUARD?

■ **INSTANT FACTS** A six-year-old child was severely injured after being struck by a car at an unguarded street crossing while walking to school alone.

■ **BLACK LETTER RULE** A police department, having assumed a duty to a special class of persons, and having gone forward with performance of that duty in the past, has an obligation to continue its performance.

■ **PROCEDURAL BASIS**

Appeal from the Appellate Division's judgment in favor of the plaintiffs.

■ **FACTS**

Florence (P) took her six-year-old child to school each day for two weeks, during which time the city police had stationed a guard at a street crossing. Florence (P), having observed this protection, ceased to take the child to school. On the day in question, the crossing guard regularly assigned there called in sick. Departmental regulations called for sending a substitute if possible and, if not, to cover the most dangerous crossings. No substitute was sent and the principal of the school was not notified. The child was struck at the unguarded crossing and suffered severe brain damage. Florence (P) recovered against the city (D) and those responsible for the operation of the car (D). The city (D) appeals.

■ **ISSUE**

Does a police department have a duty to supervise school crossings if it voluntarily assumed the regular performance of that duty in the past?

■ **DECISION AND RATIONALE**

(Jasen, J.) Yes. There is little question that the police department voluntarily assumed a particular duty to supervise the school crossing. Significantly, the duty assumed by the police department was a limited one: a duty intended to benefit a special class of persons - viz., children crossing designated intersections while traveling to and from school at scheduled times. Having witnessed the regular performance of this special duty for a two-week period, Florence (P) relied upon its continued performance. The police department, having assumed a duty to a special class of persons, and having gone forward with performance of that duty in the past, had an obligation to continue its performance. Had the police department not assumed a duty to supervise school crossings, Florence (P) would not have permitted her child to travel to and from school alone. The department's failure to perform this duty placed the child in greater danger than he would have been had the duty not been assumed, since Florence (P) would not have had reason to rely on the protection afforded her child and would have been required, in her absence, to arrange for someone to accompany her child to and from school.

[The court found that there was also proof that the city (D) was negligent in failing to provide a guard] The order of the Appellate Division should be affirmed, with costs.

Analysis:

Undertakings can create a duty to act affirmatively and with reasonable care. Liability may be imposed if the plaintiff suffers physical harm from the defendant's negligent performance and only if one of two other conditions is met either the defendant's negligent performance (or withdrawal from performance) must increase the risk to the plaintiff, or else the plaintiff must have relied upon performance. In this case, the child was struck in an unguarded crosswalk where guards have always been provided before. Liability for negligently failing to provide the guard follows because the parent relied on the guard. Reliance is possible only when the parent has knowledge of the undertaking and a choice whether to provide some other means of protection. Thus, in this case, testimony that the parent knew that a guard was regularly provided, and that she would have taken the child to school herself if she had known that the guard would not be there, is enough evidence to show reliance and therefore permits recovery.

■ **CASE VOCABULARY**

REASONABLE CARE: That degree of care which a person of ordinary prudence would exercise in the same or similar circumstances.

VIZ.: That is to say.

CHAPTER EIGHTEEN

The Duty to Protect From Third Persons

Posecai v. Wal–Mart Stores, Inc.

Instant Facts: A woman sued a store for failing to provide security guards after she was attacked and robbed in the store's parking lot.

Black Letter Rule: A very high degree of foreseeability is required to give rise to a duty to post security guards, but a lower degree or foreseeability may support a duty to implement lesser security measures.

Marquay v. Eno

Instant Facts: Three former high school girls sued the school district for sexual abuse which certain teachers allegedly committed against them.

Black Letter Rule: Failure to report abuse in accordance with the statute could give rise to liability, provided the plaintiff can show that reporting would have prevented the subsequent abuse.

Tarasoff v. Regents of University of California

Instant Facts: A murdered woman's parents sued the University (D) because therapists employed there failed to warn their daughter of death threats made towards her by a patient.

Black Letter Rule: Once a therapist does in fact determine, or under applicable professional standards reasonably should have determined, that a patient poses serious danger of violence to others, he bears a duty to exercise reasonable care to protect the foreseeable victim of that danger.

Brigance v. Velvet Dove Restaurant, Inc.

Instant Facts: A minor who was injured in a car accident is suing the restaurant who served the minor-driver of the car alcoholic beverages.

Black Letter Rule: One who sells intoxicating beverages for on the premises consumption has a duty to exercise reasonable care not to sell liquor to a noticeably intoxicated person.

Posecai v. Wal-Mart Stores, Inc.

(Assaulted Woman) v. *(Store)*
752 So.2d 762 (La.1999)

IN DECIDING WHETHER TO IMPOSE A DUTY IN A PARTICULAR CASE, THE COURT MUST MAKE A POLICY DECISION IN LIGHT OF THE UNIQUE FACTS AND CIRCUMSTANCES PRESENTED

■ **INSTANT FACTS** A woman sued a store for failing to provide security guards after she was attacked and robbed in the store's parking lot.

■ **BLACK LETTER RULE** A very high degree of foreseeability is required to give rise to a duty to post security guards, but a lower degree or foreseeability may support a duty to implement lesser security measures.

■ **PROCEDURAL BASIS**

Appeal from the lower court's verdict and award in favor of the plaintiff.

■ **FACTS**

After Mrs. Posecai (P) finished shopping at Sam's (D), she returned to her car, which was parked in the store's (D) parking lot. A man hiding under her car grabbed her ankle, pointed a gun at her, and robbed her of $19,000 in jewels [pretty fancy for Sam's!]. Posecai (P) sued Sam's (D), claiming it was negligent in failing to provide security guards in the parking lot. Evidence showed that Sam's was adjacent to, but was not in, a high-crime area, and that during the previous six years, there had been three robberies on Sam's premises. During that same time period, there were 83 predatory offenses at 13 businesses in the same block as Sam's (D). The court assessed almost $30,000 in damages against Sam's (D), and this appeal followed.

■ **ISSUE**

Did the defendant possess the requisite degree of foreseeability for the imposition of a duty to provide security patrols in its parking lot?

■ **DECISION AND RATIONALE**

(Marcus, J.) No. Jurisdictions have resolved the foreseeability issue in a variety of ways, but four basic approaches have emerged. The specific harm rule, which is now somewhat outdated; a prior similar incidents test, which can lead to arbitrary results; the totality of the circumstances test, which tends to place a greater duty on business owners to foresee the risk of criminal attacks on their property; and finally, a balancing test, which seeks to address the interests of both business proprietors and their customers by balancing the foreseeability of harm against the burden of imposing a duty to protect against criminal acts of third persons. We agree that a balancing test is the best method for determining when business owners owe a duty to provide security for their patrons. The economic and social impact of requiring businesses to provide security on their premises is an important factor. Security is a significant monetary expense for any business and further increases the cost of doing business in high crime areas that are already economically depressed. Moreover, businesses are generally not responsible for the endemic crime that plagues our communities, a societal problem that even our law enforcement and other government agencies have been unable to solve. At the same time, business owners are in the best position to appreciate the crime risks that are posed on their premises and to take reasonable precautions to counteract those risks. The greater the foreseeability and gravity of the harm, the greater the duty of care that will be imposed on the business. A very high degree of foreseeability is required to give rise to a duty to post security guards, but a lower degree of foreseeability may support a duty to implement lesser security measures such as using surveillance cameras, installing improved lighting or fencing, or trimming shrubbery. In the present case, there were only three predatory offenses on Sam's (D) premises in the six and a half years prior to the robbery of Posecai (P). It is also relevant that Sam's only operates during daylight hours and must provide an accessible parking lot to the multitude of customers that shop at its store each year. We conclude that Sam's did not possess the requisite degree of foreseeability for the imposition of a duty to provide security patrols in its parking lot. Reversed.

Analysis:

A threshold issue in any negligence action is whether the defendant owed the plaintiff a duty. Whether a duty is owed is a question of law. In deciding whether to impose a duty in a particular case, the court must make a policy decision in light of the unique facts and circumstances presented. The court may consider various moral, social, and economic factors, including the fairness of imposing liability, the economic impact on the defendant and on similarly situated parties; the need for an incentive to prevent future harm; the nature of the defendant's activity; the potential for an unmanageable flow of litigation; the historical development of precedent; and the direction in which society and its institutions are evolving. The Court looked at each of the four basic approaches to foreseeability, and decided that the balancing test was the most appropriate. Courts have generally agreed that the specific harm rule is too restrictive in limiting the duty of protection that business owners owe their invitees, and that the prior similar incidents test can lead to arbitrary results because it is applied with different standards regarding the number of previous crimes and the degree of similarity required to give rise to a duty. The totality of the circumstances test is the most common approach used in other jurisdictions, and it takes additional factors into account, such as the nature, condition, and location of the land, as well as any other relevant factual circumstances bearing on foreseeability. This approach has been criticized, however, as being too broad a standard, effectively imposing an unqualified duty to protect customers in areas experiencing any significant level of criminal activity. The balancing test standard is indeed the best method for determining when business owners owe a duty to provide security for their patrons, as the Court decided. In determining the duty that exists, the foreseeability of harm and the gravity of the harm must be balanced against the commensurate burden imposed on the business to protect against that harm. That way, in cases where there is a high degree of foreseeability of harm and the probable harm is great, the burden imposed upon the defendant may be substantial. Alternatively, in cases in which a lesser degree of foreseeability is present or the potential harm is slight, less onerous burdens may be imposed. Thus, under this test, the high degree of foreseeability necessary to impose a duty to provide security will rarely, if ever, be proven in the absence of prior similar incidents of crime on the property.

■ CASE VOCABULARY

FORESEEABILITY: The reasonable anticipation that harm or injury is a likely result from certain acts or omissions.

IMMINENT HARM: Such an appearance of threatened and impending injury as would put a reasonable and prudent man to his instant defense.

PRIOR SIMILAR INCIDENTS TEST: Foreseeability is established by evidence of previous crimes on or near the premises.

SPECIFIC HARM RULE: A landowner does not owe a duty to protect patrons from the violent acts of third parties unless he is aware of specific, imminent harm about to befall them.

TOTALITY OF THE CIRCUMSTANCES TEST: This method takes additional factors into account, such as the nature, condition, and location of the land, as well as any other relevant factual circumstances bearing on foreseeability.

Marquay v. Eno

(Sexually Abused High School Girls) v. *(High School Teachers)*

139 N.H. 708, 662 A.2d 272 (1995)

SCHOOLS SHARE A SPECIAL RELATIONSHIP WITH STUDENTS ENTRUSTED TO THEIR CARE, WHICH IMPOSES UPON THEM CERTAIN DUTIES OF REASONABLE SUPERVISION

■ **INSTANT FACTS** Three former high school girls sued the school district for sexual abuse which certain teachers allegedly committed against them.

■ **BLACK LETTER RULE** Failure to report abuse in accordance with the statute could give rise to liability, provided the plaintiff can show that reporting would have prevented the subsequent abuse.

■ **PROCEDURAL BASIS**

The federal district court certified questions to the Supreme Court.

■ **FACTS**

Three women (P) who were students in the same school district (D) each filed separate complaints alleging that they were exploited, harassed, assaulted, and sexually abused by one or more employees of the school district (D). Each plaintiff also alleges that a host of school employees, including other teachers, coaches, superintendents, principals and secretaries either were aware or should have been aware of the sexual abuse. The women (P) sued the school district (D) and its allegedly abusing employees. The federal district court where the suits were brought certified a number of questions to this Court.

■ **ISSUE**

Do sexually abused children have a cause of action against the school employees for failure to report abuse about which they either knew or should have known?

■ **DECISION AND RATIONALE**

(Horton, J.) Yes. The first certified question asks whether the statute which requires that any person "having reason to suspect that a child has been abused or neglected shall report" it, creates a private right of action in favor of abused children against those who have violated the statute's reporting requirement. We hold that the reporting statute does not support a private right of action for its violation because we find no express or implied legislative intent to create such civil liability. First, we note that where the legislature has intended that civil liability flow from the violation of a statute, it has often so provided. Where, as here, civil liability for a statutory violation would represent an abrupt and sweeping departure from a general common law rule of nonliability, we would expect that if the legislature, which is presumed to recognize the common law, intended to impose civil liability it would expressly so provide. Here there was no expressed intent. Nor can we divine any implied intent. We now turn to the negligence per se question. Use of a statute to establish the standard of care is limited to situations where a common law cause of action exists, and then, only if the statute is "applicable." Whether a statutory standard is applicable depends, in part, on whether the type of duty to which the statute speaks is similar to the type of duty on which the cause of action is based. Because the duty to which the statute speaks—reporting of abuse—is considerably different from the duty on which the cause of action is based—supervision of students—we hold that a violation of the reporting statute does not constitute negligence per se in an action based on inadequate supervision of a student. The plaintiffs also argue that all school district employees have a common law duty to protect students whom they know or should know are being sexually abused by another school employee. We hold that some employees owe such a duty while others do not. The duty owed by some defendants is based on their relationship to the students; for other defendants the duty derives from their relationship to the alleged abusers. As a general rule, a person has no affirmative duty to aid or protect another. Such a duty may arise, however, if a special relationship exists. The women (P) argue that a special relationship exists between educators and school children, imposing a duty upon educators to protect students whom they know or should know are being sexually abused by another school employee. We agree with the majority of courts from other jurisdictions that schools share a special relationship with students entrusted to their care, which imposes upon them certain duties of reasonable supervision. The scope of the duty imposed is limited by what risks are reasonably foreseeable. Major factors influencing our conclusion that a special relationship exists between schools and students include the compulsory character of school attendance, the expectation of parents and students for and their reliance on a safe school environment, and the importance to society of the learning activity which is to take place in public schools. For these reasons, we conclude that the social importance of protecting the plaintiffs' interest outweighs the importance of immunizing the defendant from extended liability. While the impairment of protection creates an affirmative duty, it also circumscribes the limits of that duty. Thus the existence of a duty is limited to those periods when parental protection is compromised. That is not to say that employees with a special relationship to a student may not be liable for injuries that occurred off school premises or after school hours, if the student can show that the employee's negligent acts or omissions, within the scope of his or her duty, proximately caused injury to the student. This is a question for the jury. We note that the principal or superintendent rarely has primary supervisory authority over a student. Because, however, it is the school to which parents turn over custody of their children and from which they expect safety, and because the principal and superintendent are charged with overseeing all aspects of the school's operation, we hold that a duty of supervision is owed to each student. Where the principal or superintendent knows or should know that a particular school employee poses a threat to a student, entrustment of the student to the care of that employee will not satisfy the duty of reasonable supervision. Therefore, we hold that employees with supervisory powers of hiring and firing might be liable for negligent hiring or retention of a person they knew or should have known was an abuser, and in this type of action the reporting statute would be applicable. Accordingly, under these circumstances, failure to report abuse in accordance with the statute could give rise to liability, provided the plaintiff can show that reporting would have prevented the subsequent abuse. Remanded.

Analysis:

At first glance, the cases appear to be inconsistent on this issue. It has held that the violation of a penal statute is an actionable wrong only when the Legislature expressly so provides, or when the purpose and language of the statute compel such inference. On the other hand, the Court has also held that the breach of a statutory duty results in liability when the plaintiff is in a class the statute is designed to protect and the injury is of the type that the statute is intended to prevent. The apparent inconsistency arises from a failure to distinguish two distinct bases of civil liability: (1) statutorily expressed or implied causes of action; and (2) negligence per se. The former is the principle that whether or not the common law recognizes a cause of action, the plaintiff may maintain violation of that statute to give rise to civil liability. The doctrine of negligence per se, on the other hand, provides that where a cause of action does exist at common law, the standard of conduct to which a defendant will be held may be defined as that required by statute, rather than as the usual reasonable person standard. The doctrine of negligence per se, however, plays no role in the creation of common law causes of action. Thus, in many cases, the common law may fail to recognize liability for failure to perform affirmative duties that are imposed by statute. School attendance impairs both the ability of students to protect themselves and the ability of their parents to protect them. It is this impairment of protection from which the special relationship between school and student arises and from which the duty of supervision flows. The Court declined, however, to accept the women's (P) argument that every school employee shoulders a personal duty simply by virtue of receiving a paycheck from the school district. Instead, the duty falls upon those school employees who have supervisory responsibility over students and who thus have stepped into the role of parental proxy. Thus, those employees who share such a relationship with a student and who acquire actual knowledge of abuse or who learn of facts which would lead a reasonable person to conclude a student is being abused are subject to liability if their level of supervision is unreasonable and is a proximate cause of a student's injury.

■ CASE VOCABULARY

CERTIFIED: A method of taking a case from a district court to the Supreme Court in which the former court may request instructions as to any question of law.

EXPRESSED INTENT: Wishes or desires which are stated or declared in direct terms.

IMPLIED INTENT: Wishes or desires are gathered by implication or necessary deduction from the circumstances.

NEGLIGENCE PER SE: The unexcused violation of an applicable statute.

PROXIMATE CAUSE: That which, in a natural and continuous sequence, unbroken by any efficient intervening cause, produces injury, and without which the result would not have occurred.

Tarasoff v. Regents of University of California

(Parents of Murdered Woman) v. *(Employer of Therapists)*
17 Cal.3d 425, 131 Cal.Rptr. 14, 551 P.2d 334 (1976)

A THERAPIST OWES A LEGAL DUTY NOT ONLY TO HIS PATIENT, BUT ALSO TO HIS PATIENT'S WOULD-BE VICTIM

■ **INSTANT FACTS** A murdered woman's parents sued the University (D) because therapists employed there failed to warn their daughter of death threats made towards her by a patient.

■ **BLACK LETTER RULE** Once a therapist does in fact determine, or under applicable professional standards reasonably should have determined, that a patient poses serious danger of violence to others, he bears a duty to exercise reasonable care to protect the foreseeable victim of that danger.

■ PROCEDURAL BASIS

Appeal from the superior court's ruling which sustained the defendant's demurrers to plaintiffs' second amended complaints without leave to amend.

■ FACTS

Prosenjit Poddar confided his intention to kill Tatiana Tarasoff to a psychologist, Dr. Moore, who was employed by the University of California at Berkley (D). On Moore's request, the campus police briefly detained Poddar, but released him when he appeared rational. Dr. Powelson, Moore's superior, directed that no further action be taken to detain Poddar. No one warned Tatiana of the threats made on her life, and two months later Poddar killed her. Tatiana's parents (P) brought suit against the therapists, the campus police, and the Regents of the University of California as their employer. The superior court concluded that the facts did not set forth causes of action against the defendants, and sustained the defendant's demurrers to the Tarasoffs' (P) second amended complaints without leave to amend. This appeal followed.

■ ISSUE

Does a therapist have a duty to protect a foreseeable victim from dangers posed by their patients?

■ DECISION AND RATIONALE

(Tobriner, J.) Yes. Although the Tarasoffs' (P) pleadings assert no special relation between Tatiana and the therapists (D), they establish as between Poddar and the therapists (D) the special relation that arises between a patient and his doctor or psychotherapist. Such a relationship may support affirmative duties for the benefit of third persons. Thus, for example, a hospital must exercise reasonable care to control the behavior of a patient which may endanger other persons. A doctor must also warn a patient if the patient's condition of medication renders certain conduct, such as driving a car, dangerous to others. The University (D) contends, however, that imposition of a duty to exercise reasonable care to protect third persons is unworkable because therapists cannot accurately predict whether or not a patient will resort to violence. In support of the argument, amicus representing the American Psychiatric Association and other professional societies cite numerous articles which indicate that therapists, in the present state of the art, are unable reliably to predict violent acts; their forecasts, amicus claims, tend consistently to overpredict violence, and indeed are often more wrong than right. We recognize the difficulty that a therapist encounters in attempting to forecast whether a patient presents a serious danger of violence. Obviously we do not require that the therapist in making that determination, render a perfect performance; the therapist need only exercise "that reasonable degree of skill, knowledge, and care ordinarily possessed and exercised by members of that professional specialty under similar circumstances." Within the broad range of reasonable practice and treatment in which professional opinion and judgment may differ, the therapist is free to exercise his or her own best judgment without liability; proof, aided by hindsight, that he or she judged wrongly is insufficient to establish negligence. Amicus contends, however, that even if a therapist does in fact predict that a patient poses a serious danger of violence to others, the therapist should be absolved of any responsibility for failing to act to protect the potential victim. In our view, however, once a therapist does in fact determine, or under applicable professional standards reasonably should have determined, that a patient poses serious danger of violence to others, he bears a duty to exercise reasonable care to protect the foreseeable victim of that danger. While the discharge of this duty of due care will necessarily vary with the facts of each case, in each instance the adequacy of the therapist's conduct must be measured against the traditional negligence standard of the rendition of reasonable care under the circumstances. The ultimate question of resolving the tension between the conflicting interest of patient and potential victim is one of social policy, not professional expertise. In sum, the therapist owes a legal duty not only to his patient, but also to his patient's would-be victim and is subject in both respects to scrutiny by judge and jury. For the foregoing reasons, we find that the Tarasoffs' (P) complaints can be amended to state a cause of action against the therapists and the University, as their employer, for breach of a duty to exercise reasonable care to protect Tatiana. We conclude, however, that the police defendants do not have any such special relationship to either Tatiana or to Poddar sufficient to impose upon them a duty to warn respecting Poddar's violent intentions.

Analysis:

In analyzing this issue, one must bear in mind that legal duties are not discoverable facts of nature, but merely conclusory expressions that, in cases of a particular type, liability should be imposed for damage done. The assertion that liability should be denied because the defendant bears no duty to the plaintiff begs the essential question of whether the plaintiff's interests are entitled to legal protection against the defendant's conduct. Duty is not sacrosanct in itself, but only an expression of the sum total of those considerations of policy which lead the law to say that the particular plaintiff is entitled to protection. Whenever one person is by circumstances placed in such a position with regard to another that if he did not use ordinary care and skill in his own conduct he would cause danger of injury to the person or property of the other, a duty arises to use ordinary care and skill to avoid such danger. Departure from this fundamental principle only occurs upon the balancing of a number of considerations. The most important of these considerations in establishing duty is foreseeability. As a general principle, a defendant owes a duty of care to all persons who are foreseeably endangered by his conduct, with respect to all risks which make the conduct unreasonably dangerous. However, when the avoidance of foreseeable harm requires a defendant to control the conduct of another person, or to warn of such conduct, the common law has traditionally imposed liability only if the defendant bears some special relationship to the dangerous person or to the potential victim. The Court found that the risk that unnecessary warnings may be given is a reasonable price to pay for the lives of possible victims that may be saved.

■ CASE VOCABULARY

AFFIRMATIVE ACTS: Positive, forthcoming actions taken.

AMICUS: A group with a strong interest in or views on the subject matter of an action, but which is not a party to the action.

DEMURRER: An allegation of a defendant, which, admitting the matters of fact alleged by the complaint to be true, shows that as they are therein set forth they are insufficient for the plaintiff to proceed upon.

DUE CARE: That degree of care which an ordinarily prudent person would have exercised under the same or similar circumstances.

Brigance v. Velvet Dove Restaurant, Inc.

(Passenger) v. *(Booze Server)*
725 P.2d 300 (Okl.1986)

THE OLD COMMON LAW RULE OF A TAVERN OWNER'S NONLIABILITY IS UNREALISTIC AND INCONSISTENT WITH MODERN TORT THEORIES

■ **INSTANT FACTS** A minor who was injured in a car accident is suing the restaurant who served the minor-driver of the car alcoholic beverages.

■ **BLACK LETTER RULE** One who sells intoxicating beverages for on the premises consumption has a duty to exercise reasonable care not to sell liquor to a noticeably intoxicated person.

■ **PROCEDURAL BASIS**

Appeal from the trial court's dismissal of the plaintiff's claim.

■ **FACTS**

Jeff Johnson drove a group of minors to the Velvet Dove Restaurant (D), where they were served intoxicating beverages. Johnson was later involved in a one-car accident in which Shawn Brigance (P) was injured. (Presumably, Brigance (P) was a passenger.) Brigance (P) brought suit against the Restaurant (D), alleging that the alcohol served to Johnson caused him to become intoxicated, or increased his earlier intoxication, which in turn caused the car accident. The trial court dismissed the claim, and this appeal followed.

■ **ISSUE**

Can a tavern owner who furnishes alcoholic beverages to another be held civilly liable for a third person's injuries that are caused by the acts of an intoxicated patron?

■ **DECISION AND RATIONALE**

(Hodges, J.) Yes. In recent years, many states have retreated from the common law rule of nonliability for a liquor vendor, regarding it as antiquated and illogical. Several states with dram shop laws have also recognized a new common law right of action against a vendor of liquor. Many of the jurisdictions which now recognize a civil right of action do so on the theory that when alcoholic beverages are sold by a tavern keeper to a minor or to an intoxicated person, the unreasonable risk of harm to members of the traveling public may readily be recognized and foreseen. This is particularly evident in current times when traveling by car to and from the tavern is so commonplace and accidents resulting from drinking are so frequent. We find that on the basis of the clear trend in this area we are free to establish a civil cause of action by an injured third person against a commercial vendor of liquor for on the premises consumption. We believe the application of the old common law rule of a tavern owner's nonliability in today's automotive society is unrealistic, inconsistent with modern tort theories and is a complete anachronism within today's society. We thus hold that one who sells intoxicating beverages for on the premises consumption has a duty to exercise reasonable care not to sell liquor to a noticeably intoxicated person. It is not unreasonable to expect a commercial vendor who sells alcoholic beverages for on the premises consumption to a person he knows or should know from the circumstances is already intoxicated, to foresee the unreasonable risk of harm to others who may be injured by such person's impaired ability to operate an automobile. However, even if a commercial vendor for on the premises consumption is found to have breached its duty, a plaintiff must still show the illegal sale of alcohol led to the impairment of the ability of the driver which was the proximate cause of the injury and there was a causal connection between the sale and a foreseeable ensuing injury. In adopting a new rule of liability which creates a civil cause of action, we specifically hold that the law hereby established will be applied prospectively to all causes of action occurring from and after the date the mandate issues herein, except that the rule of liability also applies to the parties in this case. Reversed and remanded.

Analysis:

At common law, a tavern owner who furnishes alcoholic beverages to another is not civilly liable for a third person's injuries that are caused by the acts of an intoxicated person. Such rule is principally based upon concepts of causation that, as a matter of law, it is not the sale of liquor by the tavern owner, but the voluntary consumption by the intoxicated person, which is the proximate cause of resulting injuries, so that the tavern owner is therefore not liable for negligence in selling the liquor. Ordinarily the question of causation in a negligent tort case is one of fact for the jury and becomes one of law only where there is no evidence from which the jury could reasonably find a causal nexus between the negligent act and the resulting injuries. As shown by the modern trend, the old common law rule of nonliability has been changed by judicial opinion. Inherent in the common law is a dynamic principle which allows it to grow and to tailor itself to meet changing needs. The development of the law of torts is peculiarly a function of the judiciary. Because duty and liability are matters of public policy, they are subject to the changing attitudes and needs of society. In the "horse and buggy" days, the common law may not have been significantly affected by the sale of liquor to an intoxicated person; the common law of nonliability was satisfactory. With today's car of steel and speed, it becomes a lethal weapon in the hands of a drunk driver.

■ CASE VOCABULARY

CAUSAL NEXUS: A connection which ties the act to the result.

DRAM SHOP LAWS: A State Act which imposes liability on the seller of intoxicating liquors when a third party is injured as a result of the intoxication of the buyer where the sale has caused or contributed to the intoxication.

MANDATE: A judicial command or order issued upon the decision of an appeal.

CHAPTER NINETEEN

Emotional Harm

GTE Southwest, Inc. v. Bruce

Instant Facts: Employees sued their employer for intentional infliction of emotional distress because of the extremely abusive nature of their supervisor.

Black Letter Rule: To establish a cause of action for intentional infliction of emotional distress in the workplace, an employee must prove the existence of some conduct that brings the dispute outside the scope of an ordinary employment dispute and into the realm of extreme and outrageous conduct.

Homer v. Long

Instant Facts: A husband sued his wife's therapist after the therapist used confidential information to seduce the emotionally fragile woman.

Black Letter Rule: There are situations in which conduct directed principally at one person has been regarded as extreme and outrageous as to another, but normally the other person must be present to witness the conduct in order to recover.

Grube v. Union Pacific R.R.

Instant Facts: Grube (P) sued his employer, Union Pacific Railroad (D), for negligent infliction of emotional injury, after the train he was operating as engineer collided with an automobile.

Black Letter Rule: A worker within the zone of danger of physical impact will be able to recover for emotional injury caused by fear of physical injury to himself, whereas a worker outside the zone will not.

Boucher v. Dixie Medical Center

Instant Facts: Parents sued the hospital after their son went into a coma and suffered severe brain damage following hand surgery.

Black Letter Rule: The parents of a tortiously injured adult child cannot recover for loss of the child's consortium.

Sacco v. High Country Independent Press, Inc.

Instant Facts: Sacco (P) sued her former employer for falsely accusing her of stealing from the company, and causing the police to swear out a criminal complaint.

Black Letter Rule: An independent cause of action for negligent infliction of emotional distress will arise under circumstances where serious or severe emotional distress to the plaintiff was the reasonably foreseeable consequence of the defendant's negligent act or omission.

Potter v. Firestone Tire And Rubber Co.

Instant Facts: The Potters (P) sued Firestone (D) after toxic chemicals from the plant were dumped in a landfill and then leached into the drinking water.

Black Letter Rule: A toxic exposure plaintiff need not meet the more likely than not threshold for fear of cancer recovery in a negligence action if the plaintiff pleads and proves that the defendant's conduct in causing the exposure amounts to oppression, fraud, or malice, which authorizes the imposition of punitive damages.

GTE Southwest, Inc. v. Bruce

(Employer) v. *(Emotionally Abused Employees)*

998 S.W.2d 605 (1999)

GENERALLY, INSENSITIVE OR EVEN RUDE BEHAVIOR DOES NOT CONSTITUTE EXTREME AND OUTRAGEOUS CONDUCT

■ **INSTANT FACTS** Employees sued their employer for intentional infliction of emotional distress because of the extremely abusive nature of their supervisor.

■ **BLACK LETTER RULE** To establish a cause of action for intentional infliction of emotional distress in the workplace, an employee must prove the existence of some conduct that brings the dispute outside the scope of an ordinary employment dispute and into the realm of extreme and outrageous conduct.

■ **PROCEDURAL BASIS**

Appeal from the Court of Appeals' affirmance of the trial court's judgment for the plaintiff.

■ **FACTS**

Bruce (P) and several other plaintiffs worked for GTE (D) under Morris Shields. They alleged that over a period of years, Shields engaged in a pattern of grossly abusive, threatening, and degrading conduct, regularly using the harshest vulgarity, verbally threatening and terrorizing them [a real sweetheart!]. He frequently yelled and screamed at the top of his voice, and pounded his fists when requesting the employees to do things [who wouldn't bend over backwards to help?]. He would physically intimidate the employees, charging at them with his fists balled up, stopping very close to their faces. He would force them to clean their offices daily, even though regular janitorial services were provided by others. There was also testimony that he would often call one employee into his office to stand in front of him while he simply stared at her for up to thirty minutes [pervert!]. The testimony detailed many abuses of this kind. The trial court entered judgment on the jury's verdict for Bruce (P) and the other plaintiffs. The Court of Appeals affirmed, and this appeal followed.

■ **ISSUE**

Was Shields' conduct extreme and outrageous such as to support a claim of intentional infliction of emotional distress?

■ **DECISION AND RATIONALE**

(Not Stated) Yes. To recover damages for intentional infliction of emotional distress, a plaintiff must prove that: (1) the defendant acted intentionally or recklessly; (2) the conduct was extreme and outrageous; (3) the actions of the defendant caused the plaintiff emotional distress; and (4) the resulting emotional distress was severe. In addition, a claim for intentional infliction of emotional distress cannot be maintained when the risk that emotional distress will result is merely incidental to the commission of some other tort. Accordingly, a claim for intentional infliction of emotional distress will not lie if emotional distress is not the intended or primary consequence of the defendant's conduct. Generally, insensitive or even rude behavior does not constitute extreme and outrageous conduct.

Similarly, mere insults, indignities, threats, annoyances, petty oppressions, or other trivialities do not rise to the level of extreme and outrageous conduct. Thus, to establish a cause of action for intentional infliction of emotional distress in the workplace, an employee must prove the existence of some conduct that brings the dispute outside the scope of an ordinary employment dispute and into the realm of extreme and outrageous conduct. Shields' ongoing acts of harassment, intimidation, and humiliation and his daily obscene and vulgar behavior, which GTE (D) defends as his "management style," went beyond the bounds of tolerable workplace conduct. Occasional malicious and abusive incidents should not be condoned, but must often be tolerated in our society. But once conduct such as that shown here becomes a regular pattern of behavior and continues despite the victim's objection and attempts to remedy the situation, it can no longer be tolerated. It is the severity and regularity of Shields' abusive and threatening conduct that brings his behavior into the realm of extreme and outrageous conduct. Affirmed.

Analysis:

In determining whether certain conduct is extreme and outrageous, courts consider the context and the relationship between the parties. In the employment context, some courts have held that a plaintiff's status as an employee should entitle him to a greater degree of protection from insult and outrage by a supervisor with authority over him than if he were a stranger. This approach is based partly on the rationale that, as opposed to most casual and temporary relationships, the workplace environment provides a captive victim and the opportunity for prolonged abuse. In contrast, several courts have adopted a strict approach to intentional infliction of emotional distress claims arising in the workplace. These courts rely on the fact that, to properly manage its business, an employer must be able to supervise, review, criticize, demote, transfer, and discipline employees. This Court agreed with the second approach, and, as a result, required that the behavior must be in the realm of extreme and outrageous conduct.

■ CASE VOCABULARY

EXTREME AND OUTRAGEOUS CONDUCT: Above and beyond insulting; shocking to the conscious.

INTENTIONAL INFLICTION OF EMOTIONAL DISTRESS: A tort in which emotional distress is the intended or primary consequence of the defendant's conduct.

Homer v. Long

(Patient's Husband) v. *(Patient's Seducer/Therapist)*

90 Md.App. 1, 599 A.2d 1193 (1992)

NORMALLY, THIRD PERSONS MUST BE PRESENT TO WITNESS THE EXTREME AND OUTRAGEOUS CONDUCT IN ORDER TO RECOVER FOR SUCH CONDUCT DIRECTED PRINCIPALLY AT ANOTHER PERSON

■ **INSTANT FACTS** A husband sued his wife's therapist after the therapist used confidential information to seduce the emotionally fragile woman.

■ **BLACK LETTER RULE** There are situations in which conduct directed principally at one person has been regarded as extreme and outrageous as to another, but normally the other person must be present to witness the conduct in order to recover.

■ **PROCEDURAL BASIS**

Not Stated.

■ **FACTS**

Mr. Homer (P) and his wife had been married many years when she was hospitalized for depression. While she was hospitalized, Dr. Long (D), her therapist, used confidential information and took advantage of her dependent, needy and vulnerable condition to seduce her [oh, that should cheer her right up!]. Homer's (P) wife's personality subsequently changed and they were ultimately divorced. Mr. Homer (P) sued Dr. Long (D) for, among other things, intentional or reckless infliction of distress.

■ **ISSUE**

Can conduct directed principally at one person be regarded as extreme and outrageous as to another person not present to witness the conduct?

■ **DECISION AND RATIONALE**

(Wilner, C.J.) No. To recover damages for intentional infliction of emotional distress, a plaintiff must prove that: (1) the defendant acted intentionally or recklessly; (2) the conduct was extreme and outrageous; (3) the actions of the defendant caused the plaintiff emotional distress; and (4) the resulting emotional distress was severe. Whether, for purposes of this tort, the conduct is extreme and outrageous depends, at least in part, on the context in which it is viewed. Intrinsically, of course, it is extreme and outrageous; it also violates clear standards set by the medical community itself. But the essence of the requirement is that the conduct must not simply be extreme and outrageous from the perspective of society at large, or from the perspective of someone else, but must also be so as to the plaintiff. Outrageous conduct directed at A does not necessarily give B a cause of action. There are situations in which conduct directed principally at one person has been regarded as extreme and outrageous as to another, but normally the other person must be present to witness the conduct in order to recover. The requirement of presence has been relaxed by some courts in particularly compelling circumstances, as, for example, where a parent sued the defendant for sexually molesting or kidnaping the plaintiff's child. We see no reason not to apply the general rule here. The emotional and economic trauma likely to arise from the seduction of one's spouse is not limited to the case where the

---

seducer is the spouse's therapist. The conduct may be just as outrageous and the harm may be just as great where the seducer is a neighbor, a good friend, a relative, an employee or business associate of Mr. Homer's (P), or indeed anyone in whom Mr. Homer (P) has imposed trust or for whom he or she has special regard.

Analysis:

This opinion was somewhat confusing as to what the Court was actually ruling. Basically, the Court held that although there are situations in which outrageous conduct directed at A can give B a cause of action, this is not one of those cases. The Court decided to follow the general rule which allows for a third party to recover for extreme and outrageous conduct towards another only if the third party was present to witness the conduct. In this case, it is not addressed, however it could be assumed, that Mr. Homer (P) was not present while his wife was being seduced by Dr. Long (D). Where the extreme and outrageous conduct is directed at a third person, the defendant may know that it is substantially certain, or at least highly probable, that it will cause severe emotional distress to the plaintiff. Since the mental effect can reasonably be anticipated by the defendant, it seems reasonable that he should be held accountable for any harm caused by his actions. Some argument has been made that the distinction between the wife who sees her husband shot down before her eyes, and the one who hears about it five minutes later, may be a highly artificial one. However, an argument in justification is the obvious necessity of drawing a line somewhere short of the widow who learns of the killing ten years afterward, when the genuineness and gravity of her distress may very reasonably be doubted.

■ CASE VOCABULARY

CAUSAL CONNECTION: Proof that the wrongful conduct caused the resulting emotional distress.

INTENTIONAL CONDUCT: Purposeful actions.

RECKLESS CONDUCT: Careless, heedless, inattentive to duty.

Grube v. Union Pacific R.R.

(Train Engineer) v. *(Railroad Employer)*
256 Kan. 519, 886 P.2d 845 (1994)

FEAR FOR ONE'S SAFETY IS AN ESSENTIAL ELEMENT OF THE ZONE OF DANGER TEST

■ **INSTANT FACTS** Grube (P) sued his employer, Union Pacific Railroad (D), for negligent infliction of emotional injury, after the train he was operating as engineer collided with an automobile.

■ **BLACK LETTER RULE** A worker within the zone of danger of physical impact will be able to recover for emotional injury caused by fear of physical injury to himself, whereas a worker outside the zone will not.

■ **PROCEDURAL BASIS**

Appeal from the trial court's judgment for the plaintiff.

■ **FACTS**

Ernest Grube (P) was employed by Union Pacific Railroad Company (D). He was operating as engineer when his train collided with an automobile trapped upon a railroad crossing. One of the occupants in the automobile died and two others suffered serious injury as a result of the collision. Grube (P) saw the trapped car before the collision, and remembers the driver of the car, a young man, looking at the approaching train with an expression of shock, fright and fear. Grube (P) sustained no physical injury as a result of the collision, but when the train eventually stopped, he ran back to the scene attempting to render aid. He felt the pulse of the driver and touched the deceased, attempting to find a pulse. At the accident scene, Grube (P) exhibited physical manifestations of his emotional distress; he became physically ill. Grube (P) testified that he had no thoughts of fear of physical injury at the time of the accident, but was reacting and not thinking at the time and merely doing his job. The other employee in the cab of the engine with Grube (P), however, ducked down before impact out of fear of possible explosion at the time of impact [so brave!]. Grube (P) claimed against his employer, Union Pacific (D), seeking damages for negligent infliction of emotional injury with accompanying physical manifestations. The jury returned a verdict for Grube (P) in the amount of $121,500.

■ **ISSUE**

Is fear for one's safety an essential element of the zone of danger test?

■ **DECISION AND RATIONALE**

(Davis, J.) Yes. Section 1 of FELA imposes liability on railroads for injuries sustained by their employees in the course of their employment. *45 U.S.C. Sec. 51.* Kansas law is clear in its requirement that a plaintiff demonstrate some physical impact/injury in order to recover for negligent infliction of emotional distress. The United States Supreme Court has made clear, however, that federal common law governs such claims under FELA. The "zone of danger test" was developed in prior case law to address the concerns courts experienced with the recognition of a cause of action for emotional injury when not related to any physical trauma. Under this test, a worker within the zone of danger of physical impact will be able to recover for emotional injury caused by fear of physical injury to himself, whereas a worker outside the zone will not. Grube (P) acknowledged that he expressed no fear at the time of the collision, but argues that the zone of danger test adopted by the Supreme Court does not require a contemporaneous expression of such fear. He points out that many times people react to dangerous situations automatically and only later come to the realization of the danger they were in at the time of the peril. This point is well taken, and we do not believe that the zone of danger test necessarily requires that there be fear for one's personal safety expressed contemporaneously with the collision. However, fear for one's safety is an essential element of the zone of danger test and must be expressed at or near the time of the danger in order for a plaintiff to prevail in an action. In this case, Grube (P) failed to establish that he feared for his own personal safety at any time. His emotional injury did not result from fear of his personal safety, but rather from his experiences relating to the others affected by the impact. Grube (P) nevertheless argues that the physical impact he experienced when he was thrown against the console of the engine at the time of the collision brings him within the zone of danger test. However, as Union Pacific (D) points out, there was no evidence that this action caused Grube (P) any physical or emotional injuries. He suffered no bruises or abrasions as a result of the impact. We therefore reverse the judgment of the trial court and enter judgment for Union Pacific (D).

Analysis:

The zone of danger test was adopted by the Supreme Court to alleviate concerns with recognizing a cause of action for emotional injury when there was no related physical trauma. One such concern was that these claims could inundate judicial resources with a flood of relatively trivial claims, many of which may be imagined or falsified, and that liability may be imposed for highly remote consequences of a negligent act. A more significant concern was that emotional injuries may occur far removed in time and space from the negligent conduct that triggered them. There are no necessary limits on the number of persons who might suffer emotional injury because of the negligent act. Thus, many courts note that recognition of this cause of action raises the real possibility of nearly infinite and unpredictable liability for defendants. The problem with Grube's (P) position is that, as the Court noted, the record fails to establish that he expressed fear for his own personal safety at *any* time. His fear was for the youth whose face he saw before impact and whose face he touched afterwards. As a result of this fear, Grube (P) became physically ill immediately after the collision. There is ample evidence to establish that Grube (P) experienced his severe emotional problems because of his concern about the lawsuit and his involvement in an accident in which a man died and others were injured. The courts have agreed that the entire damages may include emotional distress resulting from concern or fear for the safety of another person, so long as the plaintiff establishes that he or she suffered imminent apprehension of personal physical harm. Thus, the Court's ruling that Grube (P) cannot recover is justified based upon the record. If Grube (P) had indicated that he was fearful at any time for his own safety the outcome would perhaps have been different. However, Grube's (P) own testimony sunk him in this case.

■ CASE VOCABULARY

FELA: The Federal Employers' Liability Act is the federal law imposing liability on railroads for injuries sustained by their employees in the course of employment.

IMMINENT APPREHENSION: Urgent, immediate fear of personal injury.

NEGLIGENT INFLICTION OF EMOTIONAL INJURY: Failure to use due care to prevent circumstances which cause emotional injury to another.

ZONE OF DANGER: The area to which the consequences of a tortfeasor's conduct reach and cause imminent apprehension of physical harm.

Boucher v. Dixie Medical Center

(Parents of Quadriplegic) v. *(Hospital)*

850 P.2d 1179 (Utah 1992)

THERE IS NO RIGHT OF RECOVERY BASED ON THE RELATIONSHIP BETWEEN PARENTS AND THEIR ADULT CHILD IN LOSS OF CONSORTIUM CLAIMS

■ **INSTANT FACTS** Parents sued the hospital after their son went into a coma and suffered severe brain damage following hand surgery.

■ **BLACK LETTER RULE** The parents of a tortiously injured adult child cannot recover for loss of the child's consortium.

■ **PROCEDURAL BASIS**

Appeal from the trial court's dismissal of the plaintiffs' complaint.

■ **FACTS**

The Bouchers' (P) eighteen-year-old son, Daniel, was admitted into Dixie Medical Center (D) with a severely injured hand. He lapsed into a coma during the post-operative recovery period following surgery for his hand. He remained in a coma for ten days before awakening as a severely brain-damaged quadriplegic who will need extensive care for the rest of his life [now that's a complication!]. The Bouchers (P) were present at the hospital and observed their son's condition both before and after he awoke from the coma. The Bouchers (P) claimed damaged for (1) negligent infliction of mental distress and (2) loss of their child's consortium or society, in addition to the claim of Daniel Boucher himself. The trial court dismissed the complaint, and this appeal followed.

■ **ISSUE**

Can the parents of a tortiously injured adult child recover for loss of the child's consortium?

■ **DECISION AND RATIONALE**

(Hall, J.) No. [The Supreme Court in this opinion concluded that the Boucher (P) parents could not recover for negligent infliction of mental distress because they were not in the zone of danger. The Court then considered the loss of consortium claim as follows.] The Bouchers' (P) second claim presents an issue of first impression in this court: Should Utah judicially adopt a cause of action that allows the parents of a tortiously injured adult child to recover for loss of the child's consortium? Loss of consortium claims are based on the recognition of a legally protected interest in personal relationships. Accordingly, if one member of the relationship is tortiously injured the noninjured party has a cause of action to recover for damage to their relational interest, in other words, the loss of the injured party's company society, cooperation and affection. In the instant case, we are asked to recognize a right of recovery based on the relationship between parents and their adult son. For the reasons set forth below, we decline to adopt such an approach. The majority of jurisdictions that have addressed the issue have declined to recognize a cause of action for loss of filial consortium. Indeed, our research reveals only one jurisdiction that has expressly recognized the specific right the Bouchers (P) urge this court to adopt: a judicially created right to recover for the loss of an adult child's consortium. Utah's Married Woman's Act has been construed to abolish the claim of spousal consortium. Allowing recovery for the loss of an adult child's consortium and denying recovery for the loss of a spouse's consortium would lead to anomalous results. In many instances, the marital relationship is closer and more involved than the relationship between parents and their adult children and therefore should be granted greater or equal protection. However, we cannot recognize a filial consortium claim and extend the same right of recovery to a plaintiff who suffers a loss of consortium because his or her spouse has been tortiously injured. The adoption of the Bouchers' claim, therefore, would invite inequitable applications of the consortium doctrine. The Bouchers (P) also contend that because Utah allows recovery for the loss of society and affection in wrongful death cases, it is logical to extend this theory of damages to cases involving nonfatal injuries. However, we view wrongful death cases as distinguishable from consortium cases. In wrongful death cases, the party that suffers the actual physical injury has no cause of action and the legislature has prescribed the parties who have a right to recover for the loss of the deceased's society and affection. Therefore, there is no danger of expansive liability and no need for the judiciary to attempt to fashion rational limits on relational interests. We decline to adopt a cause of action that allows the parents of a tortiously injured adult child to recover for the loss of consortium. The trial court, therefore, did not err in dismissing the Bouchers' (P) claims of negligent infliction of emotional distress and loss of filial consortium. Affirmed.

Analysis:

A review of the case law reveals little support for the adoption of a cause of action for the loss of filial consortium. At common law, the father of a tortiously injured child did have a cause of action to recover the value of the child's loss of services and the medical expenses incurred on the child's behalf. However, this action was based on a father's right to his minor children's services and a father's obligation to pay his minor children's medical expenses. This right of recovery, therefore, did not extend beyond these two elements of damages, nor did it extend to injuries involving adult or emancipated children. These common law principles have undergone some modification. However, no widely accepted development has occurred that allows recovery in cases involving adult children, nor has any widely accepted development occurred that allows recovery for the loss of a child's society and affection. Consortium claims have the potential for greatly expanding the liability that can flow from one negligent act, and courts that have adopted consortium claims have been unable to develop rational limits on this liability. The recognition of consortium claims may also impact the cost and availability of insurance. Finally, given these concerns and the fact that the legislature has previously acted in this area, the legislature is the appropriate body to determine if Utah should recognize consortium claims.

■ CASE VOCABULARY

CONSORTIUM: The fellowship, company, cooperation and aid of one another in a relationship.

EMANCIPATED: Freed from the control of another.

WRONGFUL DEATH: A wrongful act, neglect, or default which results in death.

Sacco v. High Country Independent Press, Inc.

(Former Employee) v. *(Former Employer)*
271 Mont. 209, 896 P.2d 411 (1995)

A CAUSE OF ACTION FOR NEGLIGENT INFLICTION OF EMOTIONAL DISTRESS WILL ARISE UNDER CIRCUMSTANCES WHERE REASONABLY FORESEEABLE CONSEQUENCES OF A DEFENDANT'S NEGLIGENT ACT OR OMISSION CAUSE SERIOUS OR SEVERE EMOTIONAL DISTRESS TO THE PLAINTIFF

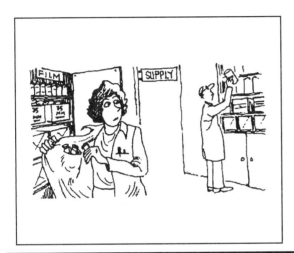

■ **INSTANT FACTS** Sacco (P) sued her former employer for falsely accusing her of stealing from the company, and causing the police to swear out a criminal complaint.

■ **BLACK LETTER RULE** An independent cause of action for negligent infliction of emotional distress will arise under circumstances where serious or severe emotional distress to the plaintiff was the reasonably foreseeable consequence of the defendant's negligent act or omission.

■ **PROCEDURAL BASIS**

Appeal from the trial judge's grant of summary judgment for the defendants.

■ **FACTS**

Dianne Sacco (P) was an employee at the High Country Independent Press (D) newspaper. When she left her employment, Sacco (P) alleges that the company and its officers/stockholders falsely told police sergeant Dighans that Sacco (P) had stolen photographic negatives and proof sheets. This led Dighans to swear out a criminal complaint. Sacco (P) asserted a number of theories against various defendants, including a theory of negligent infliction of distress against Dighans. The trial judge gave summary judgment for the defendants, and this appeal followed.

■ **ISSUE**

Is negligent infliction of emotional distress an independent cause of action?

■ **DECISION AND RATIONALE**

(Nelson, J.) Yes. After thoroughly reviewing our own case law and the authorities from other jurisdictions, we conclude that it is appropriate that we join a multitude of jurisdictions in recognizing both negligent and intentional infliction torts as independent causes of action with recovery for damages based upon satisfaction of the standard we set forth in the instant case. An independent cause of action for negligent infliction of emotional distress will arise under circumstances where serious or severe emotional distress to the plaintiff was the reasonably foreseeable consequence of the defendant's negligent or intentional act or omission. Based upon the logic and analysis in other cases, and the state of our prior case law, we conclude that it is appropriate to clarify the existing law on negligent infliction of emotional distress and to delineate a better approach to such claims. Therefore we adopt the following standard for determining whether a plaintiff has demonstrated a cause of action for the negligent infliction of emotional distress. A cause of action for negligent infliction of emotional distress will arise under circumstances where serious or severe emotional distress to the plaintiff was the reasonably foreseeable consequence of the defendant's negligent act or omission. The difference between the negligent and intentional versions of the cause of action lies, not in the elements of the tort,

---

but in the nature and culpability of the defendant's conduct. That being the case, when a cause of action for intentional infliction of emotional distress is pled, the plaintiff may request relief in the form of punitive damages to address the culpability of the defendant's conduct. Serious or severe emotional distress to the plaintiff which was the reasonably foreseeable consequence of the defendant's negligent or intentional act or omission will be addressed in both causes of action, as stated above, through a prayer for relief in the form of compensatory damages. Accordingly, we hold that the District Court erred in granting Dighans' (D) motion for summary judgment on the issue of negligent infliction of emotional distress, and we remand for further proceedings consistent with the new standard enunciated above.

Analysis:

The Court's enunciation of a new standard for determining whether a plaintiff has demonstrated a cause of action for the negligent infliction of emotional distress has alleviated concerns which historically followed claims for emotional distress. Concern over a floodgate of claims for emotional distress, particularly fraudulent claims, is eased by the necessity to prove that the emotional distress suffered is severe or serious. Additionally, concern over seemingly unlimited liability for defendants is eliminated by the necessity of demonstrating that the plaintiff's serious or severe emotional distress was the reasonably foreseeable consequence of the defendant's negligent act or omission. The requirement that the emotional distress suffered as a result of the defendant's conduct be "serious" or "severe" ensures that only genuine claims will be compensated. A jury is capable of determining whether the emotional distress claimed to have been sustained is "serious" or "severe." In cases other than where proof of mental distress is of a medically significant nature, the general standard of proof required as support for a claim of mental distress, is some guarantee of the genuineness in the circumstances of the case. This standard is not as difficult to apply as it may seem in the abstract, for the jurors are best situated to determine whether and to what extent the defendant's conduct caused emotional distress by referring to their own experience. In addition, there will doubtless be circumstances in which the alleged emotional injury is susceptible of objective ascertainment by expert medical testimony.

■ CASE VOCABULARY

COMPENSATORY DAMAGES: Those damages directly referable to the tortious act; actual damages.

CULPABILITY: Implies fault rather than guilt, it is disregard of the consequence which may ensue from the act, and indifference to the rights of others.

PRAYER FOR RELIEF: Request contained in a complaint or petition that asks for relief to which the plaintiff thinks he or she is entitled.

PUNITIVE DAMAGES: Compensation in excess of actual damages; a form of punishment to the wrongdoer and excess enhancement to the injured.

SWEAR OUT A COMPLAINT: Officially file charges against another person for a wrong incurred.

Potter v. Firestone Tire and Rubber Co.

(Contaminated Family) v. *(Toxic Waste Dumpers)*
6 Cal.4th 965, 25 Cal.Rptr.2d 550, 863 P.2d 795 (1993)

IF A TOXIC EXPOSURE PLAINTIFF PLEADS AND PROVES THAT THE DEFENDANT'S CONDUCT AMOUNTS TO "OPPRESSION, FRAUD, OR MALICE," THE PLAINTIFF NEED NOT MEET THE "MORE LIKELY THAN NOT" THRESHOLD FOR HIS FEAR OF CANCER CLAIM

■ **INSTANT FACTS** The Potters (P) sued Firestone (D) after toxic chemicals from the plant were dumped in a landfill and then leached into the drinking water.

■ **BLACK LETTER RULE** A toxic exposure plaintiff need not meet the more likely than not threshold for fear of cancer recovery in a negligence action if the plaintiff pleads and proves that the defendant's conduct in causing the exposure amounts to oppression, fraud, or malice, which authorizes the imposition of punitive damages.

■ **PROCEDURAL BASIS**

Appeal from the court of appeal's affirmance of the trial court's award for the plaintiffs.

■ **FACTS**

Firestone (D) contracted for disposal of industrial wastes produced by its tire manufacturing plant in a Class II sanitary landfill operated by the City. Class II landfills prohibit disposal of toxic substances because of the danger that they will leach into the groundwater. Firestone (D) assured the city that no such waste would be sent to the landfill. Official plant policy required proper disposal of hazardous wastes in a Class I landfill, however that program was costly. When a new production manager came to Firestone (D) to make the plant more profitable, he became angered at the costs of the hazardous waste disposal program [why do things the *right* way when you can do it the *cheap* way instead?]. As a result, Firestone's (D) hazardous waste materials, including serious toxins, were deposited in the landfill. The Potters (P), who lived near the landfill, discovered that toxic chemicals had contaminated their domestic water wells. At least two of the chemicals are known human carcinogens and others are strong suspects. The Potters (P) sued Firestone (D) on theories that included negligent infliction of emotional distress. The trial court awarded $269,500 for psychiatric illnesses and the cost of treating them, $142,975 for the cost of medical monitoring of the Potters (P), and punitive damages of $2.6 million.

■ **ISSUE**

Does a toxic exposure plaintiff need to meet the more likely than not threshold for fear of cancer recovery in a negligence action?

■ **DECISION AND RATIONALE**

(Baxter, J.) No. The physical injury requirement is a hopelessly imprecise screening device and, as such, the absence of a present physical injury does not preclude recovery for emotional distress engendered by fear of cancer. We next consider whether recovery of damages for emotional distress caused by fear of cancer should depend upon a showing that the Potter's (P) fears stem from a

---

knowledge that there is a probable likelihood of developing cancer in the future due to the toxic exposure. This is a matter of hot debate among the parties and amici curiae. We would be very hard pressed to find that, as a matter of law, a plaintiff faced with a 20 to 30 percent chance of developing cancer cannot genuinely, seriously and reasonably fear the prospect of cancer. Nonetheless, we conclude, for public policy reasons, that emotional distress caused by the fear of a cancer that is not probable should generally not be compensable in a negligence action. One concern weighing in favor of a more likely than not threshold is the unduly detrimental impact that unrestricted fear liability would have in the health care field. As amicus curiae California Medical Association points out, access to prescription drugs is likely to be impeded by allowing recovery of fear of cancer damages in negligence cases without the imposition of a heightened threshold. Another policy concern to consider is that allowing recovery to all victims who have a fear of cancer may work to the detriment of those who sustain actual injury and those who ultimately develop cancer as a result of toxic exposure. That is, to allow compensation to all plaintiffs with objectively reasonable cancer fears, even where the threatened cancer is not probable, raises the very significant concern that defendants and their insurers will be unable to ensure adequate compensation for those victims who actually develop cancer or other physical injuries. Another reason in support of the imposition of a more likely than not limitation is to establish a sufficiently definite and predictable threshold for recovery to permit consistent application from case to case. Finally, while a more likely than not limitation may foreclose compensation to many persons with genuine and objectively reasonable fears, it is sometimes necessary to limit the class of potential plaintiffs if emotional injury absent physical harm is to continue to be a recoverable item of damages in a negligence action. Policy considerations aside, we hold that a toxic exposure plaintiff need not meet the more likely than not threshold for fear of cancer recovery in a negligence action if the plaintiff pleads and proves that the defendant's conduct in causing the exposure amounts to oppression, fraud, or malice, which authorizes the imposition of punitive damages. Thus, for instance, fear of cancer damages may be recovered without demonstrating that cancer is probable where it is shown that the defendant is guilty of despicable conduct which is carried on with a willful and conscious disregard of the rights or safety of others. In our opinion, Firestone's (D) conduct brings this case within the "oppression, fraud or malice" exception for recovery of fear of cancer damages. [The Court remanded for reconsideration but not necessarily denial of punitive damages. It approved the award of medical monitoring costs without regard to whether future cancer was more likely than not.]

Analysis:

A carcinogenic or other toxic ingestion or exposure, without more, does not provide a basis for fearing future physical injury or illness which the law is prepared to recognize as reasonable. The fact that one is aware that he or she has ingested or been otherwise exposed to a carcinogen or other toxin, without any regard to the nature, magnitude and proportion of the exposure or its likely consequences, provides no meaningful basis upon which to evaluate the reasonableness of one's fear. For example, nearly everybody is exposed to carcinogens which appear naturally in all types of foods. Thus everyone is a potential fear of cancer plaintiff, and the enormity of the class of potential plaintiffs cannot be overstated. Indeed, a single class action may easily involve hundreds, if not thousands, of fear of cancer claims. With this consideration in mind, the tremendous societal cost of otherwise allowing emotional distress compensation to a potentially unrestricted plaintiff class demonstrates the necessity of imposing some limit on the class. Proliferation of fear of cancer claims in the absence of meaningful restrictions might compromise the availability and affordability of liability insurance for toxic liability risks. Unless meaningful restrictions are placed on this potential plaintiff class, the threat of numerous large, adverse monetary awards, coupled with the added cost of insuring against such liability (assuming insurance would be available), could diminish the availability of new, beneficial prescription drugs or increase their price beyond the reach of those who need them most. The general rule that the Court announces requires a plaintiff to do more than simply establish knowledge of a toxic ingestion or exposure and a significant increased risk of cancer. The plaintiff must further show that based upon reliable medical or scientific opinion, the plaintiff harbors a serious fear that the toxic ingestion or exposure was of such magnitude and proportion as to likely result in the feared cancer. However, the Court's exception for recovery when the defendant's conduct amounts to oppression, fraud, or malice appears to be a fair and reasonable alternative to arrive at a just result.

■ CASE VOCABULARY

AMICUS CURIAE: A friend of the court; one who gives information to the court on some matter of law which is in doubt.

CARCINOGEN: A cancer-causing agent.

MORE LIKELY THAN NOT THRESHOLD: A greater than fifty percent likelihood of the event occurring.

OPPRESSION, FRAUD, OR MALICE: Intentional deception resulting in injury to another.

TOXIC EXPOSURE PLAINTIFF: A plaintiff who was exposed to toxic substances as the result of the defendant's wrongful conduct.

CHAPTER TWENTY

Prenatal Harms

Remy v. MacDonald

Instant Facts: Remy (P) sued her mother, MacDonald (D), for injuries sustained when MacDonald's (D) negligent operation of an automobile caused her premature birth.

Black Letter Rule: A mother is not liable for her child's prenatal injuries caused by the mother's negligence.

Chaffee v. Seslar

Instant Facts: Seslar (P) sued Dr. Chaffee (D) for child-rearing costs after a procedure to prevent her from conceiving a child proved unsuccessful.

Black Letter Rule: A parent may recover the child-rearing expenses for an unwanted child when the parent successfully proves a physician's medical malpractice.

Remy v. MacDonald

(Infant) v. *(Mother)*
440 Mass. 675, 801 N.E.2d 260 (2004)

A MOTHER IS NOT LIABLE FOR HER BABY'S PRENATAL INJURIES

■ **INSTANT FACTS** Remy (P) sued her mother, MacDonald (D), for injuries sustained when MacDonald's (D) negligent operation of an automobile caused her premature birth.

■ **BLACK LETTER RULE** A mother is not liable for her child's prenatal injuries caused by the mother's negligence.

■ PROCEDURAL BASIS

On appeal to review a trial court grant of summary judgment for the defendant.

■ FACTS

MacDonald (D) was thirty-two months pregnant when she negligently caused a two-car accident. As a result, Remy (P) was born prematurely and suffered permanent breathing difficulties. Remy (P) sued her mother for her injuries, but a trial court granted MacDonald (D) summary judgment.

■ ISSUE

May a child, born alive, maintain a cause of action in tort against her mother for personal injuries sustained before birth because of the mother's negligence?

■ DECISION AND RATIONALE

(Greaney, J.) No. In order for Remy (P) to succeed on her negligence claims, she must establish MacDonald's (D) legal duty of care. While MacDonald (D) always has a duty to exercise reasonable care to avoid injury to others, the imposition of a precautionary duty upon a mother to her unborn child is "unadvisable or unworkable." During gestation, many personal choices, both dangerous and nondangerous, may risk harm to an unborn fetus, including exposure to chemicals, participation in sports, consumption of medication, or the refusal to take recommended medication. Recognizing a duty to one's unborn child would require courts to analyze the degree of a mother's knowledge of her pregnancy to determine when the duty arises, and to scrutinize the reasonableness of the mother's actions, many of which would be incidents of normal life. The recognition of this duty would threaten to place the unborn fetus's rights ahead of the mother's rights, and no established social policy exists to justify such a duty. While Remy (P) could recover from a third-party for her prenatal injuries, the unique relationship between a mother and her unborn child presents special circumstances that militate against the mother's liability. Accordingly, "there are inherent and important differences between a fetus, in utero, and a child already born, that permits a bright line to be drawn around the zone of potential tort liability of one who is still biologically joined to an injured plaintiff." Affirmed.

Analysis:

The court's denial of prenatal liability against a mother seems to naturally flow from the Supreme Court's 1973 decision in *Roe v. Wade*. Underpinning the court's reasoning is the threat that prenatal liability will have on the mother's rights in light of the rights of her unborn fetus. If the mother owed her unborn child a duty to reasonably protect her from injury, one may argue that abortion, while not criminally sanctionable, would give rise negligence claims against the mother. Such a result would clearly conflict with the Court's decision in *Roe v. Wade*.

Chaffee v. Seslar

(*Doctor*) v. (*Patient*)
751 N.E.2d 773 (Ind.Ct.App.2001)

THE RIGHT TO ENGAGE IN FAMILY PLANNING IS A PROTECTABLE PRIVACY RIGHT

■ **INSTANT FACTS** Seslar (P) sued Dr. Chaffee (D) for child-rearing costs after a procedure to prevent her from conceiving a child proved unsuccessful.

■ **BLACK LETTER RULE** A parent may recover the child-rearing expenses for an unwanted child when the parent successfully proves a physician's medical malpractice.

■ **PROCEDURAL BASIS**

On appeal to review a trial court's denial of the defendant's motion to strike.

■ **FACTS**

With Seslar's (P) consent, Dr. Chaffee (D) performed a procedure to prevent Seslar (P) from conceiving a child. The procedure was unsuccessful and Seslar (P) bore a healthy child. Seslar (P) sued Chaffee (D) for the costs associated with rearing the child. After the court denied Chaffee's (D) motion to strike the claims for child-rearing costs, Chaffee (D) appealed.

■ **ISSUE**

May a plaintiff in a medical malpractice action recover child-rearing expenses resulting from an unwanted pregnancy after a botched sterilization?

■ **DECISION AND RATIONALE**

(Judge undisclosed.) Yes. A person's constitutional right to privacy under the Fourteenth Amendment includes one's rights to family planning and birth control. Claims for "wrongful pregnancy" are no different than other forms of medical malpractice and require the plaintiff to prove the elements of the claim. Once the elements are proven, the plaintiff may recover all damages naturally flowing from the defendant's negligence, including child-rearing costs. The expense of rearing an unwanted child are foreseeable damages, given that the sole purpose for the procedure here was to avoid an unwanted pregnancy and those damages, if proven, naturally flow from Chaffee's (D) breach.

Although child-rearing expenses are highly speculative, juries are often called upon to determine the measure of complex, speculative damages such as pain and suffering, mental anguish, and future medical expenses. Child-rearing expenses are less speculative than those permissible damages because the use of public and private statistics can establish the average cost of rearing a child. Seslar's (P) recovery is not predicated on the birth of her child, but rather on the infringement on her right of financial security and desire to effectuate the privacy rights related to her family size and right of procreation. An award of damages does not act as a measure of her love and care for her child, but instead is a measure of the deprivation of these rights. Similarly, Seslar (P) is not compelled to mitigate her child-rearing expenses by considering abortion or adoption to avoid her damages. Such a requirement would render Seslar's (P) Fourteenth Amendment privacy rights meaningless and would compound the damages by threatening her religious or moral beliefs. The defendant may, however, offer evidence of the benefits received from raising a child to limit the damages to which he may be exposed. Reversed.

Analysis:

While the court recognizes a cause of action for wrongful pregnancy, many courts have been reluctant to do so when the case involves an unwanted, although healthy, child. Those courts reason that public policy requires that the parents should not recover under such facts because the cost of rearing a child are to difficult to calculate and the potential psychological effect on the child resulting from a valuation of his or her life is too great to recognize as a matter of law.

■ CASE VOCABULARY

MITIGATION–OF–DAMAGES DOCTRINE: The principle requiring a plaintiff, after an injury or breach of contract, to use ordinary care to alleviate the effects of the injury or breach.

MOTION TO STRIKE: A party's request that the court delete insufficient defenses or immaterial, redundant, impertinent, or scandalous statements from an opponent's pleading.

RIGHT OF PRIVACY: The right to personal autonomy. The U.S. Constitution does not explicitly provide for a right of privacy, but the Supreme Court has repeatedly ruled that this right is implied in the "zones of privacy" created by specific guarantees.

CHAPTER TWENTY–ONE

Death

Smith v. Whitaker

Instant Facts: The executor of Robbins' estate brought suit for wrongful death after she was struck and killed by a truck with faulty brakes.

Black Letter Rule: Where all of the essential elements of a punitive damages claim are established, such a claim may be sustained without proof of pain and suffering.

Smith v. Whitaker

(Executor) v. *(Truck Driver)*

160 N.J. 221, 734 A.2d 243 (1999)

AN AWARD OF AT LEAST NOMINAL DAMAGES ORDINARILY IS REQUIRED TO SUSTAIN A PUNITIVE DAMAGES AWARD

■ **INSTANT FACTS** The executor of Robbins' estate brought suit for wrongful death after she was struck and killed by a truck with faulty brakes.

■ **BLACK LETTER RULE** Where all of the essential elements of a punitive damages claim are established, such a claim may be sustained without proof of pain and suffering.

■ **PROCEDURAL BASIS**

Appeal from the Appellate Division's affirmance of the jury's award to the plaintiff.

■ **FACTS**

Whitaker (D), driving a Coastal oil truck, was unable to stop at an intersection due to maladjusted brakes. The truck hit the vehicle of Helen Robbins, a sixty-year old widow. Immediately after the collision, Robbins appeared to be unconscious. She was pronounced dead at the hospital. Coastal's (D) vehicle had failed safety inspections that called for removal from service, but Coastal (D) continued to operate the vehicle in the "out-of-service" condition. Smith (P), the executor of Robbins' estate, brought claims (1) under the wrongful death act and (2) under the Survivor's Act. The trial court dismissed the claim for pain and suffering (under the Survivor's Act) because there was no evidence that Robbins was conscious [doesn't mean it didn't hurt!]. The jury awarded $44,000 under the Wrongful Death Act for pecuniary loss to Robbins' survivors, including funeral expenses. The trial court then permitted evidence on Smith's (P) punitive damages claim. On that, the jury awarded $1.25 million. The Appellate Division affirmed, and this appeal followed.

■ **ISSUE**

Does a plaintiff's inability to establish conscious pain and suffering in a survival action involving instantaneous death bar a claim for punitive damages?

■ **DECISION AND RATIONALE**

(Stein, J.) No. The critical issue before this Court is whether Smith (P) established a valid claim for punitive damages under the Survivor's Act in the absence of an underlying award of compensatory damages for pain and suffering. As a rule, a claim for punitive damages may lie only where there is a valid underlying cause of action. In a negligence action, the maintenance of a valid claim requires the plaintiff to show a breach of duty and resulting damage. In this case, Coastal (D) stipulated negligence and causation, leaving only the issue of damages for the jury's determination. Coastal (D) argues that because pain and suffering comprise the sole compensable injury in a survival action, no punitive damages may be awarded in the absence of an underlying award of compensatory damages for pain and suffering. As Coastal (D) notes, the primary damages recoverable in a survival action sounding in tort are for the decedent's pain and suffering that is conscious. Many states have allowed recovery for conscious pain and suffering whenever it can be shown the injured person survived her injuries, however briefly. In this case, Smith (P) was unable to establish compensable pain and suffering due to the unfortunate circumstance that Robbins apparently was killed immediately upon impact with Coastal's (D) vehicle. The question is whether a plaintiff's inability to establish conscious pain and suffering in a survival action involving instantaneous death bars a claim for punitive damages. We have previously held that in some cases involving egregious conduct, a punitive damages claim may constitute the plaintiff's sole basis for recovery, at least where some injury, loss, or detriment to the plaintiff has occurred. The true loss, injury, and detriment suffered by the plaintiff, in this case her death, is not necessarily coextensive with the compensatory damages awarded, which is merely a monetary amount awarded in court to compensate or indemnify a plaintiff. When the value of a real legal injury cannot be measured in money, a plaintiff who has been substantially harmed may not be able to establish an entitlement to compensatory damages. Under such circumstances, a defendant should not be freed of responsibility for aggravated conduct because of the fortuitous circumstance that an injured plaintiff cannot prove compensatory damages. Rather, where a plaintiff suffers substantial legal injury due to a defendant's egregious conduct, nominal damages, supporting a claim of punitive damages, may be awarded to vindicate the invasion of the plaintiff's rights. We recognize that an award of at least nominal damages ordinarily is required to sustain a punitive damages award. Even where a plaintiff has suffered a harm inestimable in terms of dollars and cents, an award of nominal damages serves to confirm the jury's finding that the plaintiff has suffered a harm cognizable at law. That deficiency is not significant in these circumstances, however, where the elements of causation and the defendant's negligence were established in the related wrongful death action. Thus, the only additional finding by the jury that was required to support a valid survival claim was a finding that Robbins was harmed. That a negligently-caused death constitutes a legally cognizable injury is irrefutable. Thus, where the other elements of a survival claim have been established in a related action pursuant to the Wrongful Death Act, we hold that to require an award of funeral expenses, compensatory damages for pain and suffering, or even nominal damages to support a claim for punitive damages under the Survivor's Act would be superfluous. Accordingly, where all of the essential elements of a punitive damages claim are established, such a claim may be sustained without proof of pain and suffering.

Analysis:

At common law, no civil remedy was available for a personal injury resulting in death, either to the decedent's estate or the decedent's dependents. The rigors of this harsh and technical rule were relaxed and ameliorated by the Wrongful Death Act, first, and later by the Survivor's Act. Although both types of actions arise from the identical occurrence (the death of the plaintiff), they serve different purposes and are designed to provide a remedy to different parties. The fundamental purpose of the wrongful death action is to compensate survivors for the pecuniary losses they suffer because of the tortious conduct of the defendant. An award of damages in a wrongful death action is not a matter of punishment for an errant defendant or of providing for the decedent's next of kin to a greater extent than the decedent himself would likely have provided. The amount of recovery is based upon the contributions, reduced to monetary terms, which the decedent might reasonably have been expected to make to his or her survivors. Consistent with its remedial purpose, damages under the Act are expressly limited to the pecuniary injuries resulting from such death, together with the hospital, medical and funeral expenses incurred for the deceased. Further, courts interpreting the Act have consistently held that it permits recovery only of a survivor's calculable economic loss and that the Act does not support an award of punitive damages. Survival actions, like wrongful-death actions, were unknown at common law. The death of the plaintiff gave his representative no remedy against the tortfeasor. In 1855, the Survivor's Act was passed, allowing a decedent's representatives the right to bring an action for trespass to person or property in the same manner as if the decedent had been living. Unlike a wrongful death action, which is a derivative action arising in favor of beneficiaries named under that act, the Survivor's Act preserves to the decedent's estate any personal cause of action that the decedent would have had if he or she had survived. The Survivor's Act was intended to be supplementary to the Wrongful Death Act and to afford complete and adequate redress to the estates of those who were injured in person or property by injuries causing death, by allowing the decedent's estate to recover any loss to the decedent that accrued between injury and death. The Survivor's Act, in contrast to the Wrongful Death Act, contains no express limitation on the types of damages recoverable under the statute. A majority of states have decided that punitive damages are recoverable in a survival action, the typical reasoning being that logic dictates that if a wrongdoer may be punished if his victim lives, then surely he should not escape retribution if his wrongful act causes a death.

■ **CASE VOCABULARY**

COMPENSATORY DAMAGES: Those damages directly referable to the tortious act for which the injured party should be compensated.

NOMINAL DAMAGES: A trivial sum awarded, frequently $1.00, as recognition that a legal injury was sustained, though slight; in actuality the amount is usually so small as to not really constitute damages.

PUNITIVE DAMAGES: Compensation in excess of actual damages, which is a form of punishment to the wrongdoer and an excess enhancement to the injured.

SURVIVOR'S ACT: A statute that preserves for a decedent's estate a cause of action for infliction of pain and suffering and related damages suffered up to the moment of death.

WRONGFUL DEATH ACT: A statute that creates a cause of action for any wrongful act, neglect, or default that causes death, which is brought by the executor or administrator of the decedent's estate, or by his surviving family, and is intended to compensate the family for the loss of the economic benefit that it would have received in the form of support, services, or contributions had the decedent lived.

CHAPTER TWENTY–TWO

Vicarious Liability

Hinman v. Westinghouse Electric Co.

Instant Facts: The defendant was sued after one of its employees, who was driving home from work, ran over a policeman and permanently injured him.

Black Letter Rule: Where the employer and employee have made the travel time part of the working day by their contract, and the employee is using the time for the designated purpose of returning home, the doctrine of respondeat superior is applicable.

Edgewater Motels, Inc. v. Gatzke

Instant Facts: Gatzke (D) negligently started a fire in his hotel room after smoking a cigarette while he filled out his expense account during a business trip.

Black Letter Rule: The smoking of a cigarette, if done while engaged in the business of the employer, is within the employee's scope of employment because it is a minor deviation from the employee's work-related activities, and thus merely an act done incidental to general employment.

Lisa M. v. Henry Mayo Newhall Memorial Hospital

Instant Facts: A young, pregnant woman was sexually assaulted by a hospital technician after she went to the hospital for an injury she sustained in a fall.

Black Letter Rule: A sexual tort will not be considered engendered by the employment unless its motivating emotions were fairly attributable to work-related events or conditions.

Kastner v. Toombs

Instant Facts: Kastner (P), an employee of Clearwater, was injured in the cave-in of a ditch which an employee of Toombs (D) was hired by Clearwater to dig.

Black Letter Rule: There is no reason for a rule of exclusive liability in situations in which a servant acting within the scope of his employment for two masters negligently causes injury to another; rather, the question of how the loss so caused should be distributed should be determined in accordance with principles of contribution and indemnity.

District of Columbia v. Hampton

Instant Facts: A mother sued family services after her child was beaten to death while living in foster care.

Black Letter Rule: Foster parents are not deemed to be agents or employees of state family service agencies.

O'Banner v. McDonald's Corp.

Instant Facts: A man sued a McDonald's restaurant after he slipped and fell in the restroom and injured himself.

Black Letter Rule: In order to recover on an apparent agency theory, a plaintiff would have to show that he actually did rely on the apparent agency in going to the establishment where he was allegedly injured.

Pusey v. Bator

Instant Facts: Pusey was shot and killed by Bator (D), a security guard assigned to protect private property.

Black Letter Rule: An employer remains liable for injuries caused by its independent contractors when the employer is under a nondelegable duty to take special precautions to prevent a peculiar risk of harm to others.

Otero v. Jordon Restaurant Enterprises

Instant Facts: A bar patron sued after the metal bleachers he was sitting on, which the restaurant hired an independent contractor to build, collapsed and injured him.

Black Letter Rule: An owner of property is liable for the negligence of an independent contractor in building or making repairs to structures on that property, once the owner resumes possession.

Hinman v. Westinghouse Electric Co.

(Run-over Policeman) v. *(Crazy Driver's Boss)*
2 Cal.3d 956, 88 Cal.Rptr. 188, 471 P.2d 988 (1970)

AN EMPLOYER, HAVING FOUND IT IN THE INTERESTS OF HIS ENTERPRISE TO PAY FOR TRAVEL EXPENSES AND TO GO BEYOND THE NORMAL LABOR MARKET, SHOULD BE REQUIRED TO PAY FOR THE RISKS INHERENT IN HIS DECISION

■ **INSTANT FACTS** The defendant was sued after one of its employees, who was driving home from work, ran over a policeman and permanently injured him.

■ **BLACK LETTER RULE** Where the employer and employee have made the travel time part of the working day by their contract, and the employee is using the time for the designated purpose of returning home, the doctrine of respondeat superior is applicable.

■ FACTS

Herman was employed by Westinghouse Electric Co. (D) as an elevator constructor's helper. His work was assigned from the Westinghouse (D) office and he did not go to the office before or after work; instead he went from home directly to the job site and after work returned home from the job site. For this particular job, Herman received an hour and a half per day as his round-trip travel time and $1.30 for his travel expense. Westinghouse (D) had no control over the method or route of transportation used by Herman. One day, Hinman (P), a Los Angeles policeman, was standing on the center divider of a freeway inspecting a possible road hazard when he was struck by a car driven by Herman. As a result of the accident, Hinman (P) received permanent injuries. The city paid his medical expenses and disability pension. The trial judge refused instructions that Herman was acting within the scope of his employment at the time of the accident and instead instructed the jury that whether he was acting within the scope of his employment depended upon a number of factors including among others "whether his conduct was authorized by his employer, either expressly or impliedly; the nature of the employment, its object and the duties imposed thereby; whether the employee was acting in his discharge thereof; whether his conduct occurred during the performance of services for the employer, either directly or indirectly, or of himself; whether his conduct, even though not expressly or impliedly authorized, was an incidental event connected with his assigned work." Following these instructions, the jury found that Herman was not within the scope of his employment and hence gave a verdict for Westinghouse (D).

■ ISSUE

Is the doctrine of respondeat superior applicable in situations where the employer and employee have made the travel time part of the working day by their contract, and the employee is using the time for the designated purpose of returning home?

■ DECISION AND RATIONALE

(Peters, J.) Yes. Liability of the employer may not be avoided on the basis of the "going and coming" rule. Under the "going and coming" rule, an employee going to and from work is ordinarily considered outside the scope of employment so that the employer is not liable for his torts. The "going and coming" rule is sometimes ascribed to the theory that the employment relationship is "suspended" from the time the employee leaves until he returns or that in commuting he is not rendering service to his employer. Nevertheless, there are exceptions to this rule. Exceptions will be made to the "going and coming" rule where the trip involves an incidental benefit to the employer, not common to commute trips by ordinary members of the work force. Prior case law also indicate that the fact that the employee receives personal benefits is not determinative when there is also a benefit to the employer. There is a substantial benefit to an employer in one area to be permitted to reach out to a labor market in another area or to enlarge the available labor market by providing travel expenses and payment for travel time. It cannot be denied that the employer's reaching out to distant or larger labor markets increases the risk of injury in transportation. In other words, the employer, having found it desirable in the interests of his enterprise to pay for travel time and for travel expenses and to go beyond the normal labor market or to have located his enterprise at a place remote from the labor market, should be required to pay for the risks inherent in his decision. We are satisfied that, where, as here, the employer and employee have made the travel time part of the working day by their contract, the employer should be treated as such during the travel time, and it follows that so long as the employee is using the time for the designated purpose, to return home, the doctrine of respondeat superior is applicable. We conclude that as a matter of law the doctrine is applicable and that the trial court erred in its instructions in leaving the issue as one of fact to the jury.

Analysis:

Earlier authorities sought to justify the respondeat superior doctrine on such theories as "control" by the master of the servant, the master's "privilege" in being permitted to employ another, the third party's innocence in comparison to the master's selection of the servant, or the master's "deep pocket" to pay for the loss. The modern justification for vicarious liability, however, is a rule of policy, a deliberate allocation of a risk. The losses caused by the torts of employees, which as a practical matter are sure to occur in the conduct of the employer's enterprise, are placed upon that enterprise itself, as a required cost of doing business. They are placed upon the employer because, having engaged in an enterprise which will, on the basis of past experience, involve harm to others through the torts of employees, and sought to profit by it, it is just that he, rather than the innocent injured plaintiff, should bear them. Additionally, the employer is better able to absorb these potential losses, and distribute them, through prices, rates or liability insurance, to the public. As such, the losses are shifted to society and to the community at large.

■ CASE VOCABULARY

EXPRESS AUTHORIZATION: Authorization which has been made known explicitly and in declared terms.

"GOING AND COMING" RULE: An employee going to and from work is ordinarily considered outside the scope of employment such that his employer is not liable for his torts.

IMPLIED AUTHORIZATION: Authorization which is determined by deduction or inference from known facts and circumstances.

RESPONDEAT SUPERIOR: This doctrine stands for the proposition that when an employer is acting through the facility of an employee or agent, and tort liability is incurred during the course of this agency due to some fault of the employee, then the employer must accept the responsibility.

VICARIOUS LIABILITY: The imputation of liability upon one person for the actions of another.

Edgewater Motels, Inc. v. Gatzke

(Fire-Damaged Motel) v. *(Fire-Starting Motel Guest)*

277 N.W.2d 11 (Minn.1979)

NO HARD AND FAST RULE CAN BE APPLIED TO RESOLVE THE "SCOPE OF EMPLOYMENT" INQUIRY; RATHER, EACH CASE MUST BE DECIDED ON ITS OWN INDIVIDUAL FACTS

■ **INSTANT FACTS** Gatzke (D) negligently started a fire in his hotel room after smoking a cigarette while he filled out his expense account during a business trip.

■ **BLACK LETTER RULE** The smoking of a cigarette, if done while engaged in the business of the employer, is within the employee's scope of employment because it is a minor deviation from the employee's work-related activities, and thus merely an act done incidental to general employment.

■ **PROCEDURAL BASIS**

Appeal from the trial judge's judgment N.O.V. for the defendant.

■ **FACTS**

Gatzke (D), a district manager for Walgreen's (D), stayed in the Edgewater Motel (P) while he was in Minnesota supervising the opening of a Walgreen-owned restaurant. Gatzke (D) lived at the Edgewater (P) at the company's expense. He was allowed to call home at company expense, and his laundry, living expenses, and entertainment were all items of reimbursement. There were no constraints as to where he would perform his duties or at what time of day they would be performed. Near midnight one night, Gatzke (D) left work with others on the job. Gatzke (D) and Hubbard went to a restaurant to have a drink. Over the course of an hour, Gatzke (D) consumed a total of four brandy Manhattans, three of which were "doubles." [rough day?] Gatzke (D) and Hubbard spent part of the time discussing the operation of the newly opened restaurant. Gatzke (D) also spoke to the bartender about the mixing and pricing of drinks, as he was interested in learning the bar business because the new Walgreen (D) restaurant served liquor. Around 1:30 a.m., Gatzke (D) and Hubbard walked back to the Edgewater Motel (P). Gatzke (D) apparently looked and acted sober at that time. He went straight to his room, and then "probably" sat down at a desk to fill out his expense account, as was his habit. While Gatzke (D) completed the expense account he "probably" smoked a cigarette. The record indicates Gatzke (D) smoked about two packs of cigarettes per day. A maid testified that the ash trays in Gatzke's (D) room would generally be full of cigarette butts and ashes when she cleaned the room. She also noticed that at times the plastic wastebasket next to the desk contained cigarette butts [now *that's* safe!]. After filling out the expense form, Gatzke (D) went to bed. A fire broke out soon thereafter [surprise!]; Gatzke (D) escaped the burning room, but the fire spread rapidly and caused $330,360 in damages to the motel. Dr. Anderson, a fire reconstruction specialist, testified that the fire started in, or next to, the plastic wastebasket located to the side of the desk in Gatzke's (D) room. He also stated that the fire was caused by a burning cigarette or match. After the fire, the plastic wastebasket was a melted to a "blob." Dr. Anderson stated that x-ray examination of the remains of the basket disclosed the presence of cigarette filters and paper matches. The jury found Gatzke (D) to be guilty of 60% of the negligence and the motel guilty of the remainder. It also found Walgreen (D) liable for Gatzke (D).

The trial judge concluded, however, that Gatzke (D) was not within the scope of his employment, and rendered judgment N.O.V. for Walgreen's.

■ ISSUE

Can an employee's smoking of a cigarette constitute conduct within his scope of employment?

■ DECISION AND RATIONALE

(Scott, J.) Yes. The question of whether smoking can be within an employee's scope of employment is a close one, but after careful consideration of the issue we are persuaded by the reasoning of the courts which hold that smoking can be an act within an employee's scope of employment. It seems only logical to conclude that an employee does not abandon his employment as a matter of law while temporarily acting for his personal comfort when such activities involve only slight deviations from work that are reasonable under the circumstances, such as eating, drinking, or smoking. We hereby hold that an employer can be held vicariously liable for his employee's negligent smoking of a cigarette if he was otherwise acting in the scope of his employment at the time of the negligent act. The record contains a reasonable basis from which a jury could find that Gatzke (D) was involved in serving his employer's interests at the time he was at the bar. More importantly, even assuming that Gatzke (D) was outside the scope of his employment while he was at the bar, there is evidence from which a jury could reasonably find that Gatzke (D) resumed his employment activities after he returned to his motel room and filled out his expense account form. The expense account was, of course, completed so that Gatzke (D) could be reimbursed by Walgreens for his work-related expenses. The filling out of the expense form can be viewed as serving a dual purpose; that of furthering Gatzke's (D) personal interests and promoting his employer's business purposes. Accordingly, it is reasonable for the jury to find that the completion of the expense account is an act done in furtherance of the employer's business purposes. Additionally, the record indicates that Gatzke (D) was an executive type of employee who had no set working hours. It was therefore reasonable for the jury to determine that the filling out of his expense account was done within authorized time and space limits of his employment. In light of the above, we hold that it was reasonable for the jury to find that Gatzke (D) was acting within the scope of his employment when he completed his expense account. Accordingly, we set aside the trial court's grant of judgment for Walgreens and reinstate the jury's determination that Gatzke (D) was working within the scope of his employment at the time of his negligent act.

Analysis:

To support a finding that an employee's negligent act occurred within his scope of employment, it must be shown that his conduct was, to some degree, in furtherance of the interests of his employer. Other factors to be considered in the scope of employment determination are whether the conduct is of the kind that the employee is authorized to perform and whether the act occurs substantially within authorized time and space restrictions. No hard and fast rule can be applied to resolve the "scope of employment" inquiry. Each case must be decided on its own individual facts. The initial question raised by this factual situation is whether an employee's smoking of a cigarette can constitute conduct within his scope of employment. The courts which have considered the question have not agreed on its resolution. A number of courts which have dealt with the instant issue have ruled that the act of smoking, even when done simultaneously with work-related activity, is not within the employee's scope of employment because it is a matter personal to the employee which is not done in furtherance of the employer's interest. Other courts which have considered the question have reasoned that the smoking of a cigarette, if done while engaged in the business of the employer, is within an employee's scope of employment because it is a minor deviation from the employee's work-related activities, and thus merely an act done incidental to general employment. This was the view this Court adopted.

■ CASE VOCABULARY

ISSUE OF FIRST IMPRESSION: Refers to the first time a question of law is considered for determination by a court.

JUDGMENT N.O.V.: Literally: not withstanding the verdict. A judgment which reverses the determination of the jury, and is granted when a judge determines that the jury verdict had no reasonable support in fact or was contrary to law.

NEGLIGENCE: Failure to exercise that degree of care which a reasonable person would exercise under the same circumstances.

REASONABLE PERSON: A hypothetical person who exercises those qualities of attention, knowledge, intelligence and judgment which society requires of its members for the protection of their own interest and the interests of others.

SCOPE OF EMPLOYMENT: An act of a servant done with the intention to perform it as a part of or incident to a service on account of which he is employed.

Lisa M. v. Henry Mayo Newhall Memorial Hospital

(Pregnant Woman) v. *(Pervert Technician's Employer)*

12 Cal.4th 291, 48 Cal.Rptr.2d 510, 907 P.2d 358 (1995)

IF AN ASSAULT WAS NOT MOTIVATED OR TRIGGERED BY ANYTHING IN THE EMPLOYMENT ACTIVITY BUT WAS THE RESULT OF ONLY PROPINQUITY AND LUST, THERE SHOULD BE NO VICARIOUS LIABILITY

■ **INSTANT FACTS** A young, pregnant woman was sexually assaulted by a hospital technician after she went to the hospital for an injury she sustained in a fall.

■ **BLACK LETTER RULE** A sexual tort will not be considered engendered by the employment unless its motivating emotions were fairly attributable to work-related events or conditions.

■ **PROCEDURAL BASIS**

Appeal from the Court of Appeal's reversal of the trial court's grant of summary judgment for the defendant.

■ **FACTS**

Lisa M. (P), nineteen years old and pregnant, was injured in a fall and sought treatment in a Hospital's (D) emergency room. The examining physicians ordered obstetrical ultrasonic imaging examinations. Tripoli (D), the ultrasound technician, performed these exams and then, on the pretense that additional testing was appropriate, scanned Lisa M.'s (P) pubic area, and inserted the ultra sound wand and then his fingers into her vagina. When Lisa M. (P) discovered from her obstetrician that this procedure was not proper [ya think?!], she sued Tripoli (D) and the Hospital (D). The trial court granted summary judgment to the Hospital (D); the Court of Appeal reversed.

■ **ISSUE**

Is a hospital technician's sexual battery of a patient within the scope of his employment?

■ **DECISION AND RATIONALE**

(Werdegar, A.J.) No. Was Tripoli's (D) sexual battery of Lisa M. (P) within the scope of his employment? The injurious events were causally related to Tripoli's (D) employment as an ultrasound technician in the sense they would not have occurred had he not been so employed. Tripoli's (D) employment as an ultrasound technician provided the opportunity for him to meet Lisa M. (P) and be alone with her in circumstances making the assault possible. The employment was thus one necessary cause of the ensuing tort. But, in addition to such "but for" causation, respondeat superior liability requires that the risk of the tort have been engendered by, typical of or broadly incidental to, or, viewed from a somewhat different perspective, a generally foreseeable consequence of, the Hospital's (D) enterprise. At the broadest level, the Hospital (D) argues that sex crimes are never foreseeable outgrowths of employment because they, unlike instances of nonsexual violence, are not the product of "normal human traits." We are not persuaded that the roots of sexual violence and exploitation are in all cases so fundamentally different from those other abhorrent human traits as to allow a conclusion sexual misconduct is per se unforeseeable in the workplace. In reaching our conclusion we have consulted the three identified policy goals of the respondeat superior doctrine—preventing future injuries, assuring compensation to victims, and spreading the losses caused by an enterprise equitably—for additional guidance as to whether the doctrine should be applied in these circumstances. In this case, however, we have drawn no firm direction from consideration of the first two policy goals. Hospital liability might induce precautionary measures but the impact might be destructive rather than beneficial. As to compensation for victims, hospital liability might entail consequential costs that are not clear. Third and finally, we attempt to assess the propriety of spreading the risk of losses among the beneficiaries of the enterprise upon which liability would be imposed. As the Hospital (D) points out, this assessment is another way of asking whether the employee's conduct was so unusual or startling that it would seem unfair to include the loss resulting from it among other costs of the employer's business. We conclude the connection between Tripoli's (D) employment duties—to conduct a diagnostic examination—and his independent commission of a deliberate sexual assault was too attenuated, without proof of the Hospital's (D) negligence, to support allocation of Lisa M.'s (P) losses to the Hospital (D) as a cost of doing business. Consideration of the respondeat superior doctrine's basis in public policy, therefore, does not alter our conviction that an ultrasound technician's sexual assault on a patient is not a risk predictably created by or fairly attributed to the nature of the technician's employment. The judgment of the Court of Appeals is reversed and the matter remanded for other proceedings. [Concurring and dissenting opinions omitted.]

Analysis:

It must be noted, to begin with, that California no longer follows the traditional rule that an employee's actions are within the scope of employment only if motivated, in whole or part, by a desire to serve the employer's interests. While the employee thus need not have intended to further the employer's interests, the employer will not be held liable for an assault or other intentional tort that did not have a causal nexus to the employee's work. If an employee inflicts an injury out of personal malice, not engendered by the employment, the employer is not liable. Because an intentional tort gives rise to respondeat superior liability only if it was engendered by the employment, the Court's disavowal of motive as a singular test of respondeat superior liability does not mean the employee's motive is irrelevant. An act serving only the employee's personal interest is less likely to arise from or be engendered by the employment than an act that, even if misguided, was intended to serve the employer in some way. Respondeat superior liability should apply only to the types of injuries that are as a practical matter sure to occur in the conduct of the employer's enterprise. The employment, in other words, must be such as predictably to create the risk employees will commit intentional torts of the type for which liability is sought.

■ CASE VOCABULARY

CAUSAL NEXUS: In this case, the idea that the tort committed was engendered by the tortfeasor's employment.

CONSEQUENTIAL COSTS: Those costs which are caused by an injury but are not a necessary result of the injury.

FORESEEABILITY: The consequences which a person of ordinary prudence would reasonably expect might occur.

PER SE: Not requiring extraneous evidence or support to establish its existence.

SUMMARY JUDGMENT: Preverdict judgment rendered by the court in response to a motion by one of the parties, who claims that there is no real dispute and there is no need to send the case to the jury for consideration.

Kastner v. Toombs

(Water Pipe Layer) v. *(Ditch Digger)*

611 P.2d 62 (Alaska 1980)

THE BORROWED SERVANT RULE AS AN EXCEPTION TO THE DOCTRINE OF RESPONDEAT SUPERIOR HAS IMPARTED UNNECESSARY COMPLEXITY TO THE LAW OF AGENCY

■ **INSTANT FACTS** Kastner (P), an employee of Clearwater, was injured in the cave-in of a ditch which an employee of Toombs (D) was hired by Clearwater to dig.

■ **BLACK LETTER RULE** There is no reason for a rule of exclusive liability in situations in which a servant acting within the scope of his employment for two masters negligently causes injury to another; rather, the question of how the loss so caused should be distributed should be determined in accordance with principles of contribution and indemnity.

■ **PROCEDURAL BASIS**

Appeal from the trial court's grant of summary judgment for the defendant.

■ **FACTS**

Kastner (P), an employee of Clearwater Drilling, was hired to lay the pipe for a new water line. Toombs (D) leased a backhoe to Clearwater for digging the pipe ditch. Toombs (D) was paid an hourly rate to furnish both the backhoe and its operator. Clearwater demanded a six-foot ditch. The backhoe operator warned that this would risk a cave-in if the ditch was not shored up, but Clearwater instructed the operator to proceed anyway. The ditch did cave in and Kastner (P) was injured [buried six feet under!]. He here sues Toombs (D), claiming he should be held vicariously liable for the operator's negligence in digging. The trial court gave summary judgment for Toombs (D) on the ground that he was not vicariously liable for any negligence of the operator while he was working for Clearwater.

■ **ISSUE**

Does the borrowed servant rule create exclusive liability in situations in which a servant acting within the scope of his employment for two masters negligently causes injury to another?

■ **DECISION AND RATIONALE**

(Matthews, J.) No. Under the doctrine of respondeat superior, a master is liable for the torts of his servants committed while acting in the scope of their employment. Current legal thinking bases this doctrine on the concept that a business should pay for the losses which it causes. Its foundation is the desire to include in the costs of operation inevitable losses to third persons incident to carrying on an enterprise, and thus distribute the burden among those benefitted by the enterprise. In essence, the enterprise may be regarded as a unit for tort purposes. Employees' acts sufficiently connected with the enterprise are in effect considered as deeds of the enterprise itself. Where, through negligence, such acts cause injury to others, it is appropriate that the enterprise bear the loss incurred. The borrowed servant rule carves out an exception to the doctrine of respondeat superior. Under the borrowed servant rule, a servant who is loaned by one master to another is regarded as acting for the borrowing master, and the loaning master is not held responsible for the servant's negligent acts. This result is reached even though the loaned servant is still employed by his first master and is acting within the scope of his employment. A servant may act for two masters simultaneously. Nevertheless, if the borrowed servant rule applies, only one of them is held vicariously liable for the servant's tort. In our opinion, the borrowed servant rule as an exception to the doctrine of respondeat superior has imparted unnecessary complexity to the law of agency. We see no reason for a rule of exclusive liability in situations in which a servant acting within the scope of his employment for two masters negligently causes injury to another. The question of how the loss so caused should be distributed should be determined in accordance with principles of contribution and indemnity. These principles have been devised to answer questions concerning the allocation of losses among potentially responsible parties. These principles may not be easy to apply in every case, but they are at least directly responsive to the problem, while the various approaches taken under the borrowed servant rule are not. There is considerable authority supporting the position which we have taken. For example, Professor Mecham has argued that dual liability is the simplest and most practical solution to the borrowed servant problem. *Outline of the Law of Agency.* In Harper & James, *The Law of Torts,* dual liability is referred to as a sensible result. Reversed and remanded.

Analysis:

The function of the borrowed servant doctrine is to determine which of two potentially liable masters will have to pay for the loss caused by the servant's act. The ultimate question in borrowed servant cases is not whether a master-servant relationship exists; it is, rather, which among two masters should be liable for the servant's tort. The traditional approach to the borrowed servant problem emphasizes the factor of control. The rationale is that the master having the right of control would be the one in the best position to prevent the injury. Unsatisfactory results are reached here, however, because typically both the general employer and the special employer have significant elements of control. The courts, in applying the control test, have failed to define what is meant by control. Are the courts speaking of broad control such as the power to discharge the employee, which is usually retained by the general employer, or of the detailed, on-the-spot control, which is usually exercised by the special employer? The courts that emphasize control in the broad sense make the general employer liable, whereas if detailed on-the-spot control is emphasized the special contractor is held liable.

■ CASE VOCABULARY

BORROWED SERVANT RULE: A servant who is loaned by one master to another is regarded as acting for the borrowing master, and the loaning master is not held responsible for the servant's negligent acts.

CONTRIBUTION: The legal right enjoyed by one required to compensate a victim for his injury to demand reimbursement from another person jointly responsible for that injury.

INDEMNITY: Refers to a total shifting of the economic loss to the party chiefly responsible for that loss.

MASTER: An employer who has control over his employees.

SERVANT: One who works for, and is subject to the control of, the master or employer.

District of Columbia v. Hampton

(Department of Human Services) v. (Beaten Child's Mother)

666 A.2d 30 (D.C.1995)

WHETHER A PRINCIPAL–AGENT RELATIONSHIP EXISTS IN A GIVEN SITUATION DEPENDS ON THE PARTICULAR FACTS OF EACH CASE

■ **INSTANT FACTS** A mother sued family services after her child was beaten to death while living in foster care.

■ **BLACK LETTER RULE** Foster parents are not deemed to be agents or employees of state family service agencies.

■ **PROCEDURAL BASIS**

Appeal from the jury's finding for the plaintiff.

■ **FACTS**

Two-year-old Mykeeda Hampton was taken from her mother's (P) care by the Department of Human Services (DHS) (D) on the ground that the mother (P) was not properly caring for the child. DHS (D) placed the child with a foster parent, Geraldine Stevenson. Stevenson left Mykeeda with her two sons for over ten hours, during which time she was beaten to death by one of the boys [a much better environment, huh?]. Mykeeda's mother (Hampton) (D) brought this survival action asserting (1) that the DHS (D) was negligent in selecting or supervising Stevenson as a foster parent and (2) that Stevenson was an agent of the DHS (D) so it is vicariously liable. The jury found for Hampton (P), and this appeal followed.

■ **ISSUE**

Are foster parents deemed to be agents or employees of state family service agencies?

■ **DECISION AND RATIONALE**

(Terry, A.J.) No. [The Court first concluded that the evidence did not support the first argument, then addressed vicarious liability.] The DHS (D) maintains that Geraldine Stevenson was not its agent but an independent contractor, and thus any negligence on her part cannot be imputed to it under the doctrine of respondeat superior. As it relates to foster care, this is an issue of first impression for this court, and one that has not been addressed by many other courts. The trend of recent case law, however, seems to be that foster parents are not deemed to be agents or employees of state family service agencies. In this case there was very little testimony about the actual relationship between Mrs. Stevenson and the DHS (D) social workers, and none suggesting that the DHS (D) had a right to control Stevenson's daily performance of her foster care duties. In fact, as the DHS (D) points out, Mrs. Stevenson testified that she controlled many areas of her foster children's lives and that she was responsible for making all day-to-day decisions about their care. Without any evidence that DHS (D) actually controlled the manner in which Mrs. Stevenson cared for Mykeeda, no reasonable jury could have found that Mrs. Stevenson was the District's agent. Mrs. Hampton (P) argues that the many rules and regulations concerning foster homes demonstrate that the DHS (D) reserved the right to control a foster parent. The list of "basic requirements" for a foster home, implicitly gives the DHS (D) the right to control such matters as the sleeping arrangements for a foster child, the temperature of the foster

---

home, the diet of the foster child, and certain aspects of the foster parents' health. The DHS (D) also reserves the right to inspect a foster home at any time. Finally, the DHS (D) has the right to remove the foster child from the foster home at any time and without prior notice. These regulations obviously show that the DHS (D) has the authority to dictate many aspects of a foster child's life in a foster home. But that does not establish that the foster parent is under the actual control of the DHS (D) to a degree sufficient to make him or her the DHS's (D) agent. For these reasons, we hold that the evidence was insufficient to prove that Mrs. Stevenson was the DHS's (D) agent, and that the trial court therefore erred in allowing Mrs. Hampton's (P) respondeat superior claim to go to the jury. Judgment reversed for entry of judgment N.O.V.

Analysis:

Subject to limited exceptions, the rule is that the employer is not vicariously liable for the torts of an independent contractor. The issue arises most commonly in a business setting, in which one person (or business) hires another—the independent contractor—to do some particular work. Whether a master-servant (or principal-agent) relationship exists in a given situation depends on the particular facts of each case. The person asserting the relationship—in this case, Mrs. Hampton (P)—has the burden of proof. This Court has recognized several factors to be considered in determining whether such a relationship exists: (1) the selection and engagement of the servant, (2) the payment of wages, (3) the power to discharge, (4) the power to control the servant's conduct, and (5) whether the work is part of the regular business of the employer. The Court has often held, however, that of these five factors, the determinative factor is usually the fourth: the right to control an employee in the performance of a task and in its result, and not the actual exercise of control or supervision. If the employer can only determine what is acceptable as the end result, that is a sign that the employee is an independent contractor. But control is only one factor. If the employee runs his own business and works for others as well as for the employer, he is not likely to be a servant. If he provides his own tools or uses special skills, that is also likely to indicate that he is an independent contractor. Additionally, employees who are ordinarily independent contractors may become servants if sufficient control is retained by the employer. Retained control may also show that the employer himself was negligent. If the employer fails to exercise reasonable care to control the independent contractor, the employer may then be liable because it is negligent, whether or not it would also be vicariously liable. In this case, the Court found that the evidence presented simply did not constitute the necessary burden that Mrs. Hamilton (P) was required to prove to show that Stevenson was the DHS's (D) agent. Simply put, the right to inspect and the right to set standards by which a foster parent performs her duties are not indicia of control. They in no way indicate that the DHS (D) had the right to control the day-to-day performance of the foster parent.

■ CASE VOCABULARY

AGENT: One who, by mutual consent, acts for the benefit of another.

INDEPENDENT CONTRACTOR: One who makes an agreement with another to do a piece of work, retaining in himself control of the means, method and manner of producing the result to be accomplished, neither party having the right to terminate the contract at will.

PRINCIPAL: One who has permitted or directed another to act for his benefit and subject to his direction or control.

SURVIVAL ACTION: A statute that preserves for a decedent's estate a cause of action for infliction of pain and suffering and related damages suffered up to the moment of death.

O'Banner v. McDonald's Corp.

(*Injured Patron*) v. (*Restaurant*)

173 Ill.2d 208, 218 Ill.Dec. 910, 670 N.E.2d 632 (1996)

ACTUAL RELIANCE MUST BE ESTABLISHED IN ORDER TO RECOVER ON AN APPARENT AGENCY THEORY

ARE YOU ALL RIGHT ??.!

■ **INSTANT FACTS** A man sued a McDonald's restaurant after he slipped and fell in the restroom and injured himself.

■ **BLACK LETTER RULE** In order to recover on an apparent agency theory, a plaintiff would have to show that he actually did rely on the apparent agency in going to the establishment where he was allegedly injured.

■ **PROCEDURAL BASIS**

Appeal from the Appellate Court's reversal of the circuit court's grant of summary judgment for the defendant.

■ **FACTS**

Reginald O'Banner (P) brought an action to recover damages for personal injuries he allegedly sustained when he slipped and fell in the bathroom of a McDonald's (D) restaurant. In his complaint, O'Banner (P) named as defendants McDonald's Corporation and certain "unknown owners." McDonald's (D) promptly moved for summary judgment on the grounds that the restaurant was actually owned by one of its franchisees and that it neither owned, operated, maintained, nor controlled the facility. The circuit court entered summary judgment in favor of McDonald's (D), and O'Banner (P) challenged this decision in the appellate court, theorizing that even though McDonald's (D) was a franchisor, it could nevertheless be held liable for the franchisee's negligence under principles of respondeat superior. O'Banner (P) argued that there was sufficient evidence in the record to establish that the franchisee served as McDonald's (D) actual agent. In the alternative, O'Banner (P) contended that McDonald's (D) could be vicariously liable for the acts and omissions of the franchisee based on the doctrine of apparent agency. The appellate court rejected the actual agency theory based on the documentary evidence, but held that there remained genuine issues of material fact with respect to O'Banner's (P) alternative theory of apparent agency. Accordingly, it reversed and remanded for further proceedings.

■ **ISSUE**

Did O'Banner (P) establish the required elements enabling him to recover on an apparent agency theory?

■ **DECISION AND RATIONALE**

(Harrison, J.) No. In this appeal before us, the issue of actual agency has not been pursued. The sole question before us is whether the appellate court erred in reversing and remanding based on the theory of apparent agency. In order to recover on an apparent agency theory, O'Banner (P) would have to show that he actually did rely on the apparent agency in going to the McDonald's (D) where he was allegedly injured. No amount of liberal construction can alter the fact that the record before us is devoid of anything remotely suggesting that the necessary reliance was present here. The pleadings and affidavit submitted by O'Banner (P) in the circuit court state only that he slipped and fell in the restroom of a McDonald's (D) restaurant. They give no indication as to why he went to the restaurant in the first place. The fact that this was a McDonald's may have been completely irrelevant to his decision. For all we know, O'Banner went there simply because it provided the closest bathroom when he needed one or because some friend asked to meet him there. If O'Banner (P) had any basis to support his position, he was obliged to present it to the circuit court. He did not do so, and the time for substantiating any claim of reliance has passed. The appellate court was therefore wrong to reverse the circuit court's entry of summary judgment in McDonald's (D) favor based upon the apparent agency doctrine. For the foregoing reasons, the judgment of the appellate court is reversed, the judgment of the circuit court is affirmed, and the cause is remanded to the circuit court for further proceedings consistent with this opinion. [A dissenting opinion is omitted].

Analysis:

Apparent agency, also known in some states as apparent authority, is based on principles of estoppel. The idea is that if a principal created the appearance that someone is his agent, he should not then be permitted to deny the agency if an innocent third party reasonably relies on the apparent agency and is harmed as a result. Under the doctrine, a principal can be held vicariously liable in tort for injury caused by the negligent acts of his apparent agent if the injury would not have occurred but for the injured party's justifiable reliance on the apparent agency. The fundamental obstacle to O'Banner's (P) recovery in this case concerns this element of reliance. Even if one concedes that McDonald's (D) advertising and other conduct could entice a person to enter McDonald's (D) restaurant in the belief it was dealing with an agent of the corporation itself, that is not sufficient. As the Court stated, in order to recover on an apparent agency theory, O'Banner (P) would have had to show that he actually did rely on the apparent agency in going to the McDonald's (D) where he was allegedly injured. He did not do so, thus the Court was correct in holding that summary judgment was appropriate in this case.

■ CASE VOCABULARY

ACTUAL AGENCY DOCTRINE: A relation in which one person, the agent, acts on behalf of another with the express authority of the latter, the principal.

APPARENT AGENCY DOCTRINE: A doctrine involving the accountability of a principal for the acts of his agent which operates to make a principal liable for actions of the agent on behalf of the principal when a third person in good faith believes that such authority exists.

ESTOPPEL: A bar which precludes a person from denying the truth of a fact which has, in contemplation of law, become settled by the facts and proceedings of judicial or legislative officers, or by the act of the party himself, either by conventional writing, or by representations, expressed or implied.

RELIANCE: Dependence, confidence, trust, repose of mind upon what is deemed sufficient support or authority.

Pusey v. Bator

(Trespasser) v. *(Armed Security Guard)*
94 Ohio St.3d 275, 762 N.E.2d 968 (2002)

EMPLOYING ARMED SECURITY GUARDS IS INHERENTLY DANGEROUS

■ **INSTANT FACTS** Pusey was shot and killed by Bator (D), a security guard assigned to protect private property.

■ **BLACK LETTER RULE** An employer remains liable for injuries caused by its independent contractors when the employer is under a nondelegable duty to take special precautions to prevent a peculiar risk of harm to others.

■ **PROCEDURAL BASIS**

On appeal to review a decision of the Ohio Court of Appeals affirming a directed verdict for the defendant.

■ **FACTS**

Wilson, on behalf of Greif Brothers, entered into a contract with a security firm to provide uniformed security officers on Greif Brothers' property. The contract did not specify whether the guards were to be armed or unarmed, but upon learning that some of the guards were armed, Wilson never requested that the guards be unarmed. Bator (D) was one of the assigned guards. On the day in question, Bator (D) witnessed Pusey and another man walking through the Greif Brothers parking lot. He radioed another guard working at another location on the property, and then, unarmed, confronted the plaintiffs. After the plaintiffs became angry, Bator (D) returned to his station and retrieved a gun from his briefcase. When he showed the gun to the plaintiffs, Pusey made a quick movement and Bator (D) shot him. Pusey died at the hospital. Pusey's mother (P) sued Bator (D), the security firm, and Greif Brothers for wrongful death. After Bator (D) and the security firm settled, Grief Brothers moved for a directed verdict. The court granted the directed verdict, and the Ohio Court of Appeals affirmed.

■ **ISSUE**

Is the inappropriate use of a weapon by an armed security guard hired as an independent contractor inherently dangerous, such that an employer is liable for the negligence?

■ **DECISION AND RATIONALE**

(Douglas, J.) Yes. "[A]n employer is generally not liable for the negligent acts of an independent contractor." However, when the employer owes a nondelegable duty to others, such as when the employer's business involves inherently dangerous activities, the employer may remain liable. An employer's business is inherently dangerous when it creates a peculiar risk of harm to others unless special precautions are taken. To establish a nondelegable duty, the risk of harm must be foreseeable in advance due to the inherent nature of the work, such that special precautions must reasonably be taken.

The use of armed guards to protect private property is inherently dangerous. It is reasonably foreseeable that injuries to others may occur with the inappropriate use of a weapon unless special precautions are taken to avoid the risk of harm. The inappropriate use of a weapon is not a normal, routine matter of customary human activity, but instead presents a special danger arising out of the particular situation. Therefore, "when an employer hires an independent contractor to provide armed security guards to protect property, the inherently-dangerous-work exception is triggered such that if someone is injured by the weapon as a result of a guard's negligence, the employer is vicariously liable even though the guard responsible is an employee of the independent contractor." If the jury determines that Pusey's death was caused by Bator's (D) negligence, Greif Brothers is liable for the damages. Reversed and remanded.

Analysis:

The court's decision to establish armed security services as an inherently dangerous activity as a matter of law has troubled many commentators. While the risk that a trespasser may be shot by an armed security guard may be reasonably foreseeable, wouldn't it also be reasonable to assume that an armed security guard would take reasonable precautions in the discharge of his weapon?

■ CASE VOCABULARY

INDEPENDENT CONTRACTOR: One who is hired to undertake a specific project but who is left free to do the assigned work and to choose the method for accomplishing it.

INHERENTLY DANGEROUS: Requiring special precaution at all times to avoid injury; dangerous per se.

NONDELEGABLE DUTY: A duty that may be delegated to an independent contractor by a principal, who retains primary (as opposed to vicarious) responsibility if the duty is not properly performed.

VICARIOUS LIABILITY: Liability that a supervisory party (such as an employer) bears for the actionable conduct of a subordinate or associate (such as an employee) because of the relationship between the two parties.

Otero v. Jordon Restaurant Enterprises

(Injured Bar Patron) v. *(Bar)*
119 N.M. 721, 895 P.2d 243 (1995)

PROPERTY OWNERS HAVE A NONDELEGABLE DUTY TO MAINTAIN SAFETY IN AREAS OVER WHICH THEY HAVE CONTROL

■ **INSTANT FACTS** A bar patron sued after the metal bleachers he was sitting on, which the restaurant hired an independent contractor to build, collapsed and injured him.

■ **BLACK LETTER RULE** An owner of property is liable for the negligence of an independent contractor in building or making repairs to structures on that property, once the owner resumes possession.

■ **PROCEDURAL BASIS**

Appeal from the trial court's grant of partial summary judgment in favor of the plaintiff.

■ **FACTS**

Jordon Restaurant Enterprises (D) hired an independent contractor to expand the premises of its restaurant and bar. As part of the expansion project, the contractor assembled metal bleachers where patrons of the restaurant and bar could be seated to view a large-screen television. Approximately four months after the bleachers were installed, they collapsed. Otero (P), a patron, fell and was injured. Jordon (D) conceded in the trial court that the cause of the collapse was the contractor's faulty and negligent assembly of the bleachers. Before trial, Otero (P) filed a motion for partial summary judgment, seeking an adjudication that Jordon (D) was vicariously liable, or jointly and severally liable, for the contractor's negligence in assembling the bleachers. The trial court granted Otero's (P) motion, ruling that, as a matter of law, Jordon (D) was liable for the contractor's negligence and that Jordon (D) had a nondelegable duty to maintain safety in areas over which it had control.

■ **ISSUE**

Is an owner of property liable for the negligence of an independent contractor in building or making repairs to structures on that property, once the owner resumes possession?

■ **DECISION AND RATIONALE**

(Apodaca, C.J.) Yes. Section 422 of the Restatement imposes liability on the owner of premises who entrusts to an independent contractor the construction, repair, or other work on his land, or on a building or other structure on it. It states that an owner is subject to the same liability, as though he had retained the work in his own hands, to others on or outside the land for physical harm caused to them by the unsafe condition of the structure after he has resumed possession of the land upon its completion. The owner is in a position to prevent or minimize risks by hiring a financially responsible contractor, by making arrangements for indemnification from the contractor, and by requiring the contractor to follow safety procedures and remedy dangerous conditions. In adopting Section 422 of the Restatement, we necessarily reject Jordon Restaurant's (D) argument that an owner's liability should be limited to situations in which the owner himself is at fault. An owner of property is liable for the negligence of an independent contractor in building or making repairs to structures on that property, once the owner resumes possession. Jordon Restaurant (D) additionally argues that, despite Section 422, it should not be held liable for the contractor's negligence because such negligence was only "collateral negligence." We disagree with this contention. The concept of "collateral negligence" is set out in Section 426 of the Restatement. Section 426 states that "an employer of an independent contractor, unless he is himself negligent, is not liable for physical harm caused by any negligence of the contractor if (a) the contractor's negligence consists solely in the improper manner in which he does the work, and (b) it creates a risk of such harm which is not inherent in or normal to the work, and (c) the employer had no reason to contemplate the contractor's negligence when the contract was made." Here, however, Jordon Restaurant (D) had a nondelegable duty to exercise reasonable care that the bleachers were in a safe condition. The contractor's negligent assembly, therefore, made the completed structure unsafe and affected the result that the owner was under a duty to attain - a result of reasonably safe premises. This was not a situation involving an unsafe condition created only while the work was ongoing. Judgment affirmed.

Analysis:

Section 422 of the Restatement makes it impossible for a possessor of land to escape liability for the non-performance of his duty to maintain his land in a safe condition, so long as he is in possession of it, by delegating the task of doing the work necessary to the performance of that duty to an independent contractor. Liability is imposed on the owner of the premises despite the fact that the owner was not personally at fault in creating the unsafe condition. Unlike strict liability, a nondelegable duty operates, not as a substitute for liability based on negligence, but to assure that when a negligently caused harm occurs, the injured party will be compensated by the person whose activity caused the harm and who may therefore properly be held liable for the negligence of his agent, whether his agent was an employee or an independent contractor. To the extent that recognition of nondelegable duties tends to insure that there will be a financially responsible defendant available to compensate for the negligent harms caused by that defendant's activity, it ameliorates the need for strict liability.

■ CASE VOCABULARY

ADJUDICATION: The determination of a controversy and a pronouncement of a judgment based on evidence presented.

COLLATERAL NEGLIGENCE: Negligence which is not the principal cause of the injury or accident; rather, it is secondary, or on the side.

JOINT AND SEVERAL LIABILITY: The sharing of rights and liabilities among a group of people collectively and also individually; the injured party may sue some or all of the defendants together, or each one separately, and may collect equal or unequal amounts from each in satisfaction of his damages.

CHAPTER TWENTY-THREE

The Development of Common Law Strict Liability

Weaver v. Ward

Instant Facts: While in the midst of a military drill, Weaver's musket accidentally discharged and wounded Ward.

Black Letter Rule: A defendant is strictly liable for trespass.

Brown v. Kendall

Instant Facts: A man attempted to separate two fighting dogs with a stick. During his attempt, he struck another man standing behind him with the stick when he raised it to beat the dogs.

Black Letter Rule: The plaintiff must prove that the defendant was negligent and at fault for the injury to recover for trespass.

Bamford v. Turnley

Instant Facts: An adjoining landowner brought suit against his neighbor for operating brick kilns on the neighbor's property, which the landowner claimed emitted foul stenches that made the landowner's family sick and were otherwise extremely annoying.

Black Letter Rule: A landowner's unusual or uncommon use of his land that interferes with adjoining property owners' enjoyment and use of their land subjects the landowner to liability for nuisance.

Rylands v. Fletcher

Instant Facts: A mine owner brought a suit for damages against a neighboring mill operator for digging a mill pond, which first flooded abandoned mine shafts and then ultimately flooded the operating mine.

Black Letter Rule: A landowner is strictly liable for damage to adjoining land resulting from the un-natural or abnormal use of his land.

Weaver v. Ward

(Injured Soldier) v. *(Soldier Responsible for Injury)*

Hob. 134, 80 Eng. Rep. 284 (K.B.1616)

IN THE "GOOD OLD DAYS" STRICT LIABILITY WAS IMPOSED FOR "TRESPASS"

■ **INSTANT FACTS** While in the midst of a military drill, Weaver's musket accidentally discharged and wounded Ward.

■ **BLACK LETTER RULE** A defendant is strictly liable for trespass.

■ **PROCEDURAL BASIS**

Writ of trespass brought before the Kings Bench for injuries sustained during a military exercise.

■ **FACTS**

Weaver (D) and Ward (P) were both soldiers in the army. They were involved in a mock-battle designed as a military exercise and were members of the same regiment. During the exercise, Weaver (D) accidentally discharged his musket and fired upon Ward (P). Ward (P) was injured and brought a writ of trespass to recover for the injuries. Ward (P) demurred to Weaver's (D) account of the accident and the court gave judgment in his favor.

■ **ISSUE**

Will a defendant be liable for trespass when he had no intent to commit the trespass, or when the trespass occurred purely by accident?

■ **DECISION AND RATIONALE**

Yes. Although intent is relevant in felony cases, it is not relevant in trespass cases. For a man to be guilty of a felony, he must have committed the act with felonious intent, or a felonious mind. Therefore, in the case of two soldiers skirmishing in front of the King, or two masters of defense battling, if one should accidentally be killed by the other, there will be no felony. Likewise, if a lunatic kills a man in a crazed rage, there will be no felony. But trespass requires no intent and will lie regardless of accident. The combatants mentioned above and the lunatic would still be liable in trespass. Trespass only exists to compensate the victim for his damages; it lies without regard to fault. The only situation that might excuse a defendant for trespass is if the injury or damage was inevitable and the defendant was utterly without fault. Weaver (D) did not prove such a circumstance in this instance. Judgment for Ward (P).

Analysis:

This is an early example of a writ of trespass and the applicable law. At the time this opinion was written, trespass was a strict liability offense. Regardless of fault, accident or intent, trespass would lie if the complainant could show that the defendant's injury was the result of a direct and forcible action of another. Trespass would not lie if the injury sustained was an indirect, or consequential, result of the defendant's actions. In such a situation, case was the correct writ, and case required some showing of fault. Note that the court briefly refers to a situation where trespass might not lie—in a situation where the defendant was judged "utterly without fault." Although it might appear at first glance that the court was blending the requirements of trespass and case, a careful look at the next sentence in the case will disabuse you of this notion. The court was merely observing that if the injury was inevitable regardless of the defendant's actions, the defendant might be excused and trespass might not lie.

■ **CASE VOCABULARY**

DEMURRER: Generally, an answer made by the defendant acknowledging that the facts set forth in the plaintiff's complaint are true, but that the plaintiff is not entitled to a remedy. [In this case, it was Ward, the plaintiff, who demurred to Weaver's version of the facts. Although that is not the way we understand demurrers today, maybe those wacky English did it differently in 1616.]

WRIT OF TRESPASS: An application to the court to provide a remedy in the form of damages for an injury sustained as a direct result of another's actions.

Brown v. Kendall

(Injured Man) v. *(Dog-Beater)*
60 Mass. (6 Cush.) 292 (1850)

LIABILITY IN TRESPASS EVOLVES FROM STRICT LIABILITY TO LIABILITY BASED UPON FAULT

■ **INSTANT FACTS** A man attempted to separate two fighting dogs with a stick. During his attempt, he struck another man standing behind him with the stick when he raised it to beat the dogs.

■ **BLACK LETTER RULE** The plaintiff must prove that the defendant was negligent and at fault for the injury to recover for trespass.

■ **PROCEDURAL BASIS**

Appeal to Massachusetts Supreme Court of a verdict for Brown (P) in an action for trespass.

■ **FACTS**

Kendall (D) was beating two fighting dogs in an attempt to separate them. He was using a four-foot stick to help him separate the fighting dogs. He was moving along with the dogs and raised his stick to strike at them. In the process of raising the stick, Kendall (D) accidentally struck Brown (P) in the eye and Brown (P) brought an action for trespass to recover for the injury inflicted. Kendall (D) died in the interim and his executrix was summoned in his stead. Kendall (D) requested the judge to instruct the jury that if he was using ordinary care but Brown (P) was not [i.e., if Kendall (D) was not negligent] then Brown (P) could not recover. The judge refused to so instruct the jury. Instead, he instructed them that if Kendall (D) was doing a necessary act, or had a duty to separate the dogs, and was using ordinary care, then he would not be liable. But if Kendall (D) was under no duty to separate the dogs, but was doing so voluntarily, he had to use extraordinary care or else be liable. Under these instructions, the jury found in favor of Brown (P) and Kendall's (D) estate brought exceptions.

■ **ISSUE**

Will a defendant be liable for trespass when the plaintiff has shown neither negligence or fault on the part of the defendant?

■ **DECISION AND RATIONALE**

(Shaw, C.J.) No. A plaintiff who wants to recover for trespass bears the burden of proving that the defendant was at fault for the injury. This is an action for trespass. The traditional rule is that trespass will lie if the injury complained of is the immediate result of some act of the defendant. If the injury is consequential or indirect, then the correct remedy is case. However, these are only the rules regarding which action, if any, will lie in a particular circumstance. We do not think the cases stand for the prospect that trespass lies in *any case* where the injury complained of is the direct result of an act, regardless of whether the act was wilful, intentional or careless. [That, by the way, is exactly what the older cases stand for!] Instead, we believe that the plaintiff must come prepared to show either that the act was unlawful, or the defendant was at fault before he can prevail on a trespass claim. This being the rule, the instructions requested by Kendall (D) should have been given by the trial court. The jury should have been instructed that if both Kendall (D) and Brown (P) were using ordinary care at the time of the incident, or if Kendall (D) was using ordinary care but Brown (P) was not, then Brown (P) could not recover. In other words, Brown (P) could recover only if he showed that Kendall (D) was negligent in his actions and was therefore at fault for the injuries. The trial court should not have focused on whether the act of separating the dogs was necessary or not—rather, the inquiry should have been whether Kendall (D) was exercising the degree of care in the circumstances which prudent and cautious men would exercise. If he was, then he was free from blame and should not have been liable for the injuries. If he was not, then he was at fault for the injury complained of and Brown (P) could recover. The members of the court are of the opinion that the want of due care must be alleged and proven by the plaintiff in such cases. It was, therefore, incumbent upon Brown (P) to show that Kendall (D) was not using ordinary care when he sought to separate the dogs and accidentally hit Brown (P) with the stick. Unless it appears to the jury that the defendant in such cases is chargeable with some negligence, fault, or carelessness, the plaintiff cannot recover. New trial is ordered.

Analysis:

This case reflects an important shift in the law of torts. Rather than being strictly liable for direct and forcible injuries, after *Brown,* a defendant would only be liable if the plaintiff could prove that he was negligent or careless, or in some other way was at fault for the injury. Understand that, prior to *Brown,* the burden of proving ordinary or extraordinary care was on the defendant in case actions. *Brown* made it clear that the plaintiff bore the burden of proof with respect to the defendant's lack of due care. Of course, if the plaintiff could show that the defendant acted carelessly, or did not act as a reasonable man would have in the circumstances, then the plaintiff was pretty close to proving negligence and fault. Certainly, if the plaintiff could prove that the defendant acted intentionally or unlawfully, that would be another way of establishing liability. *Brown* is important because the court expressly rejected strict liability for trespass claims and instead put in place a fault-based system that became the basis for modern tort liability.

■ CASE VOCABULARY

BURDEN OF PROOF: The obligation of a party to affirmatively establish that which he has alleged to be true.

DICTA: That portion of a court opinion that does not reflect the holding or the necessary analysis. Dicta can be viewed as surplus language that is not necessary for the court's holding.

Bamford v. Turnley

(Adjoining Property Owner) v. *(Kiln Operator)*

3 B. & S. 66, 122 Eng.Rep. 27 (Exch.Ch.1862)

UNCOMMON OR ABNORMAL USES OF LAND THAT INTERFERE WITH ADJOINING LANDOWNERS' USE AND ENJOYMENT OF THEIR PROPERTY SUBJECTS THE LANDOWNER TO LIABILITY

■ **INSTANT FACTS** An adjoining landowner brought suit against his neighbor for operating brick kilns on the neighbor's property, which the landowner claimed emitted foul stenches that made the landowner's family sick and were otherwise extremely annoying.

■ **BLACK LETTER RULE** A landowner's unusual or uncommon use of his land that interferes with adjoining property owners' enjoyment and use of their land subjects the landowner to liability for nuisance.

■ **PROCEDURAL BASIS**

Appeal of a verdict for the defendant in an action brought by a landowner for damages caused by his neighbor's operation of brick kilns on his own land.

■ **FACTS**

Turnley (D) made bricks in brick kilns located upon his own land. Bamford (P) brought an action for damages because he claimed the brick kilns produced "unwholesome vapours, smokes, fumes, stinks and stenches" [his words, not ours!] that entered his land. Bamford (P) further complained that the stench was "corrupted, offensive, unwholesome, unhealthy and uncomfortable," and that he, his family and servants were greatly annoyed by it and had in fact become ill because of the smell. At trial, Turnley (D) admitted to making the bricks on his land but claimed that the kilns were temporary, as he planned to use the bricks to make his own house on the land. He also claimed that the kilns were located as far away from Bamford's (D) land as possible and that his use of his land was reasonable under the circumstances. The trial judge ruled that if the spot chosen for the kilns was "convenient and proper" and the making of bricks was a reasonable use of Turnley's (D) own land, then a verdict should be returned for Turnley (D). Judgment was entered for Turnley (D) and Bamford (D) appealed. [It appears that the verdict was upheld by the court. The opinion that follows appears to be a dissent of sorts.]

■ **ISSUE**

May a landowner be held liable for nuisance for an uncommon and extraordinary use of his land that interferes with adjoining land owners' ability to use and enjoy their property?

■ **DECISION AND RATIONALE**

(Bramwell, B.) Yes. In my opinion, the judgment here should be reversed and Turnley (D) should be liable for the non-reciprocal harms he has caused his neighbor. This sort of situation, if it had been done maliciously or wantonly, would be actionable as a nuisance. Turnley (D) has, by putting his land to an uncommon and extraordinary use, interfered with Bamford's (P) use and enjoyment of his land. At the very least, such a situation requires Turnley (D) to justify or excuse his conduct. It is true that

---

some acts, which may be technically viewed as nuisances, are so common and ordinary that they are not generally actionable. Such is the case with situations like emptying a cesspool or burning weeds. True, if done maliciously or wantonly to annoy a neighbor, such conduct may be actionable as a nuisance. But generally, these are necessary and common uses of land, and may be considered to inflict reciprocal harms upon adjoining landowners. By that I mean that each landowner is likely to find himself in the position of needing to do such acts periodically, as they are necessary for the use, maintenance and enjoyment of land generally. In cases of such reciprocal harm, where the use is one that is necessary for the common and ordinary enjoyment of the land, an action for nuisance will not lie absent a showing of intent or maliciousness. But this principle cannot be extended to the instant case. Turnley (D) has subjected Bamford (P) and his family to a non-reciprocal harm, and one that serves Turnley (D) himself. He cannot justify his behavior by showing that the burning of bricks is a common, necessary or ordinary use for land. It does not matter to me that the use is temporary—temporary could mean one day, one year or five years. Neither is it a justification that the use is one for the public good. As a preliminary note, I believe that a law that allows an individual to inflict harm upon another without compensation in the name of the "public good" is a bad law. But I do not believe that is what the laws surrounding "public good" actually accomplish. Actions for the public good are generally analyzed based on the balance of loss and gain to all. Here, it is only Turnley (D) who gains while Bamford (P) and his family bear the loss. It cannot be said that Turnley's (D) actions are for the public good. In cases, such as the railroad, where the action of putting in and running a railway benefit all, we still require the railroad to compensate those whose property must be used to provide the railway. In my way of thinking, if Turnley's (D) actions benefit only him, then they are not for the public good. Alternatively, if Turnley's (D) actions are for the public good, then his gain should enable him to compensate Bamford's (P) loss. The judgment should be reversed.

Analysis:

This case, although not technically a strict liability case, represents an early judicial attempt to impose liability for abnormal land uses that inflict intangible harms upon neighboring landowners. The law of nuisance deals with land uses that interfere with another's use and enjoyment of his own land. Nuisances typically involve intangible interference by gases, smoke, sound or light. The focus in the instant case was that the harm inflicted upon the neighbors was non-reciprocal. Baron Bramwell was suggesting that liability should attach when a landowner puts his land to use in an uncommon or extraordinary way and such use negatively interferes with adjoining neighbors' ability to use and enjoy their property, at least where the harm inflicted was non-mutual or non-reciprocal.

■ CASE VOCABULARY

BRICK KILN: A structure used for making bricks out of clay and other materials by placing them inside the oven-like kiln and baking them at high temperatures to cure them.

NUISANCE: An unusual, unreasonable or unlawful use of property by the landowner that interferes with other property owners' use and enjoyment of their own property.

Rylands v. Fletcher

(Mine Owner) v. *(Pond Digger)*

L.R. 3 H.L. 330 (House of Lords 1868)

A LANDOWNER WILL BE STRICTLY LIABLE FOR HARMS RESULTING FROM THE UNNATURAL OR ABNORMAL USE OF HIS LAND

■ **INSTANT FACTS** A mine owner brought a suit for damages against a neighboring mill operator for digging a mill pond, which first flooded abandoned mine shafts and then ultimately flooded the operating mine.

■ **BLACK LETTER RULE** A landowner is strictly liable for damage to adjoining land resulting from the unnatural or abnormal use of his land.

■ PROCEDURAL BASIS

Action for damages resulting from the flooding of a mine by a neighboring mill pond. The case was first considered by the Court of Exchequer, then reviewed by the Exchequer Camber and finally reviewed by the House of Lords.

■ FACTS

Rylands (P) operated a mine in Lancaster County in England. Fletcher (D) operated a mill nearby. Fletcher (D) engaged a contractor to dig a reservoir or mill pond to supply water for the operation of the mill. The contractors dug the pond over top of some old abandoned mine shafts. The mine shafts had been filled in, but inadequately, and looked just like solid earth. When the pond was filled with water, the weight of the water caused the filling in the shafts to break down and the shafts were flooded. They in turn led to other mine shafts in an intervening mine, which in turn led to mine shafts in Rylands' (P) mine. Rylands' (P) mine was flooded and damaged. He sought damages for the flooding. The case went before an arbitrator, then was considered by the Court of Exchequer, the Exchequer Chamber and ultimately ruled upon by the House of Lords. At each step, there were separate opinions, which are reflected in the Decision and Rationale Section.

■ ISSUE

Is a landowner liable regardless of fault for damages to another's land resulting from the landowner's unnatural or abnormal use of his own land? [We know the term should technically be "non-natural," but the case says "unnatural" so there it is.]

■ DECISION AND RATIONALE

(In the Court of Exchequer, Bramwell, B.) Yes. It does not matter that Fletcher (D) did not intend to cause the harm. It matters only that Fletcher (D) caused water to flow upon Rylands' (P) property and damage resulted. Such action may be considered either a trespass or a nuisance and liability should result.

(In the Court of Exchequer, Martin, B.) No. There was no trespass, as the damage was not the direct result of Fletcher's (D) activities. It was at most indirect and consequential. There was no nuisance, as nuisance can be understood to mean that the landowner has used his land in a way that was hurtful or injurious to the senses and the use has negatively impacted his neighbors' ability to use their own land.

The making of a pond is a lawful act and is not a nuisance to anyone. There should be no liability in this case.

(In the Exchequer Chamber, Blackburn, J.) Yes. We believe that Baron Bramwell was correct and that Rylands (P) is entitled to recover. The problem is that Fletcher (D) brought onto his property a substance that was harmless enough, but likely to do mischief if it escaped from his property. What is the liability of a landowner who acts in this manner? We believe he has an absolute duty to keep such a substance on his property at his own peril, rather than a duty to merely use all reasonable care to keep it bound within his property. A landowner is prima facie answerable for all damage that results from the escape of a substance upon his land which is likely to do mischief once it escapes. This is the settled law with respect to cattle owners. They keep their cattle at their own peril and are strictly liable for any damage done by an escaped animal, regardless of the precautions they have taken to prevent such an escape. We think the same principle should be applied to a landowner who brings upon his land any substance that will damage his neighbor's property if it escapes, like filth, water or stenches. A landowner is bound to use anything on his own land so that it does not hurt another. We are of the opinion that Rylands (P) is entitled to recover for his damages.

(In the House of Lords, Lord Cairns, L.C.) Yes. The principles upon which this case should be determined are simple. A landowner is entitled to put his land to any lawful, natural use. If, in doing so, an accumulation of water occurs naturally and escapes and causes damage to a neighbor, the landowner will not be liable. But if the accumulation of water or other substances is the result of the non-natural use of the land by the landowner, we are of the opinion that the landowner acts at his own peril.

(In the House of Lords, Lord Cranworth) Yes. The rule was correctly stated by Blackburn, J. in the lower opinion. The rule is if a person brings anything upon his land, which if it escapes is likely to cause damage to his neighbor, that person keeps the substance at his peril. If the substance does escape, regardless of the precautions the landowner took to prevent such an occurrence, the landowner will be strictly liable for the resulting damage.

Analysis:

The rule in *Rylands v. Fletcher* was pretty harsh—it applied regardless of whether the substance involved was inherently dangerous and regardless of any fault or intention on the defendant's part. The basic concept was to compensate those who were injured by a landowner's inconsistent, uncommon or unusual land use. The opinions are a little confusing because different writers seem to use the term "un-natural land use" in different ways. One way of viewing *Rylands* is that it imposes strict liability on a landowner who brings upon the land something that wouldn't naturally be found there if the substance escapes and damages another's property. An alternative way of viewing the rule in *Rylands* is that the landowner will be strictly liable for non-natural uses of his land, meaning uses that are inconsistent or abnormal in the surrounding area. Either way, it is clear that *Rylands* imposed strict liability for abnormal or non-natural land uses that caused damage to surrounding property. Although the American courts did not generally adopt *Rylands* in the extreme form, it represents, it is clear that at least some jurisdictions have applied strict liability in abnormal land use cases, and in some other limited cases. American courts tended at first to reject *Rylands* and adopt instead the negligence, fault based rules of *Brown v. Kendall*. But there has been a gradual shift to recognize strict liability for abnormally dangerous activities.

■ CASE VOCABULARY

ARBITRATOR: A neutral party chosen by the disputing parties or appointed by the court to hear the facts of the case and render a decision.

PRIMA FACIE: That which appears on the face of something, is presumed from the facts, or is evident at first sight.

CHAPTER TWENTY–FOUR

Tort Liability for Defective Products

Moorman Manufacturing Co. v. National Tank Co.

Instant Facts: Moorman Manufacturing (P) seeks economic damages ten years after a steel grain storage tank it purchased from National Tank (D) developed a crack.

Black Letter Rule: Damages to a product, caused by a defect in quality and limited to economic losses, may be recovered under contract law theories, but not under the theory of strict tort liability.

Lee v. Crookston Coca–Cola Bottling Co.

Instant Facts: Lee (P) had a Coca–Cola bottle explode in her hand and now seeks damages for her injuries.

Black Letter Rule: A case may be submitted to the jury under both negligence and strict tort liability theories even though all of plaintiff's evidence is circumstantial.

Knitz v. Minster Machine Co.

Instant Facts: Knitz (P) was operating a press when it accidentally activated and severed two of her fingers.

Black Letter Rule: A product design is in a defective condition to the user or consumer if (1) it is more dangerous than an ordinary consumer would expect when used in an intended or reasonably foreseeable manner, or (2) if the benefits of the challenged design do not outweigh the risk inherent in such design.

Honda of America Mfg., Inc. v. Norman

Instant Facts: Karen Norman drowned when her vehicle became submerged in water and she was unable to free herself from the automatic seatbelt mechanism.

Black Letter Rule: Under the common law, to establish products liability, a claimant must prove that an economically and technologically feasible alternative design was available and would have prevented or significantly reduced the risk of death without substantially reducing the utility to the intended users of the product.

McCarthy v. Olin Corporation

Instant Facts: A man boarded a train and began shooting at passengers using a special ammunition specifically designed by its manufacturer to cause as much damage to the victim as possible. The victims are suing the manufacturer for defective design and other claims.

Black Letter Rule: When a product is dangerous by design, the mere fact someone is injured by it will not cause the manufacturer to be liable; there must be something wrong with the product that causes injury, and if nothing is wrong there will be no liability.

Liriano v. Hobart Corporation

Instant Facts: A supermarket worker, Liriano (P), was severely injured by a guardless meat grinder and now sues his employer and the manufacturer for his injuries.

Black Letter Rule: (1) Obvious hazards still require warnings because the warning not only notifies persons of the hazard, it also provides notice of less hazardous alternative ways of proceeding. (2) Cause-in-fact of a plaintiff's injury from an obviously hazardous product will be presumed from the plain fact that the injury occurred in the first place, leaving it to the defendant to rebut the cause-in-fact in order to keep the case from the jury.

Lewis v. Lead Industries Ass'n

Instant Facts: Parents of children who may have been exposed to lead pigment sued all manufacturers of lead pigment and a trade association promoting lead pigment for civil conspiracy.

Black Letter Rule: Civil conspiracy is the combination of two or more persons or entities for the purpose of accomplishing by concerted action either an unlawful purpose or a lawful purpose by unlawful means.

Turpin v. Merrell Dow Pharmaceuticals, Inc.

Instant Facts: The mother of Turpin (P) took a drug named Bendectin, and manufactured by Merrell Dow Pharmaceuticals (D), during her pregnancy with Turpin (P). Turpin (P) was born with limb defects and now sues for damages.

Black Letter Rule: Courts are required to scrutinize very closely all evidence and testimony offered by experts in complicated scientific trials involving such evidence to make sure plaintiffs have met their requisite burden of proof before allowing the case to go to the jury.

Bowling v. Heil Co.

Instant Facts: Bowling (P) was killed when the box on a dump truck descended and crushed him while he was attempting to fix a glitch with the truck.

Black Letter Rule: The comparative fault or negligence of a party who sues a manufacturer for product liability under strict liability in tort shall not be considered in assessing liability or damages, but assumption of risk by the plaintiff is a complete defense.

Hughes v. Magic Chef, Inc.

Instant Facts: Vincent Hughes (P) was severely burned when a stove made by Magic Chef, Inc. exploded due to a buildup of propane gas inside the oven.

Black Letter Rule: (1) Assumption of risk is not to be treated as an affirmative defense when giving a jury instruction, rather it is subsumed by contributory negligence. (2) In instructing on the defense of misuse, the jury is to be instructed to consider the knowledge level of the ordinary user, not the plaintiff's level of knowledge.

Reid v. Spadone Machine Co.

Instant Facts: Reid (P) was operating a cutting machine manufactured by Spadone Machine Co. (D) with another worker. The other worker activated the machine while Reid's (P) hand was under the blade resulting in the loss of three of Reid's (P) fingers.

Black Letter Rule: A finding that the manufacturer should have reasonably foreseen the use that led to the injury will preclude the defense of superseding proximate cause by a third party.

Boyle v. United Technologies Corporation

Instant Facts: Boyle's (P) son David A. Boyle, a military pilot was killed after his helicopter crashed into the sea and Boyle (P) now sues based on defective product.

Black Letter Rule: Liability for design defects in federal government procured equipment cannot be imposed under state tort law so long as (1) the U.S. approved reasonably precise specifications; (2) the equipment conformed to those specifications; and (3) the supplier warned the U.S. about the dangers in the use of the equipment that were known to the supplier but not to the U.S.

Newmark v. Gimbel's Inc.

Instant Facts: Mrs. Newmark (P) was given a permanent at one of Gimbel's (D) beauty shops. The solution used in giving the permanent caused Newmark's (P) scalp to blister and her hair to fall out.

Black Letter Rule: There is an implied warranty of fitness of the products a retail service provider uses in providing those services the same as if the customer had purchased the product themselves.

United Blood Services, Division of Blood Systems, Inc. v. Quintana

Instant Facts: Mrs. Quintana (D) received several units of infected blood and plasma as a result of a gunshot wound. The blood was procured from a volunteer donor by United Blood Services (P) and caused Quintana (D) to develop the AIDS virus.

Black Letter Rule: The presumption that the standard of care adopted by a profession constitutes due care for those practicing in that profession may be rebutted by a showing that such standard of care is unreasonably deficient in light of readily available practices that would be better.

Moorman Manufacturing Co. v. National Tank Co.

(Tank Purchaser) v. *(Tank Maker)*

91 Ill.2d 69, 61 Ill.Dec. 746, 435 N.E.2d 443 (1982)

ECONOMIC DAMAGES TO A PRODUCT CAUSED BY QUALITY DEFECTS IN THAT PRODUCT MAY ONLY BE RECOVERED UNDER CONTRACT LAW

■ **INSTANT FACTS** Moorman Manufacturing (P) seeks economic damages ten years after a steel grain storage tank it purchased from National Tank (D) developed a crack.

■ **BLACK LETTER RULE** Damages to a product, caused by a defect in quality and limited to economic losses, may be recovered under contract law theories, but not under the theory of strict tort liability.

■ **PROCEDURAL BASIS**

Appeal to the Supreme Court of Illinois after the state appellate court applied strict tort liability in finding for the Defendant.

■ **FACTS**

Moorman Manufacturing Co. (Moorman) (P) purchased a steel grain storage tank from National Tank Co. (National) (D) for use in Moorman's (P) feed processing plant. About ten years later, a crack developed in the tank. Moorman (P) now sues on theories of strict tort liability, misrepresentation, negligent design and express warranty.

■ **ISSUE**

Can solely economic damages limited to the purchased product, caused by a defect in quality, and such as to not cause a sudden risk of personal injury or damage to other property, be recovered in strict tort liability?

■ **DECISION AND RATIONALE**

(Thomas J. Moran, J.) No. The tort law of products liability stems from the contract cause of action for breach of warranty. This theory required that the plaintiff be in privity with the defendant. As the law developed, however, most courts abandoned the privity requirement in implied-warranty actions and ultimately abandoned the fiction of warranty in favor of strict liability in tort. This State formerly adopted strict liability to allow a plaintiff to recover for personal injuries. Whether a consumer could recover under strict liability for solely economic loss is a separate question first addressed in *Santor v. A & M Karagheusian, Inc.* The court in that case held that a plaintiff who'd purchased some carpeting made by the defendant could recover purely economic damages when there was no privity between the parties. However, in *Seely v. White Motor Co.,* the California Supreme Court refused to apply strict liability to allow recovery for solely economic harm. Rather, the court allowed recovery based on express warranty, stating that economic losses are not recoverable in strict tort liability. With respect to the ruling in *Santor,* the California court said, "Only if someone had been injured because the rug was unsafe...would there have been any basis for imposing strict liability in tort." Subsequent decisions have gone both ways, with most courts denying recovery in strict tort liability for solely economic losses. We believe the majority of courts are correct and that the language of section 402A should be limited to unreasonably dangerous defects resulting in physical harm to the ultimate user or consumer, or to his property. We believe the framework provided by the Uniform Commercial Code (UCC), including implied and express warranties, rules on disclaimers, notice requirements, limitations on the extent of a manufacturer's liability, and a statute of limitations are adequate. This even though the warranty rules may frustrate just compensation for physical injury. While these rules provide for much flexibility in the commercial setting, they do not allow a manufacturer's strict liability for economic loss to be disclaimed because a manufacturer should not should not be allowed to define the scope of its own responsibility for defective products. Thus, adopting strict liability in tort for economic loss would effectively eviscerate section 2–316 of the UCC. Besides, a large purchaser, such as Moorman (P) in the instant case, can protect itself against the risk of unsatisfactory performance by bargaining for a warranty. Or, it could choose to accept a lower price in lieu of warranty protections. We believe it is better for a consumer to be limited to a comprehensive scheme of remedies under the UCC, rather than to require the consuming public to pay higher prices so the manufacturer's can insure against the possibility that some of their products will not meet the business needs of some of their customers. We do hold, however, that strict liability in tort still applies to physical injury to a plaintiff's property, and to personal injury, when a product is defective and unreasonably dangerous. On the other hand, contract law, which protects expectation interests, provides the proper standard when a defect of quality is involved. "Economic loss" has been defined as "damages for inadequate value, costs of repair and replacement of the defective product, or consequent loss of profits—without any claim of personal injury or damage to other property..." as well as the "diminution in the value of the product because it is inferior in quality and does not work for the general purposes for which it was manufactured and sold." These definitions are consistent with the policy of warranty law to protect expectations of suitability and quality. We hold that, where only the defective product is damaged, economic losses caused by defects of quality falling under the ambit of a purchaser's disappointed expectations cannot be recovered under a strict liability theory. Here, the damages were limited to the defective tank and were gradual in nature. This was not the type of sudden and dangerous occurrence best served by the policy of tort law that the manufacturer should bear the risk of hazardous products. The damages here are better handled by contract law. [The Court also held that economic losses, though recoverable for intentional misrepresentations, were not recoverable for innocent ones, and that in this case the statute of limitations had run on the warranty claim.] Reversed.

Analysis:

Why shouldn't a party be able to recover under strict tort liability for damages to the products they've purchased as some courts have previously held they should? For example, say X purchases a blender. After using the blender for six months, the motor suddenly burns up and it quits working. X sues the blender manufacturer under strict tort liability. The law of tort usually requires that some wrong have been committed or some duty have been breached. Certainly, from X's standpoint there has been a wrong perpetrated or a duty shirked. But what if the company is not at fault for the defective blender? In such a situation, the law of tort is not really the perfect fit. Rather, the product will usually be backed by either an express implied warranty, guaranteeing it will function satisfactorily for a stated length of time, certainly longer than six months. Change the facts a little: say the blender was used for 7 years and then breaks. The warranty has run out after the first 3 years. Should X be able to recover? If the answer is yes, when do we draw the line? After 10 years? Or 15? What the Court is saying is that there are other types of law, specifically contract law and the UCC that were meant for such situations. Strict tort liability can apply, but only if someone has suffered personal injury caused by the defective product, or if there has been some property damage (other than to the defective product itself). Tort law is specifically intended to cover these situations.

■ CASE VOCABULARY

DIMINUTION: To decrease, or cause a decrease, in value, quality, or quantity.

Lee v. Crookston Coca-Cola Bottling Co.

(Injured Waitress) v. *(Beverage Bottler)*
290 Minn. 321, 188 N.W.2d 426 (1971)

CIRCUMSTANTIAL EVIDENCE ALONE IS SUFFICIENT TO GET A CASE TO THE JURY ON BOTH NEGLIGENCE AND STRICT TORT LIABILITY THEORIES

■ **INSTANT FACTS** Lee (P) had a Coca-Cola bottle explode in her hand and now seeks damages for her injuries.

■ **BLACK LETTER RULE** A case may be submitted to the jury under both negligence and strict tort liability theories even though all of plaintiff's evidence is circumstantial.

■ **PROCEDURAL BASIS**

On appeal from jury verdict in favor of defendant.

■ **FACTS**

Lee (P) was working as a waitress when a Coca-Cola bottle exploded in her hand. The evidence showed that the bottle had not struck anything, or been subjected to temperature extremes or mishandling. The trial judge refused to submit a claim based on strict tort liability. The jury returned a verdict for Crookston Coca-Cola Bottling Company (Bottler) (D).

■ **ISSUE**

Is circumstantial evidence alone sufficient to allow a plaintiff's case to be submitted to the jury under both strict tort liability and negligence?

■ **DECISION AND RATIONALE**

(Rogosheske, J.) Yes. The rule of strict liability imposes liability, without proof of negligence or privity of contract, upon a manufacturer or seller for injury caused by a dangerously defective product. For recovery under strict liability, a plaintiff need only prove that (1) the product was in fact in a defective condition, unreasonably dangerous for its intended use; (2) such defect existed when the product left the control of the defendant; and (3) the defect was the proximate cause of the injury sustained. However, this does not mean a defendant is held liable regardless of circumstances. The mere fact of injury during use of the product is usually insufficient proof to show existence of a defect at the time defendant relinquished control. The narrow question presented here though, is whether circumstantial evidence, the core of the res ipsa loquitur doctrine, is sufficient to take the case to the jury on the theory of strict liability as well as on the theory of negligence. It is certainly evident that the circumstantial evidence in this case is enough to justify submission of the issue of liability on the theory of res ipsa. The Bottler's (D) expert testified that there are three causes of bottle failure: Thermo-shock, internal pressure, and external force. Here, the only possible cause, according to the testimony, was internal pressure. Failure from internal pressure due to excessive carbonation is ordinarily unlikely because the bottle is designed to withstand much greater pressure than is normally applied. However, due to a bottler's customary reuse of bottles, sometimes for years, the capacity of different bottles to withstand internal pressure varies widely. Some bottles could develop defects over longer periods of time because of "rough" handling over the years. This may be only a plausible explanation in this case given the testimony that thermo-shock and external force did not occur. But absent expert opinion, as in a case of this type, circumstantial evidence may be the only available means of establishing a claim of either negligence or defective product. Under strict liability the elements of proof are very simple. The jury need not infer that the bottler (D) was negligent in order to impose liability. It is sufficient that the bottler (D) placed a dangerously defective product on the market. A plaintiff is not required to show exactly what defect caused the accident, but may rely on circumstantial evidence from which a jury may infer that it is more probable than not that the product was defective when it left the control of the defendant. Here the jury could have found, based on the evidence, that the bottler (D) was not negligent. This finding does not preclude recovery under strict liability though. Strict liability does not require negligence, just that the bottle was defective when it was put on the market. Such a finding would compel a verdict for Lee (P), absent any valid defenses. The trial court's refusal to instruct on strict liability deprived Lee (P) of a legitimate choice of theories on which to submit the case and is, thus, reversible error.

Analysis:

In the Court's opinion it brings up the doctrine of *res ipsa loquitur.* From your introductory torts class you may remember that the doctrine is used when there is a general allegation of negligence, but a lack of specific proof. The requirements of the doctrine are that the defendant was in control of the situation; that injury would not normally occur absent some sort of negligence; and that the plaintiff did not contribute to the injury. After these three elements are proved there is an inference of negligence on the part of the defendant. The doctrine is similar to strict tort liability in that it does not require the plaintiff to present specific evidence of negligence by the defendant, where strict liability does not require any proof of negligence on the part of the defendant. It is helpful to illustrate strict liability because *res ipsa* lies somewhere in the middle, between negligence and strict liability, in that while negligence is still part of *res ipsa,* it is a very general allegation of negligence. Under strict liability, while technically no negligence need be proven, in the truest sense, there has to be some sort of "negligence," otherwise the injury would not have occurred. Thus, under strict liability, the defendant may rebut an inference of liability by showing that something material occurred to the product after it left the defendant's control. Similarly, under *res ipsa,* the requirements of exclusive control by the defendant, and lack of contribution to the injury by the plaintiff, prevent liability when it is less than reasonably certain the defendant caused the injury.

■ CASE VOCABULARY

RES IPSA LOQUITUR: "The thing speaks for itself." The doctrine in tort law that provides that the simple fact that an injury occurred leads to an inference of negligence.

Knitz v. Minster Machine Co.

(Press Operator) v. *(Press Maker)*
69 Ohio St.2d 460, 432 N.E.2d 814 (1982)

A PRODUCT DESIGN IS DEFECTIVE IF THE BENEFITS OR ADVANTAGES OF THE DESIGN DON'T OUTWEIGH THE RISK INHERENT IN SUCH DESIGN

■ **INSTANT FACTS** Knitz (P) was operating a press when it accidentally activated and severed two of her fingers.

■ **BLACK LETTER RULE** A product design is in a defective condition to the user or consumer if (1) it is more dangerous than an ordinary consumer would expect when used in an intended or reasonably foreseeable manner, or (2) if the benefits of the challenged design do not outweigh the risk inherent in such design.

■ **PROCEDURAL BASIS**

Appeal to the State Supreme Court from a grant of summary judgment by the trial judge against Knitz (P).

■ **FACTS**

Minster Machine Company (Minster)(D) manufactured an industrial press originally activated with a two-hand button tripping device that kept the operator's hands out of the danger area. This press was sold by Minster (D) to the Toledo Die and Manufacturing Company (Toledo). Toledo also purchased an optional foot pedal activation device that was in use at the time of the injury. Knitz (P) was a press operator for Toledo. Knitz (P) attempted to move the foot pedal activation device and while doing so leaned on the bottom portion of the die with her hand. Her foot then accidentally activated the foot pedal, causing the press to descend and amputate two of her fingers. There was another safety device intended to pull the operator's hands back, but it was not attached.

■ **ISSUE**

Is a product defective when it is more dangerous than a consumer would expect when used as intended or in a reasonably foreseeable manner, or when the benefits of the product design do not outweigh the design's inherent risks?

■ **DECISION AND RATIONALE**

(Brown, William B., J.) Yes. This Court has adopted the rule known as the "consumer expectation test." This test holds that "A product is in a defective condition unreasonably dangerous to the user or consumer if it is more dangerous than an ordinary consumer would expect when used in an intended or reasonably foreseeable manner." The standard reflects the commercial reality that implicit in a product's presence on the market is a representation that it will safely do the jobs for which it was built. However, this rule does not cover situations where the consumer would not know what to expect, because he would have no idea how safe the product could be made. This is the case here. In such cases, the policy underlying strict liability in tort, requires that a product may be found defective in design, even if it satisfies ordinary consumer expectations, if through hindsight the jury determines that the product's design embodies excessive preventable danger, or, in other words, if the jury finds the risk of danger inherent in the challenged design outweighs the benefits of such design. Accordingly, we hold that a product design is in a defective condition to the user if (1) it is more dangerous than an ordinary consumer would expect when used in an intended or reasonably foreseeable manner, or (2) if the benefits of the challenged design do not outweigh the risk inherent in such design. Factors relevant to the evaluation of the defectiveness of the product design are the likelihood that the product design will cause injury, the gravity of the danger posed, and the mechanical and economic feasibility of an improved design. Here, Knitz (P) provided an expert opinion that the press was defective because of the failure of Minster (D) to design the press with adequate guarding that would keep it from being activated with the operator's hands under the press. In light of this, Knitz (P) has made out a genuine issue of fact as to whether the press design was defective. Reversed and remanded.

Analysis:

This opinion represents a change in the law of strict tort liability as it relates to product design defects. Rather than rely on the consumer expectations test as the measure for all design defect cases, the Court has formulated what has come to be called the "risk-utility test." This development is largely a result of the work of two people—Page Keeton and Dean John Wade. Dean Wade has advocated the use of seven factors to be applied in the risk-utility test: (1) the usefulness and desirability of the product; (2) probability and magnitude of potential injury; (3) availability of substitutes; (4) manufacturer's ability to eliminate the unsafe characteristic of the product; (5) the consumer's ability to avoid danger; (6) the consumer's probable awareness of the danger; and (7) the manufacturer's ability to spread the loss. The last factor has largely been omitted by most courts adopting the Wade analysis. What the risk-utility test is, in effect, is a cost benefit analysis form the standpoint of the manufacturer and the user. If a company sells a product that could be rendered much safer at a small cost in both financial terms and utility terms, it is clear under the risk-utility test that liability will exist. However, if the cost of reducing the risk is high and the detriment to the utility of the product is high, liability will most likely not lie. Of course most cases will fall in between, but the test does fill a void left by the consumer's expectation test, and identified by the Court in *Knitz*.

■ **CASE VOCABULARY**

SUB JUDICE: Presently before the court; e.g. the "case at bar" or the "instant case."

Honda of America Mfg., Inc. v. Norman

(Car Manufacturer) v. *(Decedent's Estate)*

104 S.W.3d 600 (Tex.App.Ct.2003)

A RIGHT–HIP SEAT BELT RELEASE MECHANISM IS NO BETTER THAN A LEFT–SHOULDER RELEASE MECHANISM

■ **INSTANT FACTS** Karen Norman drowned when her vehicle became submerged in water and she was unable to free herself from the automatic seatbelt mechanism.

■ **BLACK LETTER RULE** Under the common law, to establish products liability, a claimant must prove that an economically and technologically feasible alternative design was available and would have prevented or significantly reduced the risk of death without substantially reducing the utility to the intended users of the product.

■ **PROCEDURAL BASIS**

On appeal to review a jury verdict for the plaintiffs.

■ **FACTS**

Karen Norman accidentally backed her Honda Civic down a boat ramp into the water in Galveston Bay. Norman's vehicle was equipped with an automatic seat belt that engaged mechanically when the doors were closed and a manual lap belt. Unable to free herself from the automatic seatbelt, Norman died as her car sank. At the time of the accident, Norman's blood alcohol exceeded the state limit. The seatbelt mechanism in Karen's car was equipped with a mouse running along the door rail that, when operating properly, moves forward with the door is opened or the ignition is switched off. Additionally, the car was equipped with an emergency release button that permitted the operator to manually disengage the seatbelt. However, the car also had an emergency locking retractor that, when the vehicle experienced rapid deceleration or substantial tilting, would lock the seatbelt in place to secure the occupants in their seats. The Normans (P) sued Honda of America Manufacturing in products liability, alleging that the vehicle had a design defect because when the emergency locking retractor engaged, occupants were unable to reach the emergency release button, and the button was improperly located to enable occupants to release the seatbelt in emergency situations that were likely to occur. A jury found Karen 25% negligent and returned a verdict for the plaintiffs.

■ **ISSUE**

Did the plaintiffs meet their burden of proving an economically and technologically feasible alternative seat belt and release system?

■ **DECISION AND RATIONALE**

(Keyes, J.) No. Under the common law, to establish products liability, a claimant must prove that the product was defectively designed so as to be unreasonably dangerous, taking into consideration the utility of the product and the risks involved in its use. To do so, the Normans (P) must show that an economically and technologically feasible alternative seat belt and release system was available and would have prevented or significantly reduced the risk of Karen's death, without substantially reducing the utility to the intended users of the product. Honda (D) argues the Normans (P) failed to meet this burden.

At trial, the Normans (P) offered the testimony of two experts. Horton, a mechanical engineer, testified that there were three potential alternative designs that could have been used in the vehicle, including a timer programmed to reverse the mouse if it did not travel its entire cycle within an established period of time. Horton, however, failed to state that such a hypothetical alternative was available or economically or technologically feasible. The Normans (P) failed to prove that a timer-controlled mouse was a safer alternative design. The second expert, Laughery, testified that the placement of the emergency button over the driver's left shoulder was not sufficient, because at the time the vehicle was manufactured, Toyota placed the emergency release to the lower right side of the driver's seat, which was easier to access by a restrained driver. From Toyota's earlier use of this alternative, Laughery testified that he knew it was technologically feasible, and he presumed it was economically feasible because of Toyota's decision to utilize that alternative. However, while Toyota's use of the alternative may establish its technological feasibility, it does not establish its economic feasibility. To establish economic feasibility, the plaintiffs must prove the cost of incorporating the technology. The plaintiffs did not meet their burden.

Even if the plaintiffs' evidence could permit a reasonable inference of technological and economic feasibility, they failed to prove that the alternative mechanism would have prevented or significantly reduced the risk of death without imposing an equal or greater risk of harm. The location of the emergency release button was chosen to enable third parties outside the vehicle easier access to the button in the event the driver was immobilized and the vehicle could not be easily accessed. No evidence was offered to prove that the right-hip mechanism would save more lives than the left-shoulder release button. The plaintiffs have not met their burden. Reversed.

Analysis:

The analysis used by the court in this case is often referred to as a risk-utility analysis. Under this approach, a manufacturer need not make its products in the safest manner possible, but rather must only take reasonable measures to ensure that its products are the safest alternative to meet the risks of danger presented while maintaining the utility of the product to the consumer. This principle is driven largely by economics. While a manufacturer can often improve the safety of its product, the cost associated with doing so may only marginally increase safety but make the product too expensive for the consumer.

■ CASE VOCABULARY

DESIGN DEFECT: A product imperfection occurring when the seller or distributor could have reduced or avoided a foreseeable risk of harm by adopting a reasonable alternative design, and when, as a result of not using the alternative, the produce is not reasonably safe.

PRODUCTS LIABILITY: A manufacturer's or seller's tort liability for any damages or injuries suffered by a buyer, user, or bystander as a result of a defective product.

McCarthy v. Olin Corporation

(*Shooting Victim*) v. (*Ammunition Maker*)

119 F.3d 148 (2d Cir.1997)

___

FOR A PRODUCT TO HAVE A DESIGN DEFECT THERE MUST BE SOMETHING WRONG WITH THE PRODUCT'S DESIGN THAT IS NOT CONTEMPLATED BY THE CONSUMER

___

■ **INSTANT FACTS** A man boarded a train and began shooting at passengers using a special ammunition specifically designed by its manufacturer to cause as much damage to the victim as possible. The victims are suing the manufacturer for defective design and other claims.

■ **BLACK LETTER RULE** When a product is dangerous by design, the mere fact someone is injured by it will not cause the manufacturer to be liable; there must be something wrong with the product that causes injury, and if nothing is wrong there will be no liability.

___

■ **PROCEDURAL BASIS**

Appeal from the Federal District Court's granting of Olin Corporation's (D) motion for dismissal for failure to state a claim upon which relief can be granted.

■ **FACTS**

On December 7, 1993, a man named Colin Ferguson boarded a New York City commuter train and began firing a gun at the passengers. Six people were killed and nineteen others, including Kevin McCarthy (P1) and Maryanne Phillips (P2), were wounded. The assailant's pistol was loaded with Winchester "Black Talons," manufactured by the Olin Corporation (Olin)(D). The injuries to McCarthy (P1) and Phillips (P2) were enhanced because of the special design of the Black Talon bullets. The Black Talon is a hollowpoint bullet designed to bend and spread into six ninety-degree angle razor-sharp petals or "talons" that increase the wounding power of the bullet by stretching, cutting and tearing tissue and bone as it travels through the victim. The Black Talon was designed and manufactured by Olin (D) and went on the market in 1992. It was originally developed for law enforcement agencies, but was also marketed to the general public until a public outcry in 1993 caused Olin (D) to remove the Black Talon from the public market and restrict its sales to law enforcement personnel. The assailant allegedly purchased the ammunition before it was withdrawn by Olin (D).

■ **ISSUE**

Can a plaintiff assert a valid cause of action for design defect stemming from a product that caused injury when it performed exactly as it was designed to perform?

■ **DECISION AND RATIONALE**

(Meskill, J.) No. McCarthy (P1) first alleges that Olin (D) is strictly liable because the Black Talon was defectively designed in that the design of the bullets is inherently dangerous and results in enhanced injuries beyond ordinary bullets. The district court rejected this argument because the bullets' performance was an intentional and functional design of the product. We agree. To state a cause of action for design defect, plaintiffs must allege that the bullet was unreasonably dangerous for its intended use. A defectively designed product is one which, at the time it leaves the seller's hands, is in a condition not reasonably contemplated by the ultimate consumer. This rule is tempered by the fact that some products must be dangerous in order to be functional. Here, McCarthy (P1) and Phillips (P2) concede that the bullets performed precisely as intended by the manufacturer and the assailant, Colin Ferguson. Many products, however well designed, may cause death or injury. Guns and bullets are two of them. There must, however, be something wrong with the product, and if nothing is wrong there will be no liability. McCarthy (P1) and Phillips (P2) have not alleged that the bullets were defective. As a matter of law, a product's defect is related to its condition, not its intrinsic function. Here, the Black Talons did exactly what they were intended to do and were therefore not in a defective condition. McCarthy (P1) and Phillips (P2) next allege that under the risk/utility test Olin (D) should be held strictly liable because the risk of harm posed by the Black Talons outweighs the ammunition's utility. But as the district court correctly saw, the risk/utility test is inapplicable because the risks arise from the intended function of the product, not any defect. The risk/utility test requires there be something wrong with the product before determining if it is unreasonably dangerous or defective. Accordingly, we hold that McCarthy (P1) and Phillips (P2) have failed to state a cause of action under New York's strict products liability law. It is also argued that Olin (D) should be held liable in negligence for marketing the ammo to the general public because of its severe wounding power; that Olin (D) should have restricted sales to law enforcement for whom the bullets were originally designed. Also alleged is that Olin (D) should have known that its advertising of the ammo, which highlighted its ripping and tearing capacity, would attract criminals like the assailant here. But New York law doesn't impose a legal duty on manufacturers to control the distribution of potentially dangerous products such as ammunition. Accordingly, even if Olin (D) could foresee the results here, Olin (D) is not legally liable for such misuse. The complaint therefore does not state a valid cause of action in negligence either. Affirmed.

Analysis:

The Plaintiffs in this case were quite obviously attempting to exploit the "deep pockets" of the Olin Corporation (D) because the assailant, Colin Ferguson, was judgment-proof. To do so, they attempted to establish Olin's (D) moral culpability and bootstrap it into a valid cause of action at law. In doing so, McCarthy (P1) and Phillips (P2) allege that the risk of harm posed by the Black Talon outweighs its utility. There is absolutely no rational logic in this assertion. The utility of the product lies solely in the fact that it poses a greater risk, even probability, of harm to those it is used against. This was the specific goal of Olin (D) in designing the ammunition. The reality is that some products are not only inherently dangerous—such as knives—they are also meant to cause harm. Once these products are produced, all a manufacturer can hope is that they are used in a responsible manner. The truth of the matter is that whether or not Black Talons were available, Mr. Ferguson would still have been on the train indiscriminately firing on random passengers. As the Appeals Court recognized, liability cannot be imposed on the manufacturer simply because a person commits a crime with its product. While it is up to each individual to decide if Olin (D) bears any moral blame for the results of Mr. Ferguson's actions, the Court seems to indicate that, for what its worth, it does feel that Olin (D) bears some moral blame. This is illustrated by the Court's statement that "although it may have been foreseeable by Olin that criminal misuse of the Black Talon bullets could occur, Olin is not *legally* liable for such misuse," and its further concentration on the *legal* duty of Olin (D) in the opinion.

Liriano v. Hobart Corporation

(*Grinder Operator*) v. (*Grinder Manufacturer*)

170 F.3d 264 (2d Cir.1999)

A WARNING HAS TWO PURPOSES: TO CAUSE AWARENESS OF DANGER AND TO POINT OUT LESS DANGEROUS ALTERNATIVES

■ **INSTANT FACTS** A supermarket worker, Liriano (P), was severely injured by a guardless meat grinder and now sues his employer and the manufacturer for his injuries.

■ **BLACK LETTER RULE** (1) Obvious hazards still require warnings because the warning not only notifies persons of the hazard, it also provides notice of less hazardous alternative ways of proceeding. (2) Cause-in-fact of a plaintiff's injury from an obviously hazardous product will be presumed from the plain fact that the injury occurred in the first place, leaving it to the defendant to rebut the cause-in-fact in order to keep the case from the jury.

■ **PROCEDURAL BASIS**

Appeal from a plaintiff's verdict in a product liability personal injury case, with both issues certified to the New York Court of Appeals before being answered by the Federal Circuit Court herein.

■ **FACTS**

Luis Liriano (P) was working at Super Associated (Super) (D1), a super market. While working his hand was severely injured by a meat grinder manufactured by Hobart Corporation (Hobart) (D2) and owned by Super (D1). The grinder had been originally sold to Super (D1) equipped with a safety guard, but the guard had been removed while in Super's (D1) possession. The grinder bore no warning indicating it should be operated only with the guard in place. Liriano (P) sued Hobart (D2), who brought a third-party claim against Super (D1). The only claim that went to the jury was the failure-to-warn claim. The jury found for Liriano (P) while attributing a degree of responsibility to all three parties. Both Hobart (D2) and Super (D1) appealed, arguing (1) there was no duty to warn, and (2) even if there was a duty, the evidence was insufficient to get the failure-to-warn claim to the jury. The federal court certified both questions to the New York Court of Appeals, which rejected the first argument and declined to answer the second.

■ **ISSUE**

(1) Does an injury hazard require a warning despite the hazard being extremely obvious to the user/consumer? (2) Does a plaintiff injured by an extremely obvious hazard that he was not warned of have to prove the failure to warn was the cause-in-fact of his injuries?

■ **DECISION AND RATIONALE**

(Calabresi, J.) (1) Yes. (2) No. More than a hundred years ago, Judge Oliver Wendell Holmes, Jr., writing for a majority of the Supreme Judicial Court of Massachusetts, held that a pile of coal on the side of a Boston street was warning enough for any and all passersby that there was a coal hole nearby. He held that because of the obviousness of the coal holes existence, given the propensity for Boston residences to have piles of coal next to these holes, that any person who falls into such a whole is bound at their peril to know of the hole. Accordingly, the defendant in that case could, as a matter of law, rely on the plaintiff's responsibility to know of the danger presented. Justice Knowlton disagreed. His opinion delved farther into the facts of the case and showed that the plaintiff's failure to appreciate the peril might have been foreseen by the defendant and hence the failure by the defendant to warn of the hole might constitute negligence, a question a jury should decide. It is this latter view of obvious dangers that has held sway in the intervening years, a view the New York courts have several times endorsed. Looking more closely at the facts at hand, Liriano (P) was only seventeen years old, was a new immigrant to the United States, and had been on the job for only one week. Liriano (P) had never received instruction on operating the meat grinder and had used it only twice or thrice previously. Also, the mechanism that caused the injury was not visible to the operator. It could be argued that such a set of facts was not so remote that a court should say, as a matter of law, that Super (D1) and Hobart (D2) could not have foreseen them and guarded against them by giving a warning. Meat grinders are obviously very dangerous. People may therefore disagree as to whether a failure to warn of such a fact would be enough to raise a jury issue. But warnings do more than simply point out the presence of danger. It can also have the equally important purpose of drawing the user's attention to the existence of alternatives that eliminate or mitigate the danger. It thus follows that the duty to warn is not necessarily obviated merely because a danger is clear. One who grinds meat can therefore benefit not only from being told that his activity is dangerous, but also from being told there is a safer way. Though most people who use grinders will know—as a matter of law—that guardless grinders are dangerous, it doesn't follow that a sufficient number of them will—as a matter of law—also know that protective guards are available, that using them is a realistic possibility, and that they may ask that such guards be used. It is precisely these last pieces of information that the reasonable manufacturer may have a duty to convey even if the danger of using a grinder were itself deemed obvious. Given these facts, a jury could find that providing such a warning is a reasonable and prudent course of action that a manufacturer of meat grinders has a duty to follow. Thus, even if New York would consider the danger of meat grinders to be obvious as a matter of law, that obviousness does not substitute for the warning. Hobart (D2) also raises the argument that Liriano (P) failed to present any evidence that Hobart's (D2) failure to place a warning on the machine was causally related to his injury in that, whether or not there was a warning, Liriano (P) may still have operated the machine as he did and suffered the same injuries. But this argument assumes that Liriano (P) has the burden to show that the failure to warn was a but-for cause of his injury. Liriano (P) does not bear that burden. When it is clear, as a general matter—as it is here—that the kind of negligence the jury attributed to the defendant tends to cause the exact type of injury the plaintiff suffered, rather than require the plaintiff to prove his case is of the ordinary kind, the law presumes normality and requires the defendant to adduce evidence that the case is an exception. Accordingly, it is up to Hobart (D2) to adduce evidence showing that Liriano's (P) injury did not occur as the normally expected result of Hobart's (D2) failure to warn. In other words, here there is a rebuttable presumption that Hobart's (D2) negligence was in fact a but-for cause of Liriano's (P) injury. The district court did not err. Affirmed in all respects.

Analysis:

The Restatement of Products Liability provides that an item is defective when it has a defect of design or manufacture, and also when the maker has failed to provide a warning of foreseeable harm. Warning failures were originally thought of as not only implicating negligence, but also strict liability. The grounds for thinking of warning failures as strict liability cases is that a product that does not carry a reasonable warning when having one could make it safer is an unreasonably dangerous product. However, since the requirement is that the warning meet a standard of reasonableness, the inquiry in such a case essentially collapses into a typical negligence analysis. The end result is that, even though many courts have—and still do—used the language of strict liability, warning cases are more like negligence cases. A manufacturer's duty to warn means it only has to provide a reasonable warning against foreseeable risks. Accordingly, a manufacturer will be held liable only where the risk could have been mitigated or eliminated by the nonexistent warning or portion of the warning *and* if the item without the missing warning was not reasonably safe.

■ CASE VOCABULARY

BUT–FOR CAUSATION: The cause that in the absence of the event in question could not have occurred. Also known as "cause-in-fact" and "actual cause."

Lewis v. Lead Industries Ass'n

(*Parent*) v. (*Trade Association*)

342 Ill.App.3d 95, 793 N.E.2d 869, 276 Ill.Dec. 110 (2003)

A CLAIM OF CIVIL CONSPIRACY DOES NOT REQUIRE DETAILED PROOF OF CAUSATION

■ **INSTANT FACTS** Parents of children who may have been exposed to lead pigment sued all manufacturers of lead pigment and a trade association promoting lead pigment for civil conspiracy.

■ **BLACK LETTER RULE** Civil conspiracy is the combination of two or more persons or entities for the purpose of accomplishing by concerted action either an unlawful purpose or a lawful purpose by unlawful means.

■ **PROCEDURAL BASIS**

On appeal to review a trial court decision dismissing the plaintiffs' cause of action.

■ **FACTS**

Lewis (P) and others were parents of children who may have been exposed to lead and may have developed medical problems as a result. The plaintiffs proposed a class action against Lead Industries Association (D), a trade association that promoted lead pigments in paint, and the manufacturer of the lead pigment, alleging a failure to warn of the harmful consequences of lead paint. The court dismissed the plaintiffs' failure to warn claims because causation was not properly alleged since the plaintiffs failed to identify which manufacturer made the pigments to which the children were exposed.

■ **ISSUE**

Did the plaintiffs sufficiently allege a civil conspiracy, such that dismissal of their cause of action was erroneous?

■ **DECISION AND RATIONALE**

(Judge undisclosed.) Yes. In their complaint, the plaintiffs alleged a civil conspiracy between the manufacturers and Lead Industries Association (D) to market, produce, and promote lead pigment and conceal the dangerous properties of the pigment from the public. "Civil conspiracy is the combination of two or more persons or entities for the purpose of accomplishing by concerted action either an unlawful purpose or a lawful purpose by unlawful means." Thus, an agreement to conspire is insufficient to sustain a cause of action for civil conspiracy, for some action in furtherance of the agreement is required. Here, the plaintiffs identified in their complaint a complete list of all producers of lead pigment and sufficiently alleged an agreement to conspire and tortious conduct in furtherance of the agreement. It is immaterial that the plaintiffs may not be able to identify which of the defendants actually caused the alleged exposure. Because civil conspiracy extends liability beyond the active tortfeasor to all who conspired with that tortfeasor, it is of little importance which defendant was the active tortfeasor. Accordingly, the plaintiffs' complaint stated a proper cause of action. Reversed.

Analysis:

A claim of civil conspiracy relieves the plaintiff of a significant challenge in proving toxic exposure. Generally, when a plaintiff sues for toxic exposure, she must prove who manufactured the toxic substance to properly allocate liability. When the facts support a conspiracy, however, all conspirators are equally liable for the damages directly caused by one defendant. Accordingly, proof of the conspiracy relieves the plaintiff of the burden of proving which defendant actually manufactured the substance, assuming liability cannot be attributed to an unrelated third party.

■ CASE VOCABULARY

CIVIL CONSPIRACY: An agreement between two or more persons to commit an unlawful act that causes damage to a person or property.

Turpin v. Merrell Dow Pharmaceuticals, Inc.

(Maimed Child) v. *(Drug Manufacturer)*

959 F.2d 1349 (6th Cir.1992)

IN SCIENTIFIC CASES BASED PRIMARILY ON EXPERT TESTIMONY COURTS HAVE A DUTY TO CLOSELY INSPECT THE REASONING OF THE QUALIFIED SCIENTIFIC EXPERTS BEFORE ALLOWING A CASE TO GO TO THE JURY

■ **INSTANT FACTS** The mother of Turpin (P) took a drug named Bendectin, and manufactured by Merrell Dow Pharmaceuticals (D), during her pregnancy with Turpin (P). Turpin (P) was born with limb defects and now sues for damages.

■ **BLACK LETTER RULE** Courts are required to scrutinize very closely all evidence and testimony offered by experts in complicated scientific trials involving such evidence to make sure plaintiffs have met their requisite burden of proof before allowing the case to go to the jury.

■ **PROCEDURAL BASIS**

Appeal of a diversity case after the district court granted defendant's motion for summary judgement after concluding the plaintiff had not met her burden of proof.

■ **FACTS**

Merrell Dow Pharmaceuticals, Inc. (Dow)(D) manufactured and sold a drug named Bendectin from 1956 until 1983 when it stopped marketing the drug of its own accord. Bendectin was produced and sold as a morning sickness anti-nauseant and was prescribed to over 30 million pregnant women who commonly took the drug during their first trimester. About seven weeks after becoming pregnant, Betty Turpin, mother of Brandy Turpin (Brandy)(P), ingested Bendectin to combat morning sickness. The initial development of a fetus' fingers and toes occurs some four to eight weeks after conception. Seven moths after first taking the drug Betty Turpin gave birth to Brandy (P). Brandy (P) was born with severely deformed hands and feet. Betty Turpin had taken no other drugs during the course of her pregnancy, nor can Brandy's (P) deformities be traced to any known genetic disorders. Brandy (P) now sues Dow (D) on the theory that Bendectin caused her birth defects.

■ **ISSUE**

Did the district court err in closely scrutinizing the expert testimony and scientific evidence and then granting summary judgment for the Defendant?

■ **DECISION AND RATIONALE**

(Merritt, C.J.) No. We agree with the trial judge that courts have a duty to inspect the reasoning of qualified scientific experts in deciding whether a highly complex case based almost entirely on expert testimony should proceed to the jury. Based on the record below we also agree that whether Bendectin was the cause of Brandy's (P) birth defects is not known and is not capable of being proved to the requisite degree of legal probability based on the scientific evidence currently available. There are two important questions here: How hard should courts examine the reasonableness of scientific theories and inferences before deciding if the evidence warrants giving the case to the jury? And, if we apply a "hard look" doctrine, what exactly are the general scientific experiments and studies capable of showing about whether Bendectin causes birth defects in a particular case? We believe that close judicial analysis of such technical and specialized matter is necessary not only because of the likelihood of juror misunderstanding, but also because expert witnesses are not necessarily unbiased scientists all of the time. Both sides here appear to accept the fact that limb defects generally appear in less than one in 1,000 live births. Dow's (D) proof consists in large measure of the 35 extant studies on the statistical relationship between Bendectin and the incidence of various birth defects. It is clear that none of these studies conclude that a causal connection exists. In addition to the 35 studies, Dow (D) offers as evidence the testimony of Dr. Lamm that no one has detected a decrease in birth defects since Bendectin was removed from the market. Brandy (P) claims that these 35 studies are based on samples that are too small to prove the absence of causation in light of the infrequency of instances of birth defects in general; that they do not adequately isolate the incidences of limb defects; that they do not control for many other factors such as smoking and the use of other drugs; and that the 95% level of confidence used in the studies does not conform to the 51% needed to meet the preponderance of the evidence standard, where if a 51% confidence level was used the studies would show a connection. In essence, Brandy (P) maintains that the studies do not prove or disprove anything concerning the connection between Bendectin and limb reduction defects like that here. The two experts who testified for Brandy (P) though, used these studies as the basis for their own recalculations, using a lower confidence interval, and claim they show a higher relative risk. Both concluded from these recalculations that there is some association between Bendectin and limb reduction defects. But Dow (D) overstates the persuasive power of these studies. An analysis of this evidence shows that it is possible that Bendectin causes defects even though the studies don't detect a significant association. Because limb reduction defects are so extremely rare, it would take a much larger study that is carefully controlled in order to instill any confidence in the results. There are also many other errors, as pointed out by Brandy (P), in the studies that rob them of any real reliability in using them to make a prediction for Bendectin and limb defects. What Brandy's (P) hypothesis comes down to is that the studies show that the compounds connected with Bendectin are capable of causing limb defects in humans, not that they do cause such defects. Put another way, the decisive weakness in the studies Brandy (P) cites is that they do not support a finding that Bendectin more probably than not caused her birth defect. Only one expert, Dr. Palmer, even testified that the drug did cause the defect. We cannot find, however, that this testimony is anything more than a personal belief or opinion. The grounds for his opinion are subject to the same flaws as those of the other experts. Dr. Palmer's conclusions go far beyond the known facts that form the premise for his conclusions. Such personal opinion is not admissible. The analytical gap between the evidence presented and the inferences to be drawn on the ultimate issue of human birth defects is too wide. Under such circumstances, a jury should not be asked to speculate on the issue of causation. Affirmed.

Analysis:

Much of the case involves statistics, or more accurately, the discussion of confidence intervals in statistical regressions. A regression is a statistical analysis using one dependent variable and multiple independent variables. The goal of such a study is to find how significant the independent variables are in determining the value of the dependent variable. The more data points that are collected and plugged into the formula the more accurate or reliable the findings will be. This reliability is expressed as the confidence interval. More accurately, a confidence interval is a range of values that tell you what result you would get in any one random study. For instance, in *Turpin* there is cited the *Atlanta Study* on the causal connection between Bendectin and birth defects. The confidence interval in this study was from 0.65 to 2.13. That means that the statistician could predict with 95% confidence that Bendectin either reduces the chance of birth defects (represented by a value below 1) or increases the chance of birth defects (represented by a value above 1). As anyone can plainly see, this will provide absolutely no guidance to a juror in deciding whether Bendectin caused Brandy's (P) birth defect. The only way to increase the predictability of the study would be to increase the number of data points, which in this case means a great increase in the number of mothers included in the study.

Bowling v. Heil Co.

(Man Crushed by Dump Truck Box) v. *(Manufacturer of Dump Hoist System)*

31 Ohio St.3d 277, 511 N.E.2d 373 (1987)

COMPARATIVE NEGLIGENCE IS NOT CONSIDERED IN A PRODUCT LIABILITY CASE BASED UPON STRICT TORT LIABILITY

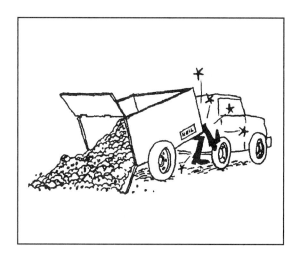

■ **INSTANT FACTS** Bowling (P) was killed when the box on a dump truck descended and crushed him while he was attempting to fix a glitch with the truck.

■ **BLACK LETTER RULE** The comparative fault or negligence of a party who sues a manufacturer for product liability under strict liability in tort shall not be considered in assessing liability or damages, but assumption of risk by the plaintiff is a complete defense.

■ **PROCEDURAL BASIS**

Appeal to the Ohio Supreme Court after the Appeals Court affirmed the ruling of the trial court in allowing the jury to consider Bowling's (P) contributory negligence.

■ **FACTS**

Heil Co. (Heil) (D) manufactured the dump hoist system (the system that raises and lowers the box on a dump truck) that was installed on a dump truck owned by Rogers. Brashear borrowed the truck for some personal use. He and Bowling (P) had dumped some gravel, but the box would not return to the down position. In order to correct the problem, Bowling (P) leaned in between the overhead box and the truck chassis below to see what was wrong. While in this position Bowling (P) grabbed the control lever on the pump valve assembly and manipulated it, causing the box to rapidly descend and crush Bowling (P), instantly killing him. This action is against Heil (D) and various others involved in the hoist assembly and controls. The jury found that Bowling (P) was guilty of contributory negligence, but not assumed risk and assessed damages at $1.75 million. Included in the verdict was a setoff for the level of Bowling's (P) fault.

■ **ISSUE**

Is contributory or comparative negligence by a plaintiff in a strict product liability case to be considered by a court in order to reduce the amount of damages awarded the plaintiff?

■ **DECISION AND RATIONALE**

(Brown, Herbert R., J.) No. Under Ohio law governing products liability, there are two affirmative defenses available, both based upon a plaintiff's misconduct. First, an otherwise strictly liable defendant has a complete defense if the plaintiff assumed the risk caused by the product defect. Second, such a defendant also has a complete defense if the plaintiff misused the product in an unforeseeable manner. The court below held that even though a plaintiff's passive contributory negligence provides no defense to a product liability action, his contributorily negligent affirmative action does provide a defense. Section 402A provides that contributory negligence is not a defense when such negligence is simply a failure to discover a defect, or to guard against the possibility it exists. However, if the user or consumer discovers a defect and is aware of the danger, and nevertheless proceeds unreasonably to make use of the product and is injured by it, he is barred from recovery. The court of appeals has therefore carved out a middle ground: contributory negligence consisting of "affirmative action." There is no such middle ground. "Affirmative action" by the plaintiff is covered because failure to guard against a defect can be "affirmative action." Indeed such would describe the conduct of Bowling (P) in this case. Under section 402A, a plaintiff's contributory negligence amounts to a voluntary assumption of a known risk or it does not. If it does, then the defendant has complete defense. If it does not, the contributory negligence of the defendant provides no defense. The jury found that Bowling (P) was contributorily negligent, but that he had not assumed a known risk. Therefore, Bowling's (P) actions do not provide Heil (D) with a defense to the strict liability claim. As illustrated in comment c to Section 402A, there are several policies and goals underlying the rule in strict liability cases. Most notably, that those who manufacture products have to treat the cost of injuries caused by those products as a part of the costs of production; a cost they can obtain insurance against. Also, as Dean Prosser has stated, the costs of damaging events caused by defective products can best be borne by those who make the products because they have the ability to effect loss spreading by shifting these costs to the consumers who purchase the products by charging higher prices. This is the opposite of the principles of negligence, where the loss is borne by the one that caused it. It must therefore be emphasized that strict liability is at odds with traditional notions of due care. While some courts do consider contributory negligence in strict liability cases, we feel that the better reasoned decisions are those that decline to inject a plaintiff's negligence into the fray. We thus hold that the principles of comparative negligence or comparative fault have no application to a products liability case based upon strict liability in tort. We therefore reverse the judgment of the court of appeals with respect to its reduction of Bowler's (P) verdict by the thirty percent found by the jury to be attributable to contributory negligence.

Analysis:

In his opinion Justice Brown cites with approval the words of Justice Mosk to support the court's position that in strict liability cases contributory negligence by the plaintiff is irrelevant: "The defective product is comparable to a time bomb ready to explode, it maims its victims indiscriminately, the righteous and the evil, the careful and the careless." Strictly speaking this may very well be the case. But it is clear, on the facts of this case, that the utilization of a little common sense on the part of Bowling (P) would have avoided this tragedy. Why should manufacturers have to pay for the results of the obviously negligent actions of consumers? Also, Ohio law has two affirmative defenses a manufacturer can use in defending a strict product liability case. The first is where the "plaintiff voluntarily and knowingly assumed the risk occasioned by the defect." Bowling (P) knew, or at least should have known that there was a chance of the dump truck box coming down unexpectedly. By positioning himself between the raised box and the truck chassis he was obviously in a clear danger zone should the box fall. Bowling (P) then "manipulated" the mechanism that controls the up and down motion of the box. At this point, there was a significant chance the box would fall. If these actions do not constitute voluntarily and knowingly assuming the risk occasioned by the defect then what type of conduct would? Is it possible that because the court was sympathetic to the plight of Bowler's (P) family, it decided to rely on the jury's verdict in not only reinstating the entire award, but in allowing the verdict of liability to stand?

■ CASE VOCABULARY

AFFIRMATIVE DEFENSE: A defense that raises new arguments and facts that, if proved true, will defeat a finding of guilt or liability, even if all of the facts or elements alleged by the prosecution or plaintiff are also proved true.

Hughes v. Magic Chef, Inc.

(Injured Cook) v. *(Manufacturer of Stove)*

288 N.W.2d 542 (Iowa 1980)

MISUSE OF PRODUCT IS NOT AN AFFIRMATIVE DEFENSE; IT IS THE PLAINTIFF'S BURDEN TO PROVE THAT THE USE MADE OF THE PRODUCT BY THE PLAINTIFF WAS REASONABLY FORESEE-ABLE BY THE MANUFACTURER

■ **INSTANT FACTS** Vincent Hughes (P) was severely burned when a stove made by Magic Chef, Inc. exploded due to a buildup of propane gas inside the oven.

■ **BLACK LETTER RULE** (1) Assumption of risk is not to be treated as an affirmative defense when giving a jury instruction, rather it is subsumed by contributory negligence. (2) In instructing on the defense of misuse, the jury is to be instructed to consider the knowledge level of the ordinary user, not the plaintiff's level of knowledge.

■ **PROCEDURAL BASIS**

Appeal from a jury verdict for the Defense in a strict product liability suit after the trial court's refusal to grant Plaintiff's motion for a new trial.

■ **FACTS**

Vincent Hughes (P) was using a stove manufactured by Magic Chef, Inc. (Magic) (D) when the propane tank fueling the stove ran out of gas. After the propane tank was refilled, the two pilot lights on the cook top of the stove were re-lit, but the third inside the oven broiler cavity was not. Two days later when Hughes (P) attempted to use the stove it exploded, severely injuring him. Experts testified that because the third pilot light wasn't lit, the gas that supplied the light built up over the intervening two days and ignited when Hughes (P) tried to use the stove, causing the explosion that caused the injuries. Hughes (P) brought this strict liability action against Magic (D), alleging the stove was unreasonably dangerous. Magic (D) raised the affirmative defenses of assumption of risk and misuse of product.

■ **ISSUE**

(1) Is misuse of a product to be treated as an affirmative defense in the giving of jury instructions? (2) Did the court err in including a specific reference to what the Plaintiff knew or should have known about the pilot light in its instruction to the jury regarding misuse?

■ **DECISION AND RATIONALE**

(Uhlenhopp, J.) (1) No. (2) Yes. This Court has previously held in *Rosenau* that in an ordinary negligence case, the defense of assumption of risk is not to be pled and submitted as a separate defense. Instead, the elements of assumed risk are to be included in the contributory negligence instruction. Separate instructions could tend to confuse the jury and cause it to render inconsistent verdicts. Hughes (P) argues that this same reasoning applies to the products liability defenses of misuse of product and assumption of risk. But this argument fails to recognize the different natures of those two issues. Misuse bars recovery when the product is used in a way not reasonably foreseeable to the defendant. Assumption of risk is a defense to a strict liability action when the plaintiff has voluntarily and unreasonably proceeded to encounter a known danger. Misuse has to do with the producer's responsibility. If a product is misused, the maker is not liable from the outset. Assumption of risk has to do with the user's culpability; he is barred from recovering if he proceeds in the face of a known danger. While we recognize that often both misuse and assumption of risk will be present in one case, we reject the idea that a plaintiff cannot do one without the other. Although we do not agree with Hughes' (P) attempt to apply *Rosenau* to this case, we do agree that the trial court erred in giving an instruction on misuse as a defense in this strict liability action. Misuse is not an affirmative defense, but rather has to do with an element of the plaintiff's case. To treat misuse as an affirmative defense distinct and additional to the plaintiff's burden of proving he used a product in a reasonably foreseeable manner, there would be the possibility of inconsistent jury findings in the same case. There would also be the problem of a shifting burden of proof on the issue. Misuse is to be treated in connection with the plaintiff's burden of proving an unreasonably dangerous condition and legal cause. The plaintiff always has the burden to prove the legal cause of the injury was a product defect that rendered the product unreasonably dangerous in a reasonably foreseeable use. Hughes (P) also asserts that the "misuse" instruction erroneously held him to a "reasonableness" standard in the use of the product. We do not find it necessary to resolve this issue though because the misuse instruction is objectionable on another ground; it gives undue emphasis to what Hughes (P) personally knew or should have known. It stands to reason that if an ordinary user would reasonably be aware that a certain use of a product is dangerous, use of the product in that manner is less foreseeable by the maker than a normal, presumably safe use. But this does not mean that just because the ordinary user knows a certain use is dangerous, such a use is not reasonably foreseeable by the maker. It therefore follows that knowledge that can be reasonably attributed to the ordinary user is to be considered as a factor in deciding if the manner in which the plaintiff used the product was reasonably foreseeable. Here the trial court erred in directing the jury to consider what Hughes (P) knew or ought reasonably to have known about the pilot light. This has little relevance to the issue of whether Magic (D) should reasonably have foreseen the use to which the stove was put. The personal characteristics or knowledge of users becomes relevant only when the characteristics or knowledge are attributable to a substantial group of users. By using Hughes (P) as the reference point, the jury was invited to consider a matter of little relevance to the issue it had to resolve—whether Magic (D) should have reasonably foreseen that users would use the stove without lighting all the pilot lights after an interruption in gas service. We therefore hold that on retrial misuse is not to be treated as an affirmative defense in the instructions. Instead the instructions have to put the burden of proof on Hughes (P) to establish that the use made of the stove was reasonably foreseeable by Magic (D). The instruction may reference knowledge attributable to the ordinary user, but it must make clear that this is but one factor in determining whether the use here was reasonably foreseeable by Magic (D). Reversed.

Analysis:

This case is a good illustration of the fact that a manufacturer can reasonably foresee that their product could be misused. In other words, just because a product is "misused" does not mean the maker could not reasonably have foreseen the misuse. Thus, the Court's concern with inconsistent verdicts. For instance, a jury could find that a consumer misused the product—a finding that should bar recovery. But in the same case, the jury could find that even though the plaintiff misused the product, such misuse was reasonably foreseeable by the defendant manufacturer—a finding that would mean the defendant is liable. By holding that misuse is not an affirmative defense, but rather is part of the plaintiff's burden in proving that the use the product was put to was reasonably foreseeable by the defendant, inconsistent jury verdicts are avoided. What it all boils down to is that even if somebody misuses a product, they can still recover for injuries if they can prove the manufacturer could reasonably foresee the misuse. This is akin to saying that manufacturers are required to design products and provide warnings with the realities of use in mind. Their products, therefore, must be safe for reasonably foreseeable misuses.

Reid v. Spadone Machine Co.

(Machine Operator) v. *(Machine Maker)*

119 N.H. 457, 404 A.2d 1094 (1979)

THE NEGLIGENCE OF A THIRD PARTY IS NOT A VALID DEFENSE IF THE USE LEADING TO INJURY WAS REASONABLY FORESEEABLE BY THE MANUFACTURER

■ **INSTANT FACTS** Reid (P) was operating a cutting machine manufactured by Spadone Machine Co. (D) with another worker. The other worker activated the machine while Reid's (P) hand was under the blade resulting in the loss of three of Reid's (P) fingers.

■ **BLACK LETTER RULE** A finding that the manufacturer should have reasonably foreseen the use that led to the injury will preclude the defense of superseding proximate cause by a third party.

■ **PROCEDURAL BASIS**

Appeal from a general jury verdict finding Defendant liable for making a defective product.

■ **FACTS**

Spadone Machine Co. (Spadone)(D) manufactured a "guillotine-type" cutting machine for cutting blocks of molded plastic. The machine had several safety devices. Originally it could only be activated by pressing two buttons simultaneously, thus requiring the operator's hands to be out of the blade area. However, some workers at the Davidson Rubber Company made a bar that allowed both buttons to be actuated at once with one hand free to manipulate the plastic stock. To avoid this danger, Spadone (D) moved the switch to the side of the machine so that the operator would have to walk to the side and activate it. The machine was intended to be operated by one person, but some of the workers at Davidson would work together with one pushing the side-button and one manipulating the plastic stock. Reid (P) was working with another when he reached under the blade without using the push-stick available and his co-worker pressed the buttons causing the blade to descend and cut off three of Reid's (P) fingers. Davidson Rubber Co. knew of the two-person use and its danger, but let it go on. The trial court denied Spadone's (D) motion to use as a defense Davidson's conduct as a superseding cause.

■ **ISSUE**

When there is a finding that the manufacturer should have foreseen the improper use of a product that led to an injury are the actions of a third party in modifying the product available to the manufacturer as a defense?

■ **DECISION AND RATIONALE**

(Grimes, J.) No. The evidence supports a finding that the machine was defectively designed. Spadone's (D) placement of the buttons on the side required the operator to leave the feeding area open while he actuated the blade, which could be found to have not only permitted, but encouraged two-person operation. This, coupled with inadequate warnings against two-person use, could be found to have made the machine unreasonably dangerous. There was evidence that the placement of the bar

---

across the buttons on the front of the machine could have been avoided by placing one button on each side facing out, thus requiring inward pressure in opposite directions. This design would have discouraged two-person use. In comparison, moving the buttons to one side left open the feeding area and made one-person operation slower. The natural tendency was to use two operators to save time. At trial, Spadone (D) sought to argue that the Davidson Rubber Company's conduct, negligence, and misuse of the machine was the sole proximate cause of Reid's (P) injury, a position that would bar recovery against Spadone (D) because Davidson's conduct would be the sole proximate cause. Spadone (D) submits that the trial court's refusal to allow this argument is reversible error. We are not convinced. With respect to a non-party third person's conduct—Davidson in this case—the manufacturer's sole defense is that of total nonliability based upon the third person's conduct as a superseding cause. The availability of this defense, however, depends on the foreseeability of the alleged misuse or negligence and, on the nature of the alleged design defect. In New Hampshire, the manufacturer is under a general duty to design his product reasonably safely for the foreseeable uses. Thus, before a defendant may argue a third party's negligence or misuse as a superseding cause, he must prove that the misuse was not reasonably foreseeable. But here the jury found the machine defective in design because two-person use was foreseeable. Spadone's (D) failure to guard against such use made the machine's design defective. Thus, that same use cannot be a superseding cause assuming Davidson was negligent in not preventing that use. Remanded.

Analysis:

This case illustrates that a plaintiff's negligence, alteration or misuse that is not reasonably foreseeable could be a superseding cause of plaintiff's injuries. Such a finding will bar recovery against the manufacturer. This applies even when the unforeseeable misuse, negligence or alteration is accomplished by third parties. The occurrence in *Reid*—removal of safety devices by workers—is common. As is the removal of safety devices by employers. If such alteration or misuse is foreseeable by the manufacturer, it is not a superseding cause that will allow the manufacturer to avoid liability because the product is defective. Also, if the alteration was not the but-for cause of the injury then it is irrelevant.

■ CASE VOCABULARY

PROXIMATE CAUSE: The cause that produced the result without which the event would not have occurred.

SUPERSEDING CAUSE: An intervening event or development that will break the chain of causation and null the cause for which the original tortfeasor is responsible with the effect of barring recovery against the original tortfeasor.

Boyle v. United Technologies Corporation

(Pilot's Father) v. *(Helicopter Maker)*
487 U.S. 500, 108 S.Ct. 2510, 101 L.Ed.2d 442 (1988)

IN AREAS OF UNIQUELY FEDERAL INTEREST, STATE LAW IS PREEMPTED AND REPLACED BY FEDERAL LAW PRESCRIBED BY THE FEDERAL COURTS

■ **INSTANT FACTS** Boyle's (P) son David A. Boyle, a military pilot was killed after his helicopter crashed into the sea and Boyle (P) now sues based on defective product.

■ **BLACK LETTER RULE** Liability for design defects in federal government procured equipment cannot be imposed under state tort law so long as (1) the U.S. approved reasonably precise specifications; (2) the equipment conformed to those specifications; and (3) the supplier warned the U.S. about the dangers in the use of the equipment that were known to the supplier but not to the U.S.

■ PROCEDURAL BASIS

Appeal of a federal diversity action to the U.S. Supreme Court from a reversal by the Circuit Court of Appeals of a jury verdict awarding Plaintiff $725,000.

■ FACTS

David A. Boyle, son of Boyle (P), was a United States Marine Corps helicopter copilot. He was killed when his helicopter crashed off the coast of Virginia during a training exercise. Although he survived the impact of the crash, he was unable to escape the helicopter and drowned. Boyle (P) sued the Sikorsky division of United Technologies Corporation (Sikorsky)(D) and presented two theories of liability at trial: that (1) Sikorsky (D) had defectively repaired a device called a servo in the craft's automatic flight control system, which allegedly malfunctioned and caused the crash; and (2) Sikorsky (D) had defectively designed the co-pilots emergency escape system; the escape hatch opened out instead of in and was therefore ineffective underwater due to the high water pressure; and that access to the escape hatch handle was obstructed by other equipment. After Boyle (P) won a jury verdict, the Court of Appeals reversed and remanded with instructions that judgment be entered for Sikorsky (D), partly because it was protected by the "military contractor defense."

■ ISSUE

Does the "military contract defense" protect the manufacturer of products specially designed for, and approved by, the government from liability for injuries caused by a defect in those products?

■ DECISION AND RATIONALE

(Scalia, J.) Yes. Boyle (P) contends that in the absence of legislation specifically immunizing Government contractors from liability for design defects, there is no basis for judicial recognition of such a defense. We disagree. A few areas, those involving uniquely federal interests, are so committed by the Constitution and the laws of the United States to federal control that state law is preempted and replaced, by federal law prescribed by the courts—so-called "federal common law." We have held that obligations and rights of the United States under its contracts are governed by federal law. The present case does not involve an obligation to the U.S. under its contract, but rather liability to third persons.

That liability may be styled one in tort, but it arises out of contract. A similarly peculiarly federal area is the civil liability of federal officials for official actions. The present case involves an independent contractor, rather than a federal official, performing its obligation under a procurement contract, but there is obviously implicated the same interest in getting the Government's work done. We think the rationale for considering these areas to be of uniquely federal interest applies as well to civil liabilities arising out of a federal procurement contract. We have previously held so in a case involving a federal performance contract; we see no basis for distinguishing between that and a procurement contract. As support, it is plain that the interest of the Federal Government is implicated by suits like this one, though it be between private parties. Imposition of liability on Government contractors will effect the terms of Government contracts. This will have a direct effect on the interests of the United States. We cannot, however, stop by deciding that the procurement of equipment is an area of uniquely federal interest. Displacement of state law still requires a significant conflict to exist between an identifiable federal policy or interest and the operation of state law, or that state law would frustrate specific objectives of federal legislation. For example, should the U.S. contract for the purchase and installation of an air conditioner, a state law imposing upon the maker of the unit a duty to include a certain safety feature would not be a duty identical to anything promised the government, but neither would it be contrary. The contractor could comply with both the federal specifications and state law. State law would thus not be preempted. Here, however, the state imposed duty of care forming the basis for the contractor's liability (the failure to provide the craft with the type of escape hatch deemed necessary by Boyle (P)) conflicts with the duty imposed by the Government contract (the duty to make helicopters with the specified type of escape hatches). The Court of Appeals, in its search for a way to decide if a conflict is significant, relied on the *Feres* doctrine, under which the Federal Tort Claims Act (FTCA) does not cover injuries to armed service personnel in the course of military service. Military contractor liability would conflict with this doctrine, the Appeals Court reasoned, because the costs of contractor liability would be passed through to the Government, thus defeating the immunity for military accidents conferred upon the Government itself. We do not adopt this analysis because in applying it to cases like the present it logically produces results that are both too broad and too narrow. Too broad because it would prohibit suits for injuries caused to military personnel by generic or standard equipment purchased by the Government, not pursuant to any special specifications. Too narrow because the *Feres* doctrine only covers service related injuries and thus would not provide for immunity for injuries caused by the military to civilians. For instance, a civilian's suit against the maker of a fighter plane because the plane's noise is too loud. Clearly, the character of the fighter planes used by the U.S. military cannot be regulated by state tort law no matter the status of the plaintiff. There is, however, a statutory provision that suggests the outlines of "significant conflict" between federal interests and state law in the area of government procurement. The FTCA excepted from tort liability "any claim based upon the exercise or performance or failure to exercise or perform a discretionary function or duty by a federal agency or an employee of the Government. . . ." We think the selection of the correct design for military hardware is clearly a discretionary function under the FTCA provision. Also, to permit "second-guessing" of these discretionary judgments through state tort suits against contractors would have the same effect sought to be avoided by the FTCA exemption. The financial burden of the tort suits would just be passed onto the Government. Therefore the purpose of the FTCA exemption would be defeated. In sum, we are of the view that state law that holds Government contractors liable for design defects in military equipment does in some circumstances present a "significant conflict" with federal policy and must be preempted. Therefore, liability for design defects in military equipment cannot be imposed, pursuant to state law, when (1) the United States approved reasonably precise specifications; (2) the equipment conformed to those specifications; and (3) the supplier warned the United States about the dangers in the use of the equipment that were known to the supplier but not to the United States. The first two conditions assure that the suit involves an area where the policy of the "discretionary function" would be frustrated—i.e., that the design feature was considered by the Government and not merely by the contractor itself. The third condition keeps contractors from simply hiding knowledge of risks, since without the condition conveying such knowledge might disrupt the contract, but withholding it would produce no liability. Remanded.

Analysis:

The thrust of the Court's decision and reasoning is that allowing state law tort claims against government contractors would defeat the "discretionary exemption" of the FTCA. The discretionary exemption keeps the Federal Government from being held liable for the discretionary decisions of its agencies and employees that end up causing harm. As Justice Scalia illustrated, decisions made by the Government in setting the specifications for military hardware are highly discretionary. Exercise of this discretion, to a large degree, results in the setting of military specifications, the requirements equipment must meet or exceed before being accepted by the Government. Contractors manufacture equipment in line with these specifications. When a design or other defect in such equipment causes injury to military personnel, the FTCA "discretionary exemption" will provide tort immunity to the Government and the contractor. The contractor is included because otherwise, the costs incurred from the suit would simply be passed on to the Government, thus rendering the exemption moot. However, when the Government has purchased standard, off-the-shelf or generic equipment that it has had no part in setting the specifications for, the exemption will not extend to immunize the manufacturer. There are no worries of the contractor passing on litigation costs exclusively to the Government because, presumably, such items are purchased on a free and open market and are demanded by all, and therefore all will share the burden.

Newmark v. Gimbel's Inc.

(Customer) v. *(Store Owning Beauty Shop)*

54 N.J. 585, 258 A.2d 697 (1969)

PRODUCTS USED BY COMMERCIAL ENTITIES IN THE PROVISION OF RETAIL SERVICES CARRY AN IMPLIED WARRANTY OF FITNESS WITH RESPECT TO THE CUSTOMER

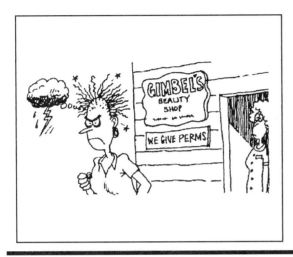

■ **INSTANT FACTS** Mrs. Newmark (P) was given a permanent at one of Gimbel's (D) beauty shops. The solution used in giving the permanent caused Newmark's (P) scalp to blister and her hair to fall out.

■ **BLACK LETTER RULE** There is an implied warranty of fitness of the products a retail service provider uses in providing those services the same as if the customer had purchased the product themselves.

■ **PROCEDURAL BASIS**

Appeal to the State's highest court after the appeals court reversed the dismissal of Plaintiff's warranty claim by the trial court.

■ **FACTS**

Mrs. Newmark (P) went to a beauty shop owned by Gimbel's, Inc. (Gimbel's)(D) where she had a standing appointment. Her regular operator, Valante, recommended she get a permanent and Newmark (P) accepted. During the treatment Newmark (P) repeatedly felt a "burning" and Valante took steps to diminish it. However, her forehead later blistered and her hair fell out. A dermatologist diagnosed her with contact dermatitis resulting from the application of the permanent solution. Valante stated that the solution could damage a scalp that had scratches on it or could cause a sting if the solution were rubbed into the scalp. He applied the solution as it came from the original package and his experience had shown that a tingling or burning sensation was fairly common. The label on the package contained a caveat for the beauty operator that cautioned the operator in using the solution, including an instruction to ask the patron if she has ever had a sensitivity to such waving lotion. Newmark (P) did not see the label and there is no indication that Valante asked her about any previous experience with such solutions. It does appear, however, that Newmark (P) had four permanent waves without any ill effects after this incident. Newmark's (P) warranty claim against Gimbel's (D) was dismissed by the trial court, holding that Gimbel's (D) was rendering a service, not making a sale. The Appellate Division reversed, holding that there might be an implied warranty as to the solution applied.

■ **ISSUE**

Are commercial entities that sell services that include the use of outside products exempt from warranty claims when those products are defective?

■ **DECISION AND RATIONALE**

(Francis, J.) No. If Gimbel's (D) had simply sold Newmark (P) the permanent solution, there would have unquestionably been an implied warranty of fitness of the product. What Gimbel's'(D) argument boils down to is that if, in addition to recommending the use of the solution and supplying it for use, they also applied it, such fact that they applied it would have the effect of lessening their liability to the patron by eliminating warranty and by limiting their responsibility to the issue of negligence. We disagree. On the contrary, by also administering the product, they might increase the scope of their liability. The transaction here has two parts: the rendering of service, and the supplying of goods for a consideration. We therefore agree with the Appellate division that an implied warranty of fitness of the products used in giving the permanent wave exists with no less force than it would have in the case of a simple sale. The fact that the customer did not specifically pay for the product, but instead had the price included in the flat rate for the permanent, is of no relevance. Common sense demands that such patron be deemed a consumer as to both manufacturer and beauty parlor operator. When a patron responds to the parlor's solicitation she does so confident that any product used in the shop has come from a reliable origin and can be trusted not to injure her. The ministrations and the products used on her are under the control and selection of the operator; the patron is a mere passive recipient. It seems to us that the policy considerations for imposing warranty liability in the case of ordinary sales are equally applicable to a commercial transaction such as that existing in this case between a beauty parlor operator and a patron. Gimbel's (D) claims that to hold them to strict liability would be contrary to *Magrine v. Krasnica.* We cannot agree. *Magrine* was injured during a visit to the dentist when a hypodermic needle, concededly being used with due care, broke off in his gum. The parties agreed the needle broke as the result of a defect. It was held that the strict liability in tort doctrine did not apply to the professional, such as a dentist or doctor, because the essence of the relationship with the patient was the furnishing of professional skill and services. We accepted the view that a dentist's bill for services should be considered as representing pay for that alone. The use of instruments or the administration of medicines or the providing of medicines for use at home cannot give the ministrations the cast of a commercial transaction. Accordingly, the liability of the dentist in ordinary cases must be tested by the principles of negligence. Gimbel's (D) suggests that there is no doctrinal basis for distinguishing the beauty parlor from the dentist or doctor, and therefore the liability for all should be tested by the same rules. But there is a vast difference in the relationships. The beautician is engaged in a commercial enterprise; the dentist and doctor in a profession. The former fulfills not a need, but a form of aesthetic convenience or luxury, involving the rendition of non-professional services. The demand for the doctor stems from need. Doctors and dentist exercise their best judgment in making a diagnosis and then making a recommendation for treatment. Each patient requires individual treatment, not some mechanically identical procedure. Doctors and dentists provide no implied warranty of relief or cure. Thus their paramount function ought to be regarded as the furnishing of opinions and services, which bears such a necessary and intimate relationship to public health and welfare that their obligation ought to be grounded in a duty of competence and care toward patients. The function of these professionals is so important as to outweigh on the policy scale any need for the imposition upon them the rules of strict liability in tort. Affirmed and remanded for a new trial.

Analysis:

What possible rationale could support holding the hairdresser strictly liable for the defective products she purchases from the distributor and uses in her business, but not for the defective products a doctor purchases from medical supply and engineering companies and uses on and in patients? It can certainly be argued that neither the hairdresser, nor the doctor has done anything wrong or is at fault (provided there is no negligence of course). The proper remedy, it seems reasonable to say, is to sue the manufacturer under strict tort liability. Instead, the Court in *Newmark* chose to draw a distinction between doctors, dentists, and presumably other "professionals" and those who minister to the desires or wishes of regular consumers by providing non-essential services. The Court says that, as a matter of public policy, the function of doctors and dentists is so essential that it would be unwise to impose strict liability in tort upon them, especially for the defects in products they use in their practice.

United Blood Services, Division of Blood Systems, Inc. v. Quintana

(Blood Provider) v. *(Blood Receiver)*

827 P.2d 509 (Colo.1992)

A PLAINTIFF IN A PROFESSIONAL NEGLIGENCE CASE MAY INTRODUCE EVIDENCE TENDING TO SHOW THAT THE STANDARD OF CARE ADOPTED BY THE PROFESSION AS A WHOLE IS DEFICIENT

■ **INSTANT FACTS** Mrs. Quintana (D) received several units of infected blood and plasma as a result of a gunshot wound. The blood was procured from a volunteer donor by United Blood Services (P) and caused Quintana (D) to develop the AIDS virus.

■ **BLACK LETTER RULE** The presumption that the standard of care adopted by a profession constitutes due care for those practicing in that profession may be rebutted by a showing that such standard of care is unreasonably deficient in light of readily available practices that would be better.

■ **PROCEDURAL BASIS**

Appeal from a jury verdict in favor of United Blood Service (P) after the trial court ruled testimony by one of Quintana's (D) experts inadmissible.

■ **FACTS**

United Blood Services (UBS)(P) [UBS was the defendant in the original trial] is a non-profit blood bank that relies strictly on volunteer donors for blood, which it then processes in the form of whole blood or blood components such as fresh frozen plasma that it provides to hospitals. In April 1983 UBS (P) received blood from a donor and then processed the blood before transferring it to Southwest Memorial Hospital in Cortez, Colorado. About a month later Mrs. Quintana (D) suffered a gunshot wound and was taken to Southwest Memorial where she received several units of whole blood and fresh frozen plasma that had been collected and processed by UBS (P). Quintana (D) thereafter developed AIDS. It was later determined that the donor of the unit of blood collected in April 1983 and given to Quintana (D) tested positive for AIDS. UBS (P) learned from the donor's physician that the donor was in a high-risk group for AIDS. Quintana (D) predicated her negligence claim on UBS's (P) failure to properly screen the donor and failure to properly screen the donated blood through surrogate testing. UBS (P) filed a motion to preclude one of Quintana's (D) expert witnesses, Dr. Conant, a dermatologist, from rendering an expert opinion on the standard of care applicable to UBS's (P) blood banking operations. Dr. Conant had extensive experience in AIDS research and had treated several thousand patients who suffered from AIDS or AIDS related illnesses. He was prepared to testify that the threat of the spread of AIDS through the blood supply was acute and that there were many options available to the blood banking profession to make the blood supply safer through donor and blood screening techniques, but the blood banking community had inexcusably failed to incorporate these techniques, instead preferring to place the privacy of donors over the safety of the blood supply and transfusion recipients. In excluding Dr. Conant's testimony, the trial court ruled that, pursuant to § 13–22–104(2), 6A C.R.S. (1987), the blood banking industry's function is "the performance of a medical service" and therefore the procedures used by UBS (P) in 1983 to protect the blood supply against AIDS contamination must be evaluated according to the professional standard of the blood banking community, not the general standard of reasonable care. Because Dr. Conant was not directly practicing in the industry, the court ruled he could not testify as to the proper standard of care in the industry. Evidence at trial indicated that in April 1983 UBS (P) had revised its donor screening in response to the Food and Drug Administration's recommendations. These screening procedures, however, did not include the aggressive questioning and physical examination of donors as recommended by the National Hemophilia Foundation, one of the organizations whose recommended procedures Dr. Conant was prepared to cite. Nor did UBS (P) employ surrogate testing as had been instituted by source plasma centers in early 1983. It was also established at trial that the donor of the blood given to Quintana (D) was served with a written interrogatory under oath prior to trial that asked several questions, of which an affirmative response to any one would have disqualified the donor as being a high risk for carrying the AIDS virus. The donor was asked if he were given these questions on the day in 1983 when the blood was donated, would any of the answers have been "yes." The donor responded "yes" to the interrogatory. The trial court also excluded testimony by Quintana's (D) other experts who would have testified similarly to Dr. Conant. The trial court's instructions to the jury were in accord with its evidentiary rulings—that the industry standard of care governed the case. So instructed, the jury returned a verdict in favor of UBS (P).

■ ISSUE

When the plaintiff alleges that an entire industry's standard of care was lacking are plaintiff's experts from outside the defendant's industry allowed to testify regarding the proper standard of care in that industry?

■ DECISION AND RATIONALE

(Quinn, J.) Yes. A defendant practicing in a profession is entitled to be judged by the standard of care applicable to the professional school to which the defendant belongs, but that standard is not always conclusive proof of due care. If such standard were deemed to be conclusive proof of due care, the profession itself would be allowed to set the measure of its own legal liability, a prospect that could lead to standards far below those that are proper. Though there is a presumption that adherence to the applicable standard of care adopted by a profession constitutes due care for those practicing that profession, the presumption is rebuttable. It can be rebutted by competent evidence that the standard of care to which the defendant adheres is unreasonably deficient by not incorporating readily available practices and procedures substantially more protective against the harm caused to the plaintiff than the standard of care adopted by the defendant's school of practice. Such proposition may be established through opinion testimony of a qualified expert in the same school or an expert in another school provided the expert is sufficiently familiar with the standard of care in the school in question. If this expert opinion testimony rises to the level of showing the professional standard of care adopted by the school of practice to which the defendant adheres is unreasonably lacking, the issue of whether such standard of care constitutes due care is a question for the jury to resolve under appropriate instructions. Section 13–22–104(2) expressly categorizes the blood banking function as "the performance of a medical service," and clearly contemplates that such function is to be measured by a professional standard of care. Any alleged negligence of a blood bank in performing those operations can occur only by reason of the action or inaction of its officers and employees functioning as health care professionals. We therefore hold that UBS's (P) conduct in acquiring and testing the blood used in treating Quintana (D) must be judged by a professional standard of care established by expert testimony. Though the trial court was correct in applying the professional standard of conduct to UBS's (P) conduct, it erroneously applied that standard in a way that precluded Quintana (D) from showing that the blood banking community's standard of care was itself unreasonably deficient. This error was tantamount to permitting the blood banking community to establish its own standard of legal liability despite the expert opinion evidence tending to show that the blood banking community had adopted unreasonably deficient practices and procedures in place of substantially more protective and readily available safeguards. Remanded for new trial.

Analysis:

In order for a defendant to be liable for a defective product, there must first be a product. Is blood a product? Exactly what is and isn't a product? Under the Restatement a product is any commercially distributed tangible personal property or items sufficiently analogous to allow for application of the same rules. It is true that most products one runs across will be tangible, but some things that are tangible are not considered products and vice versa. For example, electricity cannot be held or seen [except in the form of an arc, like lightning], but it has been treated as a product in strict liability cases. Contrast electricity with blood, which most everyone thinks of as a tangible item, however, those dealing in it commercially have always been statutorily shielded from strict liability. This seems to reflect a public policy that the blood supply is too important to hamper by allowing those responsible for maintaining it to face strict liability in tort suits. As the *UBS* case shows though, those supplying blood and blood products do remain liable in traditional negligence, albeit under the negligence standard of the blood banking industry.

CHAPTER TWENTY-FIVE

Settlement and Apportionment

Gleason v. Guzman

Instant Facts: A concussed tort victim signs a release, but later sues the tortfeasor when the injury unexpectedly causes epilepsy.

Black Letter Rule: Tort victims who signed general releases while mistaken about their injury may rescind the release later if they mistook the injury's present nature, but not if they mistook the injury's future prognosis.

Ascheman v. Village of Hancock

Instant Facts: When a drunken driver injured himself in a crash, his family sued the municipal bar for negligently serving him. The municipality seeks contribution from the driver.

Black Letter Rule: If a drunk driver's family sues a bar for loss of support under statues prohibiting serving intoxicated patrons, the bar cannot demand contribution from the driver.

Safeway Stores, Inc. v. Nest-Kart

Instant Facts: When a defective supermarket cart injures a shopper, the court finds the supermarket 80% responsible in negligence and the manufacturer 20% responsible in strict product liability. The supermarket claims apportionment proportional to comparative fault is inapplicable between negligent and strictly liable defendants.

Black Letter Rule: In "comparative fault" jurisdictions, if one co-tortfeasor is negligent and another co-tortfeasor is strictly liable, damages should be apportioned proportional to each defendant's degree of fault.

Hymowitz v. Eli Lilly and Company

Instant Facts: When a DES victim sues a manufacturer but is unsure whether she was injured by that manufacturer's DES, the manufacturer disclaims liability.

Black Letter Rule: In DES cases, where it is impossible to determine which defendant manufacturer's DES caused any given plaintiff's injuries, any defendant manufacturer which participated in marketing DES may be held liable proportional to its market share of the national DES market.

Cartel Capital Corp. v. Fireco of New Jersey

Instant Facts: When a business burns because of a defective fire extinguisher, the business settles with the manufacturer and gets judgement against the servicer. Then, the servicer sues the settling manufacturer for contribution.

Black Letter Rule: Under New Jersey law, if a joint tortfeasor settles with the plaintiff, and the plaintiff obtains judgement against its co-tortfeasors, the co-tortfeasors may seek contribution to the extent they paid more than their share of responsibility, but the plaintiff's claim at trial must be reduced by the settling tortfeasor's share of responsibility.

D'Amario v. Ford Motor Co.

Instant Facts: After the plaintiff's minor son was injured in a one-car accident, his injuries were enhanced when the car burst into flames.

Black Letter Rule: In a crashworthiness case against a product manufacturer, evidence of the driver's initial negligence is irrelevant and inadmissible.

Board of County Comn'rs of Teton County v. Bassett

Instant Facts: In a jurisdiction which abolished joint and several liability, police negligently opened a roadblock, allowing a fugitive driver to ram another car. The court ruled the fugitive cannot be included in apportioning fault, and the police appeal.

Black Letter Rule: In a jurisdiction which has abolished joint and several liability, apportionment of fault must include the fault of reckless/intentional/criminal tortfeasors.

Turner v. Jordan

Instant Facts: After a psychiatrist fails to protect a nurse from a known violent patient's assault, the court concludes liability should be allocated between the psychiatrist and patient.

Black Letter Rule: When a joint tort involves an intentional tort by one tortfeasor and negligent failure to prevent that intentional tort by another, fault cannot be allocated between them.

Gleason v. Guzman

(*Tortfeasor*) v. (*Tort Victim*)
623 P.2d 378 (Colo.1981)

TORT VICTIMS MAY RESCIND RELEASES SIGNED IF MISTAKEN ABOUT INJURY'S NATURE

■ **INSTANT FACTS** A concussed tort victim signs a release, but later sues the tortfeasor when the injury unexpectedly causes epilepsy.

■ **BLACK LETTER RULE** Tort victims who signed general releases while mistaken about their injury may rescind the release later if they mistook the injury's present nature, but not if they mistook the injury's future prognosis.

■ PROCEDURAL BASIS
Appeal from appellate court's denial of summary judgement for defendants in tort action seeking rescission of release, and damages.

■ FACTS
Gleason (D), a truck driver employed by Coin Fresh (D), dropped a vending machine from his truck, striking Ms. Guzman (P), a minor, in the head. Guzman (P) was diagnosed with temporal lobe contusion [meaning, she was struck on the head], and complained of headaches, vomiting, and disorientation, but was treated and believed cured. Since Guzman (P) was a minor, her family sued on her behalf, and received a settlement of $6,114 in exchange for a general release, signed by her guardian (father). [It is possible the father, who was uneducated and spoke little English, did not understand what he was signing.] Later, almost 4 years after the accident, Guzman (P) experienced epileptic seizures. Guzman (P) sued Gleason (D) and Coin Fresh (D) for negligent personal injury. The defendants raised as an affirmative defense the release Guzman (P) signed, and moved for summary judgement. Guzman (P) countered, moving to set aside the release on the ground it was executed under a mistake as to the injury's nature. At trial, the judge granted defendants summary judgement. Guzman (P) appealed. On appeal, the appellate court reversed the summary judgement entry. Gleason (D) and Coin Fresh (D) appeal, contending (i) Guzman (P) made no mistake about the injury actually suffered, but only about future complications, and (ii) the release was a general release encompassing injuries both known and unknown.

■ ISSUE
May a tort victim who signed a general release while mistaken about the injury later rescind the release?

■ DECISION AND RATIONALE
(Quinn) Yes. Tort victims who signed general releases while mistaken about their injury may rescind the release later if they mistook the injury's present nature, but not if they mistook the injury's future prognosis. [Procedurally, the court holds a lawsuit involving a motion to set aside a release ineligible for jury trial.] Since these arguments are presented in the context of a summary judgement review, the issue is whether the record shows a genuine issue as to any material fact. Cases addressing mistakes in the settlement of personal injury claims reflect a tension stemming from the general need for finality in the contractual settlement of suits, as opposed to the recognized need to alleviate the unintended and unfair effects of human error. These policies lean in different directions. One approach—denying

rescission even where the injuries were unknown or unsuspected during settlement—makes the releasor assume the risk that the injuries' known nature and extent might be more severe than believed at settlement. Another approach allows rescission based on any mistake about the injured plaintiff's condition, whether the mistake relates to the injuries' nature or their further consequences. Midway between these approaches is the view that rescission is available for mistakes relating to known injuries' nature, but not for mistakes about the future course and effects of those injuries. The assumption in this last approach is that rescission must be based on mistake, and "mistake," for legal purposes, must relate to a past or present fact rather than an opinion or prophecy about the future. This last approach represents the rule in this jurisdiction, as expressed in *McCarthy v. Eddings* [plaintiff who signed release for broken arm, believing it temporary, may rescind the release when the injury was found to be permanent], *Davis v. Flatiron Materials Co.* [plaintiff, correctly diagnosed and aware of nature of condition, cannot rescind release because she was mistaken about course of recovery], and *Scotton v. Landers* [plaintiff who signed release for fractured rib may rescind general release on learning spleen was ruptured]. However, as these cases demonstrate, the analytic distinction between unknown injuries and unknown consequences does not yield a litmus-type resolution to these problems. Here, this is a marginal case, because, when the injury is post-traumatic epilepsy, it is difficult to differentiate a mistaken diagnosis from a mistaken prognosis. Knowledge of an injury's nature requires an awareness and appreciation of its extent, severity, and likely duration. These basic components of knowledge involve comprehending the injury's basic character, as distinct from a prediction or opinion about the future course of recovery. Here, the record provides adequate basis to infer the existence of a mistake in the guardian's execution of the release, because the guardian had little education, was not adept at English, and apparently believed the injury was only a "concussion." Since Guzman (P) experienced only minor symptoms after the accident, it may reasonably be inferred that, when the release was executed, the guardian believed the injury was minor, temporary, and posed no risk of complication, and there is no evidence that the guardian was informed otherwise by doctors or his lawyer. In fact, Guzman's (P) lawyer was unaware the injury posed risk of brain dysfunction, much less post-traumatic epilepsy, as is discernable from his correspondence and in-court statements. On the record, there is a genuine factual issue on whether the guardian was mistaken about the nature of Guzman's (P) injury when he executed the release. Thus, summary judgement was inappropriate. The defendants argue the release bars all Guzman's (P) claims, as a matter of law, because its terms encompass unknown injuries that may develop later. Although some jurisdictions give effect to a release which precludes recovery even for unknown injuries, the tendency of the law is to the contrary. Most courts allow for avoidance (i.e., voiding the release) in appropriate circumstances (e.g., mistake, lack of intent, etc.). Resolving the intent issue necessarily means going behind the release's language. The release will be set aside if the parties did not contemplate unknown injuries. Summary judgement for defendants reversed.

Analysis:

As this case demonstrates, the majority rule is that a release is voidable if signed under mistake, but only if the plaintiff mistook the injury's "nature," and not if he merely miscalculated the duration or difficulty of recovering from a known injury. However, some jurisdictions follow other approaches, as noted. As the case notes, it is often difficult to differentiate whether a mistaken victim was mistaken about the injury's "diagnosis" or its "prognosis." Here, for instance, it could be argued that Guzman (P) was mistaken about her injury's nature (believing it a concussion where in fact it was brain damage), and that she understood her injury but miscalculated the recovery (knew she had a head injury and concussion, but did not believe it would develop into epilepsy). Policy generally dictates that a release should be voidable in any case where the injury turns out to be more complicated than foreseen at signing. This would not disadvantage the defendant unfairly. The aim of tort is (or should be) to compensate the victim fully for injury inflicted by another. If, at settlement, the full extent of the injury were known to the plaintiff, the plaintiff would demand and obtain full compensation for all complications. Thus, the defendant is liable for, and ideally should pay, the full extent of all damages caused, whether foreseen or not. If the defendant is initially liable for all damages, but manages to temporarily escape paying the full extent of the damages, it is not unfair for the defendant to later be required to pay the remainder. Of course, defendants and insurers resist this reasoning strenuously.

■ CASE VOCABULARY

(GENERAL) RELEASE: Plaintiff's signed document releasing defendant from further liability, usually in exchange for a settlement payment.

Ascheman v. Village of Hancock

(*Drunk Driver*) v. (*Bar Owner*)

254 N.W.2d 382 (Minn.1977)

BAR SUED FOR SERVING DRUNK DRIVER CANNOT DEMAND CONTRIBUTION FROM DRIVER

■ **INSTANT FACTS** When a drunken driver injured himself in a crash, his family sued the municipal bar for negligently serving him. The municipality seeks contribution from the driver.

■ **BLACK LETTER RULE** If a drunk driver's family sues a bar for loss of support under statues prohibiting serving intoxicated patrons, the bar cannot demand contribution from the driver.

■ **PROCEDURAL BASIS**

In negligence action seeking damages, appeal from dismissal of third-party complaint.

■ **FACTS**

Floyd Ascheman ("Floyd") (D) got drunk at a municipal bar, owned by the Village of Hancock ("Village") (D), then crashed his car, injuring himself. Ascheman's wife and child ("Family") (P) sued Village (D) for loss of support, contending Village's (D) bar negligently continued serving breadwinner Floyd (D) liquor despite obvious intoxication, in violation of the Minnesota Civil Damages Act. Village (D) initiated third-party proceedings against Floyd (D), seeking (partial) contribution for his negligence in breaching his duties to support his family by getting dangerously drunk. Floyd (D) moved for summary judgement dismissing the third-party proceeding, contending he cannot be named a co-defendant because Family (P) would have had no cause of action against him. At a pretrial hearing, the judge granted Floyd (D) summary judgement and dismissed Village's (D) suit against him. Village (D) appeals, contending (i) under Minnesota case law, Family (D) would have a negligence claim against Floyd (D) for loss of support, and (ii) the Civil Damages Act should not apply where the plaintiff would share recovery with the drunk driver.

■ **ISSUE**

If a drunk driver's family sues a bar for loss of support under statues prohibiting serving intoxicated patrons, can the bar demand contribution from the driver?

■ **DECISION AND RATIONALE**

(Todd) No. If a drunk driver's family sues a bar for loss of support under statues prohibiting serving intoxicated patrons, the bar cannot demand contribution from the driver. Under Minnesota statutes, husbands are legally responsible for supporting their wives while married, and fathers are responsible for supporting minor children. Village (D) contends that, under these statutes, Family (P) could sue Floyd (D) directly for his negligence in diminishing their means of support by driving drunk, and thus Village (D) should be allowed contribution from Floyd (D) as a co-tortfeasor. However, we are unaware of any decisions which recognize familial dependents' rights to sue the head of household for negligently impairing the family's means of support. Under Minnesota case law, parents remain immune from suit by children for negligent acts involving an exercise of ordinary parental discretion involving the provision of food, clothing, or other necessities. [So you can't sue your parents for malpractice in Minnesota.] While recent Minnesota decisions limited intrafamilial immunities, they did not create a new cause of action in tort for loss of support, but merely abolished some defenses to already-existing tort claims. Here, Village (D) cannot claim common liability with Floyd (D) against Family (P), because Family (P) could never bring a direct action against him for negligence for the loss of their means of support. Further, Village (D) urges this court to relax the Civil Damage Act, contending it unjust that Floyd (D) should share in the recovery by his Family (D), and that Village (D) should be 100% liable for Floyd's (D) drunk driving. However, we decline. The Civil Damage Act's legislative intent was to suppress the illegal furnishing of liquor and provide a civil remedy to compensate breadwinners's families for the loss of their support. Here, we find Family (D) is the class intended to be protected, and find that allowing contribution by Floyd (D) would diminish his ability to support his Family (D) from the proceeds of their recovery. Affirmed (claims against Floyd (D) dismissed).

Analysis:

Another Minnesota case, *Nelson, et al v. Larsen, et al*, illustrates the *Civil Damage Act,* which provides the exclusive remedy against a bar or "dram shop" for damages arising from improper sales of alcoholic beverages, but does not create a cause of action in favor of one injured by his own intoxication. In that case, Nelson had gotten intoxicated at a local bar. After he and some friends left the bar they stopped on the side of the road so Nelson could relieve himself. As he was doing so one of the other men in the car drove it a short distance away. As Nelson was standing in the middle of the road another car driven by Larsen hit Nelson, causing him serious injury. When Nelson sued, Larsen sought contribution for any damage award from the bar that served Nelson. However, under the law contribution is appropriate only where there is a common liability enforceable against each co-tortfeasor, and common liability does not exist if the injured party (Nelson) could not bring a direct action against each of the co-tortfeasors. As stated above, one injured as a result of his own intoxication cannot rely on the *Civil Damage Act* to sue the bar. Because Nelson's voluntary intoxication precludes him from suing the bar, common liability does not exist between Nelson and Larsen. Therefore, Larsen did not have common liability with the bar and contribution is thus inappropriate. As applied to *Ascheman*, the courts decided that the mother and children could not sue Floyd (D), just as Nelson could not sue the bar. Therefore, under the principles enunciated above, because the wife and children do not have a cause of action against Floyd (D), there exists no common liability between Floyd (D) and the Village (D). Thus, the Village (D) cannot get contribution from Floyd (D).

■ CASE VOCABULARY

CONTRIBUTION: In tort, the right of a co-tortfeasor who is sued for the tort's full damages to sue a fellow co-tortfeasor for payment ("contribution") of the damages proximately caused by that fellow co-tortfeasor.

THIRD-PARTY PROCEEDINGS: In civil procedure, device by which a plaintiff/defendant named in a lawsuit seeks to add another ("third") party as a plaintiff or defendant. Usually, a named defendant seeks to add another party as co-defendant because it contends the third party is liable, partially or fully. Here, named defendant Village (D) sought to add Floyd (D) as co-defending, contending he was partially responsible for damages.

Safeway Stores, Inc. v. Nest-Kart

(Negligent Co-Tortfeasor) v. *(Strictly-Liable Co-Tortfeasor)*

21 Cal.3d 322, 146 Cal.Rptr. 550, 579 P.2d 441 (1978)

COMPARATIVE NEGLIGENCE ALLOWS COMPARATIVE APPORTIONMENT BETWEEN NEGLIGENT AND STRICTLY-LIABLE DEFENDANTS

■ **INSTANT FACTS** When a defective supermarket cart injures a shopper, the court finds the supermarket 80% responsible in negligence and the manufacturer 20% responsible in strict product liability. The supermarket claims apportionment proportional to comparative fault is inapplicable between negligent and strictly liable defendants.

■ **BLACK LETTER RULE** In "comparative fault" jurisdictions, if one co-tortfeasor is negligent and another co-tortfeasor is strictly liable, damages should be apportioned proportional to each defendant's degree of fault.

■ **PROCEDURAL BASIS**

In negligence and strict liability tort action seeking damages, appeal from post-verdict motion seeking reallocation of damages between defendants.

■ **FACTS**

Elliot (P), a shopper at [the unfortunately-named] Safeway Stores (D), was injured when a shopping cart, owned by Safeway (D), broke and fell on her foot. Elliot (P) sued the cart's owner Safeway (D), its manufacturer Nest-Kart Corp. (D) for personal injury in strict liability and negligence. At trial, the jury returned a verdict of $25,000 against both Safeway (D) and Nest-Kart (D) and made "special findings" that Safeway (D) was 80% liable (in negligence and strict liability) while Nest-Kart (D) was 20% liable (in strict liability only). Safeway (D) moved to require Nest-Kart (D) to pay 50%, contending *American Motorcycle* held that, under California's "contribution" [comparative fault] statutes, multiple tortfeasors' liability may not be apportioned according to comparative fault when one is negligent and another is non-negligent but strictly liable. The trial court granted Safeway's (D) motion and ordered Nest-Kart (D) to pay 50%. Nest-Kart (D) appeals.

■ **ISSUE**

In "comparative fault" jurisdictions, if one co-tortfeasor is negligent and another co-tortfeasor is strictly liable, can damages be apportioned proportional to each defendant's degree of fault?

■ **DECISION AND RATIONALE**

(Tobriner) Yes. In "comparative fault" jurisdictions, if one co-tortfeasor is negligent and another co-tortfeasor is strictly liable, damages should be apportioned proportional to each defendant's degree of fault. *American Motorcycle* explicitly held that California's current "contribution" [comparative fault] statutes do not necessarily prohibit apportioning liability among multiple tortfeasors on a comparative fault basis, so the trial court erred in holding otherwise. However, the question remains whether *American Motorcycle's* "comparative indemnity" [comparative fault] doctrine may be applied when some defendants are liable based only on strict liability, to apportion liability based on their degree of fault. We believe it may, based on the same basic equitable considerations. Such a holding would

---

apportion liability between strictly liable defendants and other co-tortfeasors, which does not conflict with the rationale of strict liability. Although one of the social policies served by product liability doctrine is to assign liability to a party who possesses the ability to distribute losses over an appropriate segment of society, this policy is not so absolute that it must allow negligent tortfeasors who contribute to the injury to escape all liability. It is sometimes suggested that apportionment is impossible between defendants who are negligent and those who are strictly liable, since no logical basis can be found for comparing the relative "fault" of a negligent defendant with that of a defendant whose liability rests on "no fault" strict liability. However, these suggested difficulties are more theoretical than practical, and other jurisdictions' experience demonstrates juries are fully competent to apply comparative fault principles between such defendants. We note that holding otherwise—i.e., confining the comparative indemnity [comparative negligence] doctrine to cases involving only negligent defendants—would lead to bizarre and irrational consequences, because, e.g., a manufacturer who negligently produced a product would frequently be in a better position than a non-negligent one sued for strict liability, since the negligent manufacturer could shift liability to negligent co-tortfeasors, but the non-negligent one could not. Thus, to avoid such unjustified results, we hold the comparative indemnity doctrine applies to allocate liability between negligent defendants and strictly-liable ones.

Analysis:

As the court notes, it is difficult to make a rational apportionment of "fault" for a strict liability defendant, because by definition, the strictly-liable defendant need not be at fault. Some courts skirt the analytic contradiction by referring to fault apportioned to strictly-liable defendants as "comparative causation." This seems to imply the court is saying there is an _____% chance that it was the defendant who caused the injury, but this is akin to the DES "market share" apportionment, and is certainly *not* what the court is apportioning in comparative fault cases. However, the alternative is merely to always demand each co-defendant pay a pro rata (equal) share of damages, which has no rational basis either. The holding in *Safeway* is thus a compromise between fairness and practicability. In the past at common law, before comparative negligence was accepted, some courts held that a "passive" defendant (such as a strictly liable but non-negligent products manufacturer) was entitled to (full) indemnity from the "active" negligent co-tortfeasor, which meant the strictly liable defendant would not have to pay anything as long as his negligent co-defendants were solvent. However, this system was even more arbitrary, since it in effect assigns 100% of fault to a negligent defendant and 0% to a strictly liable one, even if the "passive" defendant was actually partly at fault.

■ CASE VOCABULARY

COMPARATIVE FAULT/COMPARATIVE INDEMNITY: Same as comparative negligence, a tort system under which tortfeasors must pay the percentage of total damages which corresponds to their degree of fault.

Hymowitz v. Eli Lilly and Company

(*Drug Consumer*) v. (*Drug Manufacturer*)

73 N.Y.2d 487, 541 N.Y.S.2d 941, 539 N.E.2d 1069 (1989)

DRUG MANUFACTURERS CAN BE LIABLE PROPORTIONAL TO THEIR NATIONAL MARKET SHARE

■ **INSTANT FACTS** When a DES victim sues a manufacturer but is unsure whether she was injured by that manufacturer's DES, the manufacturer disclaims liability.

■ **BLACK LETTER RULE** In DES cases, where it is impossible to determine which defendant manufacturer's DES caused any given plaintiff's injuries, any defendant manufacturer which participated in marketing DES may be held liable proportional to its market share of the national DES market.

■ **PROCEDURAL BASIS**

In negligent personal injury action seeking damages, appeal from denial of defendant's motion to dismiss.

■ **FACTS**

In 1941, the FDA approved the anti-miscarriage drug DES. The drug was generic (not patented by any one company), and was sold by 300 companies, including Eli Lilly (D). 20 years later, it was found DES caused cancer in users' children. When DES victims, including Hymowitz (P), began suing, they had difficulty proving causation, since their mothers often did not know/remember which manufacturer's DES they had taken 20 years earlier. At trial, defendant manufacturers moved for summary judgement, contending the true tortfeasor could not be identified. The trial court denied defendants' motion, and defendants appeal.

■ **ISSUE**

In cases where it is impossible to determine which defendant/manufacturer caused any given plaintiff's injuries, are all defendants/manufacturers not liable?

■ **DECISION AND RATIONALE**

(Wachtler) No. In DES cases, where it is impossible to determine which defendant manufacturer's DES caused any given plaintiff's injuries, any defendant manufacturer which participated in marketing DES may be held liable proportional to its market share of the national DES market. The paradigm of alternative liability is *Summers v. Tice* (Cal.) [two defendants shoot at hunter, but hunter cannot determine whose bullet hit him], which held that, where two defendants breached a duty to the plaintiff, but there is uncertainty about which one caused the injury, "the burden is upon each . . . actor to prove . . . he has not caused the harm." The rationale for shifting the proof burden is that, without this device, both defendants would be silent, and plaintiffs would not recover. With alternative liability, defendants will be forced to speak and reveal the culpable party, or face joint and several liability. Thus, to use the "alternative liability" doctrine generally requires that the defendants have better access to information than the plaintiff, and that all possible tortfeasors be before the court. Also, it is recognized that "alternative liability" rests on the notion that, where there are few possible wrongdoers,

---

the likelihood that any one of them injured the plaintiff is high, so it is fair to force them to exonerate themselves. In DES cases, there are many possible wrongdoers (manufacturers), who entered and exited the market at different times, and some of whom no longer exist. Also, in DES cases, many years elapsed between purchase and injury. Thus, DES defendants are not in any better position to identify the manufacturer of any given DES, and there is no prospect of having all possible producers before the court. Further, it is increasingly unfair to require one defendant of many to disprove liability. Nor does the pure "concerted action" theory supply a basis for recovery, since the record does not show DES companies engaged in a "common plan to commit a tortious act" by negligently marketing DES without proper testing. In short, extant common law doctrines provide no relief for DES plaintiffs. While other courts which reached similar conclusions have denied recovery, we conclude the present circumstances call for a realistic avenue of recovery for DES victims, since it is unfair to deny innocent victims any relief due to DES's insidious nature, especially after the New York legislature has revived previously-barred DES cases. We stress, however, that the DES situation is a singular case. We now turn to the question of how to fairly apportion the loss caused by DES in cases where the exact manufacturer is unknown. Courts have already accepted the "market share" approach, under which defendant manufacturers are liable proportional to their share of the market for the offending product, if they have a "substantial" share of the market, and unless they can prove that their product was in fact not the one which injured the plaintiff. *Sindell v. Abbott Labs* (Cal. 1980). After *Sindell*, it was determined that the national market share is the most fair indication of market share. Later, in *Brown v. Superior Ct.* (Cal. 198_), the court clarified that, where fewer than all manufacturers are joined, liability is still limited to national market share, resulting in less than 100% recovery for the plaintiff. Other state courts also followed the "market share" approach to some degree. We conclude the best solution for allocating DES liability is a "market share" theory, which allocates liability among defendant manufacturers proportional to their share of the *national* market. We are aware that using the national market, rather than regional markets, as an index may create a disproportionate liability in this state, but we believe it more accurately reflects the risk of injury each defendant created to the public-at-large. Defendants may rebut liability by proving they did not participate in marketing DES, but not by proving they did not cause a particular plaintiff's injury. Finally, we hold that, when not all DES market participants are before the court, each defendant cannot be made to pay more than its total market share, even though this prevents plaintiffs from recovering 100% of their damages. [This court also holds it was constitutional for the New York legislature to pass a law renewing DES claims previously barred by the statute of limitations.]

■ CONCURRENCE IN PART AND DISSENT IN PART

(Mollen) I believe, contrary to the majority opinion, that defendant manufacturers who prove they did not produce the DES pill which caused any particular plaintiff's injury should exculpated. Furthermore, I would impose joint and several liability on all defendants who cannot exculpate themselves.

Analysis:

Hymowitz represents just one of many DES cases nationwide. As the opinion notes, this case, on its face, is applicable only to DES, in recognition of the peculiar 20-year lag before damages became apparent, the added hardship of finding the manufacturer of a mass-produced generic drug, and the New York legislature's intent to see DES victims compensated. However, it is possible that "market share" apportionment may be applied again in future cases which make it nearly impossible to prove which defendant of several is responsible. Like most apportionment theories, "market share" liability is a compromise between full compensation for victims and fairness for defendants, and is only a partial success in both. A defendant manufacturer which is forced to pay its percentage of market share will, in the aggregate, pay the fair amount. (E.g., if a company produced 10% of all DES consumed, and if we assume all DES batches were standardized and thus equally harmful, then it is likely that company produced 10% of DES injuries, and should pay 10% of all DES damages.) However, this means that any one company will often end up paying partly for injuries actually caused by another defendant's DES. This result is necessary under the "market share" apportionment system, because if defendants were allowed to disclaim liability in cases where they could prove the plaintiff used another defendant's DES, they would pay less than their market share. (E.g., if that same company had to pay only 10% where *its* DES caused the injury, but could avoid paying anything where another caused the injury, it would only pay 10% of the damages *caused by it.* If every company did that, plaintiffs would recover only a small fraction of their damages). On the other hand, victims are undercompensated (and defendants are not forced to overcompensate), since some DES manufacturers are insolvent, and the solvent manufacturers are not jointly and severally responsible for paying their share.

Cartel Capital Corp. v. Fireco of New Jersey

(*Co-Tortfeasor's Assignee*) v. (*Co-Tortfeasor*)

81 N.J. 548, 410 A.2d 674, 19 A.L.R. 4th 310 (1980)

IN NEW JERSEY, PRETRIAL SETTLEMENT REDUCES CLAIM AGAINST CO-TORTFEASORS, BUT CO-TORTFEASORS MAY SUE SETTLOR FOR CONTRIBUTION

■ **INSTANT FACTS** When a business burns because of a defective fire extinguisher, the business settles with the manufacturer and gets judgement against the servicer. Then, the servicer sues the settling manufacturer for contribution.

■ **BLACK LETTER RULE** Under New Jersey law, if a joint tortfeasor settles with the plaintiff, and the plaintiff obtains judgement against its co-tortfeasors, the co-tortfeasors may seek contribution to the extent they paid more than their share of responsibility, but the plaintiff's claim at trial must be reduced by the settling tortfeasor's share of responsibility.

■ **PROCEDURAL BASIS**

In business tort action for negligence and strict liability, appeal from finding of liability and dismissal of cross claim.

■ **FACTS**

When Country Burger ("Burger") (P) suffered a fire causing damages of $113,400 it threatened suit against its fire extinguishing system's manufacturer Ansul (D) and its servicer/distributor Fireco (D). Burger (P) settled with Ansul (D) for $50,000, and sued Fireco (D). At trial, the court found Burger (P) 41% responsible (for negligently leaving grease and paper by a grill), Ansul (D) 29% responsible (for manufacturing defective equipment), and Fireco 30% responsible (for negligence). Fireco (D) cross-claimed against Ansul (D) for indemnity or contribution, but the court dismissed Fireco's (D) cross claim. Burger (P) appeals from the finding of its negligence, and Fireco (D) appeals from the dismissal of its cross claim.

■ **ISSUE**

Under New Jersey law, if a joint tortfeasor settles with the plaintiff, and the plaintiff obtains judgement against its co-tortfeasors, may the co-tortfeasors seek indemnity or contribution against it?

■ **DECISION AND RATIONALE**

(Schreiber) Yes. Under New Jersey law, if a joint tortfeasor settles with the plaintiff, and the plaintiff obtains judgement against its co-tortfeasors, the co-tortfeasors may seek contribution to the extent they paid more than their share of responsibility, but the plaintiff's claim at trial must be reduced by the settling tortfeasor's share of responsibility. [First, we hold Burger (P) was not negligent in creating the fire risk, because this did not constitute an unreasonable and voluntary exposure to a known risk.] As for the contribution claim, we previously held the New Jersey Contribution Law requires contribution even among co-tortfeasors liable on different theories of recovery (i.e., negligence and strict liability). Under the (older) Contribution Law, a joint tortfeasor can seek contribution only for any excess paid over "his pro rata share," and any settlement with a joint tortfeasor reduced the plaintiff's total claim against the non-settling co-tortfeasor(s) by the pro rata share, and thus barred contribution from the settling tortfeasor. However, it is necessary to note the effect of New Jersey's (later) Comparative Negligence Act, under which "[a]ny party ... compelled to pay more than [its] percentage share may seek contribution from the other joint tortfeasors." Thus, the New Jersey Legislature has seen fit to redefine the "pro rata" allocation to the party's "percentage share" among joint tortfeasors. Thus, under the new statutory scheme, when one defendant settles, the plaintiff's claim against the remaining codefendant(s) is reduced by the amount attributable to the settling defendant's percentage. Here, since we found Burger (P) non-negligent, we find that Fireco's (D) responsibility is 50.8%, or $57,661, and Ansul's (D) is 49.2%, or $55,739. However, Ansul (D) had settled. Thus, Fireco (D) remains liable for its share, $57,661.

Analysis:

It is likely that this case only went to trial because of a contradiction in New Jersey statutory law. Under the older New Jersey Contribution law, co-tortfeasors adjudged liable could seek contribution for the amount they paid over their *pro-rata share,* while under the newer Comparative Negligence Act, they could seek contribution for the amount they paid over *share of responsibility.* Apparently, Fireco (D) had hoped to apply the old pro-rata rule, though the court wisely ruled that the later statute overruled the inconsistent earlier one. The true significance of the case is not this particular ambiguity of New Jersey law, but rather the broad principle that many jurisdictions have shifted from contribution based on pro rata share to contribution proportional to fault. Jurisdictions which made the shift have, like New Jersey, also had to hold that (i) contribution may be had between negligent and strictly liable defendants, and (ii) if one co-tortfeasor settles, the plaintiff's claim against the others must be reduced by the percentage for which the settlor was at fault.

■ CASE VOCABULARY

CROSS CLAIM: Claim made by one co-defendant against another co-defendant, often for indemnity/contribution.

D'Amario v. Ford Motor Co.

(Injured Minor's Mother) v. *(Automobile Manufacturer)*

806 So.2d 424 (Fla.2001)

LIABILITY EXTENDS TO ENHANCED INJURIES

■ **INSTANT FACTS** After the plaintiff's minor son was injured in a one-car accident, his injuries were enhanced when the car burst into flames.

■ **BLACK LETTER RULE** In a crashworthiness case against a product manufacturer, evidence of the driver's initial negligence is irrelevant and inadmissible.

■ **PROCEDURAL BASIS**

On appeal to review a jury verdict for the defendant.

■ **FACTS**

Clifford Harris, a minor, was severely injured when a car driven by an intoxicated friend crashed into a tree and burst into flames. After striking the tree, a fire started in the engine area and spread throughout the vehicle, causing an explosion. Harris lost three limbs and suffered burns on most of his body. D'Amario (P), Harris's mother, sued Ford Motor Co. (D), alleging that Harris's injuries were caused by a defective relay switch in the vehicle, which resulted in the explosion after the initial impact. Ford (D) denied liability and contended that the injuries were caused by a negligent third party, without identifying the driver as a non-party tortfeasor. At trial, the plaintiff offered expert testimony that a defect in the relay switch prevented the switch from interrupting the flow of fuel to the fuel pump, causing the explosion. Ford's (D) experts testified that the explosion was caused by an oil pan that ruptured on impact. Ford (D) then amended its affirmative defense to include evidence of the driver's intoxication and excessive speed. The parties thereafter stipulated to the driver's intoxication and that the driver's negligence caused the initial impact. After deliberation, the jury found that Ford (D) was not the legal cause of the injuries and returned a defense verdict. After the court of appeals reversed the trial court's order for a new trial and reinstated the verdict, D'Amario (P) appealed.

■ **ISSUE**

Is evidence of a driver's initial negligence relevant to an automobile manufacturer's liability for product defects that enhance the initial injuries?

■ **DECISION AND RATIONALE**

(Per curiam.) No. Under the majority view, "the fault of the person causing the accident that created the circumstances in which the second accident occurred should be compared with the role of the automobile manufacturer's negligence in designing a defective product in asserting total responsibility for the claimant's injuries." Under the minority view, on the other hand, a manufacturer "is liable only for the increased injury caused by its own conduct, not for the injury resulting from the crash itself." This view recognizes the initial negligence as remote from the enhanced injury caused by a defective part designed to protect against injury in the event of a collision. Accordingly, evidence of a driver's negligence is irrelevant to the manufacturer's liability for injuries resulting from the defective product.

Unlike cases in which a plaintiff's injuries are caused by multiple defendants' joint and concurrent negligence, crashworthiness cases involve joint and successive negligence. The injuries caused from an initial collision are separate and distinct from those caused by a defective product following the collision. In this respect, crashworthiness cases are analogous to medical malpractice cases, in which evidence of a patient's initial negligence causing his injuries is inadmissible when considering a physician's successive breach of care. Therefore, the minority view is adopted and evidence of the driver's initial negligence is irrelevant and inadmissible when determining the manufacturer's successive liability. By limiting the manufacturer's liability to injuries caused by the defective product, and not by the driver's initial negligence, this view appropriately acknowledges comparative fault principles and avoids unduly confusing the jury. Reversed.

Analysis:

If evidence of the driver's negligence could be introduced as an affirmative defense or to mitigate damages, car manufacturers would nearly always avoid liability in a crashworthiness case. Because most car accidents are caused by someone's negligence, the car manufacturer need only point to that negligence as the cause of the injuries and avoid liability for its design defects. But the initial negligence is a reasonably foreseeable precursor to the injuries caused by the manufacturer's negligence, so the manufacturer should be held accountable for the unrelated injuries that follow the crash.

■ CASE VOCABULARY

CONCURRENT NEGLIGENCE: The negligence of two or more parties acting independently but causing the same damage.

SUBSEQUENT NEGLIGENCE: The negligence of the defendant when, after the defendant's initial negligence and the plaintiff's contributory negligence, the defendant discovers—or should have discovered—that the plaintiff was in a position of danger and fails to exercise due care in preventing the plaintiff's injuries.

Board of County Comn'rs of Teton County v. Bassett

(*Police Department*) v. (*Tort/Crime Victim*)

8 P.3d 1079 (Wyo.2000)

WHERE JOINT AND SEVERAL LIABILITY IS ABOLISHED, FAULT APPORTIONMENT MUST INCLUDE "FAULT" ATTRIBUTABLE TO RECKLESS/NEGLIGENT/CRIMINAL ACTORS

■ **INSTANT FACTS** In a jurisdiction which abolished joint and several liability, police negligently opened a roadblock, allowing a fugitive driver to ram another car. The court ruled the fugitive cannot be included in apportioning fault, and the police appeal.

■ **BLACK LETTER RULE** In a jurisdiction which has abolished joint and several liability, apportionment of fault must include the fault of reckless/intentional/criminal tortfeasors.

■ **PROCEDURAL BASIS**

In negligent personal injury action seeking damages, appeal from damages apportionment.

■ **FACTS**

The Wyoming Highway Patrol ("Patrol") pursued fugitive driver Ortega (D) by car. Unable to catch Ortega (D), Patrol radioed the Sheriff's officers (D) to set a roadblock to stop Ortega (D). Meanwhile, driver Coziah (P) and passenger Bassett (P) were driving nearby. As Coziah (P) and Bassett (P) turned onto the roadblocked street, several Patrol officers and National Park Service ("Park") (D) officers saw them entering and, aware Ortega (D) was approaching the roadblock, failed to warn Coziah (P) and Bassett (P). When one of the Sheriff's officers (D) moved his car to let them pass, creating a gap in the roadblock, Ortega (D) tried to drive through the opening at 100 mph, striking and injuring Coziah (P) and Bassett (P). Coziah (P) and Bassett (P) sued Patrol (D), Sheriff's officers (D), Park (D), and Ortega (D). At trial, the judge held that Ortega (D) could not be included in apportioning liability because he acted intentionally rather than negligently, and apportioned fault as follows: Coziah (P) 0%, Patrol (D) 40%, Sheriff's (D) officers 20%, and Park (D) 40%. The defendants appeal from the finding that Ortega (D) cannot be included in apportioning fault [since without any apportionment to Ortega (D), the other defendants would be liable for 100% of damages].

■ **ISSUE**

In a jurisdiction which has abolished joint and several liability, can fault be apportioned between negligent and intentional tortfeasors?

■ **DECISION AND RATIONALE**

(Grant) Yes. In a jurisdiction which has abolished joint and several liability, apportionment of fault must include the fault of reckless/intentional/criminal tortfeasors. The question is whether Ortega (D), whose conduct was intentional or wanton and willful, should be included with the negligent actors in apportioning fault under Wyoming statutes. The current Wyoming statute provides that "each defendant is liable only to the extent of that defendant's proportion of the total *fault*." The word "fault" replaces the previous statute's term "negligence," and the statute elsewhere states that "fault" "*includes* ... conduct [that is] in any measure negligent." The concept of "fault" was intended to ameliorate the harshness of the contributory negligence doctrine by stating that a plaintiff's own negligence prevents recovery only in the proportion it causes plaintiff's damages. The use of the word "includes" is significant because it signifies a legislative intent to enlarge the statute's application and to suggest that items other than negligence are includable. Defendants (D) insist "fault" was not intended to include reckless or intentional acts, because the legislative history shows that the words "reckless," "wanton," "culpable," and "intentional" were stricken from the definition, but this argument reads more into the deletion than we think justified [unlike our own opinion, which is 100% not guilty of strained interpretation]. Also, the application of the statute to intentional/reckless actors is consistent with the statute's other purpose—to eliminate joint and several liability—since holding otherwise would leave the remaining tortfeasors jointly and severally liable. While we realize that imposing joint and several liability would provide an incentive to those with a duty to prevent intentional harms, the statutory elimination forecloses our consideration of this policy's merits. Reversed and remanded [with instructions to include Ortega's (D) fault in the apportionment].

Analysis:

Leaving aside the court's strained reading of statutory language, the court's decision is consistent with Wyoming's legislatively-mandated rejection of joint and several liability. To leave intentional/reckless/criminal co-tortfeasors out of the apportionment calculation would leave the remaining negligent co-tortfeasors liable for 100% of the damages (i.e., jointly liable). Of course, including the criminal tortfeasor into the equation often reduces plaintiffs' recovery below 100%, since many petty criminals are poor and judgment-proof. While this is arguably unfair to plaintiffs, it is consistent with the policy choice made by jurisdictions which abolished joint and several liability.

■ CASE VOCABULARY

WANTON: Grossly negligent, or suggesting an indifference to the risk.

WILFUL: Same as intentional, but not necessarily malicious.

Turner v. Jordan
(Worker) v. *(Supervisor)*
957 S.W.2d 815 (Tenn.1997)

RESPONSIBILITY FOR INTENTIONAL TORT CANNOT BE ALLOCATED BETWEEN INTENTIONAL TORTFEASOR AND PERSONS WHO NEGLIGENTLY FAILED TO PREVENT THAT INTENTIONAL TORT

■ **INSTANT FACTS** After a psychiatrist fails to protect a nurse from a known violent patient's assault, the court concludes liability should be allocated between the psychiatrist and patient.

■ **BLACK LETTER RULE** When a joint tort involves an intentional tort by one tortfeasor and negligent failure to prevent that intentional tort by another, fault cannot be allocated between them.

■ **PROCEDURAL BASIS**

In personal injury action seeking damages, post-verdict retrial to reapportion damages.

■ **FACTS**

Turner (P), a nurse, and Jordan (D), a psychiatrist, worked at a psychiatric hospital. Jordan (D) had a violent patient, Williams, who had previously attacked Jordan (D), and who had a history of violence. Jordan (D) did not warn Turner (P) about Williams's violence, and took no steps to prevent it. The patient beat Turner (P), injuring her. Turner (P) sued Jordan (D) for negligently failing to prevent attacks by the patient. At trial, the jury found Jordan (D) 100% liable in negligence, and awarded Turner (P) $1,186,000. However, the trial judge thought the fault allocation was unjustified, and ordered retrial. At retrial, Turner (P) contends (i) Jordan's (D) liability should not be reduced by the occurrence of a foreseeable act he had the duty to prevent, and (ii) tortfeasors' negligent acts should not be apportioned with a co-tortfeasor's intentional acts, for policy reasons. Jordan (D) contends that the patient's intentional tort should be apportioned with Jordan's (D) own negligence, because this limits his liability to his percentage of fault.

■ **ISSUE**

When a joint tort involves an intentional tort by one tortfeasor and negligent failure to prevent that intentional tort by another, can fault be allocated between them?

■ **DECISION AND RATIONALE**

(Anderson) No. When a joint tort involves an intentional tort by one tortfeasor and negligent failure to prevent that intentional tort by another, fault cannot be allocated between them. [We conclude Jordan (D) owed Turner (P) a duty of care, and breached that duty.] We now turn to the issue of whether Jordan's (D) negligence should have been apportioned together with Williams's intentional act in determining the extent of Jordan's (D) liability. We have previously considered apportionment between negligent tortfeasors, and between negligent and strictly liable tortfeasors, but this is our first opportunity to consider apportionment between negligent and intentional tortfeasors. Other jurisdictions have addressed the issue. In Louisiana's *Veazey v. Elmwood Plantation Assoc.* (La.1994) [apartment complex's inadequate security permits sexual assault], the Louisiana Supreme Court declined to allocate liability between negligent and intentional tortfeasors, because (i) negligent defendants should not be allowed to reduce their liability by relying on intentional torts they had a duty to prevent, (ii) such

---

allocation would reduce plaintiffs' recovery, because juries will tend to allocate most/all fault to the intentional actor, (iii) such allocation would reduce the negligent actor's incentive to use due care, and (iv) such allocation is impractical because intentional and negligent torts are different in degree, kind, and social condemnation. Kansas's caselaw follows a similar doctrine. *Kansas State Bank & Trust Co. v. Specialized Transportation Services, Inc.* (Kan.1991) [school and bus company negligently permitted driver to molest boy]. The concern in allocating such liability is that a negligent tortfeasor should not be burdened with liability in excess of fault, but the concern in not allocating liability is that plaintiff should not be penalized by allowing the defendant to use the intentional act, which it had a duty to prevent, to reduce its liability. In our view, liability should not be allocated between negligent and intentional tortfeasors where the intentional tort is the same foreseeable risk created by the negligent tortfeasor, [for the reasons stated by the Louisiana court above]. Here, we conclude the lower court erred in holding fault should be allocated between Jordan (D) and Williams, though the error was harmless here, as the jury apportioned 100% of the fault to Jordan (D). Remanded for entry of judgement consistent with jury verdict.

Analysis:

This case illustrates the common class of cases where a crime/tort victim sues the premises' owner for failing to prevent the crime/tort. Here, the court notes some valid policy reasons for its decision that negligent tortfeasors who breached their duty to prevent intentional torts/crimes cannot reduce their liability by the intentional tortfeasor's percentage of fault. To hold otherwise would indeed create the perverse result that, where the defendant has a duty to prevent intentional torts/crimes, its liability is automatically reduced whenever it breaches that duty (i.e., whenever another actually commits the tort/crime it was charged with preventing) by a certain percentage of fault apportioned to the intentional tortfeasor. This rule is particularly important to secure proper compensation for the victim when we consider that (i) juries will tend to allocate most, if not all, fault to the intentional tortfeasor, since he is the most obvious culprit, and (ii) the intentional tortfeasors in such "negligent failure to prevent" are either unknown assailants, or else apprehended but insolvent criminals.

CHAPTER TWENTY–SIX

Damages

Martin v. United States

Instant Facts: When 2 schoolboys were burned and permanently disfigured by contact with negligently-maintained power lines, the judge considers damages.

Black Letter Rule: [Omitted. This case is included to demonstrate how judges evaluate personal injury claims, and the court's other findings were omitted.]

McDougald v. Garber

Instant Facts: When medical malpractice renders a patient comatose, the malpractitioners argue the patient cannot recover separately for "lost enjoyment of life."

Black Letter Rule: Tort victims can recover for "pain and suffering" and "loss of enjoyment of life" only as part of a single award, and they cannot recover for "loss of enjoyment" if they are unaware of the loss.

Mercado v. Ahmed

Instant Facts: When an economist invents a method for valuing the "loss of life's pleasure" resulting from injuries, the judge rejects it.

Black Letter Rule: In a negligent personal injury action seeking compensation for "loss of enjoyment," an economist cannot present evidence on the value of enjoying life, unless the economist has special expertise in valuing life.

Keans v. Bottiarelli

Instant Facts: After a dental surgeon negligently caused bleeding, the judge finds the patient failed to mitigate damages by ignoring the dentist's post-operative instructions.

Black Letter Rule: If a tort victim negligently fails to mitigate damages by using reasonable care, then, upon the defendant's request, the court must reduce the recovery by the amount of reasonably-preventable damages.

State Farm Mut. Auto. Ins. Co. v. Campbell

Instant Facts: After State Farm (D) failed to settle claims against Campbell (P) for its policy limits and altered information to lessen his culpability, a jury awarded Campbell (P) $1 million in compensatory damages and $145 million in punitive damages.

Black Letter Rule: In evaluating the appropriateness of a punitive damages award, a court must weigh the reprehensibility of the defendant's conduct, the disparity between the actual harm caused and the amount of the punitive damages awarded, and the difference between the punitive damages awarded and the civil penalties imposed under state law.

Martin v. United States

(Electrocuted Boys) v. *(U.S. Government, as Maintainer of Power Lines)*
471 F.Supp. 6 (D.Ariz.1979)

COMPENSATORY DAMAGES INCLUDE COMPENSATION FOR LOST EARNINGS POTENTIAL AND PAIN

■ **INSTANT FACTS** When 2 schoolboys were burned and permanently disfigured by contact with negligently-maintained power lines, the judge considers damages.

■ **BLACK LETTER RULE** [Omitted. This case is included to demonstrate how judges evaluate personal injury claims, and the court's other findings were omitted.]

■ **PROCEDURAL BASIS**

Inquest in Federal negligent personal injury action seeking damages.

■ **FACTS**

Schoolboys Burrows (P) and Martin (P), riding a motorcycle, struck a power line maintained negligently by the U.S. government (D), and were severely burned. Burrows (P) and Martin (P) sued the U.S. government (D) for negligent tort under the Federal Tort Claims Act. At trial, the judge found the U.S. government (D) liable, and now considers damages.

■ **ISSUE**

In this case, how much compensation should plaintiff receive for crippling and disfiguring burns?

■ **DECISION AND RATIONALE**

(Burns) [Unfortunate.] Plaintiff Melvin Burrows (P) sustained severe burns to his face, head, back, butt, arms, and legs. His current medical expenses were $48,130.97, and future medical expenses will be about $49,000. Finally, we award $5,000 for psychological treatment. We now consider Burrows's (P) lost earnings capacity. As for plaintiff Martin (P), we have heard testimony from Burrows's (P) principal [who is also Burrows's father's employer, and uncle to Martin (D) (!)] that Burrows (P) is of average intelligence or higher, and probably would have become a skilled worker, perhaps a mechanic or carpenter. [Remember, this is 1979.] Another witness, a finance professor and investment counselor, opined that Burrows (P) and Martin (P) would likely gravitate into the construction trades like most of their classmates, and forecast that demand for such trades would be strong. Defendant's witness, a clinical psychologist, testified that intelligence and aptitude tests administered to Burrows (P) show he could not pursue a skilled craft, but instead would probably have become a laborer. Defendant's other witness, an economics professor, opined that neither Burrows (P) nor Martin (P) would enter the skilled trades, and that they would both have earned average wages. Based on my evaluation of the expert witnesses' testimony, experience, and credibility, I conclude Burrows (P) would have become a skilled worker. Expert testimony reveals that a skilled worker in 1978 would earn $9,450 annually for a four-year apprenticeship and $18,900 in wages and $3,900 in benefits annually during a 42-year career. One expert testified Burrows (P) may be employable as a night watchman or night mechanic not involved with the public [Again, this *is* 1979.] Based on this testimony and my observation, I conclude Burrows (P) will probably be able to work at an entry-level position for at least half his working life, which would generate income of $3,120 in 1978 dollars. Thus, in total, Burrows (P) is entitled to recover (in 1978 dollars) $6,330 annually for the four-year apprenticeship period, then $19, 680 annually for the next 42 years. I find the award can be invested at little risk and return compounded interest of 7.5%. I also find Burrows's (P) annual wage inflation rate can be estimated at 5.5%. Thus, the award for Burrows's (P) lost earning capacity is $548,029. Now we consider Burrows's (P) pain and suffering. The power line burned most of Burrows's (P) head, face, back, and buttocks, and left 6 holes in his skin. When Burrows (P) was treated for 4 months, doctors performed 4 skin grafts and attempted to fashion a functioning eyelid, which still cannot be closed. Burrows (P) lost one ear entirely and part of the other. Scalp rotations were necessary to restore hair growth and build up skin where it was burned down to the skull. These operations left Burrows's (P) face severely scarred, his mouth permanently contorted, and his facial nerves unable to smile. Burrows (P) will also require 11 additional skin grafts, which are unpleasant and risky. In addition to his physical suffering, Burrows (P) has suffered psychologically. Burrows (P) is often ridiculed by classmates and strangers, became reclusive, and may develop schizophrenic tendencies. Nor is it likely Burrows (P) will have a normal social or sexual life. I award Burrows (P) $1,000,000 in compensation for pain and suffering, based upon testimony and my observation. In sum, I award Burrows (P) $1,649,788.97 [and about the same to Martin (P)].

Analysis:

To recap, the court awarded compensation for (i) actual medical expenses, (ii) probable future medical expenses, including psychological counseling, (ii) projected lost earnings over a working lifetime (i.e., potential earnings but for the accident, minus the projected earnings which might be possible after the accident), including increases due to wage inflation, (iii) interest on the above damages, from the accident to the trial, at a rate approximating the return on a low/no risk investment, (iv) actual physical pain from the injury, recuperation, and reconstructive surgery, (v) the humiliation of being disfigured, (vi) psychological damages already endured, (vii) projected future psychological harms, and (viii) compensation for an impaired social and sexual life. These items are generally recoverable where applicable, though awards may differ widely depending on how provable the intangible and future injuries are, and how sympathetic the judge is.

McDougald v. Garber

(Comatose Patient and Husband) v. *(Negligent Doctors)*

73 N.Y.2d 246, 538 N.Y.S.2d 937, 536 N.E.2d 372 (Ct.App.1989)

BRAIN DAMAGED TORT VICTIMS CANNOT RECOVER FOR "LOST ENJOYMENT OF LIFE" IF THEY CANNOT UNDERSTAND THE LOSS

■ **INSTANT FACTS** When medical malpractice renders a patient comatose, the malpractitioners argue the patient cannot recover separately for "lost enjoyment of life."

■ **BLACK LETTER RULE** Tort victims can recover for "pain and suffering" and "loss of enjoyment of life" only as part of a single award, and they cannot recover for "loss of enjoyment" if they are unaware of the loss.

■ **PROCEDURAL BASIS**

In negligent personal injury action seeking damages, appeal from appellate court's affirmation of post-verdict order reducing nonpecuniary damages.

■ **FACTS**

Mrs. McDougald (P) underwent a C-section performed by Dr. Garber (D), assisted by anesthesiologists Armengol (D) and Kulkarni (D). During surgery, Mrs. McDougald (P) suffered oxygen deprivation, causing severe brain damage and permanent coma. Mr. McDougald (P) sued, derivatively and on behalf of Mrs. McDougald (P), alleging the injuries were caused by defendants' negligent malpractice, and sought compensation for (i) pain and suffering and (ii) loss of the pleasures and pursuits of life. At trial, the judge charged the jury that, if McDougald (P) was so neurologically impaired she was incapable of experiencing pain or emotional reactions to it, she could not recover for pain and suffering. The judge also charged the jury that McDougald (P) could recover for loss of pleasures and pursuits, even if she was unaware of the loss. The jury found all defendants liable, and awarded Mr. McDougald (P) $1.5M for loss of his wife's services, and Mrs. McDougald (P) $9,650,102, including $1M for conscious pain and suffering, a separate award of $3.5M for lost pleasures and pursuits, and compensation for lost earnings and nursing care. After trial, the defendants moved to reduce the total award. The judge granted the motion, reducing the total award to Mrs. McDougald (P) by striking the award for future nursing ($2,353,374) and reducing the separate awards for suffering and lost pleasures to a single award of $2M. McDougald (P) appealed. The Appellate Division affirmed. McDougald (P) appeals again.

■ **ISSUE**

Can tort victims recover separate awards for "pain and suffering" and "loss of enjoyment of life" if their injuries leave them unaware of pain and lost enjoyment?

■ **DECISION AND RATIONALE**

(Wachtler) No. Tort victims can recover for "pain and suffering" and "loss of enjoyment of life" only as part of a single award, and they cannot recover for "loss of enjoyment" if they are unaware of the loss. In negligent personal injury cases, damages are meant to compensate the victim, not punish the wrongdoer. The goal is to restore the injured to the position they would have occupied had the wrong not occurred. Of course, damages for nonpecuniary losses are among those which may be awarded as compensation. While such recovery rests on th legal fiction that money can compensate for injury, we accept this fiction, because money is the best this court can award. However, when awards for nonpecuniary losses overcompensate the plaintiff, they become improperly punitive. We conclude that an award for loss of enjoyment of life, given to a person whose injuries preclude awareness of the loss, does not serve to compensate the victim, and is improper. In such circumstances, monetary damages have no meaning or utility *to the victim,* who cannot derive compensating enjoyment from spending the money. We recognize this holding will sometimes create the paradox that, the greater the brain damage inflicted negligently by the defendant, the smaller the award will be. However, the force of this argument is that a greater award would punish the negligent tortfeasor, but this has nothing to do with compensating the victim meaningfully. Accordingly, we conclude that, to recover for loss of enjoyment of life, the tort victim must retain "some level of [cognitive] awareness" of the loss. However, we will not require the fact finder to determine what level of cognitive function is necessary. As long as there is "some level of awareness," the plaintiff may recover for nonpecuniary losses, which is the standard used by the trial court. Next, we consider whether loss of enjoyment of life should be considered a category of damages separate from pain and suffering, and we conclude it should not. It is undisputed that the fact finder, in assessing nonpecuniary damages, may consider the injury's effect on the plaintiff's ability to lead a normal life. Traditionally, in New York and elsewhere, this aspect of suffering is not treated as a separate category of damages, but is factored into a general award for nonpecuniary damages, commonly known as pain and suffering. Recently, there has been an attempt to segregate the suffering associated with physical pain from that associated with the mental anguish of being unable to engage in certain activities. Some courts have resisted the effort, concluding it would create duplicative and excessive awards. Other courts have allowed separate awards, noting the types of suffering involved are analytically distinguishable. If we are to depart from this traditional approach and approve a separate award for loss of enjoyment, it must be on the basis that such an approach will yield a more accurate valuation of the compensation due to the plaintiff. We have no doubt that separate awards will increase the total award, but this does not necessarily mean the goal of compensation is better served. While we do not dispute that distinctions can be found between physical/emotional suffering and mental frustration, we believe the already-imprecise estimation of nonpecuniary damages will be further distorted by trying to divide a broad award along unclear lines. We conclude the court erred, both in instructing the jury that McDougald's (P) awareness was irrelevant to her damages for lost enjoyment, and in directing the jury to consider lost enjoyment separately from pain and suffering. Reversed and remanded to recalculate nonpecuniary damages.

■ DISSENT

(Titone) The majority's holding is an illogical compromise which neither comports with fundamental principles of tort compensation nor furnishes a logically consistent framework for compensating nonpecuniary loss. I find no fault with granting an award for loss of enjoyment, separate from conscious pain and suffering, because I conclude that loss of enjoyment is objective and conceptually distinct from conscious pain. The capacity to enjoy life is unquestionably an attribute of an ordinary healthy individual, and a victim deprived of this capacity is entitled to compensation. This right exists independently of the victim's ability to apprehend the impairment.

Analysis:

Regardless of the analytical propriety of separating "conscious pain and suffering" from "mental anguish for lost enjoyment of life," the fact remains that allowing separate awards for each type of injury tends to increase the total award, so it is inevitable that personal injury lawyers will invent many logical reasons to adopt separate awards, and insurers'/defendants' lobbyists will argue strenuously against it. Conceptually, it is difficult to know which approach best ensures compensation. The majority states that a separate award for lost enjoyment tends to increase the total award, but suggests this increase is superfluous. However, this argument assumes that, with dual awards, juries will first compute pain and suffering (and include lost enjoyment in that computation), then compute a separate and duplicate award for lost enjoyment. If this is true, the bifurcated award overcompensates. But it is equally likely that, but for the separate award, juries might not include in the "pain and suffering" award a compensation for lost enjoyment, which would under compensate the plaintiff. Perhaps the ideal solution is a single award for pain and suffering, but with jury instructions that this award must include compensation for lost enjoyment.

■ CASE VOCABULARY

NONPECUNIARY DAMAGES: [a.k.a. "pain and suffering."] Non-monetary/non-economic losses, which generally include pain, mental/emotional distress, humiliation from injury or defamation, loss of enjoyment from life, and (sometimes) inconvenience.

Mercado v. Ahmed

(*Injured Boy*) v. (*Negligent Driver*)

974 F.2d 863 (7th Cir.1992)

ECONOMIST CANNOT PRESENT EXPERT TESTIMONY ABOUT VALUE OF LIFE'S ENJOYMENT

■ **INSTANT FACTS** When an economist invents a method for valuing the "loss of life's pleasure" resulting from injuries, the judge rejects it.

■ **BLACK LETTER RULE** In a negligent personal injury action seeking compensation for "loss of enjoyment," an economist cannot present evidence on the value of enjoying life, unless the economist has special expertise in valuing life.

■ **PROCEDURAL BASIS**

In negligent personal injury action seeking damages, appeal from trial judge's exclusion of expert testimony on value of living.

■ **FACTS**

Mercado (P), a six-year-old boy who apparently had physical and/or mental problems, was struck by taxi driver Ahmed (D), and severely injured [apparently, brain damaged]. Mercado (P) sued Ahmed (D) for negligent personal injury, seeking compensation for pain and suffering, and also for "loss of life's pleasures." To assess the value of lost pleasures, Mercado (P) proposed to offer testimony from an economist, but the judge excluded such testimony, finding the economist's formula flawed, unsystematic, and not generally accepted. The jury awarded Mercado (P) $50K for pain and suffering, and $29K for medical expenses. Mercado (P) appeals, contending the judge erred in excluding evidence of the value of lost pleasures.

■ **ISSUE**

In a negligent personal injury action seeking compensation for "loss of enjoyment," can an economist present evidence on the value of enjoying life?

■ **DECISION AND RATIONALE**

(Coffey) No. In a negligent personal injury action seeking compensation for "loss of enjoyment," an economist cannot present evidence on the value of enjoying life, unless the economist has special expertise in valuing life. The excluded testimony would have placed a monetary value in "the reduction in [Mercado's (P)] ability to engage in and experience the ordinary value of life that he was experiencing prior to the injury." These damages are sometimes referred to as "hedonic damages." The district court conducted an extensive voir dire to determine the methods the economist employs in valuating the "lost pleasure of living" someone like Mercado (P) suffers due to injury. The economist testified he first assumes a "percentage range" representing the degree to which a victim's capacity to experience life was diminished, which is determined in consultation with a doctor. In this case, the doctor, a psychologist, concluded Mercado's (P) injuries were "severe" and that his capacity to experience life was diminished 66%–83%. The economist then measures the impairment in occupational capacity, practical functioning, emotional stability, and social function, by focusing on how much Americans are willing to pay for reductions in health risks (e.g., prices for smoke detectors, seatbelts, etc.), and how much they are compensated for assuming extra risk (e.g., the premium paid to policemen). Through this analysis, the economist concluded that, for an average (31-year-old) person, the value of the enjoyment of life was $2.3M in 1998 dollars, or $60K per year. [I, for one, never realized before how much life I was enjoying each year]. For Mercado (P), the economist adjusted it for Mercado's (P) young age, and multiplied it by 66%–83%, concluding the value of Mercado's (P) lost pleasure is $2,207,827 to $2,762,227. The trial judge excluded the economist's testimony as lacking sufficient expertise, because (i) there is no consensus among experts that supports this method of valuing life, and (ii) the supporting research is no more than a compilation of many non-expert Americans' views about the value of life, as expressed through spending decisions. These criticisms are admittedly true. Further, we have serious doubts about the economist's assertions that the studies he relies on actually measure how much Americans value life. For example, spending on items like airbags and smoke detectors is probably influenced as much by advertising and government safety requirements as by considerations of life's value. Also, the actual valuation may be higher, because many people may want to purchase more safety devices, but are unable to afford them. More fundamentally, spending on safety items is a better reflection of how cautious a person is rather than how much he values life. Few of us, when confronted with the threat, ''Your money or your life!'' would pause and respond, ''I'm thinking.'' Most of us would empty our wallets. Why that decision reflects less the value we place on life than our decision to buy airbags is unclear. Further, the economist purports to calculate the premium paid for risky jobs, such as police work, but fails to consider whether many who perform risky work are motivated not by money but by civic duty. Finally, the economist considers the amount the government spends (or forces others to spend) to save lives, but these calculations are motivated by many political considerations. The economist has taken up a daunting task: to develop a method of specialized knowledge to assist jurors in determining the monetary value of being alive. The district court ruled that, despite the economist's training and research, his testimony would not aid the jury in evaluating the evidence and reaching a verdict (which is the true test of expert testimony under the Federal Rules of Evidence) because the economist was no more expert in valuing life than the average person. We agree, though this is less a reflection on this economist's methodology than the impossibility of any person achieving unique knowledge of the value of life. Affirmed.

Analysis:

It may well be that Professor Smith's methodology of the economics is not the best reflection of what life is worth. However, it is notable that the evidence of Prof. Smith was accepted in an earlier case in that same circuit. See *Sherrod v. Berry* (N.D. Ill. 1985). While Smith's method *is* indeed flawed, in the ways pointed out by the court and in several others, the valuation it yields is certainly no less reliable than the uninformed blind-guess opinion of an uninformed juror, which is the alternative the court proposes. Consider the dilemma of a juror asked to value Mercado's (P) life, without any further research or information. If you were the juror, could you begin to objectively determine what Mercado's (P) joy of living is worth? (The problem is not, as many commentators claim, that enjoyment or life is somehow sacred or priceless, but rather that the average juror has no data or methodology for valuing it.) That being so, the court should permit Smith to present jurors with a valuation system, to inform what is otherwise a blind guess.

■ CASE VOCABULARY

HEDONIC DAMAGES: Generally, compensation for loss of life's pleasure/happiness caused by tortious injury. The term is ambiguous, because it can mean (i) recovery for the victim's awareness that he is unable to enjoy life, or (ii) recovery for the victim's potential inability to pursue certain activities, even if the victim is unaware he is unable (as when the victim is brain damaged or comatose), or some other pain and suffering evidence.

VOIR[E] DIRE: ''To speak the truth.'' Judicial pre-trial examination to test the competence of a potential witness, juror, or item of evidence.

Keans v. Bottiarelli

(Patient) v. *(Dentist)*
35 Conn.App. 239, 645 A.2d 1029 (1994)

TORT VICTIMS MUST MITIGATE DAMAGES REASONABLY OR SUFFER REDUCED AWARD

■ **INSTANT FACTS** After a dental surgeon negligently caused bleeding, the judge finds the patient failed to mitigate damages by ignoring the dentist's post-operative instructions.

■ **BLACK LETTER RULE** If a tort victim negligently fails to mitigate damages by using reasonable care, then, upon the defendant's request, the court must reduce the recovery by the amount of reasonably-preventable damages.

■ PROCEDURAL BASIS

In medical malpractice action seeking damages, cross appeal from judgement for plaintiff, seeking to reverse reduction in award.

■ FACTS

Dentist Bottiarelli (D) extracted Keans's (P) tooth. Earlier, Keans (P) had informed Bottiarelli (D) she had a disorder which prevented clotting. Nevertheless, Bottiarelli (D) proceeded to operate on Keans (P) without consulting her hematologist, and without administering a platelet transfusion. After surgery, Bottiarelli (D) gave Keans (P) a prescription for penicillin and a pamphlet on post-operative care. Keans (P) remained in Bottiarelli's (D) office until the bleeding stopped, then returned home. Later that day, Keans (P) resumed bleeding. When Keans (P) called, Bottiarelli (D) advised her to bite down on a tea bag to facilitate clotting. Keans (P) continued to bleed, but did not call Bottiarelli (D) again. The next morning, Keans (P), feeling ill, contacted her hematologist, who told her to go to the hospital. Keans (P) required 3 day's hospitalization for anemia and clotting failure, but was not permanently injured. Keans (P) sued Bottiarelli (D) for malpractice. At trial, the judge found Bottiarelli (D) negligent for failing to consult Keans's (P) hematologist. However, the judge denied Keans (D) recovery for hospitalization expenses, finding Keans's (P) own negligence (in not using penicillin, and not following Bottiarelli's (D) instructions on postoperative care) led to the hospitalization. Bottiarelli (D) appealed the verdict, and Keans (P) cross-appeals the reduction in the award.

■ ISSUE

If a tort victim negligently fails to mitigate damages, may the award be reduced by the amount of preventable damages?

■ DECISION AND RATIONALE

(Schaller) Yes. If a tort victim negligently fails to mitigate damages by using reasonable care, then, upon the defendant's request, the court must reduce the recovery by the amount of reasonably-preventable damages. The trial court applied the doctrine of mitigation and reduced the award by the amount of the plaintiff's hospitalization expenses, in reliance on *Preston v. Keith* (Conn. 1991) [patient who failed to mitigate damages by following doctor's postoperative directions cannot recover full damages]. Connecticut's Supreme Court stated, "we have long adhered to the rule that one who is injured by the negligent act of another must use reasonable care to promote recovery and prevent . . .

increase of the injuries ... When there [is] evidence that ... a plaintiff may have failed to promote his recovery [by doing] what a reasonably prudent person would be expected to do under the same circumstances, the court, [upon request], is obliged to charge [the jury] on the duty to mitigate damages." Here, the trial court found Keans (D) failed to mitigate damages and exacerbated her initial injury by not filling her prescription for penicillin and not following Bottiarelli's (D) postoperative instructions, which caused the need for hospitalization. We conclude the trial court's reduction of damages was not "clearly erroneous," and thus we reject Keans's contention that the trial court improperly reduced her award. Judgement affirmed.

Analysis:

The rule of "mitigation"—that a plaintiff must have used reasonable care to minimize damages, and cannot recover to the extent damages should have been reasonably minimized/avoided—is accepted in every jurisdiction, so it is surprising Keans (P) challenged it here. The rule is fair, and the result is consistent with comparative negligence principles (as well as a similar rule in contract law); If the defendant negligently caused some injuries, but the plaintiff negligently caused more injuries, the defendant is liable for his own negligence, but not the plaintiff's. This provides added incentives for the plaintiff to avoid creating needless expenses, and prevents one tortfeasor from being liable for another's negligence. It may be argued the negligent defendant should be liable for all later injuries, since his negligence is the "but for" cause of all the injuries (i.e., but for Dr. Bottiarelli's (D) negligence in causing bleeding, Ms. Keans's (P) failure to follow postoperative directions would have had no effect), and it would be unfair to saddle even a negligent tortfeasor with the (unforeseeable and unpreventable) bill for damages, which were really caused by the plaintiff's own negligence.

■ CASE VOCABULARY

CROSS-APPEAL: An appeal by the appellee (winner). Here, *appellant* Bottiarelli (D) appealed the verdict, and *appellee* Keans (P) simultaneously *cross-appealed* the reduction in the award.

MITIGATION [OF DAMAGES]: In tort, a tort victim has a duty to mitigate (reduce and prevent increase of) damages by using reasonable care. If the victim's negligent failure to mitigate causes additional damages which were preventable, the victim cannot recover for those additional preventable damages.

State Farm Mut. Auto. Ins. Co. v. Campbell

(Insurance Company) v. *(Insured)*

538 U.S. 408, 123 S.Ct. 1513, 155 L.Ed.2d 585 (2003)

A $1 MILLION COMPENSATORY DAMAGES AWARD CAN'T SUPPORT $145 MILLION IN PUNITIVE DAMAGES

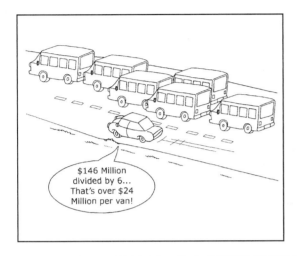

■ **INSTANT FACTS** After State Farm (D) failed to settle claims against Campbell (P) for its policy limits and altered information to lessen his culpability, a jury awarded Campbell (P) $1 million in compensatory damages and $145 million in punitive damages.

■ **BLACK LETTER RULE** In evaluating the appropriateness of a punitive damages award, a court must weigh the reprehensibility of the defendant's conduct, the disparity between the actual harm caused and the amount of the punitive damages awarded, and the difference between the punitive damages awarded and the civil penalties imposed under state law.

■ **PROCEDURAL BASIS**

Certiorari to review the excessiveness of a punitive damages verdict.

■ **FACTS**

Campbell (P) held an automobile insurance policy with State Farm Mutual Automobile Insurance Co. (D). While driving in Utah, Campbell (P) decided to pass six vans traveling slowly in front of him. As Campbell (P) was attempting to pass, Ospital, who approached from the opposite direction, was forced onto the shoulder to avoid a head-on collision. In the process, Ospital lost control of his vehicle, collided with a vehicle driven by Slusher, and died. Slusher was permanently disabled as a result of the accident. An investigation determined that Campbell's (P) unsafe pass caused Ospital's death and Slusher's injuries. Nonetheless, State Farm (D) decided to contest liability and declined offers from Ospital's estate and Slusher to settle both claims for its total policy limit of $50,000. At trial, a jury found Campbell (P) liable for the accident and returned a verdict for $185,849. State Farm (D) refused to pay the verdict in excess of its $50,000 policy limits and refused to post the supersedeas bond required for Campbell's (P) appeal. Campbell (P) subsequently obtained independent counsel and appealed the verdict. During the appeal, Campbell (P) agreed to pursue a bad faith action against State Farm (D) in exchange for an agreement by Ospital's estate and Slusher not to seek satisfaction of the judgment against Campbell (P). Ospital's estate and Slusher agreed to accept ninety percent of any proceeds received from State Farm (D) in the bad faith suit.

The Utah Supreme Court denied Campbell's (P) appeal from the wrongful death judgment, and State Farm (D) subsequently agreed to pay the full amount of the judgment against him. Campbell (P) then commenced his bad faith suit, alleging State Farm's (D) refusal to accept the settlement offer was a product of a national scheme to control the amount of claims paid. Campbell (D) offered evidence of State Farm's (D) business practices throughout the country over a twenty-year period, although little pertained to payment of third-party automobile claims similar to that asserted by Campbell (D). A jury awarded Campbell $2.6 million in compensatory damages and $145 million in punitive damages. After the compensatory damages award was reduced to $1 million and the punitive damages were reduced to $25 million, both parties appealed to the Utah Supreme Court, which reinstated the punitive damages award.

ISSUE

When compensatory damages are $1 million, is an award of $145 million in punitive damages against a defendant excessive and in violation of the Due Process Clause of the Fourteenth Amendment?

DECISION AND RATIONALE

(Kennedy, J.) Yes. Unlike compensatory damages, which serve to compensate an injured person for the wrongful conduct of another, punitive damages are aimed at deterrence and retribution against the wrongdoer. Because punitive damages serve a purpose similar to criminal sanctions, but without the procedural protections accompanying criminal punishment, a court must weigh the reprehensibility of the defendant's conduct, the disparity between the actual harm caused and the amount of the punitive damages awarded, and the difference between the punitive damages awarded and the civil penalties imposed under state law. Weighing these factors, the jury's $145 million punitive damages award was excessive.

First, State Farm's (D) conduct cannot be considered so reprehensible as to justify the award. In gauging a defendant's conduct, a court should consider whether the harm caused was physical rather than economic, whether the defendant acted with reckless disregard for the health and safety of others, whether the plaintiff was financially vulnerable, whether the conduct involved a repetitive pattern or an isolated incident, and whether the conduct was intentional. Here, while State Farm's (D) handling of Campbell's (P) insurance claims is not laudable, its conduct does not justify such an excessive punitive damages award. Rather than focusing on the particular conduct at issue in the case, the award focuses on State Farm's (D) nationwide handling of claims. A state court, however, has no authority to punish a defendant for conduct that occurred outside its territorial limits and involving parties who were directly affected by the out-of-state conduct. A defendant's dissimilar conduct, bearing no relation to the harm involved in a particular lawsuit, may not be taken into account when determining punitive damages. Due process does not permit a court to award a party punitive damages merely because the defendant may have caused some harm to others who were not proper parties to the litigation.

Second, although there is no bright-line ratio between the amount of punitive damages and the harm caused to a plaintiff, an award 145 times the actual harm suffered is excessive. Generally, anything over a single-digit ratio calls for close judicial scrutiny. Likewise, as the compensatory damages award increases, the appropriate proportion to the punitive damages award decreases, since a larger ratio is unnecessary to serve the purposes of deterrence and retribution. Here, the 145:1 ratio between the punitive award and the compensatory award is unreasonable given the $1 million compensatory damages award for plaintiff's emotional distress.

Finally, the $145 million punitive damages award is grossly in excess of the maximum $10,000 civil penalty imposed for fraud under Utah law. Applying this factor, too, the punitive damages award is excessive. Because a punitive award more closely approximating the compensatory award would be an adequate and rational punishment for the defendant's conduct, the award is excessive. Reversed and remanded.

DISSENT

(Ginsburg, J.) The Utah Supreme Court's reasoned decision on the appropriateness of the size of the punitive damages award and State Farm's (D) reprehensibility should not be superceded by the majority's views. The evidence at trial could reasonably permit the jury to conclude that State Farm (D) had engaged in a nationwide practice of denying deserving policyholders of insurance benefits, preying on those consumers unlikely to defend themselves, and destroying internal documents likely to reveal its practices. The evidence further supports that State Farm (D) had issued handbooks to insurance adjusters and State Farm (D) representatives in Utah for many years to be followed when dealing with Utah policyholders. This evidence is sufficient to give Utah a strong state interest in the litigation and to establish State Farm's (D) reprehensible conduct in the handling of Campbell's (P) claim. Because the issue of punitive damages is a matter of state law, the Court should not disturb state decisions merely because the ratio between punitive damages and compensatory damages is high.

Analysis:

The Court's fascination with the appropriate ratio between the compensatory damages and punitive damages is interesting. If punitive damages serve a separate and distinct purpose from compensatory damages, why should the amount of compensatory damages affect the amount of punitive damages? If a defendant commits intentional conduct worthy of punishment, should it matter whether the compensatory damages were substantial?

■ CASE VOCABULARY

BAD FAITH: Dishonesty of belief or purpose.

COMPENSATORY DAMAGES: Damages sufficient in amount to indemnify the injured person for the loss suffered.

PUNITIVE DAMAGES: Damages awarded in addition to actual damages when the defendant acted with recklessness, malice, or deceit.

SUPERSEDEAS BOND: A bond that suspends a judgment creditor's power to levy execution, usually pending appeal.

CHAPTER TWENTY–EIGHT

Worker's Compensation

Jaeger Baking Co. v. Kretschmann

Instant Facts: A man sought to recover workers' compensation benefits for injuries he received during an attack that occurred while he walked from a bus stop to his place of work.

Black Letter Rule: An employee may not recover under the workers' compensation statute for injuries incurred while en route from a bus stop to his employer's business.

State Industrial Commissioner v. Leff

Instant Facts: A press feeder died when the roof of the building in which he worked caved in over him after an explosion caused an adjoining building to topple over.

Black Letter Rule: If the employment requires the employee to be in a position of harm, any injury that results is said to arise out of and be in the course of employment.

Carvalho v. Decorative Fabrics Co.

Instant Facts: An employee sought recovery under workers' compensation after he suffered a rectal perforation when a coworker jokingly placed an air hose in the vicinity of his rectum.

Black Letter Rule: For purposes of the workers' compensation statute, where horseplay is customary, it should be regarded as part of the course of employment.

Harris v. Board of Educ. of Howard County

Instant Facts: Harris (P) injured her back when dragging a heavy box of laundry detergent as part of her duties for her employer.

Black Letter Rule: An employee who suffers an accidental injury that arises out of and in the course of employment qualifies for workers' compensation benefits.

Martin v. Lancaster Battery Co., Inc.

Instant Facts: A employee who suffered from several ailments as a result of his exposure to lead in a battery manufacturing plant sought to sue his employer who had intentionally altered and withheld blood test results.

Black Letter Rule: Worker's compensation is not the exclusive remedy for the aggravation of an employee's work-related injury where the employer's fraudulent misrepresentation has been alleged.

Kerans v. Porter Paint Co.

Instant Facts: Suit by an employee against her employer for injuries resulting from sexual harassment and molestation by the store manager.

Black Letter Rule: The exclusive remedy provisions of a workers' compensation statute do not bar a suit against an employer for sexual harassment and molestation inflicted by a coworker.

Jaeger Baking Co. v. Kretschmann

(Employer) v. *(Injured Employee)*
96 Wis.2d 590, 292 N.W.2d 622 (1980)

WORKERS' COMPENSATION STATUTES GENERALLY DO NOT COVER INJURIES SUSTAINED WHILE GOING TO AND COMING FROM WORK

■ **INSTANT FACTS** A man sought to recover workers' compensation benefits for injuries he received during an attack that occurred while he walked from a bus stop to his place of work.

■ **BLACK LETTER RULE** An employee may not recover under the workers' compensation statute for injuries incurred while en route from a bus stop to his employer's business.

■ **PROCEDURAL BASIS**

Not provided.

■ **FACTS**

Heinrich Kretschmann (P) was injured while walking to work when two persons attacked him on a sidewalk. The sidewalk was adjacent to the Jaeger Baking Company (Jaeger) (D) building where Kretschmann (P) worked. The attack occurred about 50 feet from the employee entrance. Although Kretschmann (P) was walking directly from a bus stop, the place where he was attacked was on the direct route used by employees in reaching the building from the employee parking lot.

■ **ISSUE**

May an employee recover under the workers' compensation statute for injuries sustained while en route from a bus stop to his employer's premises?

■ **DECISION AND RATIONALE**

(Not provided) No. An employee may not recover under the workers' compensation statute for injuries incurred while en route from a bus stop to his employer's business. In an effort to overrule our previous decisions, the legislature amended the worker's compensation statute so as to cover employees going between an employer's designated parking lot and the employer's work premises. The legislature's intent is manifest. The statute is meant to cover employee's injured while going directly from the one portion of the employer's premises to the other. It is argued that following the plain meaning of the statute will produce absurd results by distinguishing between injured employees on the basis of how they get to work. A contrary rule, however, would produce the absurd result of permitting an employee who arrives by bus to recover if he is injured close to the premises, but not if he has just alighted. It was fortuitous that Kretschmann (D) was injured at a point on the direct route from the employee parking lot to the bakery. We recognize that this is a somewhat arbitrary line, but lines must be draw somewhere. Reversed.

Analysis:

Most workers' compensation statutes cover injuries that are incurred in the course of employment and that arise out of employment. Generally speaking, workers' compensation statutes do not cover injuries sustained while going to and coming from work. There are, however, exceptions; one of which is the "premises exception" permitting employees to recover when injured in the employer's parking lot. Under the majority view, adopted by statute in Wisconsin, the premises exception is applicable when the employee is on premises not owned by the employer, but which are located between the employer's parking lot and the place of business. The court here refuses to apply the statute to the situation where an employee who is not commuting between the employer's parking lot and the place of business, but who is injured in that area. Notice that the court bases its opinion, in part, on its view that the location of Kretschmann's (D) attack was "fortuitous." Does this remind you of anything? *The arising out of* and *course of employment* requirements are often read for the proposition that the injury must be associated with the risk of employment, a concept which is akin to proximate cause. From this standpoint the opinion is well reasoned because, by establishing a parking lot isolated from the work premises, the employer reasonably incurs the risk of injury occurring between the two premises, but does not incur the risk of injury occurring between a bus stop and the work premises.

State Industrial Commissioner v. Leff

(*Administrative Agency*) v. (*Employer*)

265 N.Y. 533, 193 N.E. 307 (1934)

ACCIDENTAL INJURIES ARISE OUT OF AND ARE IN THE COURSE OF EMPLOYMENT IF THE EMPLOYMENT PLACED THE EMPLOYEE IN THE POSITION OF HARM

■ **INSTANT FACTS** A press feeder died when the roof of the building in which he worked caved in over him after an explosion caused an adjoining building to topple over.

■ **BLACK LETTER RULE** If the employment requires the employee to be in a position of harm, any injury that results is said to arise out of and be in the course of employment.

■ **PROCEDURAL BASIS**

Appeal from an order of the Appellate Division of the Supreme Court affirming an award of the State Industrial Board under the Workmen's Compensation Law.

■ **FACTS**

An employee (P) of Herman and Lillian Leff (D) died as the result of an explosion which caused the wall of an adjoining building to fall over onto and through the roof of the Leff's (D) building, crushing the Leff's (D) employee (P). The Industrial Board found that the injuries were accidental injuries arising out of and in the course of employment. The Appellate Division affirmed the award.

■ **ISSUE**

Does a worker's injury arise out of and occur in the course of employment if his employment requires him to be in a position of harm, whether foreseeable or not?

■ **DECISION AND RATIONALE**

(Per Curiam) Yes. If the employment requires the employee to be in a position of harm, any injury that results is said to arise out of and be in the course of employment. The Industrial Board found that the employee's accidental death arose out of and in the course of employment when an explosion caused the wall of an adjoining building to fall through the roof of his building. Based on our prior case we affirm this finding.

Analysis:

Worker's compensation is available only for injuries resulting from employment risks - those especially associated with the job. Injuries from personal risks - those that are not related to the employment, but happen to manifest themselves while the employee is at work - are usually non-compensable under the statutory scheme. The classification of risks, therefore, plays a crucial role in determining whether compensation will be allowed. Courts use several test to determine whether a risk anses out of the employment. The holding here implicitly uses the "positional risk" test, which holds that compensation will be allowed if the employment was a but-for cause of the injury.

Carvalho v. Decorative Fabrics Co.

(Injured Employee) v. *(Employer)*
117 R.I. 231, 366 A.2d 157 (1976)

WORKERS' COMPENSATION COVERS INJURIES ARISING FROM INNOCENT HORSEPLAY

■ **INSTANT FACTS** An employee sought recovery under workers' compensation after he suffered a rectal perforation when a coworker jokingly placed an air hose in the vicinity of his rectum.

■ **BLACK LETTER RULE** For purposes of the workers' compensation statute, where horseplay is customary, it should be regarded as part of the course of employment.

■ **PROCEDURAL BASIS**

Appeal to the Rhode Island Supreme Court, challenging the decision of the commission to deny the employee's petition on the ground that horseplay does not arise out of employment.

■ **FACTS**

Lucindo Carvalho (P) was injured when a coworker jokingly placed an air hose customarily used by employees to brush lint off their clothes near Carvalho's (P) rectum, knocking him to the floor and perforating his rectum. The commission denied compensation on the ground that Carvalho's (P) injury was the result of horseplay, an activity that did not arise out of his employment.

■ **ISSUE**

May an employee recover under the workmen's compensation statute for injuries resulting from on-the-job horseplay?

■ **DECISION AND RATIONALE**

(Bevilacqua, C.J.) Yes. For purposes of the workmen's compensation statute, where horseplay is customary, it should be regarded as part of the course of employment. Although early decisions held that injuries resulting from horseplay were not compensable on the ground that employees were not paid to play, we find these decisions contrary to the scope and intent of the statute. These decisions have, essentially, reinstituted the defenses of negligence and fault, which workers' compensation was designed to eliminate. When people are placed together in close proximity there is a natural instinct to fool around and play pranks. These activities are an incident of the employment. The claimant need only establish that the injury arose out of and in the course of employment; a causal connection must be shown. For injuries incurred during horseplay, the claimant must show that the horseplay was customary. Where the use of an air hose to clean off clothes is a daily practice, play with the hose is a risk of the employment. Such activity should be regarded as part of the course of employment, particularly where, as here, the employer places in the hands of the employee the instrumentality which was used in the horseplay and caused the injury. Reversed.

Analysis:

In line with the view of most courts, the Rhode Island Supreme Courts holds that horseplay is an accepted part of the job for purposes of workmen's compensation. The rule is justified on the basis that horseplay is just a part of life; employees are not robots and should not be expected to attend to their duties every second of every minute they are "on the clock." But courts have also recognized that horseplay can go too far, and that compensation should not be available when horseplay substantially deviates from the employment. There is caution that the distinction between acceptable and unacceptable horseplay should rest on the extent to which the employee has departed from his employment, and not on the extent of the injury. For example, courts have permitted an office worker injured in a rubber band fight with a nearby colleague to recover compensation; but have denied recovery to a video store employee injured in a staple gun fight on the basis that their employment did not involve staple guns.

Harris v. Board of Educ. of Howard County

(Injured Employee) v. *(Employer)*

375 Md. 21, 825 A.2d 365 (2003)

A WORKERS' COMPENSATION INJURY NEED NOT ARISE OUT OF UNUSUAL ACTIVITY

■ **INSTANT FACTS** Harris (P) injured her back when dragging a heavy box of laundry detergent as part of her duties for her employer.

■ **BLACK LETTER RULE** An employee who suffers an accidental injury that arises out of and in the course of employment qualifies for workers' compensation benefits.

■ **PROCEDURAL BASIS**

On appeal to review a decision of the Maryland Court of Special Appeals affirming a jury verdict for the defendant.

■ **FACTS**

Harris (P) was an employee of the Board of Education of Howard County (D). After dragging a heavy box of laundry detergent as part of her laundry duties, Harris (P) injured her back while bending down to scoop the detergent into a washer. Harris (P) completed an incident report and consulted a physician. The physician testified that Harris's (P) dragging of the laundry detergent caused her back injury. The Workers' Compensation Commission granted Harris's (P) job-related injury claim, but on review the court requested that the jury consider whether the injury arose out of "unusual activity" to qualify for benefits. The jury returned a verdict for the defendant. After the court of appeals affirmed, Harris (P) appealed.

■ **ISSUE**

Must a workplace injury arise out of unusual activity in order for the injured employee to be eligible for workers' compensation benefits?

■ **DECISION AND RATIONALE**

(Eldridge, J.) No. By statute, an employee must suffer an accidental injury that arises out of and in the course of employment to qualify for workers' compensation benefits. Nowhere in the statute is an injury excluded if it does not arise out of "unusual activity." Instead, the language of the statute is clear that any injury that is accidental and that arises out of and in the course of employment qualifies for benefits.

Although Maryland courts have previously required that the injury arise from unusual activity, those cases cannot be reconciled with the plain language of the statute, and courts may not add requirements to a statutory claim that the legislature did not intend. Other cases have included the unusual activity standard within the requirement that the injury arise out of and in the course of employment. Because those cases requiring unusual activity are relatively limited in number and directly conflict with the plain language of the statute, they are overruled. A workplace injury need not arise out of unusual activity to qualify the injured employee for benefits under the workers' compensation statute. Reversed.

Analysis:

While the unusual activity requirement would have helped the employer defend against the employee's workers' compensation claims in this case, it often could expose employers to civil liability *exceeding* the limits of workers' compensation benefits. Workers' compensation laws are designed to protect employers from large civil damages awards for work-related injuries, in exchange for a predictable but limited statutory scheme for workers' compensation benefits. A requirement that an employee's injuries arise out of "unusual activity" would potentially conflict with the "arising out of and in the course of employment" requirement and could arguably expose the employer to greater liability.

■ **CASE VOCABULARY**

COURSE OF EMPLOYMENT: Events that occur or circumstances that exist as a part of one's employment; especially, the time during which an employee furthers an employer's goals through employer-mandated directives.

Martin v. Lancaster Battery Co., Inc.

(Injured Employee) v. *(Employer)*

530 Pa. 11, 606 A.2d 444 (1992)

THE EXCLUSIVE REMEDY PROVISIONS OF WORKERS' COMPENSATION STATUTES DO NOT BAR ACTIONS AGAINST EMPLOYERS FOR THEIR FRAUD THAT AGGRAVATES A WORK-RELATED INJURY

■ **INSTANT FACTS** A employee who suffered from several ailments as a result of his exposure to lead in a battery manufacturing plant sought to sue his employer who had intentionally altered and withheld blood test results.

■ **BLACK LETTER RULE** Worker's compensation is not the exclusive remedy for the aggravation of an employee's work-related injury where the employer's fraudulent misrepresentation has been alleged.

■ **PROCEDURAL BASIS**

Appeal to the Pennsylvania Supreme Court, challenging the appellate court holding allowing a tort claim for fraudulent misrepresentation in spite of the exclusive remedy provision of the workmen's compensation statute.

■ **FACTS**

Joseph Martin (P) was an employee of Lancaster Battery Co., Inc. (LBC) (D), which was partly owned and managed by Stuart Manix (D). LBC was in the business of manufacturing wet storage batteries, a process involving extensive exposure to lead dust and fumes. Federal regulations required that employees be regularly tested for lead content in their blood. Manix (D), who oversaw the testing at LBC (D), intentionally and willfully withheld from Martin (P) the latter's test results, with Manix (D) also altering the same. Martin (P) was subsequently diagnosed with a variety of lead related ailments, the severity of which would have been substantially diminished if the test results had been accurately reported. Martin (P) sued for fraudulent misrepresentation. The trial court dismissed the action. The appellate court reversed.

■ **ISSUE**

The workers' compensation exclusive remedy provision notwithstanding, may an employee sue his employer for fraudulent misrepresentation, which exacerbated the employee's work-related injury?

■ **DECISION AND RATIONALE**

(Larsen, J.) Yes. Workers' compensation is not the exclusive remedy for the aggravation of an employee's work-related injury where the employer's fraudulent misrepresentation has been alleged. Courts so holding have reasoned that: (1) a hazard of employment does not include the risk that the employer will deprive an employee of worker's compensation rights; (2) the state has an interest in deterring this type of conduct; and (3) an employer's fraudulent concealment of diseases already developed is not a risk the employee should have to assume. Those courts that have refused to permit these type of actions have expressed a concern with employee's receiving duplicate money awards. This latter rationale is unconvincing. Martin (P) does not seek compensation for his work related injury; rather, he has alleged that his employer's fraud has aggravated his work-related injury. The legislature could not have intended to shield employers from this type of conduct. There is a difference between an employer who tolerates unsafe working conditions that result in a certain number of accidents and one who actively misleads employees already suffering as victims of workplace hazards. Aggravation of the injury relates to the fraudulent concealment; therefore, Martin's (P) action is not barred by the exclusive remedy provisions. Affirmed.

Analysis:

Workers' compensation is exclusive of all other remedies by the employee against the employer or his insurer. In fact, the basic bargain embodied by workmen's compensation statutes is that an employee gives up his right to other remedies in exchange for an "assured" and "prompt" recovery. But there are exceptions to the exclusive remedy provisions. In some circumstances, courts have allowed for employees to sue their employers for certain intentional torts. In the context of fraudulent misrepresentation of an employee's medical condition, some courts have held that worker's compensation is the only remedy when the fraud only aggravates a compensable injury. Consistent with those courts that have held the exclusive remedy provision inapplicable in the context of fraud that aggravates a work-related injury, the Pennsylvania Court bases its holding on a "dual-injury" theory. In the court's view, the first injury was the exposure to lead that caused Martin's (P) ailments. The exclusive remedy for this injury is workers' compensation. But the court holds that the second injury—the misrepresentation which aggravated the ailments—was not covered by the workmen's compensation statute.

Kerans v. Porter Paint Co.

(Sexually Harassed/Molested Employee) v. *(Employer)*

61 Ohio St.3d 486, 575 N.E.2d 428 (1991)

AN ACTION FOR A NON-PHYSICAL-INJURY TORT INFLICTED BY AN EMPLOYER OR HIS SERVANT IS NOT BARRED BY THE WORKERS' COMPENSATION EXCLUSIVITY WHEN NO WORKERS' COMPENSATION REMEDY IS AVAILABLE FOR THE PARTICULAR INJURY

■ **INSTANT FACTS** Suit by an employee against her employer for injuries resulting from sexual harassment and molestation by the store manager.

■ **BLACK LETTER RULE** The exclusive remedy provisions of a workers' compensation statute do not bar a suit against an employer for sexual harassment and molestation inflicted by a coworker.

■ **PROCEDURAL BASIS**

Appeal to the Ohio State Supreme Court, challenging the decision of the appellate court affirming the trial court's grant of summary judgment for the defendants.

■ **FACTS**

Lewis Kerans (P) and Sally Kerans (P), a decorator for Porter Paint Company (Porter) (D), filed suit against Porter (D) for injuries resulting from her sexual harassment and molestation by Al Levine, a coworker and store manager for Porter (D). The Kerans' (P) complaint against Porter (D) contained five separate counts: (1) intentionally or negligently maintaining a policy of encouraging, permitting, or condoning sexual harassment; (2) assault and battery; (3) negligent or intentional infliction of emotional distress; (4) negligent or intentional failure to provide a safe working environment; and (5) loss of consortium. The lower courts held the claim was barred by the exclusive remedy provisions of the workers' compensation statute.

■ **ISSUE**

May an employee sue her employer for injuries resulting from the sexual harassment and molestation inflicted by a coworker?

■ **DECISION AND RATIONALE**

(Resnick, J.) Yes. The exclusive remedy provisions of a workers' compensation statute do not bar a suit against an employer for sexual harassment and molestation inflicted by a coworker. While workplace injuries rob a person of resources, sexual harassment robs the person of dignity and self-esteem. Workers' compensation addresses purely economic injury; sexual harassment laws are concerned with a much more intangible injury to personal rights. For the following reasons, we reject Porter's (D) position that they are not liable for Levine's actions since they occurred outside the scope of his employment. First, federal courts have held that where an employee is able to harass another by virtue of his apparent or actual authority, the harasser's actions have taken place within the scope of employment. Their remains a issue of fact as to whether Levine had such apparent or actual authority. Second, even if the activities occurred outside the scope of Levine's employment, the Restatement imposes upon employers the duty to exercise reasonable care to control an employee from injuring others outside the scope of his employment. Based on this principal, Porter (D) had a duty to provide Mrs. Kerans (P) with a safe working environment. Here, there is an abundance of evidence that Porter (D) knew or should have known of Levine's perverse sexual proclivities, that the company was unconcerned with the threat posed by Levine, and that they took no action to remedy the problem. The grant of summary judgment was in error. Reversed.

Analysis:

In the first part of its opinion, the court holds that a sexual harassment suit is not barred by the exclusivity of worker's compensation. The court's rationale is that worker's compensation is meant to remedy an economic injury, whereas sexual harassment involves an injury to personal rights such as dignity. But this case should not be taken for the proposition that worker's compensation exclusivity provisions do not bar any sexual harassment claims. Instead, the general rule is if the harassment does not involve an accident or injury and is not the kind of tort worker's compensation was intended to remedy, then tort recovery against the employer is allowed. This rule still leaves open the possibility that an employee's sexual harassment suit will be barred if the employee is physically harmed in a manner compensable under the statute. For example, an employee that has been raped might be barred from recovering from the employer, on the ground that a rape is a physical injury, even though it is an injury of the type that might not be compensable under the statute. The greater part of the Ohio Court's opinion deals with a secondary issue that often arises in the context of sexual harassment suits - whether the employer is liable for the actions of its employees. The court here holds that an employer is liable if the harassing employee is acting within the scope of his employment, with this court tying scope of employment to the issue of authority. This is generally true whether the injured employee is seeking to recover in tort or seeking to recover under the worker's compensation statute. The Ohio Court, however, goes one step further and holds that the employer is liable in tort if he has negligently failed to control his employee from harming others while acting outside the scope of his employment. The court then holds that, in light of the fact that there was ample evidence that Porter (D) failed to address complaints regarding Levine, summary judgment was inappropriate.

CHAPTER TWENTY–NINE

Public Compensation Systems, Including Social Security

Heckler v. Campbell

Instant Facts: A disability benefits claimant appealed the decision of an administrative law judge to deny her disability benefits for a back problem.

Black Letter Rule: Even where an agency's enabling statute expressly requires it to hold a hearing, the agency may rely on its rule-making authority to determine issues that do not require case-by-case consideration.

Heckler v. Campbell

(*Secretary of Health and Human Services*) v. (*Disability Applicant*)

461 U.S. 458, 103 S.Ct. 1952 (1983)

DISABILITY BENEFITS ARE ONLY AVAILABLE TO PERSONS WHO ARE UNABLE TO ENGAGE IN ANY SUBSTANTIAL GAINFUL ACTIVITY BY REASON OF A MEDICALLY DETERMINABLE PHYSICAL OR MENTAL IMPAIRMENT

■ **INSTANT FACTS** A disability benefits claimant appealed the decision of an administrative law judge to deny her disability benefits for a back problem.

■ **BLACK LETTER RULE** Even where an agency's enabling statute expressly requires it to hold a hearing, the agency may rely on its rule-making authority to determine issues that do not require case-by-case consideration.

■ **PROCEDURAL BASIS**

Certification to the United States Supreme Court of an appellate court decision denying a court's use of medical-vocational guidelines promulgated by the Secretary of Health and Human Services to determine whether a disabled person can perform an alternative job (and therefore avoid being classified as disabled).

■ **FACTS**

In 1979, Carmen Campbell (P) applied for disability benefits because a back condition and hypertension prevented her from continuing work as a hotel maid. Following the denial, she requested a *de novo* hearing before an Administrative Law Judge. The judge determined that her problem was not severe enough to find her disabled without further inquiry, and thus considered whether she retained the ability to perform a less strenuous job. Relying on the medical vocational guidelines promulgated by the Secretary of Health and Human Services (D), the ALJ concluded that there were a significant number of jobs that Campbell (P) and others in her position could perform. Thus, he concluded that she was not disabled. The Court of Appeals, questioning the validity of the guidelines, rejected the proposition that they provide adequate evidence of a claimant's ability to perform a specific alternative occupation. The Court of Appeals then remanded the case for the Secretary to put into evidence "particular types of jobs suitable to the capabilities of Ms. Campbell" (P).

■ **ISSUE**

Can the Secretary of Health and Human Services rely on published medical-vocational guidelines to determine a claimant's right to Social Security disability benefits?

■ **DECISION AND RATIONALE**

(Powell, J.) Yes. The Social Security Act defines "disability" in terms of the effect that a physical or mental impairment has on a person's ability to function in the workplace. It only provides disability benefits to those who are unable "to engage in any substantial gainful activity by reason of any medically determinable physical or mental impairment." Further, it specifies that a person must "not only [be] unable to do his previous work but [must also be unable] to engage in any other kind of substantial gainful work which exists in the national economy." Whether a job that the claimant can do

---

exists in his or her area of the country is irrelevant; it must simply exist somewhere in the national economy. Prior to 1978, the Secretary (D) relied on vocational experts to establish the existence of suitable jobs in the national economy. This practice, however, produced some inconsistent results, so to improve both the uniformity and efficiency of this determination, the Secretary (D) promulgated some medical-vocational guidelines as a part of the 1978 regulations. The guidelines consist of a matrix of four factors—physical ability, age, education, and work experience—and set forth rules that identify whether jobs requiring specific combinations of these factors exist in significant numbers in the national economy. In practice, where a claimant's qualifications correspond to the job requirements identified by a rule in the matrix, the guidelines direct a conclusion as to whether work exists that the claimant can perform. If such work exists, the claimant is not considered disabled. The Court of Appeals discredited use of the guidelines, holding that, in addition, the Secretary (D) must bring forth individualized evidence of an ability of a particular claimant to perform an alternative job. It is this decision that we address today. The Social Security Act directs the Secretary to "adopt reasonable and proper rules and regulations to regulate and provide for the nature and extent of the proofs and evidence and the method of taking and furnishing the same" in disability cases. We do not think that reliance on the guidelines is inconsistent with the Social Security Act. It is true that the Act requires hearings and individualized determinations of disability. But this does not bar the Secretary (D) from relying on rule-making to resolve certain classes of issues. Even where an agency's enabling statute expressly requires it to hold a hearing, the agency may rely on its rule-making authority to determine issues that do not require case-by-case consideration (such as whether a particular type of job exists in the national economy). A contrary holding would require the agency to continually relitigate issues that may be established fairly and efficiently in a single rule-making proceeding. As noted, in determining whether a claimant can perform less strenuous work, the Secretary (D) must make two determinations. First, she must assess each claimant's individual abilities and then determine whether jobs exist that a person having those qualifications could perform. This involves individualized evidence. The second inquiry requires the Secretary (D) to determine an issue that is not unique to each claimant—the types and numbers of jobs that exist in the national economy. This type of general factual issue may be resolved as fairly through rule-making as by introducing the testimony of vocational experts. Finally, we consider Campbell's (P) argument that the Court of Appeals properly required the Secretary (D) to specify alternative available jobs. There is a principle of administrative law that states when an agency takes official or administrative notice of facts, a litigant must be given an adequate opportunity to respond. This principle is inapplicable, however, when the agency has promulgated valid regulations. This is because, in the rule-making proceeding, the accuracy of those facts taken notice of are fairly tested. As such, reliance on the guidelines is proper. Reversed.

Analysis:

Heckler deals with the use of the Department of Health and Human Services' medical-vocational guidelines in determining a claimant's right to Social Security disability benefits. When the Court refers to the "medical-vocational guidelines," it is referring to a set of grids or matrices set forth in 20 C.F.R. Pt. 404, Subpt. P, App. 2. These grids, as well as a set of "listings" contained in 20 C.F.R. Pt. 404, Subpt. P. App. 1, help courts to determine the existence of a disability. When a court is determining the existence of a disability, it will first look to whether the claimant has a severe impairment that limits his or her ability to work. If so, the court then turns to the listings. The listings provide automatic awards for certain disabilities. If a person's disability is on the list, then the court's job is done and benefits will be awarded according to the regulations. If the listings do not provide an automatic award, the court will then turn to the medical-vocational guidelines to determine the types and numbers of jobs that exist in the national economy. The regulations that make up the medical-vocational guidelines consist of a matrix of four factors—physical ability, age, education, and work experience—and set forth rules that identify whether jobs requiring specific combinations of these factors exist in significant numbers in the national economy. Then, as *Heckler* points out, "[i]n practice, where a claimant's qualifications correspond to the job requirements identified by a rule, the guidelines direct a conclusion as to whether work exists that the claimant can perform." If such work exists, the claimant is not considered disabled.

■ CASE VOCABULARY

HEARING *DE NOVO*: A hearing in which a previous decision of some body (such as the Department of Health and Human Services) is reviewed independent of and without deference to the decision below; the party holding the hearing examines the issue anew.

MEDICAL-VOCATIONAL GUIDELINES: A set of guidelines contained in 20 C.F.R. Pt. 404, Subpt. P, App. 2, which helps the government and Administrative Law Judges to determine whether a particular individual with particular characteristics and skills is "disabled" under the Social Security Act.

CHAPTER THIRTY

Private Insurance Solutions

Licari v. Elliot

Instant Facts: A taxicab driver who was injured in a car accident sought to have his injuries held to be "serious injuries" so as to increase his recovery under New York's no-fault law.

Black Letter Rule: Under New York's no-fault law, there is no right of recovery for non-economic loss except in the case of a serious injury; moreover, it is the trial court's responsibility (not that of a jury) to determine whether a prima facie case of serious injury has been made.

Licari v. Elliot

(*Injured Party*) v. (*Not Stated*)

57 N.Y.2d 230, 455 N.Y.S.2d 570, 441 N.E.2d 1088 (1982)

WHEN A LEGISLATURE ENACTS A NO-FAULT LAW IT MODIFIES THE COMMON LAW RIGHTS OF PERSONS IN CAR ACCIDENTS TO THE EXTENT THAT PLAINTIFFS IN SUCH ACCIDENT CASES NO LONGER HAVE AN UNFETTERED RIGHT TO SUE FOR INJURIES SUSTAINED

■ **INSTANT FACTS** A taxicab driver who was injured in a car accident sought to have his injuries held to be "serious injuries" so as to increase his recovery under New York's no-fault law.

■ **BLACK LETTER RULE** Under New York's no-fault law, there is no right of recovery for non-economic loss except in the case of a serious injury; moreover, it is the trial court's responsibility (not that of a jury) to determine whether a prima facie case of serious injury has been made.

■ PROCEDURAL BASIS

Certification to the Court of Appeals of New York of an appellate court decision that, as a matter of law, a tort claimant failed to prove a serious injury under the state's no-fault insurance law.

■ FACTS

On February 13, 1979, Licari (P), a taxi driver, was injured in a car accident, suffering a concussion, acute cervical sprain, acute dorsal lumbar sprain, and a contusion of the chest. He was released from the hospital after just a few hours, but two days later returned because he was coughing up red phlegm. The examining physician later testified that Licari (P) suffered nothing but a "very mild limitation" of movement in the back and neck areas. On March 9, 1979, just twenty-four days after his injury, Licari (P) returned to work. The only affect that the injury had on his work performance was his inability to help some customers with their luggage. He was also unable to help his wife around the house as much as he could before, and suffered from "occasional transitory headaches and dizzy spells which were relieved by aspirin." Following the close of evidence, Elliot (D) moved to dismiss Licari's (P) complaint on the ground that he had failed to establish that his injuries were "serious injuries" within the meaning of New York's insurance law. The court submitted the case to the jury, reserving decision on the motion. The jury found that such an injury had been proven. Elliot (D) filed a motion to set aside the verdict, which was denied, and an appeal followed. On appeal, the appellate division reversed the trial court's holding and Licari (P) appealed.

■ ISSUE

May a jury be permitted to decide whether a prima facie case of serious injury has been proved in a no-fault insurance case?

■ DECISION AND RATIONALE

(Jasen, J.) No. The Legislature provided that "there shall be no right of recovery for non-economic loss except in the case of a serious injury, or for basic economic loss." Although the statute sets up eight specific categories which constitute serious injury, we are only concerned with two of them.

These are whether the plaintiff suffered a serious injury which resulted in either a "significant limitation of use of a body function or system," or "a medically determined injury or impairment of a nonpermanent nature" which endured for 90 days or more and substantially limited the performance of his daily activities. While it is clear that the Legislature intended to allow plaintiffs to recover for noneconomic injuries in appropriate cases, it had also intended that the court (and not a jury) first determine whether or not a prima facie case of serious injury has been established which would permit a plaintiff to maintain a common-law tort cause of action. It is incumbent upon the court to decide in the first instance whether the plaintiff has a cause of action to assert within the meaning of the statute. By enacting the No-Fault Law, the Legislature modified the common-law rights of persons injured in automobile accidents, to the extent that plaintiffs in auto accident cases no longer have an unfettered right to sue for injures sustained. To allow a jury to make the initial decision would subvert the Legislature's intent and destroy the effectiveness of the statute. The result of requiring a jury trial where the injury is clearly a minor one would perpetuate a system of unnecessary litigation. Thus, we believe the Legislature intended that the court should decide the threshold question of whether the evidence would warrant a jury finding that the injury falls within the class of injuries that, under no-fault, should be excluded from judicial remedy. In this case, Licari (P) was able to maintain his daily routine for most of each day after returning to work. As such, it should be abundantly clear that he was not prevented from performing substantially all of his daily activities during anything close to 90 days following the occurrence of the injury. Thus, the appellate court correctly held, as a matter of law, that Licari (P) did not meet the statutory standard of serious injury. Further, it requires little discussion that Licari's (P) subjective complaints of occasional headaches hardly fulfills the definition of serious injury. He has offered no proof that his headaches in any way incapacitated him or interfered with his ability to work or engage in activities at home. To hold that this type of ailment constitutes a serious injury would render the statute meaning less and frustrate the legislative intent in enacting no-fault legislation. Finally, as to Licari's (P) contention that he suffered a "significant limitation of use of a body function or system," the evidence established only that he suffered a painful sprain which limited the movement of his neck and back. Affirmed.

Analysis:

Licari addresses the application of a no-fault insurance system to the traditional motor vehicle accident. First proposed by Professors Robert Keeton and Jeffrey O'Connell in 1965, a no-fault insurance plan provides a two-tier system for dealing with automobile accident injuries. Under the first tier of the no-fault system, claims under a certain value are wholly covered by insurance similar to medical and disability insurance. This means that a person purchases insurance to cover himself or herself in the event of injuries under a certain value. For example, if the threshold were $10,000, a car accident that results in only $7,000 in damage to a vehicle and its driver would not ever enter the tort system, but would be covered by the injured claimant's no-fault insurance. Under the second tier of the no-fault system, a claim above a certain value would be adjudicated in the traditional tort system. Thus, if, in the example above, the car accident results in $12,000 in injuries, access to the courts is not foreclosed. The Keeton-O'Connell plan includes some other ideas as well. First, no-fault insurance must be compulsory and it must cover not only the car and driver, but also all passengers and pedestrians involved. Second, the tort claims of all those who collect under the no-fault system are abolished, meaning a person with the option must choose either the settlement offered under their own system or give it up and take their chance in court. This is what *Licari* meant when it stated that "By enacting the No-Fault Law, the Legislature modified the common-law rights of persons injured in automobile accidents, to the extent that plaintiffs in automobile accident cases no longer have an unfettered right to sue for injuries sustained."

■ CASE VOCABULARY

ACUTE CERVICAL SPRAIN: A serious sprain to the cervix, or the back part of the neck (higher up on the body than the dorsal lumbar).

ACUTE DORSAL LUMBAR SPRAIN: A serious sprain to the dorsal lumbar, which is a part of the human vertebrae between the thoracic vertebrae and the sacrum (which is where the vertebrae connects with the pelvis).

CONTUSION: A non-lacerated injury (such as a severe bruise).

NO-FAULT INSURANCE: An insurance system that will, among other things, pay for a policy-holder's injuries without an adjudication of who is at fault, or who is faulted with causing the party's injuries.

NON-ECONOMIC LOSS: A loss that is not of an economic nature, such as pain and suffering (as opposed to lost wages).

SERIOUS INJURY: As defined by the court, a serious injury is "either a medically determined injury of a nonpermanent nature which prevented [a party] from performing substantially all his daily activities for not less than 90 days during the 180 days immediately following the accident," or "a significant limitation of use of a body function or system."

CHAPTER THIRTY–TWO

Communication of Personally Harmful Impression to Others

New York Times Co. v. Sullivan

Instant Facts: A city commissioner sought to sue a newspaper for defamation based on a published advertisement alleging that the police department, which the commissioner headed, engaged in a course of conduct in opposition to the civil rights movement.

Black Letter Rule: The First Amendment prohibits a public official from recovering damages for a defamatory falsehood relating to his official conduct unless he proves that the statement was made with "actual malice"—that is, with knowledge that it was false or with reckless disregard for the truth.

Gertz v. Robert Welch, Inc.

Instant Facts: An attorney filed a defamation suit against the publisher of an organ that identified him as a Communist and the architect of a frame-up against a police officer.

Black Letter Rule: So long as they do not impose liability without fault, the States may define for themselves the appropriate standard of liability for a publisher or broadcaster of defamatory falsehood injurious to a private individual.

Friedman v. Dozorc

Instant Facts: A doctor filed a suit for negligence and malicious civil prosecution against his former patient's attorney, who filed a baseless malpractice suit.

Black Letter Rule: An attorney cannot be held civilly liable to his client's adversary on the grounds that the attorney filed a baseless claim.

Solano v. Playgirl, Inc.

Instant Facts: Playgirl (D) published an issue with Solano's (D) photograph on the cover, proclaiming that the issue exposed young actors.

Black Letter Rule: To prevail on a false light claim, a plaintiff must prove (1) that the defendant disclosed to one or more persons information about or concerning the plaintiff that was presented as factual, but was actually false or created a false impression about him; (2) that the information was understood by one or more persons to whom it was disclosed as stating or implying something highly offensive and tending to damage the plaintiff's reputation; (3) that the defendant acted with constitutional malice; and (4) that the plaintiff was damaged by the disclosure.

New York Times Co. v. Sullivan

(Newspaper) v. (Commissioner of the City of Montgomery, Alabama)

376 U.S. 254, 84 S.Ct. 710 (1964)

THE FIRST AMENDMENT PROVIDES A CONSTITUTIONAL PRIVILEGE FOR DEFENDANTS IN AN ACTION FOR DEFAMATION OF PUBLIC OFFICIALS

■ **INSTANT FACTS** A city commissioner sought to sue a newspaper for defamation based on a published advertisement alleging that the police department, which the commissioner headed, engaged in a course of conduct in opposition to the civil rights movement.

■ **BLACK LETTER RULE** The First Amendment prohibits a public official from recovering damages for a defamatory falsehood relating to his official conduct unless he proves that the statement was made with "actual malice"—that is, with knowledge that it was false or with reckless disregard for the truth.

■ FACTS

The New York Times (D) published an advertisement asking for donations to help defend Dr. Martin Luther King, Jr in a perjury indictment against him. The advertisement alleged that the City of Montgomery police department arrested Dr. King seven times and ringed the campus at Alabama State College, padlocking the campus dining hall in an effort to starve students. Although not expressly named in the advertisement, L.B. Sullivan (P), Commissioner of the City of Montgomery, alleged in a suit for defamation that the advertisement's reference to the police was to be read as implicating him, and that the references to arrests were to be read as accusing him of violence and intimidation. The judge instructed the jury that the statements were libelous per se, which meant that malice, falsity and damage were presumed. The jury returned a verdict in favor of Sullivan (P), awarding him $500,000. The Supreme Court of Alabama affirmed.

■ ISSUE

In a suit for defamation of a public official, may the court instruct the jury that malice is presumed?

■ DECISION AND RATIONALE

(Brennan, J.) No. The First Amendment prohibits a public official from recovering damages for a defamatory falsehood relating to his official conduct unless he proves that the statement was made with "actual malice"—that is, with knowledge that it was false or with reckless disregard for the truth. This Court has stated that the First Amendment's safeguard was fashioned to assure unfettered interchange of ideas for the bringing about of political and social changes desired by the people. Naturally, this commitment to uninhibited and robust debate on public issues may well include attacks on government and its officials. The advertisement at issue, which dealt with a major political issue, clearly qualifies for the constitutional protection. The question here is whether it forfeits that protection because some of its factual statements are erroneous and defamatory. Erroneous statements are inevitable in free debate and must be protected so that public debate is given sufficient breathing space. We believe that neither the factual error nor the defamatory content, either alone or in conjunction with each other, suffice to remove the constitutional protections. Furthermore, the state law providing for a defense based on truth is an insufficient safeguard under the First Amendment. If truth were the only defense to an action in libel per se, as it is under Alabama law, critics of public officials would have to assure themselves of the truth of their assertions. The natural consequence of saddling the defendant with the burden on proving truth is self-censorship; critics will be deterred from voicing their views because of doubt as to whether their truth could be proved in court. Applying these principles to the present case, we find the evidence does not make a clear showing of actual malice. Reversed.

Analysis:

Adding to the privileges provided by the common law, this case established a constitutional privilege for defendants in actions for defamation of public officials. But unlike the common law privileges, the defendant need not affirmatively prove that the statements were privileged. In contrast to the view under the common law that libel *per se* was any statement that was defamatory on its face Alabama law provided that statements were libel *per se* if they slandered a person's trade or profession. At issue here was the rule allowing for the presumption of damages when a finding of libel *per se* had been made. The Court held that these presumptions ran afoul of the First Amendment when applied in a action for libel by a public official for statements relating to public conduct. The Court held that the First Amendment requires both, damages and malice to be proved in such a cause of action. But take note that the Court adopts a different definition of "actual malice" for First Amendment purposes. Under the common law view, the issue of malice focused on the publisher's reason for making the statement; the question was whether the defamatory statements were made for an improper purpose, in which case the defendant lost the protection of any privilege he may have had. In contrast, the Court's definition of malice focuses on the publisher's state of mind regarding the truth or falsity of the statements. But the First Amendment's protection does not extend to every statement made about every government employee. Instead, the First Amendment privilege applies only to those officials who appear to have substantial control over public affairs. Although not every government employee is a public official for purposes of the First Amendment, it is quite clear that just about any matter bears on the conduct of "public official." In other words, almost any subject concerning a public official is fair game, and is afforded constitutional protection. Because this was a seminal case the Court turns to democratic principles, rather than precedent, to support its holding. In a government where the people possess the sovereign power, uninhibited debate is necessary so that people make informed decisions regarding the conduct of public affairs. The Court extends the First Amendment's protection to false speech to avoid the danger of self-censorship, which would result from a critic's doubt as to whether a statement were completely true or not.

Gertz v. Robert Welch, Inc.

(*Defamed Attorney*) v. (*Publisher*)

418 U.S. 323, 94 S.Ct. 2997 (1974)

THE FIRST AMENDMENT AFFORDS NO PRIVILEGE TO THOSE WHO NEGLIGENTLY PUBLISH DEFAMATORY STATEMENTS CONCERNING PRIVATE INDIVIDUALS

■ **INSTANT FACTS** An attorney filed a defamation suit against the publisher of an organ that identified him as a Communist and the architect of a frame-up against a police officer.

■ **BLACK LETTER RULE** So long as they do not impose liability without fault, the States may define for themselves the appropriate standard of liability for a publisher or broadcaster of defamatory falsehood injurious to a private individual.

■ **PROCEDURAL BASIS**

Appeal to the United States Supreme Court, challenging the holding of the Court of Appeals which affirmed a judgment for the defendant on the ground that no "actual malice" was shown.

■ **FACTS**

Elmer Gertz (P) was an attorney who represented the family of a youth murdered by a police officer in the family's civil claim against the officer. Robert Welch, Inc. (Welch) (D) was the publisher of an organ known as the *American Opinion*, which portrayed Gertz (P) as an architect of the "frame-up" of the police officer, and as a Leninist and Communist-fronter. There was no basis for either of these conclusions. Consequently, Gertz (P) sued for defamation. Although the trial court found that Gertz (P) was not a public official or public figure, it required Gertz (P) to prove actual malice. Accordingly, it entered a judgment for Welch (D). The Court of Appeals affirmed, concluding that "actual malice" was not proved by clear and convincing evidence.

■ **ISSUE**

May a newspaper or broadcaster that publishes defamatory falsehoods about an individual who is neither a public official nor a public figure claim a constitutional privilege against liability for the injury inflicted by those statements?

■ **DECISION AND RATIONALE**

(Powell, J.) No. So long as they do not impose liability without fault, the States may define for themselves the appropriate standard of liability for a publisher or broadcaster of defamatory falsehood injurious to a private individual. In *New York Times Co. v. Sullivan* [Supreme Court holds that a newspaper was not liable for defamatory falsehoods it published about a city commissioner] we delineated the constitutional protections appropriate to the context of defamation of a public person. Under that standard, "public figures" - those who have achieved fame by reason of the notoriety of their achievements or the vigor and success with which they seek the public's attention - and those who hold public office may recover in an action for defamation only upon a clear and convincing showing that the defamatory falsehood was made with knowledge of its falsity or reckless disregard for the truth. But the reasons which justify the application of this rule to public persons are not present in an action by a private individual. First, a private individual is more vulnerable to injury because he has limited access to public channels to counteract the false statements. Furthermore, unlike public officials who accept the consequences of their involvement in government and public figures who thrust themselves into the public eye, a private individual has not voluntarily exposed himself to the increased risk of injury from defamation. We, however, find that Gertz (P) is not a public figure. Such a characterization can be met if the individual achieves such notoriety that he becomes a public figure for all purposes, or if an individual purposefully injects himself or is drawn into a particular public controversy. Gertz (D) meets neither standard. Notwithstanding, we do issue one caveat. Damages may not be presumed in an action for defamation where actual malice has not been proved. The State has no legitimate interest in compensating any plaintiff, whether he be a private individual or public person, for an injury that has not been sustained. Reversed.

Analysis:

This case sets the constitutional default standard for liability for the publication of false defamatory statements or materials. The Court rejects the application of the *New York Times* standard to a suit by a private individual. It holds that standard applicable only in suits by public officials and public figures. In place of the *New York Times* standard the Court adopts a standard of liability under which every element of a suit for defamation—publication, "of and concerning the plaintiff," and defamatory meaning—must be judged under at least a negligence standard. In other words, a private plaintiff must prove that the defendant negligently, recklessly, or intentionally defamed him. The exact level of intent is to be determined under State law. But strict liability, which was the common law rule, is flatly prohibited by the First Amendment. The States, however, remain free to adopt the *New York Times* standard for all defamation suits. One issue that has arisen in lower courts is whether negligence is to be judged by the standards of the journalism profession or against the reasonable person standard. The court bases its holding, in part, on inability of private individuals to counter defamatory statements due to their limited access to mass communication and media. Does this hold true in the age of the Internet? Regardless, the Court also relies on the fact that private individuals have not placed themselves in the spotlight and, therefore, have not assumed the risks appertaining thereto.

Friedman v. Dozorc

(Doctor) v. *(Patient's Attorney)*
412 Mich. 1, 312 N.W.2d 585 (1981)

A LAWSUIT FOR MALICIOUS CIVIL PROSECUTION REQUIRES A SHOWING OF SPECIAL DAMAGE BY THE PLAINTIFF

■ **INSTANT FACTS** A doctor filed a suit for negligence and malicious civil prosecution against his former patient's attorney, who filed a baseless malpractice suit.

■ **BLACK LETTER RULE** An attorney cannot be held civilly liable to his client's adversary on the grounds that the attorney filed a baseless claim.

■ **PROCEDURAL BASIS**

Appeal from the holding of the Court of Appeals, affirming in part and reversing in part the trial court's grant of summary judgment for the defendants.

■ **FACTS**

Anthony Serafin Jr. obtained the services of attorneys Dozorc (D) and Golden (D) in order to file an action against Dr. Friedman for the death of Mrs. Serafin, who died as a result of surgery-related complications. At trial, Dozorc (D) and Golden (D) introduced no evidence establishing that Dr. Friedman (P) violated any professional standard. Accordingly, the trial court directed a verdict for Dr. Friedman (P). Dr. Freidman (P) then instituted an action against Dozorc (D) and Golden (D) for negligence and malicious civil prosecution. The trial court granted the attorneys' motion for summary judgment. The Court of Appeals affirmed in part and reversed in part.

■ **ISSUE**

May an attorney be held civilly liable to his client's adversary on the grounds that the attorney filed a baseless claim?

■ **DECISION AND RATIONALE**

(Levin, J.) No. An attorney cannot be held civilly liable to his client's adversary on the grounds that the attorney filed a baseless claim. First, Dr. Friedman's (P) claim in negligence must fail because there is no ground to support the theory that Dozorc (D) and Golden (D) owed him a duty of care. If attorneys owed a duty to their client's adversary they would find themselves in countless situations where any action they take would violate either a duty to their client or a duty to their client's adversary. The dear conflict of interests wound place attorney's in untenable positions. Second, we hold Dr. Friedman's claim for malicious prosecution must also fail on account of his failure to allege special injury. We adhere to the proposition—rejected in several jurisdictions—that in the absence of an arrest, seizure, or special damage, the successful civil defendant has no remedy, despite the fact that his adversary proceeded against him maliciously and without probable cause. This court believes that the excessive litigiousness typical of our society should not be remedied by facilitating further causes of action. The trial court was correct in dismissing all claims by Dr. Friedman (P).

Analysis:

This case serves as an introduction to the topic of malicious civil prosecution in the context of a medical malpractice suit. The issue of countersuits brought by doctors falsely accused of malpractice is one of considerable debate. The court uses the special injury rule as a barrier to Dr. Friedman's (P) claim. Traditionally, the special injury requirement was satisfied if there was a seizure or attachment of property, or where the person himself was seized. The special injury requirement has been rejected by a number of courts, the precise tally of which is unclear. In support of its adherence to the rule, the court notes that the remedy for excessive litigation is not an expansion of liability. This case, however, is really about access to courts. Even courts that have rejected the special injury rule have found ways of limiting an attorney's liability to his client's adversary. Which ever route a court takes in limiting these types of suits, the effect is the same. One person's unfettered access to courts is favored over the other. The effect of permitting a doctor to sue his patient's attorney would be to deny a plaintiff, whose claims lie at the margins of liability, his day in court. Attorneys will be unwilling to file claims if they believe that civil liability is a real possibility in close cases. In effect, a potential plaintiff loses his right to a jury trial because the attorney will decide whether the case gets filed or not.

Solano v. Playgirl, Inc.

(Actor) v. (Publisher)

292 F.3d 1078 (9th Cir.2002)

THE PUBLICATION OF AN UNAUTHORIZED SUGGESTIVE PHOTOGRAPH MAY PLACE THE SUBJECT IN A FALSE LIGHT

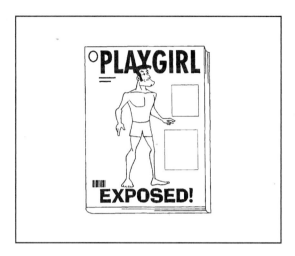

■ **INSTANT FACTS** Playgirl (D) published an issue with Solano's (D) photograph on the cover, proclaiming that the issue exposed young actors.

■ **BLACK LETTER RULE** To prevail on a false light claim, a plaintiff must prove (1) that the defendant disclosed to one or more persons information about or concerning the plaintiff that was presented as factual, but was actually false or created a false impression about him; (2) that the information was understood by one or more persons to whom it was disclosed as stating or implying something highly offensive and tending to damage the plaintiff's reputation; (3) that the defendant acted with constitutional malice; and (4) that the plaintiff was damaged by the disclosure.

■ PROCEDURAL BASIS

On appeal to review a district court order granting summary judgment to the defendant.

■ FACTS

Playgirl (D) magazine published an issue that included on the cover a photograph of Solano (P), an actor, in red swimming trunks from his role on the television show, "Baywatch." The cover also stated that the issue contained "Primetime's Sexy Young Stars Exposed." Although the only reference to Solano (P) inside the issue was a head-and-shoulders photograph showing him fully dressed, Solano (P) sued the magazine, alleging it deliberately created a false impression that he appeared nude. After the district court granted summary judgment to Playgirl (D), Solano (P) appealed.

■ ISSUE

Did Solano (P) establish a genuine issue of material fact as to whether Playgirl presented him in a false light to withstand summary judgment?

■ DECISION AND RATIONALE

(Fisher, J.) Yes. To prevail on a false light claim, a plaintiff must prove (1) that the defendant disclosed to one or more persons information about or concerning the plaintiff that was presented as factual, but was actually false or created a false impression about him; (2) that the information was understood by one or more persons to whom it was disclosed as stating or implying something highly offensive and tending to damage the plaintiff's reputation; (3) that the defendant acted with constitutional malice; and (4) that the plaintiff was damaged by the disclosure. Here, Solano (P) offered evidence that could permit a jury to conclude that the cover represented him as a "washed-up" actor willing to sell provocative photos of himself to earn a living, that some editors were concerned that the photographs possibly created a false impression, and that he was damaged by personal embarrassment. Solano (P) established a genuine issue of material fact to withstand summary judgment on his false light claims. Reversed.

Analysis:

False light claims often invoke a number of constitutional principles. The subject, often a celebrity, maintains some constitutional right of privacy, although his expectation of privacy is tempered somewhat by his public persona. On the other hand, the media has a First Amendment right to free speech. In a world of media sensationalism and the profitability to be gained by the public's fascination with celebrities, these two rights often collide in false light actions.

■ **CASE VOCABULARY**

FALSE LIGHT: In an invasion-of-privacy action, a plaintiff's allegation that the defendant attributed to the plaintiff views that he or she does not hold and placed the plaintiff before the public in a highly offensive and untrue manner.

MALICE: The intent, without justification or excuse, to commit a wrongful act.

CHAPTER THIRTY–THREE

Communication of Commercially Harmful Impressions to Others

Jeffrey v. Cathers

Instant Facts: After Cathers (D) filed a mechanic's lien on Jeffrey's (P) property, Jeffrey (P) filed an action for slander of title.

Black Letter Rule: To establish a claim for slander of title, a plaintiff must prove some interest in the property, that the words published were false, that the words were maliciously published, and that the plaintiff suffered pecuniary loss because of the false statement.

Brunson Communications, Inc. v. Arbitron, Inc.

Instant Facts: Arbitron (D) published false information concerning the number of viewers tuning into a television station owned by Brunson Communications (P).

Black Letter Rule: One who publishes a false statement harmful to the interests of another is subject to liability for pecuniary loss resulting to the other if he intends for publication of the statement to result in harm to interests of the other having a pecuniary value, or either recognizes or should recognize that it is likely to do so, and he knows that the statement is false or acts in reckless disregard of its truth or falsity.

Alyeska Pipeline Service v. Aurora Air Service

Instant Facts: Alyeska (D) induced RCA to breach its contract with Aurora (P) thereby intentionally interfering with Aurora's (P) economic benefits under the RCA contract.

Black Letter Rule: The privilege to procure a breach of another's contract, because the interest advanced is superior to the social importance to the interest invaded, is forfeited when the act is motivated by a desire to injure the contract party.

Caruso v. Local Union Number 690, International Brotherhood of Teamsters

Instant Facts: Caruso (P) sued Teamsters (D) for interference with business after publication of article in its weekly paper telling readers not patronize Caruso's (P) business.

Black Letter Rule: Liability will not be imposed for speech activities that interfere with business and cause damage.

Qualitex Co. v. Jacobson Products Co.

Instant Facts: Qualitex (P) sued Jacobson Products (D) for trademark infringement under the federal Lanham Act.

Black Letter Rule: Trademark protection applies to those product characteristics that assist consumers in identifying the source of the product, including any word, name, symbol, device, or combination thereof.

Sears, Roebuck & Co. v. Stiffel Co.

Instant Facts: Stiffel (P) sued Sears (D) for making and selling a substantially similar pole lamp to the one created by Stieffel (P).

Black Letter Rule: A State's unfair competition law cannot encroach upon, or give protection of a kind that clashes with, the objectives of the federal patent laws.

Jeffrey v. Cathers

(Property Owner) v. *(Corporate President)*
104 S.W.3d 424 (Mo.Ct.App.2003)

THE FILING OF A MECHANIC'S LIEN IS NOT ABSOLUTELY PRIVILEGED

■ **INSTANT FACTS** After Cathers (D) filed a mechanic's lien on Jeffrey's (P) property, Jeffrey (P) filed an action for slander of title.

■ **BLACK LETTER RULE** To establish a claim for slander of title, a plaintiff must prove some interest in the property, that the words published were false, that the words were maliciously published, and that the plaintiff suffered pecuniary loss because of the false statement.

■ **PROCEDURAL BASIS**

On appeal to review a trial court decision dismissing the plaintiff's claim.

■ **FACTS**

Jeffrey (P) contracted with Cathers (D), as corporate president, to perform demolition and hauling services on Jeffrey's (P) property. After Jeffrey (P) refused to pay Cathers (D) for the work, Cathers (D) filed a mechanic's lien against the property. Jeffrey (P) responded by filing suit against Cathers (D) for slander of title and requested punitive damages. After the trial court dismissed Jeffrey's (P) claim, he appealed.

■ **ISSUE**

Did the plaintiff sufficiently allege an action for slander of title based on the defendant's filing a mechanic's lien on the property?

■ **DECISION AND RATIONALE**

(Dowd, J.) Yes. To establish a claim for slander of title, a plaintiff must prove some interest in the property, that the words published were false, that the words were maliciously published, and that the plaintiff suffered pecuniary loss because of the false statement. Here, Jeffrey (P) pleaded that the mechanic's lien was filed against his property after Cathers (D) altered their contract to add notice of lien language and alleged that he had been prevented from obtaining funds that had been earlier set aside for his use. This pleading sufficiently alleges slander of title. Because Cathers' (D) filing of the mechanics' lien is not protected by an absolute privilege that would bar the action, the action should not have been dismissed. Reversed.

Analysis:

The element of malice in a cause of action for slander of title gives rise to a built-in defense for defendants. While the statement published must be false, proof of its falsity does not by itself establish slander of title. Instead, the plaintiff must also prove that the defendant acted with the intent to deceive or defraud the plaintiff or others. A good faith belief that the statement published was true will serve as a defense to a slander of title claim.

■ CASE VOCABULARY

LIEN: A legal right or interest that a creditor has in another's property, lasting usually until a debt or duty that it secures is satisfied.

PECUNIARY DAMAGES: Damages that can be estimated and monetarily compensated.

SLANDER OF TITLE: A false statement, made orally or in writing, that casts doubt on another person's ownership of property.

Brunson Communications, Inc. v. Arbitron, Inc.

(Television Station Owner) v. *(Viewership Surveyor)*

266 F.Supp.2d 377 (E.D.Pa.2003)

PECUNIARY DAMAGES MUST BE ASSERTED WITH SPECIFICITY

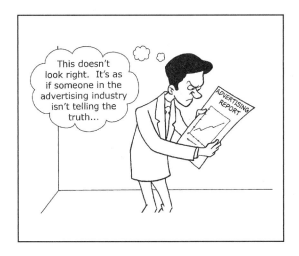

■ **INSTANT FACTS** Arbitron (D) published false information concerning the number of viewers tuning into a television station owned by Brunson Communications (P).

■ **BLACK LETTER RULE** One who publishes a false statement harmful to the interests of another is subject to liability for pecuniary loss resulting to the other if he intends for publication of the statement to result in harm to interests of the other having a pecuniary value, or either recognizes or should recognize that it is likely to do so, and he knows that the statement is false or acts in reckless disregard of its truth or falsity.

■ **PROCEDURAL BASIS**

Trial court consideration of the defendant's motion to dismiss.

■ **FACTS**

Brunson Communications (P) owned an independent television station. Arbitron, Inc. (D) purported to measure the number of viewers watching each television station in the market, but did not actually do so. Instead, Arbitron (D) published erroneous viewership information to advertisers, television stations, and others, representing the information as accurate. Brunson Communications (P) sued Arbitron (D) for commercial disparagement, alleging that Arbitron's (D) false statements caused the plaintiff to lose advertising revenue. Arbitron (D) moved to dismiss the complaint.

■ **ISSUE**

Did the plaintiff sufficiently plead a claim of commercial disparagement to withstand a motion to dismiss, when it failed to specifically identify its pecuniary loss?

■ **DECISION AND RATIONALE**

(Baylson, J.) No. Under the Restatement (Second) of Torts § 623A, "[o]ne who publishes a false statement harmful to the interests of another is subject to liability for pecuniary loss resulting to the other if (a) he intends for publication of the statement to result in harm to interests of the other having a pecuniary value, or either recognizes or should recognize that it is likely to do so, and (b) he knows that the statement is false or acts in reckless disregard of its truth or falsity." Here, although the plaintiff did not specifically reference the particular television station at issue, the allegations of the complaint sufficiently allege that the defendant made a false statement that it should have recognized would harm the plaintiff and that the defendant knew was false. However, the plaintiff has not specifically identified any pecuniary loss. To sufficiently plead disparagement damages, the plaintiff must allege "facts showing an established business, the amount of sales for a substantial period preceding publication, and amount of sales subsequent to the publication, facts showing that such loss in sale were the natural and probable result of such publication, and the facts showing the plaintiff could not allege the name of particular customers who withdrew or withheld their custom." The plaintiff here does not allege its

---

damages with sufficient specificity. The claim for commercial disparagement is dismissed without prejudice to allow the plaintiff to amend its claim. Motion granted.

Analysis:

Unlike in many cases, the court here establishes a reasonable means to calculate a party's damages in a commercial disparagement case. By comparing business revenue before the alleged act with revenue after the alleged act, a plaintiff at a minimum can establish its damages to proceed with its claim. Often times, lost revenue or lost business opportunity are not so easily proven.

■ CASE VOCABULARY

DISPARAGEMENT: A false and injurious statement that discredits or detracts from the reputation of another's property, product, or business. To recover in tort for disparagement, the plaintiff must prove that the statement caused a third party to take some action resulting in specific pecuniary loss to the plaintiff.

Alyeska Pipeline Service v. Aurora Air Service

(*Interfering Party*) v. (*Victim of Breached Contract*)
604 P.2d 1090 (Alaska 1979)

INDUCING A BREACH OF ANOTHER'S CONTRACT FOR OBJECTIVELY PROPER REASONS MAY STILL RESULT IN LIABILITY IF DONE IN BAD FAITH

■ **INSTANT FACTS** Alyeska (D) induced RCA to breach its contract with Aurora (P) thereby intentionally interfering with Aurora's (P) economic benefits under the RCA contract.

■ **BLACK LETTER RULE** The privilege to procure a breach of another's contract, because the interest advanced is superior to the social importance to the interest invaded, is forfeited when the act is motivated by a desire to injure the contract party.

■ **PROCEDURAL BASIS**

Appeal after jury trial, challenging denial of motion for summary judgment in action for damages for inducing breach of contract.

■ **FACTS**

Alyeska Pipeline Service (Alyeska) (D) entered into a contract with RCA to provide communication systems along the Alaska oil pipeline, and giving Alyeska (D) the option to terminate the contract. RCA in turn contracted with Aurora Air Service (Aurora) (P) to provide a plane, pilot, parts and service along the pipeline, and giving RCA the option to terminate Aurora's (P) services. After services under both contracts commenced, Alyeska (D) and Aurora (P) had a dispute about an earlier arrangement and Alyeska (D) exercised its option under its contract with RCA to take over the flight services itself. [Notice that by so doing, RCA no longer needs Aurora's (P) services.] As a result, RCA terminated its contract with Aurora (P). Thereafter, Aurora (P) [believing that Alyeska (D) was motivated to cause it harm] sued Alyeska (D) alleging that it induced RCA to breach its contract with Aurora (P). The trial court denied Alyeska's (D) motion for summary judgment. The court held that although Alyeska (D) was entitled to terminate RCA under the contract with it (and hence, indirectly terminate Aurora's (P) services), if it did so in bad faith, then it, Alyeska (D), could be liable to Aurora (P). The matter was submitted to the jury and it found in favor of Aurora (P). Alyeska (D) appealed.

■ **ISSUE**

Is the privilege to procure a breach of another's contract, because the interest advanced is superior to the social importance to the interest invaded, forfeited when the act is motivated by a desire to injure the contract party?

■ **DECISION AND RATIONALE**

(Connor) Yes. We hold that when bad faith motive is the basis for inducing a breach of another's contract, any privilege that may exist for procuring such breach is forfeited. Alyeska (D) makes three contentions on appeal. The first is that the right to modify the contract (in this case the right to terminate RCA), is absolute and may be exercised regardless of motive. We reject this contention. One party to a contract may sue a third party who intentionally procures the breach of that contract by the other party without justification or privilege. Recent authority even holds that a claim of unjustifiable interference can be made when the contract is terminable at will. Alyeska (D) next contends that it was permitted to terminate its contract with RCA due to overriding economic and safety interests. A privilege does exist that allows one to invade a contractual interest if the interest advanced by him is superior to the social importance to the interest invaded. The immunity afforded by this privilege may be forfeited however if one does not act in a good faith attempt to protect his own interest or that of another but, rather, is motivated by a desire to injure the contract party. Whether the justification for invading the interest was made in good faith or bad faith is a question normally reserved for the trier of fact. In this case, there was a conflicting factual issue whether Alyeska (D) was furthering its own economic and safety interests or was using them as a façade for inflicting injury on Aurora (P). This issue was correctly submitted to the jury. [The jury obviously thought Alyeska (D) intended to cause harm to Aurora (P) by going through RCA.] Alyeska (D) also claims error in not giving its proposed jury instruction that Aurora (P) had the burden of proving by a preponderance of the evidence that Alyeska's (D) actions were malicious and committed with the sole intent of injuring Aurora (P). We reject this contention and hold that the issue of whether Alyeska (D) acted in good faith or in bad faith goes to the question of justification, and that Aurora (P) did not have the burden of proof on this issue. The matter is affirmed, with the exception of an error in computing damages, which is reversed as to permit a correction.

Analysis:

This case concerns a claim for inducing a breach of contract. The contract allegedly breached was between RCA and Aurora (P), and the one who induced the breach was Alyeska (D). Inducing a breach of contract requires that the interference be improper or unjustified and that it causes at least partial breach of the contract. One of the issues in the case was whether Alyeska (D) was *justified* in terminating its own contract with RCA so that it could provide the flying services itself out of concern for economics and safety. It is a valid defense if one induces a breach to protect his own existing financial interests; however, interference cannot be justified on the ground that the interferer is competing. Alyeska's (D) motion for summary judgment was denied by the trial court because there was an issue of whether it terminated its contract with RCA in bad faith. Remember that the contract between Alyeska (D) and RCA provided that Alyeska (D) had the option of terminating the contract. Alyeska (D) claimed that it did so because of economics and safety concerns. So how can Alyeska (D) be sued? Because of an improper motive. If it terminated the RCA contract in bad faith so that Aurora (P) would lose its contract with RCA, Alyeska (D) can be held liable to Aurora (P) for inducing RCA to breach the contract. There are circumstances where one can lawfully interfere with the contractual interests of another. For example, if the reason for interfering is superior in social importance to the contractual interest invaded, there will be no liability. The case also addressed who has the burden of proof concerning lack of good faith. The court held it was Alyeska's (D) burden.

■ CASE VOCABULARY

CONTRACT TERMINABLE AT WILL: A contract that can be terminated with or without cause.

Caruso v. Local Union Number 690, International Brotherhood of Teamsters

(Business Owner) v. *(Teamsters)*
100 Wn.2d 343, 670 P.2d 240 (1983)

FREE SPEECH USED TO PERSUADE OTHERS TO INTERFERE WITH BUSINESS IS PERMITTED

■ **INSTANT FACTS** Caruso (P) sued Teamsters (D) for interference with business after publication of article in its weekly paper telling readers not patronize Caruso's (P) business.

■ **BLACK LETTER RULE** Liability will not be imposed for speech activities that interfere with business and cause damage.

■ **PROCEDURAL BASIS**

Petition for review of claims for business interference and defamation following denial of motion for summary judgment on the business interference claim and granting of motion to amend to add defamation claim.

■ **FACTS**

Caruso (P) caused the authorities to tow away delivery trucks that were blocking the entrance to a parking lot he owned, a short distance from his business, "Linoleum & Carpet City." The local teamsters union, Local Union Number 690, International Brotherhood of Teamsters (Teamsters) (D), published an article in its weekly paper, mailed primarily to union members and distributed to several universities and libraries. The article stated, in substance, "Don't patronize Carpet City in Spokane", and giving as reasons the details of the incident that resulted in the towing of the delivery trucks. [The driver of one of trucks had it in for Caruso (P) for having the truck towed.] The article was printed once on the front page of the teamster paper, twice more on page 5, and printed again in a later edition. Caruso (P) thereafter received calls at his business stating, among other things, that they would not shop there. Caruso's (P) business dropped dramatically. Caruso (P) filed suit against the Teamsters (D) seeking damages for business interference. Teamsters' (D) motion for summary judgment was denied and Caruso's (P) motion to amend his complaint to allege an additional cause of action for defamation was granted. Teamsters (D) petitioned for review contending that the publication of the articles was constitutionally protected and cannot give rise to liability for the tort of business interference.

■ **ISSUE**

Can liability be imposed for speech activities that interfere with business and cause damage?

■ **DECISION AND RATIONALE**

(Dimmick) No. We hold that the constitutional right of free speech prohibits the imposition of liability for speech activities that interfere with business and cause damage. The United States Supreme Court held in *NAACP v. Claiborne Hardware Co.* that there could be no liability for the tort of business interference as a result of speeches, marches, picketing, threats and several acts of violence causing a 7-year boycott of businesses. The court stated that the opportunity to persuade others to action is clearly protected by the First and Fourteenth Amendments. The Supreme Court relied on the holding

---

in *Organization for a Better Austin v. Keefe*, which denied liability in a case involving the peaceful distribution of leaflets intended to influence the respondent's conduct. In the case before us, the Teamsters (D) asked its members and others to boycott Caruso's (P) business. Such activity is speech in its purest form and is entitled to at least the same degree of protection afforded to "speech plus conduct" activities afforded in the *Claiborne* case. Just as there is no remedy for damage to a business subject to lawfully conducted boycott, there can be no liability for the "do not patronize" message. This is true in spite of Caruso's (P) claim that the request to not patronize was based on false information. Any claim of falsity only goes to the defamation cause of action. Dismissed as to the business interference claim, remanded for trial on the defamation claim.

Analysis:

"Persuasion" is protected speech. The constitutional right to free speech permits the persuasion of others even if to do so interferes with one's business. This case demonstrates that free speech through a newspaper article which results in boycotting of a business cannot form the basis for the tort of business interference. Note that the interference was with business. If Caruso (P) had contracts with customers to install carpeting and the articles caused the customers to breach the contracts, the rule would be the same. Free speech cannot form the basis for liability for interfering with either business or contract. This case involved speech through published articles. Past decisions upholding the right to persuade others dealt with conduct as well, such as marches, picketing, threats, acts of violence and distribution of leaflets. The court held that if such activity was entitled to protection, then so was pure speech. Many years ago, liability existed for picketing involving labor disputes. A union that encouraged its members to not go to work and picket the employer could be held liable for interference with the employer's business. Federal statutes were eventually enacted that protected the right of organized labor to strike. Thereafter, case law developed which gave protection to political and social boycotts. Some boycotts do, however, give rise to liability; secondary boycotts, where there is a refusal to deal with one's promisor, and anti-competitive boycotts, where there is a restraint of trade or monopoly, are examples.

■ CASE VOCABULARY

BOYCOTT: A refusal to do business with a person or business in protest of certain practices.

MOTION FOR LEAVE TO AMEND COMPLAINT: Seeking permission from the court to modify, change or add facts or legal theories to a complaint.

SECONDARY BOYCOTT: Refusing to do business with a secondary employer with the purpose of forcing it to stop doing business with the primary employer that is the target of the dispute.

Qualitex Co. v. Jacobson Products Co.

(Trademark Holder) v. *(Infringer)*
514 U.S. 159, 115 S.Ct. 1300, 131 L.Ed.2d 248 (1995)

A PRODUCT'S PARTICULAR COLOR QUALIFIES FOR FEDERAL TRADEMARK PROTECTION

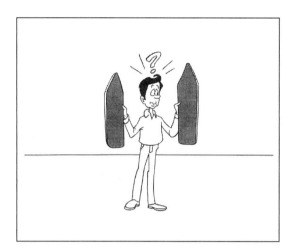

■ **INSTANT FACTS** Qualitex (P) sued Jacobson Products (D) for trademark infringement under the federal Lanham Act.

■ **BLACK LETTER RULE** Trademark protection applies to those product characteristics that assist consumers in identifying the source of the product, including any word, name, symbol, device, or combination thereof.

■ **PROCEDURAL BASIS**

Certiorari to review a decision of the Ninth Circuit Court of Appeals in the defendant's favor.

■ **FACTS**

Qualitex (P) sold distinct green and gold pressing machine pads to dry cleaners. Jacobson Products (D) started selling pads of the same colors. After Qualitex (P) registered its pad colors with the Patent and Trademark Office, it sued the defendant under the federal Lanham Act. The Ninth Circuit Court of Appeals barred Qualitex's (P) use of color as a trademark.

■ **ISSUE**

Can a seller or producer of a product register a trademark for the product's color?

■ **DECISION AND RATIONALE**

(Breyer, J.) Yes. Under the Lanham Act, a seller or producer has the exclusive right to register a trademark and prevent its competitors from using that trademark. Among the broad characteristics that qualify for trademark protection, the Lanham Act includes "any word, name, symbol, or device, or combination thereof." This language has been applied to afford trademark protection to a particular shape, a particular sound, and a particular scent. Similar to these characteristics, a particular color identifies and distinguishes one's goods and may indicate the source of the goods. Although the color of a good itself is not a characteristic that automatically tells a customer the source of the product, over time the color of a product or its packaging gains special significance in associating the product with its source by secondary meaning. This secondary meaning easily assures consumers of the product's quality and allows producers to reap the financial rewards its reputation generates. Therefore, once a product's color effectively distinguishes it from similar products, it is entitled to trademark protection.

The functionality doctrine, which precludes protection of those product features essential to the function of the product, does not apply to colors. Although a particular color may enhance the demand for a product, color does not always have such an effect. Because color is not always essential to the proper functioning of a product, the functionality doctrine does not preclude trademark protection. Reversed.

Analysis:

While color may be a permissible characteristic for a trademark, special considerations must be made before a color can obtain that protection. For instance, a charcoal manufacturer will not likely obtain a trademark on the color black. Only when the color develops a secondary meaning that identifies the product with its specific manufacturer is color eligible for trademark protection. Trademark law attempts to strike a balance between protecting the producers' financial investment in their products and the avoidance of a monopoly over the manufacture of certain products.

■ CASE VOCABULARY

INFRINGEMENT: An act that interferes with one of the exclusive rights of a patent, copyright, or trademark owner.

TRADEMARK: A word, phrase, logo, or other graphic symbol used by a manufacturer or seller to distinguish its product or products from those of others.

Sears, Roebuck & Co. v. Stiffel Co.

(Copy Cat) v. *(Pole Lamp Inventor)*

376 U.S. 225, 84 S.Ct. 784, 11 L.Ed.2d 661

THE RIGHT TO COPY AND SELL AN UNPATENTED ITEM MAY NOT BE CURTAILED BY THE STATES

■ **INSTANT FACTS** Stiffel (P) sued Sears (D) for making and selling a substantially similar pole lamp to the one created by Stieffel (P).

■ **BLACK LETTER RULE** A State's unfair competition law cannot encroach upon, or give protection of a kind that clashes with, the objectives of the federal patent laws.

■ **PROCEDURAL BASIS**

Supreme Court granted certiorari in action where injunctive relief and damages were ordered pursuant to State's unfair competition statute.

■ **FACTS**

Stiffel Company (Stiffel) (P) secured design and mechanical patents on a "pole lamp", which is a vertical tube standing between the floor and the ceiling with lamp fixtures along the outside. The pole lamps were a commercial success. Soon after Stiffel (P) brought them onto the market, Sears, Roebuck & Co. (Sears) (D) put a substantially identical lamp on the market for a retail price about the same as Stiffel's (P) wholesale price. Stiffel (P) sued Sears (D) claiming that the copying of the lamp design infringed Stiffel's (P) patents, and that by selling copies, Sears (D) had violated Illinois' unfair competition law by causing confusion among the public as to the source of the lamp. The District Court first held that Stiffel's (P) patents were invalid for want of invention. It then found that because of the confusion caused by the substantially exact lamps, Sears (D) was liable for unfair competition. It enjoined Sears (D) from selling the lamp and ordered an accounting to fix the profits and damages resulting from Sears' (D) unfair competition. Sears (D) appealed and the court of appeals affirmed, holding that Sears (D) was liable under Illinois law for copying and marketing an unpatented article. Sears (D) appealed to the United States Supreme Court.

■ **ISSUE**

Is a State's unfair competition law inconsistent with federal patent laws where it imposes liability for, or prohibits the copying of, an article which is protected by neither a federal patent or copyright?

■ **DECISION AND RATIONALE**

(Black) Yes. We hold that a State's unfair competition law cannot encroach upon, or give protection of a kind that clashes with, the objectives of the federal patent laws. We conclude that the use of the State's unfair competition law in this case is not compatible with the federal patent law. When a patent is issued under federal law, others may not make, use, or sell the patented product without authority for the term of years fixed by the patent. However, once the patent expires the monopoly created by it expires too and the right to make the article passes to the public. Because of the Supremacy Clause of the Constitution [federal law is the supreme law of the land and is controlling over any conflicting state law], a State may not extend the life of a patent beyond its expiration date or give a patent on an article that lacks the level of invention required for federal patents. Nor can a State encroach upon the federal

---

patent laws directly, or give protection of a kind that clashes with its objectives. In this case, the lower court held that Stiffel is not entitled to a patent. Accordingly, like an article on which the patent has expired, the public may make and sell an unpatented article. Sears (D) thus had every right to copy the lamp design and sell almost identical lamps to those sold by Stiffel (P). However, to allow a State by use of its unfair competition law to prevent the copying of an article which represents too slight an advance to be patented would permit the State to block off from the public something which federal law has said belongs to the public. If this were permitted, the States could allow perpetual protection to unpatented articles. [This means that the patents would never expire.] This would be too great an encroachment on the federal patent system to be tolerated. Because of the federal patent laws, a State may not prohibit the copying of the article or award damages therefore when the article is unpatented and un-copyrighted. Reversed.

Analysis:

The State's unfair competition law improperly encroached upon the federal patent laws and, pursuant to the Supremacy Clause of the United States Constitution, the federal patent laws were controlling and displaced the State law. Note that Stiffel (P) had obtained design and mechanical patents on the pole lamp, but the district court held that they were invalid. The basis for the decision was that it was for want of invention. Without a valid patent, Stiffel (P) could not sue under the federal patent laws. As a result, it attempted to seek relief under the State's unfair competition law. The Supreme Court rejected the conclusion of the court of appeals that Stiffel (P) only had to prove that there was a likelihood of confusion as to the source of the products to make a case of unfair competition. It held that the State could not give protection to an article where doing so would conflict with the objectives of federal laws. If Stiffel's (P) patent had not been declared invalid, it would have had rights under federal law. Moreover, assuming the State's unfair competition law did not give greater protections, it would have rights under the State law as well. However, because the District Court had declared the patents invalid, the use of State law to obtain rights, which, in effect, clashed with federal patent laws, was held to be in violation of the Supremacy Clause. The purpose of federal patent laws is to grant a statutory monopoly and to encourage invention by rewarding the inventor with the right to exclude others from the use of his invention for a period of years. The States must not be allowed to offer a better protection.

■ CASE VOCABULARY

COPYRIGHT: Registering rights to the author or originator of literary or artistic works.

PALMING OFF: Selling goods as the goods of another or doing business as the business of another so as to mislead the public into believing it is dealing with someone other than the actual seller.

UNFAIR COMPETITION: Misappropriating for commercial advantage the goods of another for one's own goods.

CHAPTER THIRTY–FOUR

Misrepresentation and Other Misdealings

Ultramares Corp. v. Touche, Niven & Co.

Instant Facts: After preparing an independent audit of a business to be used by potential lenders, public accountants were sued for fraudulent and negligent misrepresentation after the business collapsed.

Black Letter Rule: Traditionally, negligence could not form a basis of liability for misrepresentation under tort law.

Gauerke v. Rozga

Instant Facts: A real estate company is sued by its client and found liable under a theory of strict liability, after misrepresenting the acreage of hotel property, despite believing the representation to be true.

Black Letter Rule: A speaker may be held strictly liable for innocent misrepresentations relied upon, if the speaker professes personal knowledge.

Pinnacle Peak Developers v. TRW Investment Corp.

Instant Facts: An investment corporation is unable to recover damages under a theory of misrepresentation, despite relying on an oral representation contemporaneous to a formal written contract.

Black Letter Rule: Justified reliance is a prerequisite for the claim of misrepresentation.

Ollerman v. O'Rourke Co., Inc.

Instant Facts: A seller of property is found to have a duty to close "material facts," and is held liable for his "silent" misrepresentation.

Black Letter Rule: A seller has a duty to disclose "material facts" that are known to the vendor and not readily discernable by the purchaser.

Ultramares Corp. v. Touche, Niven & Co.

(Investors) v. *(Lazy Accountants)*
255 N.Y. 170, 174 N.E. 441 (1931)

NEGLIGENCE DID NOT TRADITIONALLY FORM A BASIS FOR LIABILITY UNDER TORT LAW

■ **INSTANT FACTS** After preparing an independent audit of a business to be used by potential lenders, public accountants were sued for fraudulent and negligent misrepresentation after the business collapsed.

■ **BLACK LETTER RULE** Traditionally, negligence could not form a basis of liability for misrepresentation under tort law.

■ **PROCEDURAL BASIS**

Appeal to the Court of Appeals of New York for a dismissal of an action for scienter fraud and negligent misrepresentation.

■ **FACTS**

Touche, Niven & Co. (Touche) (D) were public accountants who, pursuant to a contract with Stern, prepared an independent audit of the business showing a net worth of over a million dollars. Touche (D) certified the audit as accurate and prepared 32 originals. The audit was to be used by potential lenders, who, depending on Stern's financial situation, would lend money to Stem. Relying on the defendants audit, Ultramares Corp. (P) loaned $165,000 to Stern. When Stern Collapsed, the plaintiff was unable to obtain repayment of the loan. Ultramares (P) brought this action against Touche (D) for the damages suffered, claiming both scienter fraud and negligent misrepresentation. There was evidence that Touche (D) did not examine Stern's books with appropriate care and that if they had done so, discrepancies would have been revealed which would have led to a more accurate audit. The trial judge set aside the jury's verdict for Ultramares (P). The Appellate Court dismissed the fraud action but not the negligence claim.

■ **ISSUE**

Can negligence form a basis of liability for misrepresentation under tort law?

■ **DECISION AND RATIONALE**

(Cardozo, J.) No. Negligence can not form a basis of liability for misrepresentation under tort law. Touche (D) owed a legal duty to their employer, to make their certificate without fraud, and a duty from their contract to make it with care and caution proper to their calling. Fraud, includes the pretense of knowledge when there is none. Accordingly, because there was notice that the employer did not intend to keep it to himself, Touche (D) owed a duty to make the certificate without fraud. However, a different issue arises when we ask whether Touche (D) owed a duty to make the certificate without negligence. If liability for negligence exists, a thoughtless slip or blunder, the failure to detect a theft or forgery beneath the cover of deceptive entries, may expose accountants to a liability for an indeterminate amount, for an indeterminate time, to an indeterminate class. In the field of contract law, the beneficiary of a promise, clearly designated as such, is seldom left without a remedy. However, the remedy is narrower where the beneficiaries of the promise are indeterminate or general. The promise must be such as to "bespeak the assumption of a duty to make reparation directly to the individual members of the public if the benefit is lost." In the field of tort law, a manufacturer who is negligent in the manufacture of a chattel, in circumstances pointing to an unreasonable risk of serious bodily harm to those using it thereafter, may be liable for negligence though privity is lacking between the manufacturer and user. If liability for negligence is imposed in this case, it will extend to many callings other than an auditor's. Lawyers who certify their opinions as to the validity of municipal or corporate bonds, with knowledge that the opinion will be brought to the notice of the public, will become liable to the investors if they have overlooked a statute or a decision, to the same extent as if the controversy were one between client and adviser. A person making a promise having the quality of a contract will have a duty apart from the contract to an indefinite number of potential beneficiaries when performance has begun. Thus, the assumption of one relation will mean the involuntary assumption of a series of new relations. Our holding does not emancipate accountants from the consequences of fraud. It does not relieve them if their audit has been so negligent as to justify a finding that they had no genuine belief in its adequacy, for this again is fraud. It does no more than say that if less than this is proved, if there has been neither been a reckless misstatement nor insincere profession of an opinion, but only honest blunder, the ensuing liability for negligence is one that is bounded by the contract, and is to be enforced between the parties by whom the contract has been made. Remanded as to the fraud action and dismissed as to the negligence action.

Analysis:

This case serves as an introduction to misrepresentations under tort law. Fraudulent misrepresentation, fraud, or deceit, and negligent misrepresentation are torts that cause only financial harm, without causing physical harm either to persons or property. As illustrated in the case, scienter is required in order to be held liable on the basis of fraud or deceit. In other words, it is required that the accused party make a knowingly false statement, or at least made the statement with a conscious ignorance or reckless disregard of whether it was true or false. More importantly however, this court follows the traditional rule that negligence may not form a basis of liability for misrepresentations under tort law. The court opines that liability for negligence in such situation as the instant case, would unjustly impose a duty to an indefinite number of people. Therefore, in cases of honest blunder, ensuing liability for negligence is bounded by the law of contracts, not torts. Put another way, negligent misrepresentation may form a basis of liability when there is a duty to perform with reasonable care. However, this duty is limited to contracting parties.

■ CASE VOCABULARY

FRAUDULENT MISREPRESENTATION: A false representation made with scienter, intended to induce reliance upon the representation.

SCIENTER: Knowledge that a representation is either false or made with a reckless disregard as to whether it is true or false.

Gauerke v. Rozga

(Land Seller) v. *(Property Buyer)*
112 Wis.2d 271, 332 N.W.2d 804 (1983)

STRICT LIABILITY MAY BE IMPOSED FOR INNOCENT MISREPRESENTATION

■ **INSTANT FACTS** A real estate company is sued by its client and found liable under a theory of strict liability, after misrepresenting the acreage of hotel property, despite believing the representation to be true.

■ **BLACK LETTER RULE** A speaker may be held strictly liable for innocent misrepresentations relied upon, if the speaker professes personal knowledge.

■ **PROCEDURAL BASIS**

Certification to the Supreme Court of Wisconsin of a decision by the trial court finding strict liability for innocent representation.

■ **FACTS**

Rozga (D1) owned hotel property which was listed for sale with Gudim Realty (Gudim). Rozga (D1) told Gudim that according to former owners, the property was five and one-half acres, and Gudim put this information on a specification sheet. Gauerke (P) in search of a hotel property, asked Robert Frost Realty, Inc. (Frost) (D2) to act as their agent. Frost contacted Gudim, obtained the specification sheet, submitted it to the Gauerkes (P), and Gauerkes (P) eventually bought the property. However, two years later, Gauerkes (P) discovered that the property contained less than three acres. They brought this action against Rozga (D1), Frost (D2), and Gudim. Gudim settled, and Frost (D2) was held liable on a theory of strict liability for misrepresentation. Frost (D2) appeals.

■ **ISSUE**

May strict liability be imposed for an innocent misrepresentation?

■ **DECISION AND RATIONALE**

(Ceci, J.) Yes. A speaker may be held strictly liable for innocent misrepresentations relied upon, if the speaker professes personal knowledge. Frost (D2) argues that the strict responsibility theory is only applicable where the defendant could normally be expected to know the facts represented to be true without investigation. The court of appeals held that in strict liability, the innocent defendant, and not the innocent plaintiff, should bear the loss. Wisconsin law requires: 1) a representation made as of defendant's own knowledge, concerning a matter about which he purports to have knowledge, so that he may be taken to have assumed responsibility as in the case of warranty, and 2) a defendant with an expectation to gain some economic benefit from the transaction into which the plaintiff enters. In other words strict responsibility applies when a speaker indicates that he either had particular means of ascertaining the pertinent facts, or his position made possible complete knowledge, and the statement fairly implied that he had it. We agree with the court of appeals that the application of strict liability requires only that the speaker profess or imply personal knowledge. The other key element is the buyer's reliance on the statement. A factor in determining a buyer's justifiable reliance, might include

---

taking into consideration whether the fact represented is something that one would not expect the speaker to know without an investigation. Affirmed.

Analysis:

Traditionally, scienter was required in tort law, in order to be held liable for misrepresentation. Today, it is now generally accepted that negligent misrepresentations are actionable under special conditions. As illustrated by the case above, some courts may hold a defendant strictly liable for negligent misrepresentations which cause stand-alone economic harm, when the defendant undertakes to guarantee the truth of the matter represented. Accordingly, under the Wisconsin statute, two elements are required for the imposition of strict liability. The first element requires that the defendant make a statement which implies that the defendant has personal knowledge. In other words, the representation made must be construed as giving a warranty or guarantee as to the truth of the statement. The second element requires that a buyer justifiably relies on the misrepresentation. Factors to consider in determining a buyer's "justifiable reliance," include whether the buyer chose his or her conduct because of the misrepresentation, or as the court notes, whether the fact represented is something that one would not expect the speaker to know without an investigation. It is important to note that this case is distinguishable from cases of fraud where a speaker purports to have knowledge, but in fact has none. In the instant case, Frost (D2) did believe that they had appropriate knowledge as to the acreage of the property, based on a specification sheet. However, because their "knowledge" was incorrect, and because they gave a "guarantee" for its accuracy, Frost (D2) could still be liable for their innocent misrepresentation.

■ CASE VOCABULARY

NEGLIGENT MISREPRESENTATION: A false representation which, although believed to be true, was made with the failure to exercise reasonable care in ascertaining the true facts.

Pinnacle Peak Developers v. TRW Investment Corp.

(Land Developers) v. *(Investment Firm)*
129 Ariz. 385, 631 P.2d 540 (1980)

NO ACTION FOR MISREPRESENTATION WILL LIE FOR UNJUSTIFIED RELIANCE

■ **INSTANT FACTS** An investment corporation is unable to recover damages under a theory of misrepresentation, despite relying on an oral representation contemporaneous to a formal written contract.

■ **BLACK LETTER RULE** Justified reliance is a prerequisite for the claim of misrepresentation.

■ **PROCEDURAL BASIS**

On appeal from grant of summary judgment in favor of Pinnacle (D).

■ **FACTS**

TRW Investment Corporation (TRW) (P) entered into a purchase with Pinnacle Peak Developers (Pinnacle) (D) for 40 acres, which required TRW (P) to make certain off-site improvements, such as roads and electrical systems. TRW (P) was given the option to purchase additional acreage, but only if a certain portion of the off-site improvements had not been completed by the option deadline. When the option deadline was reached, the improvements had been made, and Pinnacle (D) took the position that the option for additional acreage had expired. TRW (P) took the position that Pinnacle (D) fraudulently induced TRW (P) to forego the improvements. TRW (P) claimed that it was induced to enter into the purchase and option agreement by reliance on Pinnacle's (D) misrepresentation that the off-site improvements would be no obstacle to the exercise of the option so long as there was reasonable progress on those improvements. The trial court granted summary judgement for Pinnacle (D). TRW (P) appeals.

■ **ISSUE**

Is a party with some expertise and business experience, justified in relying on an oral representation contemporaneous to a formal written agreement?

■ **DECISION AND RATIONALE**

(O'Connor, J.) No. A promise is a misrepresentation which can give rise to an action for fraud, if it is made with a present intention not to perform it. The representation must be of matters of fact which exist in the present, and not merely an agreement or promise to do something in the future. Nor can the representation which may give rise to an action for fraud, be an expression of opinion or judgment as to something which has happened or is expected to happen. The only exception to this is when a promise to perform a future act is made with the present intention on the part of the promisor, that he will not perform it. Such a representation will give rise to an action of fraud. According to the parol evidence rule, any evidence of prior or contemporaneous oral or written understandings, which would contradict, vary, or add to a written contract which was intended as the final and complete statement or integration of the parties agreement, is inadmissible. The problem raised in this case arises when the well recognized notion of promissory fraud, collides with the policies underlying certain prophylactic legal rules like the Statute of Frauds and the parol evidence rule. Both these rules are designed to prevent fraudulent claims or defenses, by excluding evidence that is easily fabricated and too hard to meet. While not meant to shield fraud, these rules may have the effect of preventing a party from showing that he or she has been deceived by an oral promise, made to induce reliance and action but without the slightest intention of keeping it. Courts are split on whether to permit parol evidence which contradicts a writing when fraud in the inducement is alleged. In practice, courts generally apply the parol evidence rule to exclude allegations of prior or contemporaneous oral promises which contradict the written agreement in cases involving formal contracts which were the result of negotiation between parties with some expertise and business sophistication. On the other hand, courts show a greater tendency to allow such evidence, in cases dealing with "informal contract" between people who lack sophistication in business. In cases involving abuse of the bargaining process, such as unconscionable contracts or contracts involving duress, courts almost always disregard the parol evidence rule. In the instant case, both parties had experience in business transactions and the written option agreement was prepared as the result of negotiations between the parties who were represented by counsel. It involved a relatively substantial and sophisticated real estate transaction. Furthermore, the written option agreement was a "formal contract". The contradiction of the written agreement and the oral representation is clear. Therefore, TRW (D) was not justified in relying on the oral representation. The facts are such that courts in most jurisdictions would exclude the evidence of the prior oral statement on the basis of a strict application of the parol evidence rule. The trial court correctly granted summary judgement to appellee on Count II quieting title to the property covered by the option agreement in appellee.

Analysis:

This case specifically analyzes "justifiable reliance", a requirement for liability under any theory of misrepresentation. In an action for misrepresentation, the plaintiff must not only rely on the misrepresentation, the plaintiff's reliance must be justified under the situation. It the instant case, the court recognized that when a promise is made to perform a future act with a present intention by the promissor not to perform, an action for fraud will rise. However, because this situation deals with a promissor's present state of mind, proof may be too much of an obstacle. A promissor's non-performance may result for other reasons such as a change of heart. Therefore, mere proof that the statement was made and then not performed, would not be sufficient proof of fraudulent misrepresentation. This obstacle is further heightened by legal rules such as the Statute of Frauds and the parol evidence rule, which may have the effect of preventing a party from showing that he or she has been deceived by an oral promise. Thus, as the opinion notes, despite the parol evidence rule, courts may generally allow evidence of an oral misrepresentation in cases dealing with "informal contract," between parties which lack sophistication in business, neither of which existed in the instant case. The courts holding reaffirms the requirement of "justifiable reliance." In effect, it held that TRW (P) had not satisfied this requirement. Even if Pinnacle (D) had made a fraudulent misrepresentation, and TRW (P) had relied on this misrepresentation, TRW's (P) reliance was not justified. The contract in this case was a "formal contract," written by the counsels of parties with business experience. Therefore, TRW (P) should not have relied on any prior oral promise.

■ CASE VOCABULARY

JUSTIFIED RELIANCE: Reliance is justified if it was reasonable for a party to rely on a representation, in consideration of the party's subjective view.

RELIANCE: Reliance on a representation occurs when a party either acts or refrains from acting because of the representation.

Ollerman v. O'Rourke Co., Inc.

(Seller) v. *(Buyer)*

94 Wis.2d 17, 288 N.W.2d 95 (1980)

SILENCE MAY BE ACTIONABLE AS A MISREPRESENTATION WHEN THERE IS A DUTY TO DISCLOSE

■ **INSTANT FACTS** A seller of property is found to have a duty to close "material facts," and is held liable for his "silent" misrepresentation.

■ **BLACK LETTER RULE** A seller has a duty to disclose "material facts" that are known to the vendor and not readily discernable by the purchaser.

■ **PROCEDURAL BASIS**

Certification to the Supreme Court of Wisconsin of trial court decision to overrule a motion to dismiss an action for "silent misrepresentation".

■ **FACTS**

Ollerman (P) after purchasing a lot from O'Rourke (D) and excavating to build a house, discovered an underground well which was uncovered and uncapped, and water was subsequently released. Ollerman (P) alleged he had spent over $2700 to cap the well and that building changes costing over $10,500 were necessitated by its presence. He alleged that O'Rourke (D) knew of the underground well but did not disclose it. The trial court overruled O'Rourke's (D) motion to dismiss. O'Rourke (D) appeals.

■ **ISSUE**

Does a seller have a duty to disclose known "material facts" of a transaction?

■ **DECISION AND RATIONALE**

(Abrahamson, J.) Yes. A seller has a duty to disclose "material facts" that are known to the vendor and not readily discernable by a purchaser. When there is a duty to disclose, silence is equivalent to a misrepresentation of fact, and a seller could be held liable for an "intentional" representation. The traditional rule for Wisconsin is that of caveat emptor. That is, a seller of real estate, dealing at arm's length with the buyer, has no duty to disclose information to the buyer, for in a free market, the diligent should not be deprived of the fruits of superior skill and knowledge lawfully acquired. Therefore the seller has no liability in an action for intentional misrepresentation for failure to disclose. Over the years society's attitudes toward good faith and fair dealing in business transactions have undergone significant change, and this change has been reflected in the law, by carved out exceptions to the traditional rule. Thus courts have held that this rule does not apply where the seller actively conceals a defect, prevents investigation, has told half-truths, has made an ambiguous statement with the intent to create a false impression, where there is a fiduciary relationship, or where the facts are peculiarly and exclusively within the knowledge of one party to the transaction, and the other party is not in a position to discover the facts for himself. The case at bar does not appear to fall into one of these well-recognized exceptions to the "no duty to disclose rule." However, there is a tendency in most courts toward a finding of a duty of disclosure in cases where the defendant has special knowledge and is aware that the plaintiff is acting under a misapprehension as to facts which could be of importance to

---

him. The attitude of courts toward nondisclosure is under going a change and it would seem that the object of the law in these cases should be to impose on parties to a transaction, a duty to speak whenever justice, equity, and fair dealings demand it. In an effort to formulate a rule embodying this trend to a more frequent recognition of a duty to disclose, the Restatement of Torts Second sets forth conditions under which a duty to disclose exists. It states that a party to a transaction is under a duty to exercise reasonable care to disclose to the other facts basic to the transaction, if he knows that the other is about to enter into it under a mistake as to the facts, and that the other would reasonably expect a disclosure of those facts. These conditions are limited to the disclosure of those facts basic to the transaction. A basic fact is defined as a fact that is assumed by the parties as a basis for the transaction itself. O'Rourke (D) contends that if this court affirms the trial court, this court would be adopting a strict policy of "let the seller beware." We do not find O'Rourke's (D) argument persuasive. Where a vendor is in the real estate business and is skilled and knowledgeable and the purchaser is not, the purchaser is in a poor position to discover a condition which is not readily discernible, and the purchaser may justifiably rely on the knowledge and skill of the vendor. Therefore, in this case, a strong argument for imposing a duty on the seller to disclose could be made on this "reliance factor." We hold that a subdivider-vendor of a residential lot has a duty to a "non-commercial" purchaser to disclose facts which are known to the vendor, which are material to the transaction, and which are not readily discernible to the purchaser. A fact is "known," if the vendor has actual knowledge of the fact or if the vendor acted in reckless disregard as to the existence of the fact. The use of the word "know" is the same as in an action for intentional misrepresentation based on a false statement. A fact is material if a reasonable purchaser would attach importance to its existence or nonexistence in determining the choice of action in the transaction in question, or if the vendor knows or has reason to know that the purchaser regards or is likely to regard the matter as important in determining the choice of action, although a reasonable purchaser would not so regard it.

Analysis:

Traditionally, the bargainer was not obliged to make affirmative revelations of known material facts. This case illustrates the modern trend away from the harsh rule of caveat emptor. As the court notes, due to the change in society's attitudes toward good faith and fair dealing, courts readily excepted many situations from the traditional rule whenever justice, equity, and fair dealing demand it. Accordingly, this court held that a seller has a duty to disclose material facts that are known to the vendor, and that silence, when there is a duty to disclose, is equivalent to a misrepresentation of fact. It is important to note that the facts must be material or basic to the transaction. In other words, this duty to disclose only pertains to facts that the seller knows or has reason to know that the purchaser regards, or is likely to regard as important in determining his or her choice of action. Furthermore, courts agree that a buyer is not justified in relying upon representations that are not material to the transaction. Therefore, "materiality" is an extension of the element of justified reliance, required for liability under misrepresentation.

■ CASE VOCABULARY

MATERIAL FACTS: Facts that a reasonable person would want to consider in determining a course of action.